God,
Scripture &
Hermeneutics

First

Theology

Kevin J. Vanhoozer

IVP Academic
An imprint of InterVarsity Press
Downers Grove, Illinois

Apollos
Nottingham, England

InterVarsity Press
P.O. Box 1400, Downers Grove, IL 60515-1426
World Wide Web: www.ivpress.com
E-mail: email@ivpress.com

APOLLOS (an imprint of Inter-Varsity Press, England)
Norton Street, Nottingham NG7 3HR, England
Website: www.ivpbooks.com
E-mail: ivp@ivpbooks.com

InterVarsity Press® is the book-publishing division of InterVarsity Christian Fellowship/USA®, a student movement active on campus at hundreds of universities, colleges and schools of nursing in the United States of America, and a member movement of the International Fellowship of Evangelical Students. For information about local and regional activities, write Public Relations Dept., InterVarsity Christian Fellowship/USA, 6400 Schroeder Rd., P.O. Box 7895, Madison, WI 53707-7895, or visit the IVCF website at <www.intervarsity.org>.

Scripture quotations, unless otherwise noted, are from the Revised Standard Version of the Bible, *copyright 1946, 1952, 1971 by the Division of Christian Education of the National Council of the Churches of Christ in the U.S.A., and are used by permission.*

Cover photograph: Michikatu Saito/Photonica

U.S. ISBN-10: 0-8308-2681-5
U.S. ISBN-13: 978-0-8308-2681-0
U.K. ISBN-10: 0-85111-267-6
U.K. ISBN-13: 978-0-85111-267-1

Printed in the United States of America ∞

Library of Congress Cataloging-in-Publication Data
Vanhoozer, Kevin J.
    First theology: God, scriptures & hermeneutics/Kevin J. Vanhoozer
      p. cm.
    Includes bibliographical references.
    ISBN 0-8308-2681-5 (pbk.: alk. paper)
    1. Theology, Doctrinal. 2. God. 3. Bible—Hermeneutics. 4. Hermeneutics—Religious aspects—Christianity. I. Title.

    BT65.V36 2002
    231—dc21

                                            2001051998

British Library Cataloguing in Publication Data

A catalogue record for this book is available from the British Library.

P   22   21   20   19   18   17   16   15   14   13   12   11   10   9   8   7   6   5   4
Y   22   21   20   19   18   17   16   15   14   13   12   11   10   09   08   07

Contents

Acknowledgments

Most of the chapters in the present volume have been published elsewhere. Some I have left essentially unchanged; others I have more or less rewritten to reflect and reinforce the main lines of argumentation in the collection as a whole. Special thanks are due to Rob Clements of Regent College, who first encouraged me to compose this unified collection and hence, with regard to my scattered thoughts, to solve the problem of the one and the many.

Chapter one, from which the collection takes its name, was originally given as the inaugural Hudson Armerding and Carl Armerding annual lecture on Scripture at Wheaton College in October 1999. It has been substantially revised for inclusion in the present volume.

The author and publisher would like to thank the following for permission to reproduce material used in this book.

Chapter two appeared in Kevin Vanhoozer, ed., *The Trinity in a Pluralistic Age: Theological Essays on Culture and Religion* (Grand Rapids, Mich.: Eerdmans, 1997), pp. 41-71.

Chapter three is a moderately revised version of a piece that first appeared in Kevin Vanhoozer, ed., *Nothing Greater, Nothing Better: Theological Essays on the Love of God* (Grand Rapids, Mich.: Eerdmans, 2001), pp. 1-29.

Chapter four was delivered as the annual lecture in theology at Tyndale House, Cambridge, and first appeared in *The Tyndale Bulletin* 48 (1998): 213-51.

Chapter five was originally delivered at the jubilee meeting of the Tyndale Fellowship for Biblical and Theological Research in 1994 and first appeared in Philip E. Satterthwaite and David F. Wright, eds., *A Pathway into the Holy Scripture* (Grand Rapids, Mich.: Eerdmans, 1994), pp. 143-81.

8

Chapter six is a much-revised version of a paper first delivered at a consultation on speech act theory and biblical interpretation in Cheltenham, England, in April 1998. It first appeared in Craig Bartholomew, ed., *After Pentecost: Language and Biblical Interpretation* (Grand Rapids, Mich.: Zondervan, 2001). Published in the U.K. and Europe by Paternoster Press, Carlisle, U.K.

Chapter seven was originally delivered at the Wheaton College Theology Conference in 1994 and first appeared in Roger Lundin, ed., *Disciplining Hermeneutics: Interpretation in Christian Perspective* (Grand Rapids, Mich.: Eerdmans, 1997), pp. 131-65, with a response by Dallas Willard.

Chapter eight first appeared in Joel Green, ed., *Hearing the New Testament: Strategies for Interpretation* (Grand Rapids, Mich.: Eerdmans, 1995,) pp. 301-28, under the title "The Reader in New Testament Interpretation." Published in the U.K. and Europe by Paternoster Press, Carlisle, U.K.

Chapter nine first appeared in A. Graeme Auld, ed., *Understanding Poets and Prophets: Essays in Honour of George Wishart Anderson* (Sheffield, U.K.: JSOT, 1993), pp. 366-87.

Chapter ten was originally delivered at the North Park Symposium on Theological Interpretation of Scripture, North Park Theological Seminary, in 2000, and first appeared in *Ex Auditu: An International Journal of Theological Interpretation of Scripture* 16 (2000): 1-29, with a response by David S. Cunningham.

Chapter eleven first appeared in D. A. Carson and John Woodbridge, eds., *God and Culture* (Grand Rapids, Mich.: Eerdmans, 1993), pp. 1-30.

Chapter twelve first appeared in Kevin Vanhoozer and Andrew Kirk, eds., *To Stake a Claim: Mission and the Western Crisis of Knowledge* (Maryknoll, N.Y.: Orbis, 1999), pp. 120-56.

Preface: First Thoughts

Ludwig Feuerbach, the influential nineteenth-century atheist, once summed up the progression of his thinking in the following manner: "God was my first thought, reason my second, man my third and last thought."[1] Feuerbach, of course, believed that "God" was actually a projection of what humans most value. Anthropology, says Feuerbach, is thus the "secret" of theology. That did not stop theologians, however, from imitating Feuerbach's progression from one starting point to another. Modern theologians in particular have been adept in talking about God on the basis of reason and human experience.

The present book starts where Feuerbach did, but seeks to keep God as our first thought. But how? When it comes to doing theology, God must be our first thought, Scripture our second thought, and hermeneutics our third and last thought. Yet matters are not really so simple, nor so linear. Doing theology involves all three thoughts, together and at once. This collection of essays represents numerous thoughts I have had over the years about what it means to do theology, about what it means to be biblical in one's theology and in one's life, about what it means to speak and to act in the name of God to God's glory.

This is a book about God and hermeneutics. It is a plea for being hermeneutical about theology, and for being theological about hermeneutics. To be precise: it is an argument for the importance of treating the questions of God, Scripture and hermeneutics as one problem. This one, admittedly complex problematic defines what I call "first theology." To engage in theological hermeneutics is to recognize the specifically theological application of the celebrated hermeneutical circle: "I must believe

---

[1]Quoted in Hans Küng, *Does God Exist? An Answer for Today* (London: Collins, 1980), p. 192.

in order to understand, but I must understand in order to believe." Theological hermeneutics recognizes that our doctrine of God affects the way we interpret the Scriptures, while simultaneously acknowledging that our interpretation of Scripture affects our doctrine of God. Such is necessarily the case when theology is viewed as "God-centered biblical interpretation."

We must not think about God—at least not for very long—apart from the authorized witness of Scripture. Similarly, we must not think about Scripture—again, at least not for very long—apart from its divine author and central subject matter. Nor must we think about hermeneutics—about interpreting Scripture—apart from Christian doctrine or biblical exegesis.

Overview of Contents

Chapter one introduces the integrative theme that unites the diverse essays in the book: the project of "first theology" or theological hermeneutics. It also introduces a number of themes that will be treated more fully elsewhere in this volume: the postmodern challenge to theology, the crucial role of the imagination in biblical interpretation and theology, the notion of Scripture as a diverse set of divine speech acts, the importance of learning wisdom by indwelling the biblical texts.

The three chapters of part one present God as a triune communicative agent who is both loving and sovereign. Together these chapters provide the theological basis for what I shall later say about Scripture and hermeneutics. Chapter two raises the question of how we identify God and asks whether the triune God is the "same" as the god(s) worshiped in other religions. The doctrine of the Trinity, I argue, uniquely identifies the Christian God as Father, Son and Spirit. The distinction between the three Persons must not, however, obscure either their eternal communion (the immanent Trinity) or their joint historical work (the "missions" of the economic Trinity). God as triune communicative agent goes out of himself for the sake of communion with what is not God: the created world.

The identity of the triune God, and the theme of communion, leads to the focus in chapter three on the love of God and on the God-world relationship. I argue that the philosopher's concept of God, built on the idea of an infinite and perfect being, needs to be open to correction from the narrative identification of the triune God's self-revelation as attested in Scripture. I further contend that the triune God is both loving (personal) and sovereign (transcendent), a claim that encounters opposition from "panentheistic" theologians who depict the world as in a real sense God's "body" and from "openness of God" theologians who maintain that God's love precludes his control. The love of God is an ideal case study in first theology: how we construe God's love clearly affects how we interpret Scripture (and vice versa).

Chapter four considers the effectual call, the Reformed doctrine that affirms the irresistible gracious drawing of the sinner toward God, as a divine communicative act that is at once loving and sovereign. The main challenge here is to show that God's communicative agency is qualitatively distinct from impersonal causation. The notion of God's effectual call to human beings provides another excellent case study with which to examine the God-world relation and to assess the difference between various forms of theism and panentheism. Furthermore, the distinction between the internal and external call of God allows me once again to focus on divine communication action and to reintroduce the theme of what God does with words.

The chapters that make up part two turn from a consideration of God himself, the communicative agent, to Scripture as a species of divine communicative action: God's word written. Chapter five analyzes the doctrine of Scripture, especially the so-called Scripture principle, and picks up the earlier suggestion that the doctrines of God and Scripture stand or fall together. This time, however, the focus is on the doctrine of providence. I argue that the Bible is itself a "mighty act" of God, an indispensable ingredient in his plan of salvation. The gospel requires both the "Word made flesh" and a word made *verbal*.

Chapter six serves as a mini-*summa* on the theme of divine communicative action in Scripture, complete with ten theses on theological hermeneutics. It also contains an extended analysis of what is arguably the most important concept in this collection of essays: illocution—"what one does in saying something." My thesis is that God's communicative action—the core concept for thinking about the God-world relation in biblical terms—is essentially a matter of divine illocutions. Even here, however, philosophy's role is ancillary; my use of philosophical concepts is ultimately governed by theological principles, specifically, a formal principle (canon) and a material principle (covenant).

The essays in part three, the longest part of the book, treat various aspects of biblical hermeneutics. It would be wrong, however, to think of this part of the book as dealing with interpretation theory as over against "God" and "Scripture." On the contrary, the main thrust of the present work is that hermeneutics, when theologically conceived, is precisely the locus where God and Scripture are best considered together. This becomes apparent in chapter seven, which treats the role of the Holy Spirit in biblical interpretation. Interpreting Scripture theologically involves more than dealing with biblical words, more even than rules for textual interpretation. Interpreters must have receptive spirits as well, a possibility that depends on the work of the Holy Spirit. Furthermore, there is no contradiction between acknowledging the work of the Spirit in biblical interpretation and affirming *sola scriptura*. For God's communicative action in and through Scripture is triune, involving both Word and Spirit.

The next three chapters represent exegetical reflections on three different texts, all taken from the Fourth Gospel. As such, they serve as practical illustrations of how my approach to theological hermeneutics works when applied to biblical texts. Chapter eight compares the process of reading Scripture to the Samaritan woman's meeting Jesus by the well (Jn 4). Chapter nine examines the process of reading Scripture in light of the witness of the Beloved Disciple to Jesus' crucifixion (Jn 21:20-24). Chapter ten focuses on the "body piercing" scene in John's Passion narrative in order to reflect on the aims and norms for reading Scripture in and for the church. It also offers five more theses on the nature of theological interpretation and makes a case for the authority of the "theological natural" sense of the text.

Chapters eleven and twelve seek to apply my theological hermeneutics to considerations of culture and apologetics respectively. Thus they may be taken as recommendations for appropriating and "performing" biblical meaning, knowledge and truth. Chapter eleven makes the twofold claim that (1) culture needs to be exegeted and interpreted and (2) interpreting the Bible involves a critical analysis of contemporary culture and the construction of a biblical counterculture. Finally, chapter twelve considers postmodern criticisms of the notions of knowledge and truth, and argues that the most compelling truth claim for the gospel requires a performative interpretation in terms of a cruciform shape of individual and community life. Interpretations are ultimately tested by the trials of life. The goal for Christian interpreters is to hold fast to the apostolic witness to the truth, and in so doing to become witnesses themselves.

Common Themes

Besides the linear progression that connects each essay to the preceding ones, there are also several cross-sectional themes.

First, these essays are decidedly trinitarian. The distinctively Christian manner of parsing "God" has, as we shall see, important implications for the way we understand both Scripture and the process of its interpretation. In short, Christian theological hermeneutics must be trinitarian.

Second, many of these essays were written with one eye on the contemporary situation, which is often described as postmodern. There are many varieties of postmodern thought, but the one I wish to resist is the deconstructive variety, characterized as "the death of God put into writing." On this view there is nothing that transcends the play of language; "meaning" and "truth" have no transcendent authority but are merely tools wielded by those who have the power to determine social conventions. These essays, however, proceed from a different premise, one that affirms "the providence of God put into writing." By this phrase I mean to highlight the central theme of "first theology": God's communicative action.

The God in whom Christians believe not only makes himself known in words but relates to human beings and does things in the world in and with and through his words. Not just writing, of course, but oral discourse too. In a sense, then, these essays are theological reflections on Isaiah 55:11, the climax of a theological ode to joy—the joy that celebrates the Word of God that is both gracious and powerful: "My word . . . shall not return to me empty, but it shall accomplish that which I purpose, and prosper in the thing for which I sent it."

God's word is a trinitarian work of love. The understanding of God that emerges from these pages is of a communicative agent who relates to and interacts with human beings in words and Spirit that together minister God's living Word, Jesus Christ. *The triune God is a personal and transcendent communicative agent.*

Third, Scripture appears in these essays as a work of trinitarian communicative action. Of central importance here is the priority of God's communicative act. God's call, covenant and command precede our answering, obeying and following. The priority of divine communicative action to human communicative response carries several important implications for biblical interpretation and hermeneutics as well.

Fourth, biblical interpreters are also communicative agents, since to engage and respond to texts and illocutions is to get caught up in the action. Communicative action is again the operative concept, for biblical interpretation, whether by the professional theologian, the minister or the layperson, ultimately calls for more than reading. Understanding and responding to God's Word written involves communicative action on our part; it involves our concrete relation to the living Word, the risen Lord, to whom the Scriptures direct us.

Finally, insofar as "first theology" involves responding to God's prior communicative action in Scripture, it calls for individual and corporate performance: for *doing* the Word. For in the final analysis, a proper response to these texts means creating a shape of life that manifests the same kind of communion as does the triune life of their divine Author. What therefore emerges is a notion of doing theology that is an intrinsic part of our Christian witness and that has Christian wisdom for its ultimate goal: a living out of the Word in the world to God's glory. Theology as God-centered biblical interpretation makes us followers and witnesses, even martyrs, to the truth of Jesus Christ.

One

First Theology

Meditations in a Postmodern Toolshed

*T*hose who wish to succeed, Aristotle famously commented, must ask the right preliminary questions. What is the right preliminary question when it comes to theology and theological method? In particular, should theology begin with God or with the Word of God? Is it even possible to begin with one or the other?

Many modern theologians devoted considerable energy to prolegomena, to that which must be said before one can do theology proper. To them it was obvious that the right preliminary question had to involve prolegomena. After all, the success of modern science seemed to follow from its commitment to the scientific method.[1] With the ebbing of modernity, however, others are inclined to answer Aristotle's query somewhat differently.

If, then, we wish to succeed theologically, may we straightaway begin talking of God, or is there something we must say, or do, beforehand? In particular, which

---

[1]I am not suggesting that modern theologians employed the scientific method, only that they sought something analogous for theology. For systematicians this often meant adopting a conceptual scheme (e.g., existentialism, process philosophy) whose categories could be used as analytic tools for determining the meaning either of Scripture or of human experience (see David Tracy, "Theological Method," in *Christian Theology: An Introduction to its Traditions and Tasks,* ed. Peter C. Hodgson and Robert H. King, 2nd ed. [Philadelphia: Fortress, 1985], pp. 35-60). In biblical studies, the scientific approach is represented by various "critical" methods.

comes first: the doctrine of God or the doctrine of Scripture? On the one hand, starting with God prompts the question, How do we know about God? just as starting with Scripture raises the question, Why *this* particular text rather than another? On the other hand, it is difficult to talk of God without appealing to the Bible, just as it is difficult to treat the Bible as Scripture without appealing to God.

It is precisely this apparent dilemma that makes of God, Scripture and hermeneutics a single problem. Yet out of this dilemma arises a new possibility for doing theology beyond prolegomena, a way of speaking of God that allows the theological matter to influence the theological method. I call this alternative approach *first theology*.

First Philosophy

First philosophy in premodernity: Metaphysics. Aristotle knew what the right preliminary question was. It was the question of "first principles," the question of the nature of ultimate reality: metaphysics. Most ancient Greek philosophers agreed. Some said "all is water"; others suggested "all is air" or "all is fire." Aristotle, for his part, argued that everything is "being." We owe to him many categories that we still use today for thinking about things: substance, essence, existence.

Determining the nature of reality was therefore the issue that the ancient world considered the most important—its "first philosophy." One can tell a good deal about an age by identifying its first philosophy. Indeed, one rough-and-ready way to distinguish the premodern, modern and postmodern eras is precisely on the basis of what each considers its first philosophy. For these revolutions in first philosophy are felt far beyond philosophy proper. They reverberate through the academy and society and are eventually felt in the church.

It is not surprising, then, given Aristotle's stature and influence in the twelfth and thirteenth centuries, that many medieval theologians tended to make metaphysics—or in their case, the question of *God's* "being"—first theology.[2] To be sure, Scripture was an important, even authoritative, source for theology, but it not the only one. Theologians such as Thomas Aquinas believed that one could gain some knowledge about God's essence and existence (about the nature of God's being) from reason alone.

First philosophy in modernity: Epistemology. Everything changes with the advent of modernity and the Enlightenment. The burning issue in the Age of Reason

---

[2]This is, of course, a generalization. A good case can be made for the priority of language and logic in medieval theology as well. For instance, T. F. Torrance calls attention to the "scientific passion"—a love for rigor and analytic discipline—that characterizes much medieval theology (see Torrance, *Theological Science* [Oxford: Oxford University Press, 1969], p. 56). Nevertheless, the point of such analysis was to gain knowledge of divine reality. The critical move made by Immanuel Kant—typical of modernity, in which knowledge of things as they are in themselves is problematized—was not as keenly felt by medieval theologians.

becomes the nature and possibility of knowledge. How can I know? How can I show that my belief is more than mere opinion? In such a critical environment, what counts is not the right preliminary questions so much as the right *procedures*. This change in philosophical priorities can be seen in the full title of René Descartes's classic, *Discourse on the Method of Rightly Conducting Reason and Reaching the Truth in the Sciences,* a work that for many represents the epitome of modernity's quest for the foundations of knowledge.[3] What justifies one's knowledge claims is no longer an appeal to authoritative sources but rather an account of how this information has been processed. In this regard the success of the natural sciences is paradigmatic; the scientific method became the envy of other disciplines too. What matters for moderns is being able to justify one's beliefs. Henceforth it's method over matter, epistemology over metaphysics. Van Harvey, in *The Historian and the Believer,* speaks for modernity when he claims that it is actually *immoral* to believe something except on the basis of sufficient evidence.[4]

Harvey was thinking primarily of historians, but the same requirement applied to exegetes, or theologians, or anyone else in the modern era. That is why, after two hundred years or so, many academics are still knee-deep in the "critical" questions concerning the reliability of the Bible. The biblical scholars who make up the so-called Jesus Seminar, for example, rely on a scientific method of sorts to distinguish the real, critically reconstructed Jesus from the Jesus of apostolic testimony. These scholars put their faith more in their critical method than in the apparent meaning of the text; accordingly, what they claim to know about Jesus is as much *in spite of* the Bible as *because of* it. In my view, however, what they know about Jesus is *less,* not more, than what those who trust the biblical witness know. Claiming to be wise, they became skeptics. One early, and particularly effective, attack on the prestige of biblical criticism was, interestingly enough, that of C. S. Lewis.

Lewis's Toolshed and the Critique of Modernity

C. S. Lewis's "Meditation in a Toolshed" is one of the short pieces he wrote for his local newspaper, the *Coventry Evening Telegraph,* in July 1945. The article is essentially a brief parable in which Lewis recalls a simple experience—going into a dark toolshed—and then provides an explanation of its meaning. Yet like Jesus' world-subverting stories, so Lewis's brief narrative is used to overturn the tables of the knowledge-changers in the temple of modernity.

The episode is quickly rehearsed. A certain man (Lewis) goes into a toolshed. The

---

[3]See J. Cottingham, ed., *The Cambridge Companion to Descartes* (Cambridge: Cambridge University Press, 1986).

[4]Van Harvey, *The Historian and the Believer: The Morality of Historical Knowledge and Christian Belief* (New York: Macmillan, 1966).

door closes behind him. It is very dark inside, apart from a single beam of light. At first he looks at the beam and sees only specks of dust floating in it. Then he steps into the light; instantly the whole previous picture vanishes. He sees neither the toolshed nor the beam of light, but green leaves moving on the branches of a tree outside, and beyond that the sun, framed in the irregular cranny at the top of the door.

A simple story, but what is it really about, and wherein lies its significance? The parable, together with Lewis's meditation, concerns nothing less than the nature of knowledge (epistemology), and its significance lies in the distinction Lewis draws between looking *at* and looking *along*. Lewis notes that in the modern world, all the prestige lies with those who look *at* things—those who are a step removed from the experience on which they bring their analytic-critical techniques to bear. To look *at* things means to contemplate them in dispassionate and disinterested—in a word, *detached*—terms. Such has been the fate of the Bible in modern times. By and large, biblical scholars look *at* the Bible—at questions of its authorship, at questions of its composition, at questions of its historical reliability—instead of *along* it.

Well, why not? If modernity is the theoretical age par excellence, an extended discourse on method, and if epistemology reigns virtually unchallenged as first philosophy, why shouldn't theology begin with a critical study of the Bible? I can think of at least two reasons. First, because this approach leads to a "great divorce"—a painful separation between the academy and the church, between scholarly and devotional ways of reading the Bible, and between reason and faith.

Second, because the critical approach promises knowledge but does not deliver. What we get instead is an abbreviated, short-circuited substitute for knowledge. Imagine, if you will, what we would come to know if, in the toolshed, we elevated "looking at" to first philosophy. In that case the "true" story about the light beam— the "metanarrative"—is that it is entirely made up of specks of dust. Any further revelation would be discounted by the authorized view, the account we get of light by looking *at* it. In Lewis's words: "The people who look *at* things have had it all their own way; the people who look *along* things have simply been brow-beaten."[5] *Looking at* thus falls prey to the besetting temptation of modern intellectual thought: the belief that our theories see all there is to be seen and know all there is to be known. The technical term for this temptation is *reductionism;* the theological term is *pride.*[6]

---

[5]C. S. Lewis, "Meditation in a Toolshed," in *God in the Dock* (Grand Rapids, Mich.: Eerdmans, 1970), p. 213.

[6]Reductionism is the tendency to think in terms of "nothing but" explanations. For example, the mind is "nothing but" brain matter in motion; love is "nothing but" a reflex of evolutionary psychology. Reductionism (the lust of the mind?) is the preeminent theoretical temptation.

Lewis elsewhere discusses this distinction between two kinds of looking in terms of the contrast between seeing and tasting. "Seeing" stands for theoretical knowledge, for knowledge gained by following methodological procedures; tasting stands for knowledge attained through personal acquaintance, for knowledge gained through firsthand experience.[7] It would be a grievous mistake to reduce all instances of the latter kind of knowing to instances of the former. What it is to know a friend, or perhaps one's child, cannot be reduced to the information gleaned by various means of analysis. Given his metaphor of the light beam, then, Lewis might perhaps rephrase my opening question in the following way: is knowing God more like *seeing* or *tasting?* In other words, should theology begin with abstract, propositional knowledge or with concrete, personal knowledge?

We shall return to this question in due course. Before we do, however, we must inquire into the fate of first philosophy in our postmodern times.

The Postmodern Toolshed and the Critique of Modernity

To some extent the epistemology of "looking at," together with the goal of comprehensive theoretical knowledge, continues to enjoy the prestige of first philosophy, at least in certain quarters of the academy. By and large, however, postmodern critics and philosophers have exploded the myth of the "innocent eye." Our supposedly neutral and disinterested procedures for looking at things—God, the world, ourselves—are in fact not neutral but biased, interested and politically charged. Jacques Derrida says that metaphysics, which purports to be a true description of ultimate reality, is really only a projection of the way white Western male academics think about the world: a "white mythology." What is happening in the postmodern toolshed is that things are not being put together but *taken apart.* In particular, belief systems are being deconstructed. The deconstructor, like an inquisitive boy who disassembles things to see how they work, pries apart worldviews in order to expose their inner workings and their rhetorical ploys. What the postmodern discovers behind various worldviews are political interests and power levers. For these postmodern disbelievers in knowledge, philosophy is not about truth but about power, rhetoric and ideology.

The postmodern critique of modern theories of objective knowledge does not mean the end of philosophy. Indeed, one of the best ways of understanding postmodernity is to determine what postmoderns most care about and how they pursue their goals. So what counts as first philosophy for postmoderns? While no clear front runner has yet emerged, there seem to be three plausible candidates.

---

[7]The English word *theory* comes from the Greek verb *theoreo,* "to behold." Theories tell us what we are looking at with the mind's eye, as it were.

Language as first philosophy: "There is nothing outside the text." The first candidate is language. "All is language." In fact I know of no postmodern who has said this (it sounds too universal, too metaphysical); nevertheless, it is not a bad first approximation of what many postmoderns think. Derrida implies something similar, I think, when he declares: "There is nothing outside the text."[8] What Derrida means, I think, is that we have no nonlinguistic access to the way things really are. We necessarily speak and think about things on the basis of a certain language, and this language is (for Derrida) largely a matter of arbitrary social convention. Our words are not actually linked to the real world; on the contrary, they acquire meaning not by referring to things but by *differing* from other words. Language for Derrida is a system of differences—a pattern of distinctions and connections—that a society of speakers *imposes* on human experience. We cannot even begin think about things, whether particular or abstract, without language. It follows, then, that whatever we think is always/already shaped by the system of language that we employ.

Language is first philosophy, then, because there is nothing that precedes it and nothing so fundamental. "There is nothing outside the text." It is important neither to misconstrue nor to caricature this statement. Derrida is not saying that baseballs and bookstores and burritos do not exist; rather, he is saying that what we know about these things is culturally, which is to say linguistically, constructed.

In the postmodern toolshed all the windows are boarded up; there is no light, only language. And language no longer represents the world, no longer lets the world in. Nothing outside the toolshed of language gets through intact; language is the contamination of thought and experience alike. The old toolshed may have a few cracks here and there in the walls, but no natural light gets through, for bits of cut glass—the prism of language—intercept every beam. Lewis's light beam itself is made up no longer of white light but of deconstructed light, of the fragmented shards of the color spectrum. In the postmodern toolshed nothing is regarded as a given of nature; instead everything is graven, "marked" by the system of language in which human experience lives and moves and has its being. In the postmodern toolshed we must be either idolmongers who mistake the distorted image for the reality or iconoclasts who question every image.

A postmodern wag would no doubt take great delight in pointing out that the etymology of *prism* comes from the Greek verb *prizo*—"to saw," an apt metaphor for the way everything can be cut down to signs in an arbitrary system of signifiers. Language, then, is a prime candidate for first philosophy in the postmodern tooldshed: "I came, I sawed, I deconstructed."

Ethics: Justice to the other. Postmoderns are typically quite sensitive to the

---

[8]Jacques Derrida, *Of Grammatology* (Baltimore: Johns Hopkins University Press, 1976), p. 158.

myriad ways that language can be wielded as an ideological weapon or as an instrument of social oppression. Rhetoric displaces logic: it is now more important to persuade people of the truth than to prove it. Rhetoric—the art of using language to persuade—is thus the bridge to our second candidate for postmodern first philosophy: ethics.

The call for ethics to serve as first philosophy in postmodernity is most commonly associated with the Jewish philosopher Emmanuel Lévinas. By *ethics* Lévinas means something very different from a system of moral values. Indeed for Lévinas ethics has nothing to do with systems at all. It is "systems"—of ideas, of values, of theology!— that Lévinas regards as oppressive and hence unethical. Whereas theoretical systems take thought captive, ethics let the "other" be. Essentially, ethics has to do with respecting the particularity of the other. For Lévinas it therefore follows that the one thing we must not do is seek to "comprehend" or theoretically explain God, others and the world.

Lévinas calls the attempt theoretically to master the world "Greek-think," largely because it is typical of our Western tradition. Philosophy has traditionally sought to "know" (see, comprehend, theorize) reality. In Lévinas's view, ethics has to do with resisting the tendency of systems of language and systems of thought to swallow things up (to "totalize"). Indeed ethics questions philosophy itself insofar as the latter is bound up with metaphysics and epistemology, both attempts to reduce all forms of otherness into the "Same," that is, into what our philosophical and political systems classify as "good" and "true."

Lewis and Lévinas agree at least in this: that modernity wrongly identifies knowing as a kind of "seeing." To "see" or to apprehend is to *grasp*—an essentially violent gesture.[9] If we "apprehend" something, then it does not remain "other." The other is precisely what *escapes* our conceptual grasp. The temptation of modernity, says Lévinas, is to reduce the real with what we can "see" or "apprehend." In his words: "The labor of thought wins out over the otherness of things and men."[10] His concern is the opposite of the apostle Paul's: it is not a matter of "taking every thought captive" but of "freeing every captive thought." For Lévinas, first philosophy consists in the ethical plea on behalf of the other not to be reduced to just another piece of a system.[11]

Aesthetics as first philosophy: The realm of make-believe. Whereas some postmoderns resist language with its potential for totalization, others prefer to play

---

[9]To use Lévinas's image: philosophy is the alchemy whereby otherness is transmuted into sameness (in Simon Critchley, *The Ethics of Deconstruction: Derrida and Lévinas* [Oxford: Blackwell, 1992], p. 6).

[10]Emmanuel Lévinas, "Ethics as First Philosophy," in *A Lévinas Reader,* ed. Seán Hand (Oxford: Blackwell, 1989), p. 79.

[11]To respect the other as other, one must not reduce the other to the category of the same-as-something-else or the same-as-me.

with it. Here we may recall that what goes on in the postmodern toolshed is that things are taken apart. Don Cupitt, a Cambridge University theologian, believes that theology today finds itself doing roughly what physics and painting were doing in the first decade of the twentieth century. *It is dismantling its own objects.* This holds even for theology's object: "God" for Cupitt is merely the product of a way of talking, an invention of discourse. He remarks that "the world of everyday life conjured up by our language is the only real world there can be for us."[12] Yet for Cupitt, the fact that "all is language" is not bad news, but rather an excellent excuse for humans to celebrate their creativity.

In a book that Cupitt has aptly entitled *The Last Philosophy,* he urges us to abandon our quest for "the way things are." Searching for "reality" will only make us unhappy. There is no "Beyond" for philosophy to tell us about. Metaphysics is just a conjuring trick with words and concepts. In short, philosophy is a literary construction, a work of art, a set of metaphors that help create a bit of order out of the chaos of experience. Metaphysics and epistemology must therefore renounce their former privileges and acknowledge that they are just as fictional as other works of creative literature.[13] Cupitt argues that our metaphysics—our metanarratives—are only elaborate fictions; once drained of truth they lose their prestige, they are "undone." What's left is talk amidst the philosophical ruins. Cupitt is nevertheless unapologetic: "I haven't got any higher world . . . to tell you about."[14]

With no hope of seeing what lies outside the toolshed, then, Cupitt contents himself with interior redecorating. His postmodern theology abandons the quest for truth—the quest for looking at things as they actually are—and instead takes up linguistic "arts and crafts." The products of such postmodern theology—stories, doctrines—bear the stamp not of revealed truth but rather "made in Jerusalem" or "made in Cambridge." It is up to us, says Cupitt, to reinvent faith for our time, to engage in "make believe."

There is a deep yet ironic inconsistency behind Cupitt's assumption that by virtue of his "last philosophy" he has effectively demythologized false truths. It is hard to reconcile Cupitt's skepticism about knowledge in general with his implicit claim to know what the truth of the human condition is. Cupitt holds that humans are ultimately biological beings. The only sort of worldview to which we have access is a talking animal's worldview. Moreover, "there's nothing wrong with being a talking

---

[12]Don Cupitt, *The Last Philosophy* (London: SCM Press, 1995), p. 6.

[13]Cupitt falls into inconsistency at this point, for try as he may, he simply cannot help but tell us what there "really" is, namely, "a beginningless, endless and outsideless stream of language-formed events" (ibid., p. 25). I leave it to the reader to determine the merits, rhetorical or otherwise, of this statement vis-à-vis ancient and modern, not to mention Christian theological, alternatives.

[14]Ibid., p. 8.

animal."[15] (C. S. Lewis would probably agree, but he would mean something different.) By adhering to biological naturalism, Cupitt has, for all intents and purposes, returned to Plato's cave, only to insist that the shadows on the wall alone are real. For those who, like Cupitt, see aesthetics as first philosophy, theology is nothing but a game of hand shadows projected on a caveman's wall.

Implications for biblical interpretation: Ideological criticism. No matter which of the three options one crowns as first philosophy, it should be obvious that postmodernity provokes a crisis for biblical interpretation, and hence for the theologian who seeks knowledge of God using Scripture as a source. As we shall see, postmodernity generates a new approach to the biblical texts as well: ideology criticism.

The vital interpretative question for postmoderns is simply this: what makes one interpretation better than any other? If language blocks our access to meaning and truth, it follows that interpretations tell us more about the readers—their interests, their biases—than about the text. If we are honest, we will stop talking about what the text means and speak instead of what we *will* it to mean. I have argued elsewhere that postmodernity represents not simply a new chapter in the hermeneutics of suspicion but a radically new suspicion of hermeneutics itself.[16] Neither interpretations nor interpretative approaches are innocent. For that matter, neither are texts. Behind every text and every interpretation are biases engendered by one's race, gender or class. The notions of meaning and truth are thus co-opted into partisan political struggles.

With this insight, postmodernity has given birth to a new form of biblical criticism that analyzes how textual meaning is at the service of political power.[17] The postmodern critic takes apart each and every biblical text, as well as each and every biblical interpretation, in order to expose the power relations that underlie the verbal relations.

Those who, like Cupitt, are inclined to make aesthetics their first philosophy respond to the pervasiveness of ideology with a call to celebrate creative reading. Let a hundred ideologies bloom, just so long as we don't take any one of them too seriously. Why not read the Bible so that it supports your preferred way of life? Everyone else's reading is just a projection of biases too. Everything is relative to the identity of the reader. Some read the Bible from a Marxist perspective, others from a capitalist; some read with a heterosexual bias, others from a homosexual perspective; still oth-

---

[15]Ibid., p. 2.
[16]See Kevin Vanhoozer, *Is There a Meaning in This Text? The Bible, the Reader and the Morality of Literary Knowledge* (Grand Rapids, Mich.: Zondervan, 1998).
[17]To analyze meaning in the service of power is to analyze "ideology." See John B. Thompson, *Ideology and Modern Culture: Critical Social Theory in the Era of Mass Communication* (Palo Alto, Calif.: Stanford University Press, 1990), p. 7.

ers read as Calvinists, others as Arminians. The postmodern gives them all permission
to lead Scripture by its nose of wax.

On the other hand, those who make ethics rather than aesthetics their first philosophy
are not as sanguine in their response to the pervasiveness of ideology. The
postmodern ethical response to the notion that texts and their interpretations are governed
by some ideology or other is to resist. For if reading is ultimately a political
affair, a power struggle, then the ethical response is to champion the otherness of the
text and to undermine interpretations that, having become too powerful, threaten to
engulf it. Walter Brueggemann, for example, advocates an approach to Old Testament
theology that is pluralistic. This means acknowledging that there is no interest-free
interpretation and committing oneself to protect the "otherness" of biblical texts
that resist being subsumed by grand interpretative schemes.[18] Following Lévinas,
postmoderns like Brueggemann typically resist any claim to have "mastered" a text.
The ethical response to ideological interpretation is to enter a plea on behalf of marginalized
readings, a plea on behalf of the oppressed.

Whose interpretation counts most, and why? In the postmodern era fewer and
fewer voices are able to answer with any confidence. This sea-change has affected
the academy too. For postmodern biblical critics, the historical-critical approach that
has dominated biblical studies for much of modernity is as ideological as any other
method. Postmoderns turn a deaf ear to modern appeals to method, science and
objectivity; these appeals are merely special pleadings on the part of special interest
groups, especially white educated males. Consequently interpretation, of the Bible
and of other texts, has in our time become a species of ideological warfare. We are,
all of us, stuck in the trenches of language, where exegetical armies clash by night.
(Here ends my reading of the contemporary world.)

First Theology
The centrality of Scripture for Christian dogmatics means that theologians have a
vested interest in debates over the practice, and the principles, of interpretation. As
we have just seen, however, what was already a complex task has become even
more complicated in postmodernity. Given the difficulty of biblical interpretation, lay
Christians may perhaps be forgiven for desiring a more immediate knowledge of
God. Yet is there a way of doing theology that avoids the task of biblical interpretation?
We thus return to our original question about starting points. What, in the vale
of the shadow of deconstruction, shall we take as our "first theology"? Can we begin
with God (divine reality, being and metaphysics) or must we begin with Scripture

---

[18]See Walter Brueggemann, *Texts Under Negotiation: The Bible and Postmodern Imagination*
(Minneapolis: Fortress, 1993), and *Theology of the Old Testament: Testimony, Dispute, Advocacy* (Minneapolis: Fortress, 1997), pp. 61-114.

(divine revelation, testimony and epistemology)?

Thinking God apart from Scripture: The "sensus divinitatis." What happens when we begin with our intuitions about the existence and nature of God, with what John Calvin calls the *sensus divinitatis?* According to Calvin, the knowledge of God has been implanted in the human mind. Why not begin, then, with the idea of God which, as Charles Hodge puts it, "lies in the mind"?[19] There is a long-standing tradition of philosophical theology that begins with the idea of a "most perfect being," from which it then deduces a number of divine attributes, such as eternity, goodness and immutability. Is the right preliminary theological question therefore a question about the concept of a being of infinite perfection? To answer in the affirmative is to pursue the philosopher's theism.

It is an open question, however, whether the God of the philosophers can be equated with the God of Abraham, Isaac and Jacob.[20] It is one thing to identify certain generic attributes of a supreme being, quite another to grasp Yahweh's covenant faithfulness, or the triune God, or the Father's readiness to forgive sinners. Calvin himself states the chief objection to this approach to doing theology, which is that the *sensus divinitatis* is corrupted by sin: "They do not apprehend God as he offers himself, . . . but measure him by the yardstick of their own carnal stupidity [and] imagine him as they have fashioned him in their own presumption."[21] The danger in beginning from the idea of divine perfection, then, is that our thinking is muddled and perverse. Thinking ourselves theologians, we become idolaters. The postmoderns clearly have a *biblical* point: what we say about God on the basis of our own ideas may well reveal more about us, our social location and our sinfulness, than it does about God.

There is a further difficulty in doing theology on the basis of our idea of a supreme being: how does one define "perfection"? Consider the models of God that are presently in vogue. Many of them reflect what our culture currently considers to be a perfection or ultimate value.[22] Though they appear to be attempts to think about God as "most perfect being," they actually begin "from below," that is, from human experience and human culture. They tend to take as authoritative only those bits of the biblical account that fit in with their preconceived ideas and pass political muster.

Sallie McFague is a case in point. She believes that theology best addresses contemporary problems by using metaphors of God that speak compellingly to the

---

[19]Of course for Calvin and Hodge the very presence of the idea of God in the human mind is a function of our creation in God's own image.

[20]It was Blaise Pascal who famously distinguished the God of the philosophers from the God of Abraham, Isaac and Jacob.

[21]John Calvin, *Institutes of the Christian Religion,* ed. John T. McNeil (Philadelphia: Westminster Press, 1960) 1.4.1 (order slightly amended).

[22]Chief among these is love. See chapter three for an assessment of certain contemporary approaches to the love of God.

contemporary situation. She explains her approach to theology in *Models of God*. Theologians should look to the Bible not for information about God but rather as a model of how theology ought to be done: metaphorically, with images. Theology "is principally an elaboration of a few basic metaphors and models in an attempt to express the claim of Christianity in a powerful, comprehensive, and contemporary way."[23] As to the "claim of Christianity," McFague identifies it with the claim that the universe is neither indifferent nor malevolent and that there is a power "which is on the side of life and fulfilment."[24] Because our global, ecological situation is different from that of the biblical authors, however, McFague declares us free to use new metaphors and images that will express this claim in a manner that better meets the needs of our time. In particular, McFague wants theologians to abandon "outmoded and oppressive" metaphors that depict God as "Father" (too patriarchal) or that pictures the God-world relation in terms of king and kingdom (too hierarchical). Theology for McFague is *mostly* fiction, but some fictions are less oppressive than others.

What regulates what McFague the theologian says about God? Not the Bible, nor the theological tradition. No, the criterion for what McFague says about God is her experience of transforming love, which she somehow connects to the story of Jesus. In the final analysis, McFague uses her own values and experience as the standard against which everyone else's (including the biblical authors') experience and idea of God are evaluated. Though she acknowledges the pluralism of ways of thinking about God, this does not trouble her, as she relies on her own pragmatic criterion— does such and such a model of God advance the cause of transformative love?—to sort the doctrinal wheat from the chaff.[25] Unfortunately, notions such as the incarnation and the atonement end up in McFague's theological dustbin. The idea that a God-man died for our sins as a representative may have made sense in terms of Platonic philosophy, but in today's terms it offers us "a salvation we do not need."[26] For McFague, images of sacrificial atonement, or of dying and rising gods, simply do not address our situation; we can therefore discard them. Indeed McFague is positively Jeffersonian in her use of Scripture: her method amounts to scissors and paste, to cutting out those portions of Scripture that do not scratch where our culture itches.

McFague finds the Bible's tendency to speak about God as "Lord" particularly irritating. The notion that God lays down the law for human beings is too oppressive for

---

[23]Sallie McFague, *Models of God: Theology for an Ecological, Nuclear Age* (Philadelphia: Fortress, 1987), p. xi.

[24]Ibid., p. x.

[25]The story of Jesus apparently expresses God's salvific power, but the real touchstone for determining just what this power is like seems to be McFague's own experience.

[26]McFague, *Models of God*, p. 54.

McFague. She prefers to think about God not as Lord but as Lover of the world, and about the world not as the Lord's realm but rather as God's body. This "body of God" model is more useful in addressing the cultural sensibilities of our time, especially as we seek to cope with our planetary ecological crisis. McFague explains the thesis of her book: "*The Body of God* begins with an analysis of the ecological or planetary crisis that we face. . . . My contribution is the model of the body, a model that unites us to everything else on our planet in relationships of interdependence. In my own journey I have discovered the body to be central to Christianity, to feminism, and to ecology. This organic model suggests . . . a postpatriarchal, Christian theology for the twenty-first century."[27]

McFague's idea of God, then, is distinctly feminine, and she is in touch with her body. This approach has little to offer by way of defense to Feuerbach's criticism that "God" is simply a projection of human values onto a heavenly figure. Nevertheless, McFague's example is instructive; it reminds us of theology's constant temptation to make God into our own image. The moral of this story is clear: a deregulated *sensus divinitatis* makes easy prey for the ideologies of the day.

Thinking Scripture apart from God: The "sensus literalis." Is it possible to reverse the above strategy and begin theology not with the doctrine of God and the *sensus divinitatis* but with Scripture and its literal meaning, the *sensus literalis?* At first glance this approach seems more promising, for what we need is an independent criterion to regulate what we say about God. This is precisely what the Greek word *canon* means: a "measuring rod," a yardstick with which to determine whether our talk of God measures up. Why not start theology with a commonsense reading of the "plain" or "natural" sense of the text?

On closer inspection, there are problems with this approach as well. In the first place, the literal sense has in the modern world dwindled into the historical sense, or rather, into the "only human" sense. Biblical scholars who start "from below," with the human words of the historical authors, find it difficult, if not impossible, to climb up Jacob's ladder so as to discover the Word of God. Such a focus on the "only human" meaning ultimately results in a loss of *canonical* functioning. The words of historical authors fail to carry divine authority.

The second problem, as postmoderns are quick to point out, is that common sense is not really common, not universal, at all; it is rather a social-cultural construction. One community's "plain" or "natural" reading may be another community's misinterpretation. In short, a focus on the *sensus literalis* leads to the same problem as did the *sensus divinitatis:* the recognition that our intuitions and interpretations alike are subject to cultural relativity at best and to sinful idolatry at worst. "Back to the

[27]Ibid., p. x.

Bible" may be a good battle cry, but the postmodern suspicion is that we are really being led back to Egypt, back to the bondage of a particular Bible teacher's or theological tradition's or denomination's interpretation.

Simply to claim that one is starting with the Bible is not to say much. In the first place, most heretics have claimed as much. Second, we have to recognize the plurality of textual kinds in the Bible. There are two testaments, four Gospels and a dozen or so major types of literary genres. Can one approach to reading the Bible do justice to its literary, historical and theological variety? While we may wish to begin with the Bible as "most perfect Word," this starting point alone does not tell us which of the many interpretative approaches to employ. What does it mean to do theology "according to the Scriptures"?

This recognition of a variety of literary kinds in the Bible is one reason that John Goldingay, like Sallie McFague, prefers to speak of "models" in the plural: *models for Scripture*.[28] Just as McFague is reluctant to let any one image or metaphor of God become predominant, so Goldingay is reluctant to let any one model or category of Scripture overshadow the others. Consider, for example, a few of the models to which one might reasonably appeal as a means for starting with Scripture: "revelation," "inspiration," "authority," "witness." The problem, says Goldingay, is that none of these terms is a biblical term for referring to the Bible as a whole, nor is any one model a suitable covering term for the whole of Scripture. Goldingay argues that each of these terms find its proper home in certain parts of the Bible only. For example, *witness* is well suited to describe biblical narrative; *inspired* applies best to the prophets; *authority* corresponds to the biblical laws and commands; finally, *revelation* covers those biblical texts that reflect on events where God made himself known. Goldingay's conclusion is that most of the ways theologians have traditionally formulated the doctrine of Scripture are themselves unbiblical. Doing theology according to the Scripture, then, is harder than it first looks.

David Kelsey's Toolshed: Models of "God and Scripture"

We seem to be at an impasse. Starting with either God or Scripture involves building on a *sensus—divinitatis* or *literalis* respectively—that is ultimately subject to ideological distortion and leads to a plurality of competing models. It is high time to go back to the drawing board, or better yet, to the toolshed, located this time in the backyard of the Yale Divinity School. David Kelsey, longtime Yale professor of theology, has made a great leap forward in what I am calling "first theology."[29] His important book

---

[28]John Goldingay, *Models for Scripture* (Grand Rapids, Mich.: Eerdmans, 1994).
[29]Kelsey does not himself employ the term "first theology," though in focusing on the link between views of God and views of Scripture he treats the very problem for which I use this phrase.

Proving Doctrine: The Uses of Scripture in Modern Theology[30] is a closely observed analysis of how diverse theologians appeal to the Bible's authority to support their theological arguments. It is a brilliant study not of what theologians say about but what they *do with* Scripture, hence the emphasis on the *uses* of Scripture.

Kelsey's book convincingly shows that theologians appeal to the Bible in very different ways. The moral is that there is no one concept of biblical authority; rather, what biblical authority actually means in practice varies from theologian to theologian.

Seeing the Bible as . . . In my opinion Kelsey has asked the right preliminary question. He has correctly perceived that theologians make an important move prior to "proving" doctrine from Scripture. Kelsey calls this move a "construal" of Scripture. Before using the Bible as authoritative, theologians make a judgement as to *how* the Bible will be brought to bear authoritatively: *as* doctrine, *as* myth, *as* history, *as* story, and so on. To view the Bible *as* such and such is to construe it. Kelsey's first achievement, then, is to have documented a number of different construals of Scripture, thus helping explain how the Bible is actually put to work as a theological authority.

More models, more plurality—alas! The real merit of Kelsey's study, however, lies in its successful identification of the crucial point where theological approaches part company. The dividing line is not simply that between conservatives and liberals, between those who affirm biblical authority and those who do not. For both conservatives and liberals have to construe Scripture. What Kelsey discovers is that theologians in fact formulate their views of God and Scripture *together.* For when one decides in what way the Bible is authoritative—*as* teaching, history, myth and so on—one also makes a judgment regarding the way God is involved with Scripture and with the Christian community. In short: theological approaches part company over the issue of the mode in which God is present in the community through his Word. Kelsey identifies three possibilities: God's presence in and through Scripture may be construed in an ideational mode (as in B. B. Warfield, where God's presence is like the presence of truth), in the mode of concrete actuality (as in Karl Barth, where God's presence is like the presence of another person) or in the mode of ideal possibility (as in Rudolf Bultmann, where God's presence is like the presence of an existential possibility).[31]

We can best see what Kelsey has in mind by examining some of his case studies. For B. B. Warfield, the Bible is authoritative Scripture because it contains revealed

---

[30]David Kelsey, *Proving Doctrine: The Uses of Scripture in Modern Theology* (Harrisburg, Penn.: Trinity Press International, 1999). The original edition was published by Fortress Press in Philadelphia in 1975, under the title *The Uses of Scripture in Recent Theology.* The two editions are identical, save for an additional six-page preface in the newer version.

[31]See Kelsey, *Proving Doctrine,* p. 161.

propositions. Warfield takes the Bible *as* doctrine and simultaneously views God *as* revealer of truth. His doctrine of God and his doctrine of Scripture imply one another. Rudolf Bultmann, to take another example, conceives faith as a mode of self-understanding and Scripture as the expression of the self-understanding of faith. On this view God is not a personal agent who does things in history so much as the power behind a new human possibility. Accordingly Bultmann does not appeal to the Bible as history but as myth that both expresses and has the power to transform human existence. The point, again, is that one's view of God and one's view of Scripture are mutually *inclusive*.

To account for this mutual implication of God and Scripture defines the task of first theology. As I am using the notion, then, *first theology concerns the nature of the relation between God and Scripture*. What we discover in Kelsey's toolshed is a theological variation of the famous hermeneutical circle. Our view of Scripture affects our view of God, just as our view of God colors our view of Scripture.

The "sensus fidelium." How does Kelsey explain a theologian's decision to interpret the God-Bible relation in one way rather than another? How is it that Christians theologians can agree *that* the text is authoritative but disagree as to the manner in which it exercises its authority—as history, as doctrine, as myth and so forth? Kelsey argues that every theologian, and every believer for that matter, makes an imaginative judgment as to what Christianity is all about based on his or her participation in the Christian community. According to Kelsey, what is of decisive importance is not textual exegesis but a "pre-text" imaginative judgment in which the theologian tries to express his or her sense of how God's presence among the faithful is tied up with the way the faithful engage with Scripture.[32] What counts as first theology for Kelsey, then, is not the *sensus literalis* but the *sensus fidelium:* the sense of the people of faith as to how God is present in their community through Scripture.

In my judgment, Kelsey's study of the uses of Scripture in recent theology represents a great methodological leap forward. It is an analytic tour de force. At the same time, despite his protestations of theological neutrality, I believe he takes two fateful steps back.[33]

First, Kelsey tends to describe a given theologian's approach in terms of one construal only. He assumes, in other words, that each theologian treats *all* of Scripture in terms of a single overarching construal. Moreover, Kelsey seems to accept such

---

[32]In Kelsey's words: "These decisions [regarding how to construe Scripture] are decisively shaped by a theologian's prior judgement about how best to construe the mode in which God's presence among the faithful correlates with the use of scripture in the common life of the church" (ibid., p. 167).

[33]In both the original and the new edition, Kelsey insists that he is making no *constructive* theological points; his analysis is (almost) purely descriptive. Methinks he doth protest too much.

mono-construals as normal, never acknowledging the possibility that some parts of Scripture may be more susceptible to certain construals than others.[34] Now it does seem to be the case that many theologians tend to gravitate toward a particular part of Scripture and then interpret the whole of Scripture in light of that part. Warfield, for example, tends to treat the whole of Scripture as doctrine. Hans Frei and others have claimed, similarly, that Karl Barth treats all of Scripture as a narrative rendering of the triune God. The natural partner of Bultmann's existentialist theology is surely the wisdom literature of the Bible, with its apparent disregard for history.

Matching theologians to the biblical genres they tend to favor makes for an interesting graduate school game. Friedrich Schleiermacher? He tends to read the whole of Scripture as if it were all psalms. Wolfhart Pannenberg? What matters to him is reading Scripture in terms of apocalyptic. And so forth. There is a serious point to this exercise, however. It serves to remind us how easy it is for systematicians to fall prey to reductionism—the temptation of thinking that the whole wealth of theological knowledge can fit into our categorical box. The problem with this one-size-fits-all approach to the Bible-theology relation is twofold: it's reductionistic, and (as Goldingay has shown) it's unbiblical. We should not read *all* of Scripture as myth, or as history, or as doctrine, or as *any* one thing only. I will return to this thought in a moment.

The second problem with Kelsey's analysis is his working assumption that one's imaginative decision about the God-Scripture relation must always be "pre-text." The *sensus fidelium*—the church's impression of what the Christian thing is all about—is learned as we participate in the Christian community, not as we exegete the text.[35] Kelsey is quite explicit about this. But should first theology rest on this *sensus fidelium*, on the community's imaginative, "pre-textual" judgment? To answer in the affirmative is to assign theological authority to the community rather than to Scripture.[36] I believe that the clues to a better way forward lie in the toolsheds we have already visited.

---

[34]The reason Kelsey does not take up this latter possibility, I believe, is that he is convinced that construals are "pre-text," that is, uninformed by textual exegesis. If the text is not the decisive factor in a theologian's imaginative construal of Scripture, then, the fact that the Bible is composed of different kinds of texts is of little significance.

[35]Interestingly, Kelsey affirms the "determinate givenness" of the structure of "tradition" (and its ability to impose certain "checks" on one's imaginative construal) but not of Scripture (*Proving Doctrine*, p. 174).

[36]The strongest argument for deferring to the believing community's judgment is that which sees the church's practices as the result of the Holy Spirit's work. Indeed it has recently been suggested, by a group of theologians connected with the Center of Catholic and Evangelical Theology, that a pneumatological ecclesiology is the best candidate for "first theology." See, for example, James J. Buckley and David Yeago, eds., *Knowing the Triune God: The Work of the Spirit in the Practices of the Church* (Grand Rapids, Mich.: Eerdmans, 2001),

Back to the Toolshed:
The Bible as Divine Communicative Action

To succeed in something, one needs the right preliminary question, and perhaps a toolbox as well. Winston Churchill once declared, in the context of waging a world war, "Give us the tools, and we will finish the job." Christian theologians too are engaged in a kind of war, a "culture war" over the nature of language and textual interpretation. The doctrine of Scripture is perhaps the greatest casualty of this war as it has been waged on the postmodern front.

The toolbox of language: Wittgenstein. What kind of tools does the theologian need to finish the job, or indeed to begin it? With what kind of toolbox should the theologian work? The philosopher Ludwig Wittgenstein drew a now famous analogy between language and a toolbox: "Think of the tools in a tool-box: there is a hammer, pliers, a saw, a screw-driver, a glue pot, nails and screws. The functions of words are as diverse as the functions of those objects."[37] Wittgenstein's point was that there are different uses of language that fit different activities or "forms of life": giving orders, reporting an event, telling a story, making a joke, thanking, greeting and so forth.[38] Wittgenstein himself believed that many, if not most, philosophical problems arise out of confusions concerning the way language is being used. In particular, he resisted reducing the many things people do with language to any one function (e.g., referring, or "picturing" the world).

Wittgenstein would probably look askance at Kelsey's suggestion, based on his analysis of how theologians actually use Scripture, that the Bible plays one "language game" only. For Kelsey too sees Scripture as doing essentially one thing, namely, *shaping Christian identity.*[39] Despite his attention to the diverse uses of Scripture, Kelsey implies that what really makes the Bible "Scripture" is this one key function. Kelsey himself, then, offers a single construal of the mode of God's presence in and through his Word. And despite their apparent fascination with plurality, I believe that postmoderns too tend to construe language, of the Bible but also more generally, in nonplural terms.

On the one hand it would seem that the toolbox of language is, for postmoderns, a Pandora's box from which cultural demons fly out. Yet on the other hand there is a

---

and Reinhard Hütter, *Suffering Divine Things: Theology as Church Practice* (Grand Rapids, Mich.: Eerdmans, 2000). A full discussion of this option is beyond the scope of the present chapter. I have, however, examined this proposal elsewhere, in Kevin Vanhoozer, *The Drama of Doctrine: A Canonical-Linguistic Approach to Christian Theology* (Louisville, Ky.: Westminster John Knox, forthcoming), chap. 4.

[37]Ludwig Wittgenstein, *Philosophical Investigations*, 3rd ed., trans. G. E. M. Anscombe (Oxford: Blackwell, 1958), §11.

[38]Ibid., §23.

[39]See Kelsey, *Proving Doctrine*, pp. 90-96.

tendency to deprive language of many of its functions (e.g., referring, representing reality) in favor of an emphasis on language's world-constructing power. In short, the tendency, at least among those influenced by Continental strains of postmodern thought, is to construe *all* language as "fiction," a plaything.[40] While language may be the first philosophy of postmodernity, it ultimately leads to a philosophy of despair. For if language is a labyrinth from which there is no exit to the real world—if there is nothing in what we say—than ultimately nothing we say really matters. Language becomes a "sickness unto death."[41]

Christians, by way of contrast, should approach the toolbox of language believing that it is a gift from God. To be sure, much of what postmoderns say about the ideological use of language is true, but it is so because of human fallenness. Language can be corrupted, just like every other good gift of creation; that is not the fault of the tool, of course, but of its user. A corrupt people can use language for corrupt purposes: for telling lies, for manipulating others, for constructing false images and concepts of God. Be this as it may, God's original intention for language—its design plan—was altogether more positive: to be a tool for exploring the world, for interacting with other people, for getting to know God. We must therefore counter the postmodern despair of language with Christian *delight,* and the main reason we can delight in language is that we believe language is God-given (and hence reliable), and that we believe there is something beyond language to which our poems, our propositions and our prayers all point: the reality of the Creator and the created order.[42]

If language does many things, why do theologians typically read the Bible under one construal only, as if Scripture were doing only one thing? This is where I must respectfully take my leave of Kelsey. His toolshed lacks some essential supplies. For it is unnecessarily reductionistic to treat everything in the Bible as if it were only one

---

[40]There are various strains of postmodernity. See, for example, the eight types of postmodern theology presented in Kevin Vanhoozer, ed., *The Cambridge Companion to Postmodern Theology* (Cambridge: Cambridge University Press, forthcoming). In particular, Nancey Murphy has identified an "Anglo-American" strain of postmodern thought that she associates with philosophers such as Wittgenstein and J. L. Austin, among others. See Nancey Murphy, *Anglo-American Postmodernity: Philosophical Perspectives on Science, Religion and Ethics* (Boulder, Colo.: Westview, 1997).

[41]This allusion to one of Søren Kierkegaard's works is intentional. I believe that Kierkegaard's critique of the so-called aesthetic or uncommitted way of life was prescient and prophetic, an impressively appropriate critique of tendencies that have come to fruition in our postmodern times. See Ronald L. Hall, *Word and Spirit: A Kierkegaardian Critique of the Modern Age* (Bloomington: Indiana University Press, 1993). I also invoke Kierkegaard as an ally on behalf of Christian truth claims in "The Trials of Truth," chapter twelve of the present work.

[42]With respect to the language-world relation, we must avoid thinking in either absolutist or anarchic terms. Language is neither a perfect nor a useless tool; it is rather an *adequate* one. While it may have rough edges, it is nevertheless able to get most jobs done—including the theological.

kind of "tool": whether narrative, or doctrine, or history, or another kind. In order to take Wittgenstein's metaphor of the toolbox seriously, then, we must be attentive to the many things that can be done with words, sentences and texts.

Holy Scripture: How God does things with biblical words. From seeing language as a tool to seeing speech as a way of doing things is but a short, but invaluable, step. What Wittgenstein and others have shown us is that words do not do one thing only—say, represent the world—but that we can do many things with words. Speaking and writing may therefore be deemed to be forms of what I shall call communicative action.[43] Furthermore, if using language is a form of action, we would do well to think about the ethical implications of doing things with words. Both speakers/authors and listeners/readers have communicative responsibilities. Communicative agents have a responsibility to make good on their claims. Yet recipients or observers of communicative action are responsible for doing justice to the words of others. In an age that has celebrated the birth and the creativity of the reader, it is not hard to see how authors figure among the marginalized voices of our times.[44] Doing justice to an author—arguably the most marginalized other in postmodenity!—means recognizing what the author has said and done in a text, rather than foisting one's own opinions and ideas onto the text.[45] I take this to be an implication of both the Golden Rule and the ninth commandment: "Thou shalt not bear false witness."

The application to theology should be obvious. Inasmuch as *sacra doctrina* is tied up with *sacra pagina,* theologians must do justice to the diverse uses of language—that is, to the different kinds of "speech acts"—in the Bible. But this is not all. One must also construe the mode of God's presence vis-à-vis the Bible. I submit that God is present in Scripture precisely as a communicative agent, its ultimate author. The agency behind the variety of communicative acts in the Bible, then, must be ascribed not only to its human authors but ultimately to God.[46] Scripture contains a wide rep-

---

[43]Communicative action pertains to what we do in conveying messages. For instance, we can inform, or warn, or question, or promise. Note that some communicative acts may be performed without benefit of words. We can warn someone simply by waving our arms. More sophisticated forms of communicative action, however, require the use of language. It is difficult to discuss, say, the nature of knowledge with body language alone. For a more extended treatment of communicative action, see chapter six of the present work, "From Speech Acts to Scripture Acts: The Covenant of Discourse & the Discourse of the Covenant."

[44]Note that the notion of responsibility for communicative action effectively weds the postmodern concern with language with the postmodern concern for ethics and respecting otherness.

[45]This is one of the principal themes in chapters eight and nine of the present work.

[46]I treat this important transition—from seeing the Bible as a collection of human speech acts to seeing it as a work of divine communicative action—more fully in chapter six of the present work. See also Nicholas Wolterstorff, *Divine Discourse: Philosophical Reflections on the Claim That God Speaks* (Cambridge: Cambridge University Press, 1995).

ertoire of what God does with human words.

If Kelsey were to examine my view, he would perhaps say that I construe the Bible *as* a rainbow of divine communicative acts. The principal advantage of this construal is that it derives not from a pre-text decision, nor from a cultural construct, but from the text.[47] The Bible itself depicts God as a speech agent: as One whose word comes to Israel via the law and the prophets, and then to the world in the person of Jesus Christ and his gospel. Of course God's power of communicative agency far surpasses ours. Whereas our words often fall flat, God is able to send his Spirit with his Word so that it will not fail to accomplish the purposes for which it was sent. Furthermore, God communicates not only information about himself but himself. What God ultimately wants to communicate to us is salvation, a share in the divine life; he wants to communicate the Spirit of Christ.

The notion of divine communicative action both clarifies the role and enriches the authority of Scripture in theology and in the Christian life. We saw earlier that theologians invariably think God and Scripture *together*. We also saw that there is a tendency to elevate one portion or aspect of Scripture above the others and to make that the model for how God relates to us through Scripture in general. By contrast, the view I am commending resists seeing the Bible's authority in terms of one model only (as only doctrine, or only history, or only myth and so on). Instead the Bible enjoys a multifaceted authority. Its promises are to be trusted, its commands obeyed, its songs sung, its teachings believed.

I submit that the best way to view God and Scripture together is to acknowledge God as a communicative agent and Scripture as his communicative action. The virtue of this construal, as far as first theology is concerned, lies in its implicit thesis that one can neither discuss God apart from Scripture nor do justice to Scripture in abstraction from its relation to God. For if the Bible is a species of divine communicative action, it follows that in using Scripture we are not dealing merely with information about God; we are rather engaging with God himself—with God in communicative action. The notion of divine communicative action forms an indissoluble bond between God and Scripture.

The recovery of the biblical-poetic imagination. I suggested earlier that there were three plausible candidates for the role of first philosophy in postmodernity. The notion of communicative action catches up the first two—language and ethics—with its suggestion that speakers and hearers alike are responsible for what is done with

---

[47]The reality may be more complex. The Bible is indeed considered "holy" by the church, and many Christians learn to treat it as such by participating in church practices. My point, however, is twofold: first, the church's perception of Scripture is not the force that *makes* it holy; second, it is the text's own claims, together with the ministry of the Spirit, that call forth the church's response.

language. What about the third candidate, aesthetics? As we have seen, postmoderns are keenly aware of the make-believe character of our texts and interpretations, each a linguistic construction in its own way. Interestingly, Kelsey points out that the determining factor of a theologian's use of Scripture is her *imaginative* construal of the mode of God's presence.[48] I believe that there is indeed a legitimate role for aesthetics, and the imagination, to play in theology. However, contra Kelsey, I believe that the imagination is both enabled and constrained primarily by Scripture. Similarly, contra the radical postmoderns, I believe that the imagination involves more than the power of fiction. Could it not be that God has designed the imagination to be not merely a faculty of fantasy—a means for seeing what *is not* there—but as a means for seeing what *is* there, particularly when the senses alone are unable to observe it?[49]

That ideology-criticism ultimately devalues the imagination is the second great irony of postmodernity. (The first is that the postmodern preaches justice for the other but ultimately emasculates the voice of the author.) It is ironic that postmoderns like Cupitt and McFague revel in metaphor and story yet ultimately drain them of significance by insisting that we cannot really believe in them because we know that they are actually fictional constructions. This highbrow skepticism with regard to the imagination finds a strange bedfellow in lowbrow popular culture. Consider the fall 2000 television lineup. According to *Time* magazine, of the thirty-six new shows, all but one were aimed at adolescents, and none of them illumined the human condition in significantly new ways. It was a sad case of "the bland leading the bland." Our souls are undernourished; we are suffering from spiritual malnutrition, from image anemia: a deficiency of vital stories in the bloodstream of the imagination, resulting in weariness, depression and a culture of death.[50]

A similarly anemic imagination characterizes too much exegetical and theological scholarship. Modern and postmodern biblical interpretation alike are dominated by various types of analysis or "undoing." The modern biblical critic looks *at* Scripture, takes it apart layer by layer, exposing its component parts. The postmodern biblical critic looks at *interpretations* of Scripture, takes them apart, exposes their ideological underpinnings. Neither way of reading is able to appreciate the text as a meaningful whole, a work of literature with imaginative integrity. To return to C. S. Lewis's distinction: neither modern nor postmodern biblical criticism looks *along* the grain of the biblical text.

---

[48]Kelsey, *Proving Doctrine*, p. 159.
[49]There is a growing bibliography on the role of the imagination in theology. See, for example, John McIntyre, *Faith, Theology and Imagination* (Edinburgh: Handsel, 1987), and Trevor Hart, "Imagination and Responsible Reading," in *Renewing Biblical Interpretation,* ed. Craig Bartholomew (Grand Rapids, Mich.: Zondervan, 2000).
[50]For a more extended attempt at theological interpretation of culture, see chapter eleven of the present work.

Lewis can serve as a helpful mentor to the theologian when it comes to reading books. What literary critics like Lewis share with theologians, at the very least, is an interest in great literature. For while the Bible is more than great literature, it is certainly not less. The question Lewis's distinction between looking at and looking along raises for biblical interpretation is whether theologians have been sufficiently attentive to the literary nature of the Bible, to its status as a complex textual act and to the role of the imagination in both structuring and recovering the biblical message.

How can we interpret Scripture so that we do not merely look at its light beams but *along* them? It is important not to overreact, either to modernity or to postmodernity. Theologians should not be coerced into a forced march behind the banner of either doctrine or story. Theologians ought to resist the forced choice between reading for propositional knowledge on the one hand and for personal knowledge on the other. Above all, theologians ought to resist having to view the God-Scripture relation in terms of either only seeing or only tasting. After all, we want not only propositional, "seeing" knowledge but personal "tasting" knowledge: "Taste *and* see that the LORD is good." In Lewis's words: "One must look both *along* and *at* everything."[51]

The various ways of "looking at" the biblical texts (at the sources, the form, the redaction, the tradition history, the rhetoric, the grammar) are functions of critical reason. "Looking along," on the other hand, is a feat and function of the imagination. It has to do with our ability to enter into different ways of seeing and experiencing and thinking. The imagination is our port of entry into other worlds. In particular, the imagination enables us to enter the world of the text, to read Scripture along its various textual grains.[52] Genuine interpretation is less a matter of looking *at* Scripture than of looking *along* Scripture, thereby seeing God, the world and ourselves as biblical texts do. One can discern what God is saying and doing in Scripture only by such looking along.

Theology must relearn the skill of seeing reality as Scripture sees it. This involves, among other things, the rehabilitation of the imagination. Calvin called the Bible the "spectacles of faith"; I would add only that these spectacles are composed not of one lens but of several. To look along the text of Scripture is to become an apprentice to the Bible's diverse literary forms. The spectacles of faith enable us to look along the text, to see our world and ourselves through the lenses of biblical history, prophecy, law, apocalyptic and Gospel. These are the texts that should be informing, and transforming, our worldview.

---

[51]Lewis, "Meditation in a Toolshed," p. 215.

[52]Paul Ricoeur distinguishes the text as structured *work* from the "world of the text." Though he does not employ or allude to Lewis's distinction between "looking at" and "looking along," I believe Ricoeur is making a similar point. We can analyze the text as work, but we gain entry to the world of the text only by an effort of sympathetic imagination.

Theological hermeneutics as first theology: The "sensus scripturalis." We are now in a position to respond to our initial query: should theology therefore begin with God or Word of God? The answer is: Neither. I have argued that Christian theologians must resist this pernicious either-or and affirm instead a both-and approach: we interpret Scripture as divine communicative action in order to know God; we let our knowledge of God affect our approach to Scripture.[53] There is a certain circularity here, to be sure, but it need not be vicious, so long as we remember that our interpretations are corrigible and that we are ultimately accountable to the text.[54] The circularity in question is that of the traveler who makes frequent round-trip voyages. We may visit the same places, but we see new things because we are wiser for our travels.

Theology, then, is God-centered biblical interpretation. It follows that hermeneutical theology (doing theology by way of biblical interpretation) and theological hermeneutics (bringing Christian doctrine to bear on the principles and practice of interpretation) are equally ultimate. I therefore propose theological hermeneutics as my candidate for first theology. Note well: I did not say "hermeneutics" full stop. I am rather advocating a distinctly Christian and theological, which is to say trinitarian, approach to biblical interpretation that begins by recognizing God as a triune communicative agent and Scripture as the written locus of God's communicative action.[55]

An objection now arises. Am I not constructing just one more model of Scripture, just one more case study for Kelsey to undertake? Is this not one more myopic system that takes thought captive and reduces the richness of Scripture to one dimension only? I think not. For while I have commended an overarching model—Scripture as God's communicative action—the concept of communicative action enables us to appreciate the wide-ranging diversity of the language and literature of the Bible in a manner that the other models do not. The rubric of communicative action embraces a

---

[53] I am convinced that there is a demonstrable and intrinsic connection between the doctrine of God and the doctrine of Scripture. The current debate over the so-called openness of God provides an apt illustration. Exegetical decisions about whether to interpret biblical predications of God literally or figuratively are informed as much by theology as by Hebrew or Greek grammar. For an analysis of one aspect of this debate, see chapter three in the present work.

[54] I have elsewhere argued that readers who have achieved linguistic and literary competence, and who seek to cultivate the interpretative virtues through the Spirit's sanctifying work, may arrive at an adequate (not absolute) knowledge of the text's determinate meaning (see Vanhoozer, *Is There a Meaning in This Text?* chaps. 6-7). Being accountable to the text is another way of speaking of the interpreter's responsibility to do justice to what the author was saying and doing with his or her words.

[55] Jesus Christ is, of course, the Word of God made flesh. The life of the incarnate Jesus therefore is God's communicative act as well. The point is, however, that one can begin with Christ only by attending to the apostolic (divinely authorized) testimony about him.

plurality of specific construals. Indeed its strength lies precisely in its ability to do justice to the many ways God is present and active in his Word: commanding, promising, warning, comforting and so on. It also enables us to conceive of an integral unity between God and Scripture, without confusing them and without reducing one to the other. Finally, the notion of divine communicative action highlights the importance of entering, via the imagination, into the many ways of seeing and thinking about God, the world and ourselves enacted by the divine Author for our benefit.

What Counts as Success in Theology?

Those who wish to succeed, I have said, must ask the right preliminary questions. Well, I have now examined the preliminary questions. Now we need to ask, what counts as success in the toolshed of theology? If theological hermeneutics is "first theology," the place to begin, what is the proper *end* of theology? To put it bluntly: what is a doctrine of Scripture, even a reconstructed one, good for? Just what counts as success in theology, and in theological hermeneutics?

Wisdom: Living along the text. The postmodern condition has awakened theologians from their dogmatic slumbers—to be precise, from the dream that doctrine or system is the be-all and end-all of theology. I have argued that the Bible is much more than a book of information, more even than divinely revealed information. It is a collection of divine communicative actions that continue to work their effects in those who read in Spirit and in truth.

How should we respond to Scripture as God's communicative action? For every communicative action there is an equal and opposite communicative reaction. Well, not quite. Readers do not always behave according to Newton's third law of motion. Yet responsive readers should respond to the biblical text in a fitting manner, a manner that is appropriate to what the text itself is doing. Because God does many things with words, our responses too will be varied: we must affirm the doctrine, obey the law, hold fast in hope to the promises, rejoice in the gospel. First theology is a matter of performance knowledge, a matter of doing the Word, of *living,* as well as *looking,* along the text.

What counts as success for human beings? Who is the person "most likely to succeed"? If we wish to succeed, we must undertake a prolegomenon of the human condition. Just what are the right preliminary questions for the human race? The classification of the human species affords a clue: *Homo sapiens.* Sapience—wisdom—is good for human beings. Wisdom is more than information, more than propositional knowledge. It is lived knowledge, performance knowledge.[56] The ultimate

---

[56]I treat the theme of performance knowledge at greater length in Vanhoozer, *Drama of Doctrine,* chaps. 4, 7 and 8.

justification for the study of theology is that doctrine is good for our selves and good for our souls.[57] Doctrine is a statement not merely of information, nor even of knowledge, but of wisdom: the wisdom of God made known in Jesus Christ. Christian doctrine yields that vital knowledge which, when applied, leads to human flourishing: abundant life.

When wisdom is not learned—that is, appropriated and acted on—it remains inert. It is of no more use than a pair of reading glasses that one looks at rather than through. If we do not look, and live, along the text, our doctrines of biblical authority will similarly be useless, and we will be left only with "cheap inerrancy": the profession of the Bible's truthfulness without a corresponding discipleship to the One who is the truth.

The right preliminary question: Rightness. Success in theology, then, is connected to success in life. If we consult not Aristotle but the Scriptures, we see that the most important right preliminary question is how to become right with God.

Asking the right preliminary question is not a sufficient condition for success, of course. We also need the correct answer. The Bible proclaims the answer. If we look along the biblical text, we will see Christ; if we live along the text, we will meet Christ and we will learn Christ. Faith comes by the hearing of the Word; human flourishing comes from the doing of the Word—from trusting the word of promise and obeying the word of command. Success in theology is a matter of becoming right with God.

When one stands in right relation to God, all one's other relations are made right too. Knowing ourselves forgiven by God, we are empowered to forgive others. This too is part of our "lived knowledge" of Scripture. Indeed it may be no exaggeration to say that the ultimate purpose of biblical interpretation is to achieve right relationships: with God, with others and with oneself. After all, Christian truth is in the service of Christian love. If I speak with the tongues of Reformers and of professional theologians, and I have not personal faith in Christ, my theology is nothing but the noisy beating of a snare drum. And if I have analytic powers and the gift of creating coherent conceptual systems of theology, so as to remove liberal objections, and have not personal hope in God, I am nothing. And if I give myself to resolving the debate between supra and infralapsarianism, and to defending inerrancy, and to learning the Westminster Catechism, yea, even the larger one, so as to recite it by heart backwards and forwards, and have not love, I have gained nothing.

First philosophies eventually come and go. So do trends in theological method. I cannot predict what the next generation will decide is of first priority and impor-

---

[57]This point has been brought home with considerable force by Ellen Charry's *By the Renewing of Your Minds: The Pastoral Function of Christian Doctrine* (Oxford: Oxford University Press, 1997).

tance. This one thing I do know: that there is no more vital task facing Christians today than responding faithfully to Scripture as God's authoritative speech acts—not because the book is holy but because the Lord is, and because the Bible is his Word, the chief means we have of coming to know Jesus Christ. Those who interpret the Bible rightly—those who look and live along the text, following the written words to the living Word—will have rightly ordered loves and rightly ordered lives. Indeed first theology matters precisely because it is tied up with our *first love*. The apostle Paul leaves us in no doubt as to either his first theology or his first love: "I count everything as loss because of the surpassing worth of knowing Christ Jesus my Lord" (Phil 3:8).

Part One

God

Two

Does the Trinity Belong in a Theology of Religions?

*On Angling in the Rubicon
& the "Identity" of God*

*R*ivers and bridges, for some reason, figure prominently in debates concerning religious pluralism and the theology of religions. Mahatma Gandhi was one of the first to use a river analogy: "One may drink out of the same great rivers with others, but one need not use the same cup." "The soul of religion is one, but it is encased in a multitude of forms. My position is that all the great religions are fundamentally equal."[1] "Same . . . one . . . equal"—do all religions refer to the same God? This question whether the Christian God is identical with the referent of the other religions is, fundamentally, a question about the identity of God.

The Three Rivers—and a Fourth
Raimundo Panikkar symbolizes the history of Christianity's relation to other religions with three sacred rivers. The Jordan, with all its historical associations to the particular events of Israel with Yahweh and Jesus with the Father, stands for exclusivism— the traditional belief that Christianity is the only true religion. The Tiber symbolizes the distinctly Western mentality of Christendom, with its medieval Crusades and its modern missions. As all roads lead to Rome, so all rivers—religions—lead to Christianity. The "Declaration on the Relation of the Church to Non-Christian Religions,"

---

[1]Quoted in Bruce Demarest, *General Revelation: Historical Views and Contemporary Issues* (Grand Rapids, Mich.: Zondervan, 1982), p. 255.

approved by the Second Vatican Council in 1965, made inclusivism the official Roman Catholic position.[2] Inclusivists take the position that Christianity embraces what is true in the other religions.

According to Panikkar, neither mentality, Jordan or Tiber, adequately recognizes or respects the "otherness" of the other religions. The Ganges, formed from many sources and dispersed in diverging outlets, represents contemporary pluralism: Christianity is one of several valid religions. Here Panikkar wishes to speak neither of doctrinal Christianity nor of institutional Christendom but of "Christianness": the mystical, spiritual core of the faith that is shared by humanity at large.[3] We will return to Panikkar, and his trinitarian solution to the problem of religious pluralism, in due course.

Yet a fourth river has been invoked. Contemporary Christians, aware of the plurality of religions, stand before what Paul Knitter calls a "theological Rubicon": "To cross it means to recognize clearly, unambiguously, the possibility that other religions exercise a role in salvation history that is not only valuable and salvific but perhaps equal to that of Christianity. . . . It is to admit that if other religions must be fulfilled in Christianity, Christianity must, just as well, find fulfillment in them."[4]

Knitter notes three principal strategies—three bridges across the Rubicon—by which theologians typically move from exclusivism or inclusivism to a pluralistic position. First, an ever-increasing awareness of historical-cultural relativity with regard to knowledge and beliefs in general. From atop this bridge, exclusivists and inclusivists alike appear presumptuous with their breathtaking truth-claims of Christian absoluteness. John Bunyan had at least a foot on this bridge when he wrote: "Every one doth think his own Religion rightest, both *Jews* and *Moors* and *Pagans;* and how if all our Faith, and Christ, and Scriptures, should be but a thinks-so too?"[5] The second bridge is theological: it is the awareness that the divine mystery exceeds our linguistic and conceptual resources. Christian formulations are not exempt; they afford no privileged access to the divine Fact. The third bridge, the shared concern for justice and human welfare, is ethicopolitical in nature and best expressed by Hans Küng: "no world peace without peace among the religions, no peace among the reli-

[2]See David Wright, "The Watershed of Vatican II: Catholic Approaches to Religious Pluralism," in *One God, One Lord: Christianity in a World of Religious Pluralism,* ed. Andrew D. Clarke and Bruce W. Winter (Grand Rapids, Mich.: Baker, 1992), pp. 207-26.
[3]See Raimundo Panikkar, "The Jordan, the Tiber and the Ganges," in *The Myth of Christian Uniqueness: Toward a Pluralistic Theology of Religions,* ed. John Hick and Paul F. Knitter (Maryknoll, N.Y.: Orbis, 1987), pp. 89-116.
[4]Paul Knitter, "Toward a Liberation Theology of Religions," in *The Myth of Christian Uniqueness: Toward a Pluralistic Theology of Religions,* ed. John Hick and Paul F. Knitter (Maryknoll, N.Y.: Orbis, 1987), p. 225.
[5]Quoted in William C. Placher, *Unapologetic Theology: A Christian Voice in a Pluralistic Conversation* (Louisville, Ky.: Westminster John Knox Press, 1989), p. 15.

gions without dialogue between the religions, and no dialogue between the religions without accurate knowledge of one another."[6]

Same and Other: Must Orthodoxy Be Oppressive?

I will take it for granted that Christian theologians can agree that the other religions should be treated with charity, justice and respect. But what exactly do these virtues entail? Is it the case that every Christian truth-claim is an assault on the integrity of other religions? Must everyone entertain the same opinion (*ortho-doxa*) as I or receive a violent reprisal? Must orthodoxy be repressive?

Introducing the "other." Who is the other? The other is that which is not "us"— "them." In the Christian West, this meant that the other was until the sixteenth century "pagan"; during the Age of Reason, "unenlightened"; in the nineteenth century, "primitive"; in the twentieth century, "different."[7] In our times, then, the other is first and foremost a hermeneutical problem, an often intractable interpretive challenge that resists our faltering attempts to understand it.

Emmanuel Lévinas accuses Western philosophy of a totalizing and totalitarian discourse. Thought is nothing less than the violence by which the other is reduced to the Same; knowledge of others becomes knowledge of oneself. "Greek" represents the language and rule of the concept, the universal.[8] In "Greek" thinking the other is subdued, captured by consciousness; difference is domesticated. Philosophy tries to reduce the many to the one, the other to the same. Because "identity" is defined in opposition to "difference," the task of philosophy is to overcome otherness. So construed, philosophy is the report of a conquest, not a genuine encounter.

For Lévinas, the face of the other ultimately eludes philosophy's grasp.[9] The other's face proclaims a difference between the other and myself that cannot be dissolved: "I cannot make him mine, nor reduce him to my cognition of him."[10] In place of totality is plurality, which abandons the logic of assimilating members to classes. The face of the other is an infinite end in itself.[11] Our capacity for grasping reality is exceeded by my infinite duty to the other: to protect the other's otherness becomes

---

[6]Hans Küng, "Christianity and World Religions: Dialogue with Islam," in *Toward a Universal Theology of Religion*, ed. Leonard Swidler (Maryknoll, N.Y.: Orbis, 1987), p. 194.

[7]I am here following Bernard McGrane's typology as explored in *Beyond Anthropology: Society and the Other* (New York: Columbia University Press, 1989).

[8]See Robert Gibbs, *Correlations in Rosenzweig and Lévinas* (Princeton, N.J.: Princeton University Press, 1992), chap. 7.

[9]See Emmanuel Lévinas, "Ethics as First Philosophy," in *The Lévinas Reader*, ed. Seán Hand (Oxford: Blackwell, 1989), pp. 75-87.

[10]Gibbs, *Correlations*, p. 165.

[11]See ibid., p. 159: "For Lévinas, the ethical obligates me in the face of an other; my objection against the universal is not ultimately for my own sake as the unique individual, but is for the sake of the other person, whose individuality is lost."

the prime ethical imperative, and perhaps a description of what it is to love.[12]

Theology and the other. That there is an other that cannot simply be assimilated by me presents a challenge that is both epistemological and ethical. How have systematic theologians responded? Pluralists level two charges against theologians who have not yet crossed the Rubicon. First, the soteriological critique: Christian theology is exclusivistic. Wilfred Cantwell Smith expresses outrage at the narrow-minded mentality of theologians of the narrow road: "It is morally not possible actually to go out into the world and say to devout, intelligent, fellow human beings: 'We are saved and you are damned.' "[13] Second, the epistemological critique: Christian theology is repressive. Interestingly, this critique is directed against the inclusivist as often as the exclusivist. Both John Hick and George Lindbeck claim, for instance, that Karl Rahner's notion of the "anonymous Christian" is as imperialistic and deeply offensive to non-Christians as exclusivism.[14] The inclusivist too forces the other into a category that the other does not acknowledge. Küng, pertinently, asks whether Christians would be happy to be termed "anonymous Muslims."[15]

There seem to be, then, two strategies that Christian theologians may adopt vis-à-vis the other: conversion or conversation. Conversion, by remaking the other into the same, does to the other in practice what "Greek" thinking does to the other in theory. David Tracy speaks for pluralists who opt for the second strategy: "I believe that we are fast approaching the day when it will not be possible to attempt a Christian systematic theology except in serious conversation with the other great ways."[16] Theology needs to encompass within its horizons the religious experience of all humanity. Wilfred Cantwell Smith is another who claims that theology is inseparable from the history of religions: "From now on any serious intellectual statement of the Christian faith must include . . . some sort of doctrine of other religions. We explain the fact that the Milky Way is there by the doctrine of creation, but how do we explain that the Bhagavad Gita is there?"[17] Pluralists such as Panikkar think that Christian theologians would do well to converse with Eastern sources now that "Greek" thinking has been exposed as a parched riverbed. What the fathers did with Greek philosophy may point the way forward for theology today. John Cobb claims that the dialogical

---

[12]See ibid., p. 184: "Love binds me and creates a responsibility for the beloved that has no limits."

[13]Quoted in Placher, *Unapologetic Theology*, p. 16.

[14]So Gavin D'Costa, "Theology of Religions," in *The Modern Theologians*, ed. David F. Ford, vol. 2 (Oxford: Blackwell, 1989), p. 282 n. 28.

[15]Küng, "Christianity and World Religions," p. 203.

[16]David Tracy, *Dialogue with the Other: The Inter-religious Dialogue*, Louvain Theological and Pastoral Monographs (Grand Rapids, Mich.: Eerdmans, 1991), p. xi.

[17]Wilfred Cantwell Smith, "The Christian in a Religiously Plural World," in *Christianity and Other Religions*, ed. John Hick and Brian Hebblethwaite (London: Collins, 1980), p. 100.

relation with the religions of Asia today represents "a similar opportunity for reconceptualization in and through engagement with Eastern wisdom.[18]

"Angling": The Nature of Dialogue

The pluralist challenge to the systematic theologian is thus to enter into dialogue in good faith with the other, with the other religions. Why dialogue? Küng's response is a model of conciseness: "'War.' I believe that this is indeed the alternative to religious dialogue."[19] Assuming for the moment that this is sufficient reason to enter into conversation with the other, we need to inquire into the nature and implication of dialogue.

Dialogue as wager and commitment. To what do we commit ourselves when we enter into interreligious dialogue? Minimally, to the formal criteria implicit in rational conversation: the willingness to validate what one proposes and the absence of constraints on what the other can say in response. Jürgen Moltmann states that in serious dialogue "there can be no valid evasion of difficult questions by recourse to a higher authority not open to critical inspection by others."[20] Moreover, to enter into a dialogue then implies the possibility that one will not emerge unchanged. Indeed the full cost of dialogue is only here exposed: we must be prepared to put our most cherished beliefs at stake. James DiNoia applies the Golden Rule to interreligious dialogue: do unto others as you would have them do unto you.

But in order to do justice to the other, must we also follow the pluralists in their assumption that interreligious dialogue presupposes a commonality of subject matter? To enter into conversation in true pluralist spirit, must one check all one's commitments at the door? The pluralist assumption that dialogue is a means to truth depends on the presupposition that all religions are really expressions of the same fundamental reality. But *is* the other best served by the pluralist presupposition that the various religions are all talking about the same thing?

The angler as paradigm for a nonpluralistic dialogue. Against the pluralists, I wish to take Izaak Walton's description of the "Compleat Angler" as an alternative paradigm for engaging the other. The opening chapters of *The Compleat Angler* consist of a dialogue between a fisherman, a hunter and a falconer concerning the relative merits of their three sports. Walton's work brings to mind another dialogue about religious pluralism: Gotthold Lessing's *Nathan the Wise*. Walton himself belonged to a

---

[18]John B. Cobb Jr., "The Religions," in *Christian Theology: An Introduction to Its Traditions and Tasks*, ed. Peter C. Hodgson and Robert H. King (Philadelphia: Fortress, 1985), p. 371.
[19]Küng, "Christianity and World Religions," p. 194.
[20]Jürgen Moltmann, "Is 'Pluralistic Theology' Useful for the Dialogue of World Religions?" in *The Myth of Christian Uniqueness Reconsidered: The Myth of a Pluralistic Theory of Religions*, ed. Gavin D'Costa (Maryknoll, N.Y.: Orbis, 1990), p. 153.

group of intellectuals, called the Great Tew, who believed in religious moderation. As has been noted, Anglers are an obvious metaphor in Walton's book for Anglicans.[21]

The Angler has commitments, but he is willing to be tolerant of others and to argue his case with humility and humor as well as conviction, as the following quotation attests: "Angling is much more ancient than the Incarnation of our Saviour; for in the Prophet *Amos* mention is made of *fishhooks . . .*" (p. 23). Walton also offers the reader a short contemplation of rivers. Sitting by the River's side, we are told, is the fittest place for Contemplation (p. 24). And on the debate over whether contemplation or action be the happiness of humanity in the world, Walton argues that both meet together in the art of Angling (p. 24). Angling—with its overtones of trying for, gaining a perspective on—stands for the contemplative attitude of one who stands on the shores of the theological Rubicon and sits on the banks of the Ganges.

On the "Identity" of God

In what follows I want to relocate the problem of religious pluralism from soteriology to theology proper. I will examine the three options—exclusivism, inclusivism, pluralism—with regard to the question, are the other religions concerned with the same reality as is the Christian faith? Crossing the theological Rubicon into a pluralistic theology of religions means taking a position on the identity of God. "Identity" is, of course, susceptible of several meanings: numeric oneness, ontological sameness or permanence in time, and the personal identity of self-continuity.

Two kinds of identity. I wish to contrast two kinds of identity, to which I shall refer, following Paul Ricoeur, by the Latin terms *idem* (= sameness) and *ipse* (= selfhood).[22] I will superimpose Ricoeur's distinction on one drawn by Robert Jenson between two kinds of God. This juxtaposition is not arbitrary, for both Ricoeur and Jenson are concerned with the question of identity through, or over, time. Jenson distinguishes two kinds of God by the different ways in which each construes eternity. Every eternity, as a union of past and future, will be one of two broad kinds: a "Persistence of the Beginning" kind or an "Anticipation of the End" kind, for religion is either an attempt to escape from or a trust in the ultimate meaningfulness of temporality.[23]

What Jenson calls the Persistence of the Beginning kind of God I shall call the God of *idem*-identity, identity under the sign of the Same. The God of *idem*-identity

---

[21]So Jonquil Bevan, introduction to Izaak Walton, *The Compleat Angler* (London: J. M. Dent, 1993), p. xviii. The following references are to this edition.

[22]Paul Ricoeur, *Oneself as Another*, trans. Kathleen Blarney (Chicago: University of Chicago Press, 1992).

[23]Robert W. Jenson, *The Triune Identity: God According to the Gospel* (Philadelphia: Fortress, 1982).

is the philosophers' God and is identified by uncovering the properties of "perfect being." This "Hellenic" interpretation of God posits a timeless ground of Being above the temporal flux: an Unmoved Mover. This supreme Substance became the immutable God of classical theism. In Aristotle and the tradition of classical logic, identity is sameness, which is exclusive of otherness. The "Hellenic" interpretation of Being as an eternal self-same unity thus leads to a monistic ontology. Every differentiation must, on this view, be regarded as a tendency toward nonbeing.

As we have seen, Lévinas reads the history of Western thought precisely as the pursuit of identity, that is, as the process of excluding difference and of reducing the other to the same. Augustine, in Jenson's opinion, relates the three persons of the Trinity to the divine substance not only equally but *identically,* so that the differences between the persons are irrelevant to the being of God.[24] Accordingly, "the inheritance of Hellenic interpretation was received as what the scholastics would come to call 'natural' theology, a supposed body of truth about [the one] God shared with the heathens."[25]

Jenson's Anticipation of the End kind of God bears a striking similarity to what Ricoeur calls *ipse*-identity in his discussion of personal identity, the identity of self-constancy rather than sameness. God identifies himself to Israel as Yahweh and ties his proper name to a promise. It follows that the identity of God is tied up with his power to do what he says rather than with the sameness of substance. The "Hebrew" interpretation of God sees God not as standing apart from time but as standing faithful *through* it. God is true not because God lies unperturbed outside but because God can be relied upon in time, and until the end of time. In Jenson's words: "The continuity of his being is not that of a defined entity, some of whose defining characteristics persist from beginning to end. It is rather the sort of continuity we have come to call 'personal': it is established in his words and commitments, by the faithfulness of his later acts to the promises made in his earlier acts."[26]

Ipse-identity—selfhood—is not merely sameness. To be a self is more than to enjoy an uninterrupted persistence in time. And yet to be a self there must be some principle of permanence through time.[27] But is there a kind of permanence in time that is not simply the continuity of the Same? Here Jenson's account can be bolstered by Ricoeur's theory of narrative identity, which relates the search for a principle of

---

[24]"When the Nicenes call the Trinity as such God, they so named him *because* of the triune relations and differences; when Augustine calls the Trinity as such God, it is *in spite* of them" (ibid. p. 119).

[25]Ibid., p. 117.

[26]Ibid., p. 40.

[27]For a philosophical discussion of the problem of self-continuity, see Terence Penelhum, "Personal Identity," in *The Encyclopedia of Philosophy,* ed. Paul Edwards (London: Collier Macmillan, 1967), 6:95-107.

permanence in time to the question "Who?" rather than "What?"[28] The principle in question is keeping one's word. The continuity of the Same is one thing, the constancy of friendship or a promise quite another. *Ipse*-identity, centered on the self's constancy to its word, does not exclude otherness but requires it.

Pluralists argue for dialogue, for an encounter with the alterity of the other rather than a reduction of the other to self. Ironically, however, most theologians who have crossed the Rubicon reduce the particularities and otherness of the gospel's narrative identification of God to a bland, homogeneous, unitive or "monistic" pluralism in which the differences in the Christian identification of God are subsumed, sometimes violently, under the intolerant category of the Same.

Are the various religions referring to the same God? Pannenberg argues that Christianity must presuppose a general idea of God as identifying the subject to which it ascribes various attributes on the basis of God's actions. In Scripture, a general idea of God *('elohim)* underlies the statement that Yahweh alone is God (Is 43:10-11). The content of this general idea seems to be the God of the philosophers—the eternal, infinite One who is the origin of the cosmos. For Pannenberg, this is the minimal condition presupposed in all religious talk about God. However, Pannenberg goes on to assert that this minimal concept of God "is not identical with the essence of God which reveals itself in his historical acts."[29] Only in his further revelation does God show us "what it means to be God."[30]

An entity may be identified by means of definite description or by proper names and titles. A definite description designates a specific individual by creating a class that has but a single member (e.g., *first, man, walk, moon*). Proper names designate an individual as well, but without giving any information about that individual (e.g., Neil Armstrong). Jenson states: "The doctrine of the Trinity comprises both a proper name, 'Father, Son and Holy Spirit,' . . . and an elaborate development and analysis of corresponding identifying descriptions."[31] There are certain central identifying descriptions of God in the Scriptures: in the Old Testament, God is known as "the one who brought Israel out of Egypt" (Deut 5:6); in the New Testament, as "the one

---

[28]Ricoeur acknowledges an aspect of sameness in personal identity too: character. Character pertains to those aspects of my existence that I am unable to change; as he puts it, "character is truly the 'what' of the 'who'" (*Oneself as Another,* p. 122). Note that the stories of God's acts do not make him what he is but reveal him for what he has been from all eternity and always will be. The narrative does not constitute God's being but reveals it. I am arguing, however, that the narratives are a necessary mediation: ontological reflection alone does not allow us to identify the Christian God over against the others.

[29]Wolfhart Pannenberg, *Systematic Theology,* trans. Geoffrey W. Bromiley (Grand Rapids, Mich.: Eerdmans, 1991), 1:394.

[30]Ibid.

[31]Jenson, *Triune Identity,* p. 4. Compare Exodus 20:2—the name of God and the narration of his works belong together.

who raised Jesus from the dead" (Rom 4:24).

Those who have crossed the Rubicon into a pluralistic theology of religion have usually done so on the basis of a different account of religious reference. The problem with identifying by definite description, they say, is that such descriptions inevitably grow into doctrines. And as world history has shown, doctrinal descriptions divide. If reference is secured by an accurate doctrinal description, it follows that most accounts of God would be false. Maurice Wiles proposes, as an alternative to doctrinal description, a "causal theory" of reference, "in which reference is secured not by a correct definition of the object in question but by the causal-historical relations which link the speaker with the intended referent."[32] What fixes reference to God according to the causal theory is the religious experience of a few mystics or saints. The experience is associated with certain soteriological effects: changed behavior and transformed character. Others who have not had this anchoring experience may nevertheless "borrow" the reference from previous speakers. Proponents of the causal theory argue that identifying descriptions are attempts to define more precisely what is already being referred to as "God." Thus one need not conclude from the fact that people are saying different things about "God" that they are referring to different "gods": "God of the Hebrews, God of the Arabs, God of the Hindus . . . could all be different names for the same being *even if there is no significant overlap in belief about His nature.*"[33]

On the idea of God as love. Descriptivists like John Searle, however, find it implausible "to suppose that in the chains of communication, when they do occur, the only intentionality which secures reference is that each speaker intends to refer to the same object as the previous speaker."[34] If this were the case, speakers could use names but would know nothing of the type of thing named by the name. It is difficult, for instance, to see how the pluralist who relies on the causal theory of reference can say, "God is love." If there is not some minimal descriptive content associated with the word *God,* how can we know whether we are referring to the

---

[32]Maurice Wiles, *Christian Theology and Inter-religious Dialogue* (London: SCM Press, 1992), p. 39.

[33]Richard B. Miller, "The Reference of 'God,'" *Faith and Philosophy* 3 (1986): 14. John Searle in *Intentionality: An Essay in the Philosophy of Mind* (Cambridge: Cambridge University Press, 1983) argues that speakers refer, and thus that reference is successful only if the intentional content corresponds to the referent. For Searle, what counts is an intentional description associated with a name (compare William Alston, "Referring to God," in *Divine Nature and Human Language* [Ithaca, N.Y.: Cornell University Press, 1989], pp. 103-17). The debate between descriptivist and causal theories of reference is highly technical. For a statement of the causal theory, see Saul Kripke, *Naming and Necessity* (Cambridge, Mass.: Harvard University Press, 1972), and for a defense of the descriptivist theory see Searle, *Intentionality,* esp. chaps. 8-9).

[34]Searle, *Intentionality,* p. 249.

power of the whole rather than to an ephemeral feeling? Jenson writes: "Only when we specify *who* or *which* allegedly is God is 'God is' a threat or a promise, a solution or a conundrum."[35]

"Love," according to George Lindbeck, loses all meaning apart from a specific context: "the significant things are the distinctive patterns of story, belief, ritual, and behavior that give 'love' and 'God' their specific and sometimes contradictory meanings."[36] Perhaps the God of Buddhists and Hindus loves the world too, but only the Christian identifies God as the One who dies on humanity's behalf. A narrative identification of God, on the other hand, can both give "love" content and ascribe love to God. The doctrine of the Trinity is the result of a narrative identification of the Christian God.[37] The Gospels "figure" God—by ascribing certain acts and a pattern of activity—as economic Trinity, as One who relates to the world through Spirit and Son. The ontological Trinity—the belief in the eternality of the triune God—is a "configuration" of this economic configuration.

Debates about religious pluralism get bogged down because they start from the *idem*-identity of the *one* God, that is, with an assumption of *sameness*. In a pluralistic theology of religions, God is identified ontologically, by extrapolation from religious experience or through philosophical reflection; the various "economic" relations are considered incidental to the *one* God rather than constitutive revelations of the divine identity. The fathers, however, identified the one God with the plurality of Father, Son and Spirit. They thought of God equally in terms of oneness and threeness, and they did so by allowing the narrative to clarify and correct the philosophical identification of God.

The "Theology of Religions"

Early modern philosophers of religion suggested that true religion is natural and rational, available to all. For philosophers such as Kant, particularities that distinguish the ecclesiastical religions are merely secondary features—accidents of history—and thus inessential. Does twentieth-century theology of religions do better in preserving differences and in negotiating the scandal of particularity? Though Christian theologians have always held "doctrines" about other religions (e.g., that other religions teach some truth, that other religions are false, that other religions are fulfilled by Christianity), it is only relatively recently, with the demise of rational religion, that a

---

[35]Jenson, *Triune Identity*, p. xi.

[36]George A. Lindbeck, *The Nature of Doctrine: Religion and Theology in a Postliberal Age* (Philadelphia: Westminster Press, 1984), p. 42.

[37]By emphasizing narrative I do not wish to exclude the normative function of other types of biblical literature in identifying God. But narrative adds a specificity to notions such as "love" and "power" that these attributes might lack without a concrete narrative depiction.

"theology" of religions has been attempted.[38]

Pluralistic theology of religions. Briefly stated, a pluralistic theology of religions aims at recognizing the validity of other religions without abandoning Christian faith. Religious pluralists believe that all religions ultimately point to the same truth. Hick's pluralistic hypothesis takes its cue from Kant: the religions are culture-relative ways of experiencing the Real. "According to the pluralistic hypothesis, when we speak of God as known within a particular religious tradition—Jahweh or Adonai, the heavenly Father or the Holy Trinity, Allah, Shiva, Vishnu and so on—we are speaking of a humanly experienced *persona* of the Real."[39] Revelation—the Real as we apprehend it—is always phenomenal; the Real *an sich* is, however, beyond human experience and categories. Otherwise we would have "either to regard all the reported experiences as illusory or else return to the confessional position in which we affirm the authenticity of our own stream of religious experience whilst dismissing as illusory those occurring within other traditions."[40] Neither of these options, however, strikes Hick as "realistic." Why not?

The pluralist begins the interreligious dialogue with a conviction of sorts about the "rough parity" between the religions. To enter into true dialogue with the other means, for the pluralist, recognizing that there is some sort of truth in the other.[41] According to the pluralist, inclusivists are just as monistic as exclusivists when it comes to religious truth claims (for example, concerning the finality of Jesus as Savior)—they simply wish to affirm that more people are saved on their view than under an exclusivist soteriological scheme.

A "world" theology of religions. Whereas Hick sees all religions as paths to the same truth, Gordon Kaufman believes that truth emerges only in the course of conversation: "I call this a 'pluralistic' or 'dialogical' conception of truth."[42] But surely Kaufman here is confusing the concept of truth with the manner in which we attain it. In the end, or better *at* the end, truth is still one for the pluralist. All religions are

---

[38]See J. A. DiNoia, *The Diversity of Religions* (Washington, D.C.: Catholic University of America Press, 1992), chap. 1. On the development of history and theology of religions see Paul Knitter, *Toward a Protestant Theology of Religions: A Case Study of Paul Althaus and Contemporary Attitudes* (Marburg: N. G. Elwert, 1974), and Heinz Schlette, *Towards a Theology of Religions* (New York: Herder & Herder, 1966). See Pannenberg, *Systematic Theology,* for the theology of the history of religions.

[39]John Hick, *An Interpretation of Religion: Human Responses to the Transcendent* (London: Macmillan, 1989), p. 258. Hick rightly sees his pluralistic hypothesis as espousing a modalistic construal of the Trinity (pp. 271-72).

[40]Ibid., p. 249.

[41]Langdon B. Gilkey, "The Pluralism of Religions," in *God, Truth and Reality: Essays in Honour of John Hick,* ed. Arvind Sharma (New York: St. Martin's, 1993), p. 111.

[42]Gordon Kaufman, "Religious Diversity and Religious Truth," in *God, Truth and Reality: Essays in Honour of John Hick,* ed. Arvind Sharma (New York: St. Martin's, 1993), p. 158.

equally valid ways to the same truth.

It thus comes as no surprise that many pluralists now openly advocate a "world" or "universal" theology of religions. Wilfred Cantwell Smith argues that a theology of religions is "universal" if it draws its data from all religions. And in N. Ross Reat and Edmund F. Perry's *A World Theology* the monistic tendency of pluralistic theologies of religions is made explicit. Their thesis is both clear and simple: the world religions are different expressions of the same central spiritual reality of humanity—"God." As the central spiritual reality of humanity, "God" is "an expression of the human necessity of affirming meaning and purpose in one's life as a whole."[43] "God" is thus undeniable and desirable. "God" is also, as all the religions acknowledge, ultimately elusive.

This last dimension, elusiveness, is vital for world theology, as the authors point out: "Each religion thus embraces in its very heart a paradox. On the one hand, each disclaims that it totally comprehends ultimate reality. On the other hand, each claims to have supreme access, understanding, and relation to ultimate reality. This paradox signifies more than any religion has discerned, or has admitted responsibly."[44] In spite of their case for a world theology, Reat and Perry claim that they do not intend "to encourage the sacrifice of particularity on the altar of universality."[45] As symbolic expressions of the same central spiritual reality, the several religions may be mutually complementary rather than mutually exclusive.[46]

Can the Trinity fit into such a schema? Interestingly, though the authors rightly recognize the Christian belief that Jesus' person and work reveals God, they claim that Christianity's "theocentricity" entails that "even the revelation of God in Christ [is] itself relative to God whose reality exceeds all that is revealed in Christ."[47] The Christian claim that Jesus is the only way and truth "contradicts the Christian theocentric axiom that God alone is absolute."[48] The doctrine of the Trinity sits uneasily in such a scheme, particularly when we learn that God's "personhood" is not a universally attested characteristic of humanity's central spiritual reality.[49]

Against pluralistic and universal theology of religions. Is a pluralistic or world theology of religions any less exclusivistic and repressive of the "other" than is orthodox theology? No, for several reasons.

---

[43]N. Ross Reat and Edmund F. Perry, *A World Theology: The Central Spiritual Reality of Hunankind* (Cambridge: Cambridge University Press, 1991), p. 9.

[44]Ibid., p. 22.

[45]Ibid., p. 311.

[46]Ibid., p. 23.

[47]Ibid., p. 206.

[48]Ibid., p. 207.

[49]I discovered only one brief reference to the Trinity in the authors' sixty-six-page chapter on Christianity.

Does world theology embrace or efface the religiously particular and the different? A number of critics argue that pluralism has by no means escaped an exclusivistic attitude but merely transposed it from Christianity to modern Western liberalism. According to Kaufman, Hick's position is "utterly monolithic" insofar as it explains that as far as religious truth claims are concerned "they all come down to *essentially the same thing*."[50] Several critics have decried pluralism's illegitimate treatment of religion as a genus.[51] To the extent that the pluralist defines the core of religion, then, the very concept of religion must be exclusivistic: some phenomena will be in, others out. For example, Küng is quite sure that "one cannot place magic or belief in witches, alchemy, or the like, on the same level with belief in the existence of God."[52] But why can we not? Because such phenomena do not correspond to the contemporary liberal intellectual tradition to which most pluralists belong.[53]

Not only does a pluralistic theology of religions keep some phenomena out, but those that are let in must conform to the prevailing interpretive framework. Gavin D'Costa charges pluralism with itself being imperialistic and absolutist inasmuch as it proposes "to incorporate religions on the system's own terms rather than on terms in keeping with the self-understanding of the religions."[54] Kathryn Tanner observes that pluralism is a form of colonialist discourse that hinders rather than helps interreligious dialogue: "In imitation of the general way colonialist discourse constructs its 'Others,' the pluralist insistence on identity in beliefs, norms, or reference as a presupposition for inter-religious dialogue undermines, I argue, respect for other religions *as other*."[55]

Is pluralistic theology a theology without a concrete religious practice to support it, or is it the expression of a new religious faith? Pannenberg worries that Smith begins his theology of religions with a knowledge of God that is independent of the

---

[50]Kaufman, "Religious Diversity," p. 162 n. 2.

[51]See John Milbank, "The End of Dialogue," in *The Myth of Christian Uniqueness Reconsidered: The Myth of a Pluralistic Theory of Religions,* ed. Gavin D'Costa (Maryknoll, N.Y.: Orbis, 1990), pp. 174-91; Alister E. McGrath, "The Christian Church's Response to Pluralism," *Journal of the Evangelical Theological Society* 35 (1992): 487-501; and especially Robert T. Osborne, "From Theology to Religion," *Modern Theology* 8 (1992): 75-88.

[52]Hans Küng, "What Is True Religion? Toward an Ecumenical Criteriology," in *Toward a Universal Theology of Religion,* ed. Leonard Swidler (Maryknoll, N.Y.: Orbis, 1987), p. 236.

[53]See John V. Apczynski, "John Hick's Theocentrism: Revolutionary or Implicitly Exclusivistic?" *Modern Theology* 8 (1992): 39-52. Robert T. Osborne argues that the idea of "religion" itself is repressive, in that it was originally a projection of Christianity onto other phenomena. It then became possible to look at Christianity as the best exemplification of "true religion." See Osborne, "From Theology to Religion."

[54]Gavin D'Costa, introduction to *The Myth of Christian Uniqueness Reconsidered: The Myth of a Pluralistic Theory of Religions,* ed. Gavin D'Costa (Maryknoll, N.Y.: Orbis, 1990), p. ix.

[55]Kathryn Tanner, "Respect for Other Religions: A Christian Antidote to Colonialist Discourse," *Modern Theology* 9 (1993): 1.

religious traditions. But where would such a knowledge come from? Knitter and other pluralists wield a liberationist-pragmatic criterion for "true" religion: the concern for human welfare, not doctrine, provides a ground both for religious cooperation and for criticism of religion. But this stance is every bit as ideological as an exclusivistic theology of religions.

Küng proposes the "humanum" as a general ethical criterion with which one can judge the truth of a religion. True religion, he says, may not commend "what appears to be inhuman."[56] Appears to whom? I would not be at all surprised if celibacy did not appear as inhumane as cannibalism to some of the "humane modernists" whom Küng has in mind. Though Küng rightly recognizes that the fundamental question is "What is good for human beings?" he fails to see the inadequacy of his answer: "what helps them to be truly human."[57] Is not the nature, meaning and goal of the humanum precisely what is disputed in the religions?

Küng, of course, has his own vision of the humanum: "whatever clearly protects, heals, and fulfills human beings in their physico-psychic, individual-social humanity."[58] But as Paul Eddy points out, it is hard to see Küng's liberationist criterion as anything other than an arbitrary preference. Either one truly does abandon any "interested" viewpoint and accepts all notions at the dialogue table, "or else one acknowledges *some* meta-criteriological touchstone by which the various dialogical viewpoints are to be evaluated."[59]

Perhaps the blandness of a pluralistic theology of religion is its worst fault—religion should never be boring! And yet Hick manages to reduce the rich tapestry of religious belief and practice to a throw rug (all synthetic with no natural fibers). Hick discounts the significance of doctrine; religious truth is not cognitive so much as transformative. What it is that transforms us is, however, very difficult to specify. J. A. DiNoia complains that pluralists tend "to homogenize cross-religious variations in doctrines of salvation in the direction of an indeterminate common goal."[60] Kenneth Surin similarly calls attention to the inevitable result—differences become *merely* cultural: "monological pluralism sedately but ruthlessly domesticates and assimilates the other—*any* other—in the name of world ecumenism."[61]

---

[56]Küng, "What Is True Religion?" p. 240.

[57]Ibid., p. 242.

[58]Ibid.

[59]Paul R. Eddy, "Paul Knitter's Theology of Religions: A Survey and Evangelical Response," *Evangelical Quarterly* 65 (1993): 243.

[60]DiNoia, *Diversity of Religions*, p. 48.

[61]Kenneth Surin, "A 'Politics of Speech': Religious Pluralism in the Age of McDonald's Hamburger," in *The Myth of Christian Uniqueness Reconsidered: The Myth of a Pluralistic Theory of Religions*, ed. Gavin D'Costa (Maryknoll, N.Y.: Orbis, 1990), p. 200.

A Trinitarian Theology of Religions?

It is surprising that the Trinity, with its unique solution to the problem of the one and the many, is not more regularly invoked in the theology of religions.[62] The present essay tries to remedy this lacuna. My intent is to bring the resources of trinitarian theology to bear on the question of religious pluralism in a more direct manner by focusing on the question of the identity of "God" rather than on soteriology.[63]

Raimundo Panikkar: The "perichoresis" of religions. Panikkar is the exception that proves the rule, a pluralist who *does* invoke the Trinity and who believes it to be at the heart of all human religions.[64] Panikkar criticizes "unitive" pluralism for some of the same reasons that I have already rehearsed, most notably for its presumption that a rational universal theory of religion is desirable. The Western search for a universal theory (monologue) is only one way of expressing human religiosity. True pluralism (dialogue) is a matter of mutually exclusive ultimate systems, which cannot, by definition, be grounded in a common denominator or resolved in a higher synthesis. Truth itself is pluralistic, by which Panikkar means that there is no one absolute truth.

Panikkar believes that Eastern thought, particularly the nondualist or advaitist tradition of Hinduism, is more congruent with Christian trinitarian thought than the dualist philosophy of the ancient Greeks. "Christianness" (symbolized by the Ganges) refers to the mystical core of religion rather than its institutional or doctrinal forms. Panikkar wishes to make a supernatural "cosmic confidence in reality," rather than a universal theory of religions, the basis for interreligious conversation and cooperation. Each concrete religion offers only a perspective, a window to the whole. It is vital that we are aware that we see the whole through a part, for only then can we concede that the other may also have a view of the whole.

The very incommensurability of the religions is the condition for a kind of trinitarian perichoresis in which each religion is a dimension of the other, since each represents the whole of the human experience in a concrete way. Both the other and I see the whole, but only under one particular aspect: "Christianity has no proper name for the Supreme Being. 'God' is a common name. . . . All this suggests the possibility of a

---

[62]D'Costa notes that the Trinity "is very rarely mentioned in Christian theologies of religion" (D'Costa, "Theology of Religions," p. 287).
[63]David Burrell, reviewing *Myth of Christian Uniqueness Reconsidered,* says that its first two chapters confirm one's suspicions "that a deeper Christian appropriation of our trinitarian faith will open such [interreligious] conversation in an illuminating manner" (*Modern Theology* 9 [1993]: 309).
[64]Raimundo Panikkar, *The Trinity and the Religious Experience of Man: Icon-Person-Mystery* (Maryknoll, N.Y.: Orbis, 1973), p. viii. Rowan Williams judges Panikkar's book on the Trinity to be "one of the best and least read meditations on the Trinity in our century" ("Trinity and Pluralism," in *The Myth of Christian Uniqueness Reconsidered: The Myth of a Pluralistic Theory of Religions,* ed. Gavin D'Costa [Maryknoll, N.Y.: Orbis, 1990], p. 3).

Christianness different from Christendom and Christianity. . . . 'Christ' is the symbol for the divine-human mystery 'which is at work everywhere and elusively present wherever there is reality.'"[65]

Against the monism of exclusivism, inclusivism and unitive pluralism alike, Panikkar proposes a view of Reality as radically free (i.e., free from being assimilated by thought). And yet reality can be trusted because it is ordered, though the order is more like the harmony of music than the hierarchy of a system: "Concord is neither oneness nor plurality. It is the dynamism of the Many toward the One without ceasing to be different and without becoming one, and without reaching a higher synthesis. . . . There is no harmonical accord if there is no plurality of sounds, or if those sounds coalesce in one single note."[66]

The Christian symbol of this harmony is, for Panikkar, the Trinity. The Father stands for the nameless Absolute. The Son is the divine Person in whom humans participate. The Spirit is the principle of unity in which the nameless Absolute and named persons participate. The Trinity is thus a symbol for "theandrism"—"that intimate and complete unity . . . between the divine and the human . . . which is the goal towards which everything here and below tends."[67] Reality is "theandric"; each being is a christophany, an intrinsic part of the whole. There are neither two realities (God and humankind) nor one (God or humankind). This is the central message of the Upanishads—"God is in all; all is in God"—that cannot be communicated in words or concepts. We know God immediately in the depths of spiritual experience.

Western theology has lost this sense of cosmic harmony through its overemphasis on the Logos (thought/consciousness) over against a true plurality of truths (Spirit as freedom). "What I am against ultimately is the total dominion of the *logos* and a subordinationism of the Spirit—to put it in Christian trinitarian words—or against any form of monism, in philosophical parlance."[68] Panikkar adopts a nondualistic, advaitic attitude that holds that reality is itself pluralistic: "Being as such, even if 'encompassed' by or 'co-existent' with the Logos or a Supreme Intelligence, does not need to be reduced to consciousness."[69] By denying the equivalence of being and consciousness, Panikkar represents one possible response to Lévinas's injunction to let the other "be" rather than assimilating it to thought. Indeed Panikkar says that if

---

[65]Panikkar, "The Jordan, the Tiber and the Ganges," pp. 106, 113. Or as Demarest paraphrases: "Christ is the non-historic Logos, confessed by Christians as Jesus but known in other religions by different names" (*General Revelation*, p. 221).

[66]Raimundo Panikkar, "The Invisible Harmony: A Universal Theory of Religion or a Cosmic Confidence in Reality?" in *Toward a Universal Theology of Religion*, ed. Leonard Swidler (Maryknoll, N.Y.: Orbis, 1987), p. 145.

[67]Panikkar, *Trinity and Religious Experience*, p. 71.

[68]Panikkar, "Invisible Harmony," p. 124.

[69]Panikkar, "The Jordan, the Tiber and the Ganges," p. 109.

the Logos is the transparency of being, the Spirit is its opaqueness. Even God has an opacity that resists total intelligibility: "This is precisely the locus of freedom—and the basis of pluralism."[70]

Geist or Gestalt: Configuring shapes of the Spirit. A number of recent works on the general topic of theology and religious pluralism have followed Panikkar's lead in dealing with the "loyalty-openness" dilemma, that is, the problem of how to be faithful to one's own religion while engaging the other in dialogue. Though they claim to be trinitarian, each is careful to maintain a certain critical distance between Christology and pneumatolgy.

We begin with Rowan Williams's "Trinity and Pluralism," an essay on Panikkar's trinitarian pluralism. The Trinity is there seen as an ever-generative source of form (Logos) and realization (Spirit). "Form," however, is never exhausted nor limited by specific realizations. *Christ* is for Panikkar the name of a specific person *and* of the shape of the potential future of all human beings. But the Spirit is the process by which this form is realized "in a diversity as wide as the diversity of the human race itself."[71] As God the Father is constitutive of the identity of Jesus, so God the Spirit is constitutive (in a different sense) of the process of the church.[72] Williams appears to agree with Panikkar that the mystery of "Christ" will be realized in forms hitherto unknown in Christianity, forms that we may well discover in our encounter with the other religions.

Like Panikkar, Michael Barnes wants to avoid a unitive pluralism. He offers a way beyond the paradigms of exclusivism, inclusivism and "monological" pluralism: a "dialogical" pluralism.[73] With Panikkar, Barnes sees the religions not as constituting competing systems but as representing different ways of being human. Each religion has a unique language and practice through which people cope with change and expiate suffering. Religions are united not on the level of beliefs but on the (deeper) interpersonal level of human religiosity. Religions understand themselves better through dialoguing with others. And at the root of Barnes's theology of religions lies a Spirit-centered theory of the interpenetration (perichoresis) of religions. Interreligious dialogue proceeds on the basis of a common human religiosity, which is the work of the Spirit.

---

[70]Panikkar, "Invisible Harmony," p. 130.

[71]Rowan Williams, "Trinity and Pluralism," in *The Myth of Christian Uniqueness Reconsidered: The Myth of a Pluralistic Theory of Religions,* ed. Gavin D'Costa (Maryknoll, N.Y.: Orbis, 1990), p. 8.

[72]See Rowan Williams, "Trinity and Ontology," in *Christ, Ethics and Tragedy: Essays in Honour of Donald MacKinnon,* ed. Kenneth Surin (Cambridge: Cambridge University Press, 1989), pp. 71-93.

[73]Michael Barnes, *Religions in Conversation: Christian Identity and Christian Pluralism* (London: SPCK, 1989), pp. 172ff.

Peter Hodgson, drawing largely on G. W. F. Hegel, similarly believes that the divine *Geist*—or, in his terminology, the divine *Gestalt*—takes different forms in different times (and religions). Hodgson claims that God is present in history in *many* shapes of freedom.

But we here encounter a problem, best stated by Langdon Gilkey, that confronts all these attempts to "deregulate" the Spirit from its specific Christian context: within the plurality around us "are forms of the religious that are intolerable . . . because they are demonic."[74] Caste, consumerism, sexism, racism—these represent the "dark side" of religion. Gilkey recognizes the pluralist's dilemma: to resist, one must assert some sort of ultimate value, but to do this is to assert a "worldview," which at least implicitly implies that other views of reality are mistaken. The pluralist wants both to relativize the religious *and* to resist the demonic.

In theory the dilemma is insoluble; but in praxis we uncover a "relative absoluteness."[75] Hodgson agrees: "The way beyond absolutism and relativism may be found . . . through engagement in some form of transformative, emancipatory praxis."[76] God is present in history precisely as the plurality of shapes of freedom.

Specifically, God is "the One who loves in freedom." Hodgson gives this Barthian formula a distinctly Hegelian twist. *Spirit* becomes a shorthand term for the process by which God enters into relationship with the world, suffers its alienation and overcomes ("transfigures") the difference. But how can we tell the difference between the divine and the demonic, between forms of freedom and forms of fascism? Apparently a form of praxis may be configured as "love in freedom" whenever it manifests the dialectical process of identity, difference and mediation, represented by the figure of Jesus: "Love entails a union mediated by relationship and hence distinction."[77] Significantly, Hodgson identifies the "world" with the moment of difference. It is precisely because the world is not-God that it is a moment in the divine life: "God is the identity of God and not-God, the event that takes place between God and the world."[78]

Does the substitution of "world" for "Son of God" as the second moment in the divine life mean that Hodgson's theology is no longer Christian? He replies that theology has traditionally manifested a "potentially idolatrous fixation" on Jesus.[79] He cites a number of reasons theologians should resist this fixation—not only the con-

---

[74]Langdon B. Gilkey, "Plurality and Its Theological Implications," in *The Myth of Christian Uniqueness: Toward a Pluralistic Theology of Religions,* ed. John Hick and Paul F. Knitter (Maryknoll, N.Y.: Orbis, 1987), p. 44.
[75]Ibid., p. 47.
[76]Peter C. Hodgson, *God in History: Shapes of Freedom* (Nashville: Abingdon, 1989), p. 41.
[77]Ibid., p. 99.
[78]Ibid., p. 106.
[79]Ibid.

ceptual difficulties of incarnation Christology but also the sad history of Jewish persecution, feminism and religious pluralism. But having loosened the ties that bind us to Jesus, Hodgson nevertheless confidently speaks of "God's loving, suffering, transformative embrace of the world,"[80] which appears not all at once but in a plurality of forms, of which none can claim exclusive validity. For Christians, the paradigmatic "shape" by which God's love for the world is discerned is the life and death of Jesus, whose cross constitutes the "divine gestalt." But "God" is present in a transfiguring way in all the many shapes of liberating praxis, not just the Christian: "God takes shape in other religions as well, and their claims are as legitimate as ours."[81]

Hodgson's treatment leads one to inquire into the basis of this configuration of God as the "one who loves in freedom." How can we know that God is love, much less that the same God is at work in all religions, apart from his self-identification as this (or that) God? After all, the divine Gestalt can be disfigured as well as configured. And is freedom a gift of the *Heilige Geist* or the necessary end point of Hegel's *Geist?* Is the mystery of love nothing more than the mystery of Hegelian dialectics?

Whose Trinity? What Spirit? Which pluralism? What seems to unite pluralistic trinitarian theologies of religion is the role of the Spirit as a "universalizer." The Spirit resists the reduction of Being (Father) to Logos (Son); consequently no one religious "form" can lay claim to have caught the fullness of reality. D'Costa remarks, "Pneumatology allows the particularity of Christ to be related to the universal activity of God in the history of humankind."[82] No friend to pluralism, D'Costa nevertheless believes (on the basis of passages such as John 16) that divine revelation is not limited to the particularities of Jesus' history—the Spirit will guide us into even *more* truth. Because the Spirit "blows where it will," the activity of the Spirit cannot be confined to Christianity.

The underlying question that must be asked of these trinitarian theologies of religion concerns the manner in which, and the extent to which, the Spirit is the Spirit of Jesus Christ. Bruce Demarest contends that what Panikkar calls "Spirit" derives more from speculative philosophy than from Christian theology. He refers to Panikkar's adoption of a pantheistic monistic Hindu perspective of humanity's essential identity with transcendent Reality as an "unholy union" of Christian faith and Eastern spirituality.[83] Tempering Demarest's assessment somewhat, we might say that Panikkar has exchanged a Western monism (of reason) for an Eastern one (of Spirit). Pan-

---

[80]Ibid., p. 107.

[81]Ibid., p. 214.

[82]Gavin D'Costa, "Christ, the Trinity and Religious Plurality," in *The Myth of Christian Uniqueness Reconsidered: The Myth of a Pluralistic Theory of Religions,* ed. Gavin D'Costa (Maryknoll, N.Y.: Orbis, 1990), p. 19.

[83]Demarest, *General Revelation,* p. 223.

ikkar would doubtless wish to distinguish metaphysical monism from his vision of
cosmic harmonic unity. But what looks like pluralism may merely be a muddier
monism, where everything is a mixture of everything else in a kind of metaphysical
perichoresis. Indeed Timothy Bradshaw has argued that if various religions hold a
common trinitarianism, it is only a subordinationist or cosmological kind that seeks
to construct a bridge between God and the world.[84]

John Milbank similarly believes that Panikkar's attempt to equate trinitarian and
New-Vedantic pluralism falls short of orthodox trinitarian theology. Panikkar's nondualist pluralism acknowledges differences as realities to be encountered but fails to
arrive at a valuation of the other insofar as the transcendent is an "indifferent" presence and power. For Milbank, only in a Christian trinitarianism "can one both fulfill
respect for the other and complete and secure this otherness as pure neighborly difference."[85]

D'Costa proposes the following axiom, designed to show that truth criteria in discussions of religious pluralism are always tradition-specific: "In relation to the
decreased specificity of an alleged neutral proposal its usefulness diminishes."[86] I
believe we can sum up the aforementioned criticisms concerning "pneumatological
pluralism" with a similar axiom: In relation to the decreased specificity of "Spirit," its
usefulness in a theology of religion diminishes.[87] If the Spirit's activity were literally
universal, we would not be able to distinguish the divine from the demonic. Williams
seems to concede this point, implicitly invoking the Reformed emphasis on the
necessity of both Word and Spirit, when he says that if the Christic principle—what
Hodgson calls the divine *Gestalt*—is to have the capacity to challenge current versions of "humanity's common good," it must do so "in the name of its own central
and *historically* distinctive Trinitarian insight."[88]

"Relating" God: From Narrative to Ontology

The Christian goal in interfaith dialogue is to invite others into the narrative that

---

[84]Timothy Bradshaw, "The Ontological Trinity," *Scottish Journal of Theology* 29 (1976): 301-10.
Bradshaw says that it is another question altogether to ask "whether the 'orthodox' formulation of triunity has parallels of its own in the history of religions" (p. 305).
[85]Milbank, "End of Dialogue," p. 188. Williams disagrees, saying that the heart of Panikkar's
ontology can be summarized by saying that "differences matter" ("Trinity and Pluralism," p. 4).
[86]Gavin D'Costa, "Whose Objectivity? Which Neutrality?" *Religious Studies* 29 (1993): 81.
[87]It is noteworthy that while John the Baptist acknowledged his diminishing role with regard
to Jesus—"He must increase, but I must decrease" (Jn 3:30)—Jesus does not similarly cede
his place to the Spirit. On the contrary, Jesus says of the Spirit, "He will bear witness to Me"
(Jn 15:26) and "He will glorify me" (Jn 16:14).
[88]Williams, "Trinity and Pluralism," p. 10. He also remarks: "Witness to the 'christic fact' as an
integrating reality proposes to the world of faiths the possibility of a kind of critical human
norm that can be used in the struggle against what limits or crushes humanity" (p. 9).

"relates" God and identifies God as One who, in his inner and outer trinitarian relations (i.e., in God's being and acts), is love. I offer the following remarks on "relating God" as a contribution to the resolution of the loyalty-openness dilemma (i.e., how to hold convictions *and* a conversation). I have argued that pluralistic theologies of religions typically work with an *idem* concept of God's identity, which seeks to do ontology without narrative mediation. I now wish to develop my earlier suggestion that the biblical narrative's identification of God as triune gives rise to an ontology wherein differences are neither reduced nor repressed but reconciled—"saved."

Narrative identity: The triune God. Following Wilhelm Dilthey, Ricoeur notes that narrative articulates personal identity as it is manifested in a life history. The identity of the character "is constructed in connection with that of the plot."[89] A "plot" is a way of "configuring" heterogeneous events and persons into a meaningful whole. Narrative (not metaphysics, as in Panikkar) thus mediates between concordance and discordance. The narrative operation has developed "an entirely original concept of dynamic identity which reconciles the same categories that Locke took as contraries: identity and diversity." The identity of the character is so dependent on the narrative operation that Ricoeur claims: "characters . . . are themselves plots."[90]

Each person's life history is "entangled" in the histories of others. "Self-constancy is for each person that manner of conducting himself or herself so that others can *count on* that person."[91] A narrative identification reveals the self in its difference with respect to the Same (character, one's permanence in time) and in its dialectic with respect to the other (fidelity, one's self-constancy through time).

I will now develop my earlier suggestion that Jenson's "God according to the Gospel" manifests the *ipse*-identity of self-constancy rather than the *idem*-identity of self-sameness. With regard to the question of divine identity, we may associate the problematic of sameness with God's oneness and the problematic of *ipseity* or selfhood with God's threeness. If character is plot, we can identify God only on the basis of his acts, configured as a certain kind of whole with an implicit ethical aim. But this is precisely what we have in Scripture. The Old Testament identifies God as the One who has kept his promises to bring Israel out of Egypt and who will keep his promise to restore Israel. The Gospels identify God as the One who raised his Son from the dead and promised to give him a cosmic kingdom. The biblical narratives confer a "dynamic identity" on God: God's identity is a matter of his self-constancy to his work. God's identity is a function not merely of the aseity

---

[89]Ricoeur, *Oneself as Another,* p. 143.
[90]Ibid.
[91]Ibid., p. 165.

of an indeterminate entity but of the ipseity of a self.[92]

Of course the narrative identity of God is complicated by the fact that there seem to be three interrelated life stories: those of Father, Son and Spirit. Here too, however, the differences as well as the relations between the three personas are articulated by narrative. Who God is, and what God is like, is a function of the entangled life histories of Father, Son and Spirit related in the Gospels. Jenson is critical of formulations that make the differences and relations between the three persons irrelevant to the identity of God. Such attempts are metaphysical interpretations of deity in terms of timelessness (the *idem*-identity associated with Persistence of a Past). Rather, it is the narrative figuration of the economic Trinity—that is, the story of the temporal missions of Jesus and the Spirit—that alone configures God's eternity.

Pannenberg criticizes theologians of both West and East for trying to derive the threeness of persons from the concept of God's essential unity, regardless of whether this unity is conceived as substance (e.g., by Augustine, Aquinas, Protestant orthodoxy) or as subject (e.g., Hegel, Barth). Pannenberg reverses the traditional order: "It is only with the question of the essence and attributes of the trinitarian God that the unity of this God becomes a theme."[93] However, Pannenberg moves beyond the tradition by expanding the economy, as it were, and considering the trinitarian relations not only in terms of origin or causality, as did the Cappadocians, but in light of the total work of Word and Spirit.

What constitutes the identity of Father, Son and Spirit is not merely the manner or origin (e.g., begetting, breathing) but the sum total of their multifarious relations. If persons are what they are in their relations to one another, it is illegitimate to reduce the richness of these relations to relations of origin alone: "The persons cannot be identical simply with any one relation. Each is a catalyst of many relations."[94] The Father is as dependent on the triumph of the Son as the Son is on his sending by the Father. Pannenberg accepts Rahner's axiom that the immanent Trinity is the economic; God is the same in his eternal essence as he is in his self-revelation in salvation history. God's unity can be determined only by a configuration of the works of the Father, Son and Spirit in salvation history. This configuration is, of necessity, narrative in nature. Ricoeur's insight that "character is plot" is thus another way of saying that God's ontological unity is derived from God's triune self-manifestation in history. The God of religious pluralism may be self-same, but the triune God of Christian faith has *character*.

If Jesus is indeed the decisive revelation of God, then God can be true to his Word

---

[92]This is not meant as a denial of divine aseity. God does not "acquire" an identity as the plot of universal history develops. Rather, the story of God's relations shows who God always was, is and will be.

[93]Pannenberg, *Systematic Theology*, 1:299.

[94]Ibid., 1:320.

only if the whole of history manifests the same cross-and-resurrection shape. The Spirit is the Spirit of the humiliated and exalted Christ. Whereas Panikkar and other pluralists try to weaken the ties that bind the Spirit to the Son, a reading of the "expanded economy" that takes account of the diverse relations of Father, Son and Spirit would, I believe, configure the Spirit as the deputy of Christ rather than as an independent itinerant evangelist.

Ontological reflection: Love and marriage. The narrative identification of the triune God leads to an ontological reflection whose climax and conclusion is the declaration "God is love." The only reason this identifying description escapes the fate of other vacuous abstractions is that God's love is given a concrete narrative specification: God's being is such that it continues to pour itself out for others, albeit in different ways. The meaning of "God is love," then, is tied to the narrative configuration of God's being as the fellowship of Father, Son and Spirit.

The narrative of the Trinity is entangled with other life histories as will. The deity of the Father is a function of his keeping both his Word and his world, insofar as he has chosen to love and identify with it. Jesus asks the Father, "Keep them in thy name" (Jn 17:11). The triune identity embraces others in a noncoercive way. The well-being of the other is constitutive of the identity of God, insofar as God has not only spoken to but *become* a Word of promise for others. The being in communion of the triune God is not the *idem*-identity of the Persistence of the Past. There are dynamic relations between the three persons, relations not merely of causality but of faithfulness (keeping, obeying, abiding, glorifying). The Father's identity is at stake in his promise to the disciples to send the Spirit and to keep them in the Father's name.

Marriage is also a being in communion constituted by a word of promise. In marriage there is a recognition of both sameness (one flesh) and otherness (two distinct persons). "This is a great mystery" (Eph 5:32)—great enough, perhaps, to illustrate the triune identity? What I am hesitantly trying to articulate is an ontology of marriage, a concrete form of love. What constitutes marriage is fidelity to one's vows, to one's word of promise. The Gospel narratives that identify God as Father, Son and Spirit call for and configure an ontological reflection that recognizes the triune life as constituted by *covenantal,* not causal, relations—relations that help us to understand who God is and what love is.

Milbank has recently argued that the only alternative to an ontology of violence, where everything is either reduced to the Same or else constituted by sheer difference and thus related conflictually, is the ontology of peace that emerges from narratives of Jesus.[95] I have here argued that the pluralistic theology of religions,

---

[95]John Milbank, *Theology and Social Theory* (Oxford: Blackwell, 1990), esp. pp. 427-30.

beginning as it does with the *idem*-identity of the one God, has not escaped the violence that reduces the Many to the Same. In the triune *ipse*-identity, on the other hand, peace and harmony are gained not by excluding the other but by God's covenant promise to be for the creature *precisely in its difference* from its Creator. Difference—internal and external to the trinitarian life—is the condition for fidelity and fellowship.

The nature of dialogue and the dilemma of "loyalty-openness." True pluralism—the kind that respects the alterity of the other rather than assimilating it—is possible only on trinitarian grounds. This follows from the fact that one's ethics and epistemology are rooted in ontology. The Trinity, then, far from hindering conversation, is the transcendental condition of interfaith dialogue with the other. Without the Trinity, theological dialogue lacks the necessary specificity (Logos, Christ) and the necessary spirit (love, Spirit) to prosper. Our Angler's dialogical dilemma is at least clearer: he must be open to differences while at the same time minding distinctives.

One may seek in charity to be, as far as is conceptually and confessionally possible, at peace with all positions, but one must then seek, in clarity, to enumerate the differences that remain. DiNoia offers a salient reminder: "Recognizing differences is not equivalent to promoting discord. It is a way of taking other people seriously."[96] Recognizing others in their alterity is thus an ethical imperative for the Christian. Tanner appeals to the doctrine of creation as a means of saving the differences: we should respect others because they are God's creatures too. "Identity in fundamental beliefs or ultimate reference is no precondition for respecting the different belief systems of various people."[97] With respect to epistemology, we must not subsume but *submit* to the other insofar as we must be willing to put our beliefs to critical tests. We must remember that our theological formulations are always provisional; none of them catches the sacred fish.

The Angler admits that there are other sports, but he nevertheless is convinced that his sport (or art, or religion) is superior—"true" not just for him but for everyone. His task is to convince others, not through violent rhetoric or manipulation but through persuasion, that the world as seen from his "angle" is possible, desirable and true. A form of dialogue modeled on trinitarian life will be less concerned with the defense of a received inheritance (the doctrinal equivalent of the Persistence of the Past) than with exploring ways to "down the otherness" (the etymological meaning of *katallage* or "reconciliation") in a noncoercive manner. Such reconciliation can be bought only with a price: our exposure to otherness, negativity, perhaps intellectual

---

[96]DiNoia, *Diversity of Religions*, p. 169.
[97]Tanner, "Respect for Other Religions," p. 15.

crucifixion. True dialogue demands the practice, and not simply the discourse, of Christian love. Indeed might we not venture, in light of these trinitarian reflections, to suggest that it is *only* by opening ourselves up to the other and to difference that we are true to our Christian distinctives?

The Incompleat Angler: Remaining Questions

I have been angling in the Rubicon, not crossing but standing knee-deep in its waters, trying to gain a perspective, casting questions. The following queries, about other positions as well as my own, continue to bait (and bite).

Love and the other. What is the nature and scope of God's love for the other? Does "God is love" entail a universal salvific will? Is there really nothing that will be excluded from the divine life? Will even the demonic be domesticated in a noncoercive way (and what biblical support is there for such a position)? And by what means are we caught up into the divine love: is it by virtue of God's being Creator, or Savior, or simply Spirit?

Spirit and Son. Inclusivists and pluralists alike claim that the Spirit is universally active and that therefore Christians must try to discern the Spirit in other religions. But if the Spirit's activity is really universal, then why restrict it to the world religions? And if the salvific will of God is truly universal, then we can no longer limit the means of salvation to the religions. How, then, can we discern God's Spirit, if it is indeed everywhere? Does not the narrative identification of the triune God present the Spirit as the Spirit of Christ—not simply the Logos but the crucified and raised Christ? How else are we to take seriously verses such as John 7:39 ("for as yet the Spirit had not been given, because Jesus was not yet glorified"), not to mention the event of Pentecost itself? Is Hegel's universal *Geist* really *der Heilige Geist?* Perhaps it is time to reclaim the Reformed emphasis on the inseparability of Word and Spirit, and in particular its doctrine of the testimony of the Spirit, for a theology of religions.

The identity of God, again. Pluralism, insofar as it claims that the various names and predications for God are only modes of speaking about the same God, is guilty of semantic Sabellianism. Pannenberg, however, sees a continuing validity in the philosophical concept and generic term *God* as a minimal identifying description (e.g., God is the Being behind beings, the origin of the cosmos). To what extent, then, are the various religions about the "same" God?

We may agree with Pannenberg that the other religions, insofar as they recognize the one God (the Creator), have a true but not exhaustive identity description of God. It is partially true, and thus it has a relative adequacy—but how relative? how adequate? Carl Braaten expresses my concern: "One of the open questions for me at this time is how Pannenberg relates the christologically motivated Christian doctrine of the Trinity to the understanding of God in the other religions of the world."[98] Does the Muslim pray to the same God as the Christian? Pannenberg does not shirk the question, but he does not answer it either: "This is a question to be decided by God, not us."[99]

Conclusion

In conclusion: the Trinity is the Christian answer to the identity of God. The one Creator God is Father, Son and Spirit. This is an identification that is at once exclusivistic and pluralistic. And because this God who is three-in-one has covenanted with what is other than himself—the creature—the identity of God is also inclusivistic. The Trinity, far from being a *skandalon,* is the transcendental condition for interreligious dialogue, the ontological condition that permits us to take the other in all seriousness, without fear and without violence.

In the course of Walton's work, the Angler convinces his dialogue partners, Hunter and Falconer, that angling is indeed the best recreation. He does not coerce but persuades.[100] Rhetoric is part of the story: the Angler is both passionate and eloquent. But what he really does is *witness,* in his discourse and in his practice, to the nature of angling in such a way that its reality is disclosed to his listeners. He invites them to enter the angler's world, and they experience there the freedom that comes from contemplation and from living in harmony with nature.

As the apostle Paul notes, however, rivers are dangerous (1 Cor 11:26). The Angler must be careful not to become engulfed in deep waters. But a river of life, identified in John 7:38-39 with the Spirit, runs through the city of God (Rev 22:1). If this Spirit is universally available, it is not because all religions drink from the same great river. It is rather because the Spirit has sprung, under the conditions of history, from a Rock (1 Cor 10:4). Life in the Spirit, "rivers of living water," shall flow from the hearts of those who believe in Jesus.

---

[98]Carl Braaten, "The Problem of the Absoluteness of Christianity," in *Worldview and Warrants: Plurality and Authority in Theology,* ed. William Schweiker and Per M. Anderson (Lanham, Md.: University Press of America, 1987), p. 65. Or as he states it elsewhere: "The question is how the experience of God apart from Christ is related to the experience of God in Christ" ("The Place of Christianity Among the World Religions: Pannenberg's Theology of Religions," in *The Theology of Wolfhart Pannenberg,* ed. Carl Braaten and Philip Clayton [Minneapolis: Augsburg, 1988], p. 310).

[99]Wolfhart Pannenberg, "Religious Pluralism and Conflicting Truth Claims: The Problem of a Theology of the World Religions," in *The Myth of Christian Uniqueness Reconsidered: The Myth of a Pluralistic Theory of Religions,* ed. Gavin D'Costa (Maryknoll, N.Y.: Orbis, 1990), p. 103.

[100]Cf. Eddy's comment: "The question of tolerance or intolerance is one of *attitude,* not truthclaim" ("Paul Knitter's Theology of Religions," p. 239).

Three

The Love of God

*Its Place, Meaning & Function
in Systematic Theology*

*T*he opposite of love, it has been said, is not hate but indifference. The God of the Christian gospel is anything but indifferent toward humanity. Humanity, of course, has not always returned the compliment. Indeed, if we are to judge from their often oblique, indistinct or awkward treatments of the subject, Christian theologians have themselves been somewhat indifferent—inattentive, neutral—with regard to the concept of the love of God.

It is no exaggeration to say that defining and situating the notion of the love of God is the perennial task, and standing challenge, of Christian dogmatics. Yet there is at present little consensus as to where the topic of the love of God belongs. Is the love of God an aspect of God's being, or should it be treated under some other heading—the Trinity, providence or atonement perhaps? What do the various headings under which the love of God is treated tell us about its meaning and function?

The love of God highlights the God-world relation in general and the incarnation in particular. It is arguably one of the central themes of Scripture. It appears that the topic of God's love involves us, once again, in first theology. For to construe the mode of God's presence among the faithful is to define the nature of God's love.

Though just what it means to predicate God's "love" remains something of a mystery, this has not impeded appeals to love in human affairs. "Love" has been the subject of poems, ballads and philosophical treatises down through the ages. It

has been a prominent theme in ethics and in theological discussions of the appropriate human response to God's gracious initiative. The frequency of the term's
use, however, stands in inverse proportion to its meaningfulness. In the 1936 film
Modern Times, a biting satire on industrial life, Charlie Chaplin sings "It's Love,"
repeating the term *love* at breakneck speed dozens of times: "It's love—love,
love—love, love, love, love, love, love. Love, love, love, love, love, love, love." A
mere repetition of the term leads inexorably to its devaluation. Hence the predicament of our modern and postmodern times: to say what love is and how it may be
affirmed of God.[1]

To assume that contemporary thinkers have any advantage in this effort over
those of antiquity is to flirt with chronological snobbery. A growing number of Christian theologians nevertheless maintain that a major advance in understanding the
love of God has been made, a step so significant as to entail a paradigm revolution in
all of Christian theology. I refer to the suggestion that God's love is to be viewed in
terms of *interpersonal relations* rather than in terms of *substantival attributes.*[2] As
early as 1962 John McIntyre identified the prime difficulty in giving full value to the
concept of the love of God as "an unduly narrow equation of the term with an
attribute."[3] More recently Vincent Brümmer has observed that in the Christian tradition "love has generally been taken to be an attitude of one person toward another,
rather than as a relation between persons."[4]

According to Sallie McFague, the essential core of Christianity is the transformative
event of new life, grounded in the life and death of Jesus of Nazareth: "the event of
God's transforming love."[5] This new paradigm for construing the love of God entails
nothing less than a revision of the God-world relationship itself, which is to say, a
revision of the whole of theology. To be precise, the revolution McFague has in mind
involves the change from seeing the God-world relation in terms of unilateral sovereignty to emphasizing bilateral fellowship. For instance, she sees the world as God's

---

[1]The love of God, as perhaps no other theological topic, is particularly vulnerable to Ludwig
von Feuerbach's suspicion that doctrines are projections of human ideals.

[2]See, for instance, Philip Clayton, "The Case for Christian Panentheism," *Dialog* 37 (1998), pp.
201-8. Cf. Vincent Brümmer's comment: "Since Aristotle our intellectual tradition has been
infected by the ontological prejudice that there are only two sorts of reality: substances and
attributes" (*The Model of Love: A Study in Philosophical Theology* [Cambridge: Cambridge University Press, 1993], p. 33).

[3]John McIntyre, *On the Love of God* (London: Collins, 1962), p. 34

[4]Brümmer, *Model of Love,* p. 33.

[5]Sallie McFague, "An Epilogue: The Christian Paradigm," in *Christian Theology: An Introduction to Its Traditions and Tasks,* ed. Peter Hodgson and Robert King, 2nd ed. (Philadelphia:
Fortress, 1985), p. 382. Note that for McFague, Christianity is itself a paradigm inasmuch as it
constitutes a comprehensive interpretation (though only one; others are available) of God's
relation with the world.

"body" and world history as the process of "inclusive love for all."[6]

On a more popular level, the authors of *The Openness of God: A Biblical Challenge to the Traditional Understanding of God* similarly maintain that a new understanding of the love of God leads to a shaking of the foundations of traditional theism. "A new way of critical reappraisal and competent reconstruction of the doctrine of God is sweeping over the intellectual landscape."[7] Clearly any concept such as the love of God that lies at the heart of such revolutionary change of theological paradigm merits serious consideration. Is it indeed the case that the concept of the love of God leads to the deconstruction of traditional Christian theism?

Historical Review: Where We Are

Revolutions in paradigm are visible only against a background of "normal science," or in the case of theology, against the backdrop of Christian tradition.[8] How, then, did early theologians understand the love of God?

The love of God as attribute and action. Classical theism—the classic model for understanding the God-world relation—has a double origin: the Bible and ancient philosophy. Theology was to a large degree the attempt to reconcile the story of God's acts in Israel's history and in the history of Jesus Christ—essentially a love story of the Creator for his creation, his community, his child—with ancient Greek notions of perfect being.

According to Plato, love is either the desire *(eros)* for something I do not have or the desire never to lose what I now have in the future. Love is "always poor," always needy. Augustine agrees with Plato that love is essentially the desire for ultimate happiness. For Augustine, however, only one's love for God will not disappoint; everything else is either destroyed or dies. Only God, then, should be loved for his own sake and not for the sake of something else. Now human beings are mortal. How,

---

[6]Sallie McFague, *The Body of God: An Ecological Theology* (London: SCM Press, 1993), p. 160. McFague acknowledges that in speaking of the world as the "body" of God, she no longer considers the body of Jesus to carry exclusive significance. Her paradigm change requires considerable revision, not only of classical theism but of classical Christology too: "The first [move] is to relativize the incarnation in relation to Jesus of Nazareth and the second is to maximize it in relation to the cosmos. In other words, the proposal is to consider Jesus as paradigmatic of what we find everywhere: everything that is is the sacrament of God" (p. 162). As we shall see, a number of the essays below find it difficult to speak of the love of God apart from the doctrine of the incarnation.
[7]Clark Pinnock, Richard Rice, John Sanders, William Hasker and David Basinger, *The Openness of God: A Biblical Challenge to the Traditional Understanding of God* (Downers Grove, Ill.: InterVarsity Press, 1994), p. 9.
[8]The language and idea of "normal science," "paradigms" and "scientific revolutions" goes back to an influential work by Thomas S. Kuhn, *The Structure of Scientific Revolutions,* 2nd ed. (Chicago: University of Chicago Press, 1970).

then, can God love us? According to Plato the gods cannot love, for they lack noth-ing.[9] It is not as though God *needs* the human creature, for it follows from the notion of perfect being that nothing can add to God's own enjoyment of himself. Yet it is clear from Scripture that God loves us. Augustine's solution to the paradox of God's love is to posit a properly divine kind of love, a gift-love: *agape.*

For the Stoics and the whole eudaemonist tradition of antiquity, happiness is a matter of uninterrupted bliss. The wise person is one who learns how not to be dis-turbed by changes in the world. The wise person lacks *pathos:* he or she is without passion, is impervious to changes that would overturn the rule of reason. Nicholas Wolterstorff observes that "Augustine stood in the Platonic tradition of seeing happi-ness as lying in the satisfaction of *eros* while the Stoics saw happiness as lying in the elimination of *eros.*"[10] Yet both agree that *pathos*—any emotional event that "dis-turbs" reason and joy—has no place in the life of the only wise God.

God's life is thus one of bliss and beneficence, or as Wolterstorff paraphrases it, a life of "non-suffering apathy."[11] In Wolterstorff's words: "God dwells eternally in bliss-ful non-suffering *apatheia.*"[12] Augustine's God "turns out to be remarkably like the Stoic sage: devoid of passions, unfamiliar with longing, foreign to suffering."[13] In the Christian tradition, God was widely held to be "impassible": not able to suffer. In the classic theological paradigm, the Bible and classical philosophy are seen to agree: a perfect being who has life in himself cannot suffer. Where the Bible appears to ascribe emotion or suffering to God, the tradition quickly concluded that such lan-guage must be figurative. Classical theism thus functions as a theological hermeneutic for construing what Scripture says about the love of God.

How, then, does God "process" the suffering of the innocent, or the suffering of his Son? God is all-knowing, to be sure, but how should we characterize God's

---

[9]See Brümmer's discussion of Plato's dialogue *Symposium* in *Model of Love,* pp. 110-20.
[10]Nicholas Wolterstorff, "Suffering Love," in *Philosophy and the Christian Faith,* ed. Thomas V. Morris (Notre Dame, Ind.: University of Notre Dame Press, 1990), pp. 205-6. Wolterstorff points out another important difference between Augustine and the Stoics. For Augustine the reality of human sinfulness implies that a certain sorrow is both fitting and appropriate. The ideal of apathy is inappropriate for Christians in this life, thought Augustine, for being apathetic would involve countenancing indifference toward sin rather than repentance.
[11]Ibid., p. 198. It is important to note that *apathy* here functions as a technical term. Augustine allowed that the wise person might experience passions such as fear and grief; his point, however, is that the wiser person will not allow these passions to unduly affect his or her reasoning. However, the experience of human sorrow would seem to compromise God's eternal bliss. When Augustine longs for apathy, therefore, he is longing not for a state of feelinglessness but for a state of unending joy.
[12]Ibid., p. 209.
[13]Ibid., p. 210. Wolterstorff locates the tension in Augustine's thought just here. On the one hand, the presence of evil properly brings about a suffering awareness (pathos) in human beings, whereas God remains blissful even when he is aware of evil.

knowledge of those occurrences that involve loss—grief, injury, pain, death? Wolterstorff believes that the root assumption behind the notion of divine impassibility is that God is unconditioned by anything not himself. If, as John of Damascus puts it, passion is "a movement in one thing caused by another," then God must, if he is unconditioned, have no passions. The question Wolterstorff presses home is simply this: if God cannot be affected by anything other than himself, then how are we to understand God's knowledge of human suffering and human loss? Is this something that God can know, or not? Can a God who does not experience suffering in some sense be said to "know" particular instances of suffering in our world? More pointedly: can a God who is unable to sympathize be said to love?

Many of the same classical emphases that characterize Augustine may be found almost a thousand years later in Thomas Aquinas. God's being and God's will are unconditioned. God cannot change, for he is perfect (the doctrine of divine immutability). God's will—either to do or to permit—is the final explanation for everything that happens (the doctrine of divine sovereignty). Is it correct to infer from these constants, however, as proponents of the new paradigm are prone to do, that "God's relation to the world [in the classical paradigm] is thus one of mastery and control"?[14]

What precisely is the love of God according to Aquinas? Question 20 of the *Summa Theologiae* treats *de amore Dei* and, significantly enough, follows question 19 on "will in God." For Aquinas, the love of God is God's willing the good. God is benevolent (*bene volere* = "good willing"). To love someone is to will that person good. Does God love the whole world? Yes, for God wills some good to each existing thing. However, God loves some things more than others, "for since his love is the cause of things . . . one thing would not be better than another but for God willing it more good."[15] Importantly, Aquinas does not believe that God *responds* to the good in a thing by loving it, but rather that God's love for a thing is the *cause* of its goodness.

On the traditional view, then, God metes out good but takes neither joy nor delight in the good he brings about (for this would make God's joy conditional on something in the world). That in which God takes delight turns out to be his own exercise of benevolence. Classical theism pictures God not as a utilitarian or pragmatist who delights in results but rather as a Kantian—a modern Stoic—who takes pleasure simply in his good will: good for goodness' sake. Wolterstorff admits that such a

---

[14]Richard Rice, "Biblical Support for a New Perspective," in *The Openness of God: A Biblical Challenge to the Traditional Understanding of God,* by Pinnock et al. (Downers Grove, Ill.: InterVarsity Press, 1994), p. 11.

[15]Thomas Aquinas, *Summa Theologiae,* ed. and trans. Thomas Gilby (London: Eyre & Spottiswoode, 1963), 5:65.

picture is coherent, but he does not find it to be biblical.[16]

For Aquinas (following Aristotle), God moves the world but is not moved by the world. This is simply another way of stating what it means for God to be immutable and impassible. God, says Aquinas, is like a stone column to which humans stand in relation. The column may be on our left or our right, in front of or behind us, but our relation to the column is in us, not in the column. Similarly, we may experience God's mercy or his wrath, but it is not God who changes, only our relation to him. "What changes is the way we experience the will of God."[17] With regard to God's will, only his goodness can move it. The concepts of immutability and impassibility here converge: God's will cannot be affected or changed by anything outside himself. God is, to use Richard Creel's fine phrase, "unsusceptible to causation."[18] This is a most important analytic point: impassibility no more means impassive than immutable means immobile. God may be unmoved (transcendent: unsusceptible to worldly causes), but he is nevertheless a mover (immanent: active and present in the world). The original intent of both concepts is to insist that no creature can move or affect or change God by dint of its own will.[19]

Twentieth-century developments: Responsiveness and relation. A number of twentieth-century developments have led to the demise of the classical paradigm that saw God's love in terms of divine sovereignty—God's ability unilaterally to will and to do good. The problem is not *that* God loves but rather *what* God's love is. What, then, is the effect of what Langdon Gilkey calls contemporary theology's "war with the Greeks" upon the notion of the love of God?[20]

Process philosophy stands out in the twentieth century for its resolute commitment to the metaphysical project—constructing a comprehensive account of the cate-

[16]It would appear that both the traditional and the revisionist views work with a combination of natural and revealed theology, that is, with a concept of divine perfection and with the biblical storyline. As to the notion of God's valuing his own good will, this is not entirely without biblical support, as the language of Ephesians 1 attests: "according to the purpose of his will" (1:5, 11); "for the praise of his glory" (1:12, 14).

[17]Richard E. Creel, "Immutability and Impassibility," in *A Companion to Philosophy of Religion*, ed. Philip L. Quinn and Charles Taliaferro (Oxford: Blackwell, 1997), p. 317. See also Creel's earlier, more comprehensive work *Divine Impassibility* (Cambridge: Cambridge University Press, 1986).

[18]Creel, "Immutability and Impassibility," p. 314.

[19]Thomas Gilby, editor of the English translation of the *Summa Theologiae*, argues that the entire structure of the *Summa* can be seen as a "going forth" and "returning home" of creation (1:43), something akin to Karl Barth's two-part reading of Christology in terms of the parable of the Prodigal Son: the "way into the far country" and "the homecoming." Gilby suggests that the love of God is essentially a matter of friendship, a sharing wherein one wills to communicate good to others.

[20]Langdon Gilkey, "God," in *Christian Theology: An Introduction to Its Traditions and Tasks*, ed. Peter Hodgson and Robert King, 2nd ed. (Philadelphia: Fortress, 1985), p. 105.

gories by which to understand all of reality, from the amoeba to the Absolute—and for its critique of the classical theistic model of the God-world relation. From a process perspective, the classical picture of a universe filled with various kinds of individual substances fails to capture the dynamic and interrelated nature of the physical world, not to mention the other, nonphysical orders of reality. Classical theism, they suggest, pictures God as a spiritual, personal substance of infinite perfection that exists over ("transcends") the world order.

George Newlands rightly comments that "faith has been a central theological motif particularly in the tradition of Luther and of modern existential thought. Hope has appeared as the new promise of a future oriented theology. . . . Love has come to the fore particularly in process thought in America."[21] Charles Hartshorne, a theologian who draws chiefly on the process philosophy of Alfred North Whitehead, has sought to rethink the nature of divine perfection. God, says Hartshorne, must be thought of not as "above it all" but as "in touch with it all." The universe is not a collection of discrete entities, each complete in itself, but rather a vast organic network where each entity is what it is thanks to its relation to other entities. God is God, says Hartshorne, not because he is above this social network but rather because he is at the heart of it. God, in short, is God because he relates to everything that happens. It is in this sense that we may affirm "God is love": "To love is to rejoice with the joys and sorrow with the sorrow of others. Thus it is to be influenced by those who are loved."[22]

Process theologians conceive of God in terms of their newer metaphysical categories: temporality, development, change, relatedness and interdependence. They see no reason to apologize for this (after all, classical theists had their metaphysical categories too), for many of these qualities are, they would argue, essential if we would understand the love of God. Love in a process world is no longer a matter of unilateral benevolence.[23] On the contrary, love means entering into a relationship in which one is willing to undergo—to suffer—change. As Paul Fiddes puts it: "To love is to be in a relationship where what the loved one does alters one's own experience."[24]

Classical theism has also been criticized by theologians proper. The twentieth cen-

---

[21] George Newlands, *Theology of the Love of God* (Atlanta: John Knox Press, 1980), p. 37.

[22] Charles Hartshorne, *A Natural Theology for Our Time* (La Salle, Ill.: Open Court, 1967), p. 75. Hartshorne called his view "panentheism" to signal that "all," while not the same as God, is nevertheless "in" God. See also his *The Divine Relativity: A Social Conception of God* (New Haven, Conn.: Yale University Press, 1948).

[23] For a critique of the traditional model of a sovereign God, see John Cobb and David Ray Griffin, *Process Theology: An Introductory Exposition* (Philadelphia: Westminster Press, 1976).

[24] Paul S. Fiddes, *The Creative Suffering of God* (Oxford: Clarendon, 1988), p. 50. On a process view, love seems to be a metaphysical as much as ethical phenomenon, inasmuch as relatedness in an essential aspect of a being's constitution.

tury has seen a renaissance of sorts in trinitarian theology. This has had a twofold effect with regard to our topic of the love of God. In the first place, trinitarian theology challenges approaches to the doctrine of God that begin with the notion of "perfect being" (the one divine nature) rather than with the economy of salvation (the three divine Persons). In the second place, a renewed interest in Eastern Orthodox approaches to the Trinity have led some to redefine God's being itself in terms of its trinitarian relations. John Zizoulas argues that the Cappadocians made *person* rather than substance the prime ontological category.[25] Love for another is thus more basic—more fundamental to reality, that is—than self-sufficiency. Thus the same theme, relationality, comes to the fore as in process thought, but for reasons wholly internal to Christian theology.

Karl Barth's theology reflects a similar tendency to begin with the concrete acts of God rather than abstract speculation on the nature of perfect being. For Barth, God is knowable only because he reveals himself through himself, that is, in Jesus Christ. Indeed all that can be known of God is known only on the basis of his revelation through Jesus Christ. Hence one can discuss God's being only on the basis of his "act" in Jesus Christ, an all-encompassing act that embraces both revelation and reconciliation. In rigorously refusing to think God except on the basis of Jesus' life, death and resurrection, Barth comes to the conclusion that God essentially is the One who goes out of himself for the sake of another. God is "the one who loves in freedom," and these two qualities, "love" and "freedom," define for Barth the whole range of divine attributes.[26]

Intriguingly for our purposes, Newlands suggests that the whole of the *Church Dogmatics* might be described as a theology of the love of God, since it is concerned with the act of God in Christ on humanity's behalf.[27] Perhaps the most startling thesis to emerge from a focus on the act of God in Jesus Christ, however, is Jürgen Moltmann's thesis that God himself suffered and "died." If the cross of Christ is the prime criterion for correct speech about God, then we must assert that God, somehow, suffers because he loved the world. A God who cannot suffer, Moltmann states, "is poorer than any human . . . he is also a loveless being."[28]

Three other twentieth-century theological developments have lent support to Moltmann's criticism of divine immutability and impassibility. Alister McGrath mentions "protest atheism" (where was God during Auschwitz?), the rediscovery of Luther's theology of the cross, and the growing impact of the "history of dogma"

---

[25]John Zizoulas, *Being and Communion: Studies in Personhood and the Church* (London: Darton, Longman & Todd, 1985).

[26]See Karl Barth, *Church Dogmatics* 2/1, trans. T. H. L. Parker, W. B. Johnston, Harold Knight and J. L. M. Haire (Edinburgh: T & T Clark, 1957).

[27]Newlands, *Theology of the Love of God*, p. 46.

[28]Jürgen Moltmann, *The Crucified God* (London: SCM Press, 1974), p. 222.

movement that sought to prise the gospel apart from its formulation in terms of Greek thought.[29] In light of this combined attack, it is becoming increasingly difficult for classical theists to defend the intelligibility of the love of God as an apathetic and unilateral benevolence.

We should not ignore the significance of sociopolitical developments in the surrounding culture as we attempt to trace the genesis of the current paradigm revolution in theology. Several movements are arguably as much sociopolitical as theological.

Marxism and other social theories have raised our collective consciousness to the plight of the oppressed. The power of ideas such as justice and solidarity can be seen in the social upheavals that have followed in their wake. Highlighting the social dimensions of sin and reconciliation, liberation theologians have raised searching questions concerning the complicity of the classical theological paradigm with certain forms of institutional oppression. The upshot for the doctrine of God has been a new emphasis on God's solidarity and identification with the poor and oppressed. The God of liberation theology, unlike his classical theistic counterpart, is not far off but active and present wherever there is liberating activity.

Feminist theologies are united by the belief that women's concerns have been systematically repressed in traditional systematic theology. Could it be that the classical view of the love of God was similarly distorted, male-authored and male-centered? The God of classical theism is a God of "royal love"—a monarchical "provide and protect" kind of love that is in fact an exercise in control (albeit benevolent). Yet a benevolent dictator is still a dictator. For many feminist theologians, the God of classical theism is a God who loves while remaining distant and unaffected—in short, a *male* projection.

Catherine LaCugna reclaims the doctrine of the Trinity on behalf of feminist theology and argues that God's being as communion excludes any suggestion that persons can be subordinate to one another. From her perspective, the basic problem with Western trinitarian theology is that it begins with a substance ontology that tries to think "being" before "person" or "relation." LaCugna believes that substantival metaphysics and patriarchal politics are mutually reinforcing: "The subordination of woman to man is but a symptom of the conceptualization of personhood deep at work in patriarchy: a perfect person is self-sufficient."[30] The point of trinitarian theology, however, is that it is

---

[29]Alister McGrath, *Christian Theology: An Introduction,* 2nd ed. (Oxford: Blackwell, 1997), p. 251. Fiddes lists similar factors as explanations for the trend toward speaking of a suffering God (see *Creative Suffering of God,* pp. 12-15).

[30]Catherine Mowry LaCugna, "God in Communion with Us," in *Freeing Theology: The Essentials of Theology in Feminist Perspective,* ed. Catherine Mowry LaCugna (San Francisco: HarperCollins, 1993), p. 91.

the essence of God to be in relationship to other persons.

And not to persons only. Sallie McFague claims that God is related to the world as spirit is to body. What the secular scientist calls evolutionary development is for McFague, from a theological perspective, the story of God's inclusive, nonhierarchical love for all. McFague proposes a number of models for imagining God's relation to the world, among them God as "lover." The love she has in mind is not *agape,* however. For many feminists it is culpably misleading to suggest that women qua women are more beholden to the ideal of love as self-sacrifice than men. Indeed some feminists believe that women can give *too much* of themselves, to the point of becoming virtual nonentities.[31] Feminist theologians and ethicists have sought new ways of defining love so that it retains the aspect of self-giving while at the same time giving "new emphasis to a mutuality or reciprocity that makes possible and completes the genuinely interpersonal and relational dimensions of love."[32]

According to McFague, love is about finding a person valuable (and being found valuable) just because of who one is. It is also about the desire to be united with the beloved. A God who simply wills good to others is not yet a lover.[33] That God loves the world means, for McFague, that God finds the world valuable and wants to reunite with it. The love of God thus implies a certain need in God for the world: for the world's loving response, for the world's wholeness, both of which are necessary to make God whole.[34] In particular, the response that God the loved needs from his beloved world is cooperation: "The model of God as lover, then, implies that God needs us to help save the world!"[35]

I have been tracing the contours of a nascent revolution in theological paradigms. The notion of the love of God in the wake of the critique of theism is, as we have seen, more up to date. The themes of relatedness, mutuality and inclusiveness have appeared, quite independently, in process, trinitarian, liberation and feminist theology. Twentieth-century theologians exegete the love of God in terms that are familiar to modern culture: sympathy, compassion, mutuality, solidarity, inclusiveness. Culture, together with the history of ideas, however, marches on—and so does the story of the love of God.

---

[31]Lisa Sowle Cahill, "Feminism and Christian Ethics," in *Freeing Theology,* p. 217.

[32]Ibid. According to William Madges, whereas Catholics stress God's self-love (i.e., trinitarian unity and community) and Protestants stress other-love (e.g., self-sacrifice), feminists have championed an alternative definition of love as mutuality (William Madges, "Love," in *A New Handbook of Christian Theology,* ed. Donald W. Musser and Joseph L. Price [Nashville: Abingdon, 1992], p. 300).

[33]Sallie McFague, *Models of God: Theology for an Ecological, Nuclear Age* (Philadelphia: Fortress, 1987), p. 130.

[34]McFague argues that we should see "change" as a divine attribute (ibid., p. 134).

[35]Ibid., p. 135.

The authors of *Christian Theology: An Introduction to Its Traditions and Tasks* assume that the Enlightenment was the watershed for paradigm change. And so it has proved for modern theology. Yet the paradigm change in Christian thinking about the love of God intersects in complex fashion with another paradigm change: from the modern to the *postmodern*. The meaning of love has undergone another permutation in postmodern writing, acquiring the sense of "excess" and "self-abandonment." Jean-Luc Marion, for example, suggests that because God, as love, gives himself, theology must abandon all metaphysical attempts to conceive God, for love is precisely that which does not have to "be." God's self-communication is pure gift, excess, and cannot be correlated with Being.[36] David Tracy, in his foreword to Marion's book, concludes that the task for contemporary theology is to think the excessive reality of an "*agape* beyond Being."[37] Tracy interprets this postmodern theme of love as excess as a retrieval of the neo-Platonist metaphor of God's love as "overflow."[38] "Love enters postmodernity first as transgression, then as excess, and finally as transgressive excess of sheer gift."[39]

It is not yet clear what the love of God will become in postmodernity. One thing, however, is certain: the love of God in postmodern theology surpasses both its medieval and modern predecessors, inasmuch as it is "beyond being" and "beyond relationality."[40]

Central Issues

The concept of the love of God is both fundamental to the doctrine of God and, oddly, disruptive of it. There seems to be no one place in a systematics in which the notion of the love of God neatly fits. What, therefore, is the significance of the place of the love of God in systematic theology for its meaning and function?

Structure. With regard to the structure of systematic theology, the love of God functions either as a discrete doctrinal topic (e.g., one of the loci) or as the structuring principle that provides a point of integration or thematic unity between individual doctrines. Somewhat surprisingly, few theologians have chosen the latter option. Instead most medieval and post-Reformation systematic theologies discuss the love of God, when they discuss it at all, as one subheading under the attributes of God.

Most discussions of the love of God in the classical paradigm take place under the

---

[36]It would be interesting to compare and contrast Anders Nygren's sense of *agape* or "gift love" with the postmodern treatment of love as "gift."

[37]David Tracy, foreword to Jean-Luc Marion, *God Without Being*, trans. Thomas A. Carlson (Chicago: University of Chicago Press, 1991), p. xv.

[38]David Tracy, *On Naming the Present: God, Hermeneutics and Church* (Maryknoll, N.Y.: Orbis, 1994), p. 56.

[39]Ibid., p. 44.

[40]Ibid.

heading "God's being." This location perhaps reflects an underlying substantival metaphysics in which beings of different kinds have different essences and properties (attributes). The prior issue is whether one discusses the being of God from the starting point of the notion of "perfect being" or from the biblical story of salvation. It may transpire, of course, that the God of infinite perfection just is the God of Abraham, Isaac and Jacob, and the classical paradigm assumes as much at the outset. As we have seen, however, the notion of "perfect being" is not absolute but subject to the vagaries of culture (compare the different views of perfection held by Aristotle in antiquity and Hartshorne in modernity).

The structure of Aquinas's *Summa Theologiae* shows that he conceives of God first as he is himself and only then as he is in relation to his creatures. Aquinas limits himself in questions 2-26 to examining attributes of God's unitive being ("the one God"). And as we have seen, he defines the love of God in terms of will: benevolence. The Trinity does not receive serious attention before question 27, after the divine ontology has largely been mapped out. Not only is God's love discussed under the heading of the will of the one God, but the Trinity is presented as a self-sufficient divine community, unrelated to the world.

According to John McIntyre, the love of God should not only be the controlling category of Christian theology but be *seen* to be so.[41] The question for the classical paradigm is whether the love of God can structure theology in this manner if it is only one of several divine attributes of an infinite, personal (though single) being. It comes closer to doing so in Barth's *Church Dogmatics,* for Barth defines God's being not in terms of substantival metaphysics but in terms of God's revelation in Christ. On the basis of God's being-in-act (e.g., incarnation), Barth concludes that God is essentially the one who goes out of himself for the sake of fellowship with another, or simply, as "the one who loves in freedom." In *Church Dogmatics* love operates as a kind of "control attribute" which regulates the other divine perfections. And with regard to the structure of his theology, Barth reserves discussion of the divine attributes to volume two. In other words, the discussion of God's being and attributes follows Barth's treatment of God's self-revelation and the doctrine of the Trinity.[42]

Meaning: Attribute, attitude, action, relation? To this point we have considered how the love of God has been implicated in a paradigm revolution in contemporary theology. What now needs to be added is that the paradigm revolution is in fact a revolution in models for understanding love.

According to McFague, all theological language is metaphorical, and its purpose

---

[41]John McIntyre, *On the Love of God* (London: Collins, 1962), pp. 32-33.
[42]Barth thus devotes the first volume of his *Church Dogmatics* to the doctrine of the Word of God.

is to articulate the nature of the God-world relation. "God loves the world." The love of God intersects with models and metaphors on two levels. First, it is a general characterization of the way God and the world should be thought of. The love of God is thus a metaphor of the God-world relation. Indeed, to a large extent the model of love functions as a control metaphor that determines much else in one's doctrine of God. However, this is not the end of the story. For what is the meaning of the love of God? Here too contemporary theologians use metaphors. Understanding the love of God depends on our ability to formulate multiple images (e.g., benevolence, mutuality) of a root metaphor—relationality.[43]

McIntyre argues that no one metaphor can give full value to the concept of God's love. Accordingly he examines six different models for viewing God's love: concern, commitment, communication, community, involvement and identification. For her part, McFague believes that there is an open-ended number of relatively adequate metaphors for depicting the God-world relationship. Among the many options, she chooses three in particular that best convey the nature of this relationship to a "nuclear, ecological age" such as ours: mother, lover, friend.[44]

Brümmer examines a number of models of human love—romantic, mystic, courtly, neighborly—but ultimately opts for a literal definition: "Love must by its very nature be a relationship of free mutual give and take, otherwise it cannot be love at all."[45] In so saying, however, Brümmer is doing no more than stating his preference for one definition of love over another. Insofar as he assumes this definition without further argumentation, moreover, his treatment of the love of God risks begging what is arguably the main question: what does it mean to predicate love of God?

The classic model of traditional theism conceives the love of God in terms of *sovereign will:* benevolence, the intent and the ability to will and to act for a person's good. Brümmer complains that the tradition conceives of the love of God as something "attitudinal rather than relational." Western thought, he opines, "has suffered from a systematic blind spot for relations."[46] His basis criticism of the traditional picture of benevolence is that such love is *impersonal.* Willing someone good, he reasons, hardly qualifies as an instance of a genuine personal relation; indeed it would be more accurate to describe it as manipulative than as mutual.[47]

---

[43]Whereas McFague treats the love of God as a metaphor, Brümmer treats it alternately as a model and a concept, McIntyre as a complex concept.

[44]See McFague, *Models of God,* chaps. 4-6.

[45]Brümmer, *Model of Love,* p. 161.

[46]Ibid., p. 33.

[47]Ibid., pp. 156-63. Fiddes agrees, adding that the notion of a personal, loving God also entails the suffering of God. Traditional theology escapes this conclusion only "by regarding love as an attitude and action of *goodwill* towards another person" (*Creative Suffering of God,* p. 17).

84

Traditional theologians, however, are unhappy with the suggestion that the conception of God's love as sovereign will is "impersonal." Augustus Strong, for instance, states, "By love we mean that attribute of the divine nature in virtue of which God is eternally moved to self-communication."[48] This self-communication originates from God (as in the incarnation) and counts as an initiative of love even if its objects fail to respond: "He came to his own home, and his own people received him not" (Jn 1:11). Note too that for Strong, and perhaps for much of the Christian tradition besides, love is not the all-inclusive divine attribute. True, "God is love"; but 1 John also tells us that "God is light" (1 Jn 1:5). Strong sees "light"—that is, divine holiness—as the broader of the attributes, for love does not include God's holiness, whereas holiness includes God's love.[49]

While the concept of the love of God does indeed tend to underline God's relatedness, the accent of holiness is on God's separation from, not relation to, the world of human beings. It remains an open question whether this emphasis on holiness makes God's transcendence (his otherness, his set-apartness) more fundamental to his being than his immanence.[50]

That God is both "love" and "light" recalls McIntyre's caution not to let any one definition of love exclude all others. A monologic approach to love is bound to be reductionistic. Does the classical model of the love of God stress divine transcendence at the expense of divine immanence and so fall prey to reductionism?

Of McIntyre's six models, two, concern and involvement, when taken together, best correspond to the classical view. God's love for the world means that his concern passes into action, his compassion into passion—a self-communication and an identification that culminate in the incarnation and the cross. McIntyre's discussion of these aspects of the love of God is useful in dismissing some of the caricatures of the classical model. Immutability, for instance, does not mean immobility, only that God is thoroughly self-consistent and reliable. Self-consistency, moreover, "is compatible with a whole variety of reactions to different situations."[51]

Vincent Brümmer speaks for many today when he questions the intelligibility of the classical model of the love of God as benevolence or "gift-love." If there is no desire in God, then presumably God does not need or desire us to return his love. But if love is not only communication but communion, then it seems wholly inadequate to suggest that God's love is a one-way phenomenon, a giving without a

[48]Augustus H. Strong, *Systematic Theology* (Valley Forge, Penn.: Judson Press, 1907), p. 268.
[49]Ibid.
[50]It is perhaps preferable, however, to see the love of God as itself both transcendent and immanent, rather than classing love on one side rather than the other.
[51]McIntyre, *On the Love of God*, p. 57. On divine impassibility, McIntyre leaves us with the intriguing suggestion that God suffers in the manner "appropriate to his nature," though he does not tell us just what this manner might be (p. 56).

receiving.[52] As we have seen, Brümmer himself defines love as a relationship in which traffic flows in both directions.

By itself, of course, the term *relation* is not very illuminating. There are many kinds of relations in the world. *Causality,* for example, covers a whole family of relations.[53] Impersonal causal relations, however, have nothing to do with loving relations, for the latter are interpersonal. Yet here too we need considerably more precision, for there are many types of interpersonal relationships (e.g., parent-child, friend-friend, friend-enemy), and some of these resemble their causal counterparts (e.g., master-slave). How do we know which of these interpersonal relationships are genuinely loving, and thus apt metaphors for the love of God?

Proponents of the relational view usually qualify such love with adjectives such as *mutual, reciprocal* or *inclusive,* though it is arguable whether these categories ever get beyond the notion of justice ("light"?). As we have seen, Brümmer offers the following stipulative definition: "Love must by its very nature be a relationship of free mutual give and take, otherwise it cannot be love at all."[54] I confess to finding this definition rather puzzling. In the first instance, Brümmer seems to have transgressed his own methodological boundaries by giving us love's "very nature" rather than a metaphor or model. More seriously, it is not clear that his definition is coherent. If love *is* the relationship, then it follows that the notion of unrequited love is impossible. For if love's overture is unrequited, then there is no reciprocity, and where there is no reciprocity there is no free mutual giving and taking, no relationship—no love. If Brümmer is correct, then it becomes difficult in the extreme to know how to love one's enemies. How can one love those who refuse to enter into relations of mutuality if love just *is* that mutual relation?

Clearly Brümmer's model on its own will not do. If, on the other hand, there is such a thing as unrequited love, then love cannot merely be identified with the relationship. The only alternative would be to argue that God's love is of such a nature that it unilaterally *creates* relationships that invariably elicit a genuine response on the part of the beloved. But that is another theological controversy.[55]

These conceptual problems lead us back to Brümmer's basic assumption, that all genuinely loving personal relations must be characterized by mutuality and reciprocity. Is it indeed the case that all genuinely loving interpersonal relations must be symmetrical? Must they be *exactly* symmetrical (and how does one determine this)? A

---

[52]See John Burnaby, *Amor Dei: A Study of the Religion of St. Augustine* (London: Hodder & Stoughton, 1938), p. 307.

[53]Aquinas followed Aristotle in distinguishing four types of causality.

[54]Brümmer, *Model of Love,* p. 161.

[55]I refer, of course, to the notion of irresistible grace. It may also be the heart of the issue. As we have seen, Brümmer's fundamental problem with the notion of unilateral love is that it *depersonalizes* us by rendering us the "objects" of divine manipulation (pp. 136-37).

mother may indeed be desirous of a response from her infant, but the quality of the infant's response may not be such as could be described in terms of "mutuality" or "reciprocity." Furthermore, it is hardly self-evident that the relation of Creator to creature should be thought of in terms of mutuality and reciprocity. And even were one to accept these qualifications, it is not entirely clear that mutuality and reciprocity alone take us beyond the concept of justice to that of love. After all, what is more mutual and reciprocal than "an eye for an eye"?

Function: Critical versus constructive. It has become a virtual given in much contemporary theology that one should interpret the Bible in such a way as to maximize the love of God. This is not quite Augustine's famous hermeneutical rule. Augustine said, "Choose the interpretation which most fosters the love of God"; the contemporary equivalent might be "Choose the interpretation which most fosters the understanding of God as love." As we have seen, however, (1) "love" is not the only model for how God relates to the world, and (2) there are at least two significant proposals for how one should understand the love of God. It may prove useful to look at two concrete examples that show how theologians use the concept of the love of God in debates about other doctrinal topics. The love of God functions in contemporary theology both as a critical and as a constructive principle.

Edward Farley, in his *Ecclesial Reflection*—a masterful deconstruction of the Scripture principle—appeals to the love of God at a critical point in his argument against the theological method of classic orthodoxy, which he dismisses as "argument by citation."[56] To be precise, Farley undermines the logic of the Scripture principle by challenging the presupposition of salvation history on which it rests: the notion that God sovereignly intervenes in human history.

The notion that God can direct salvation history—including the composition of the biblical canon—implies that God controls either all of history or only a part of it. If we say that God's sovereign will applies to only a portion of history, we must conclude that he does not will the good of (love, save) the rest of it. If, on the other hand, we say that God's sovereign will is universal, then the horrors of history have the same relation to God as the saving events. In either case, Farley reasons, classical theism founders on the problem of evil: either God is involved with only part of the world in a loving way, or everything that happens is a result of God's will, in which case we cannot say that God is love.

Farley presents us, in other words, with the following dilemma: either God is sovereign or God is love. If God is love, the implication is that God is not in control of

---

[56]Edward Farley, *Ecclesial Reflection: An Anatomy of Theological Method* (Philadelphia: Fortress, 1982). Similar points are made in Edward Farley and Peter Hodgson, "Scripture and Tradition," in *Christian Theology: An Introduction to Its Traditions and Tasks*, ed. Peter Hodgson and Robert King, 2nd ed. (Philadelphia: Fortress, 1985), pp. 61-87.

history (nor of the process of Scripture's composition). Farley expects his readers to agree with him: faced with deciding for God's control or God's love, "there is really no choice."[57] What the world needs now is love.

What, however, does Farley assume to be the meaning of the love of God? Is there really a contradiction between divine love and divine sovereignty? Not according to Thomas Aquinas. For the tradition, as we have seen, God's love means God's settled determination to will *and to effect* the good. This is precisely what Farley's God cannot do. Farley's God may want the good, but he cannot will it. Farley's God, in essence the God of process theology, can invite cooperation but cannot unilaterally intervene in human history, for good or for ill. The question for Farley is what we mean when we affirm that God is love, if God *cannot* act unilaterally for the good of humankind. For if the traditional model preserves a valid insight, God can be *love* only if he is also *Lord* (free, sovereign). Farley, of course, believes that we must choose between divine sovereignty and divine sympathy, assuming as he does that love involves vulnerability.

I have already hinted at the second way the love of God has been applied as a critical fulcrum to revise Christian tradition. Divine passibility may strike us at first glance as a somewhat marginal topic in the doctrine of God, an unlikely beachhead for a paradigm revolution in theology. As we have seen, however, the basic issue comes down to this: Can God be affected—in his being, will, nature or emotions—by something external to himself? Can not-God condition God? If God is love, and if love means sympathy ("suffering with"), then it would indeed appear that God is affected by what happens in the world—that God "suffers change." Paul Fiddes, in agreement with Hartshorne, argues that because love is "the sharing of experience," God's love for the suffering must include God's real participation in that suffering. However, while God may sorrow and suffer because of his people's unbelief and disobedience, he nevertheless remains God. Note, however, that suffering entails change: "To love is to be in a relationship where what the loved one does alters one's own experience."[58]

It is noteworthy that Fiddes sees fit to build certain bridges in the direction of process theology. Love is "essentially mutuality."[59] God and the world are, on this view of love, *partners*—a suggestion that would have probably horrified most classical theists. This way of stating the implications of relational theism also clarifies the

---

[57]Ibid., p. 156.

[58]Fiddes, *Creative Suffering of God*, p. 50. The nature of theological language, and in particular analogy, is an issue for many of the essays in the book. The challenge is to speak intelligibly of God without succumbing to anthropomorphism. Fiddes's comment provides an interesting test case: how are we to understand the notion of God's having experiences? or of suffering in a manner appropriate to his nature?

[59]Ibid., p. 173.

outstanding challenge: if God's love is seen in terms of God's suffering change by that which is not God, then can God love in this sense and remain *God?* Must Christians really choose between God as love and God as Lord?

Very few voices in the current debates are willing to give up either notion. The real issue concerns the meaning of love and lordship: How does God's love qualify (modify, temper) God's lordship? How does God's lordship qualify God's love?

These two examples pale in comparison to the larger paradigm revolution, from theism to *panentheism,* that is currently under way. In large part it is the theme of God's love that has served as the impetus for the growing tendency to abandon theistic models of the God-world relation for those that are panentheistic.[60] Again, the basic point of contention concerns the nature of God's relation to the world, and in particular whether God suffers change because of what his creatures will and do.

Like many panentheists, the authors of *The Openness of God* argue that there is "genuine interaction" and "genuine dialogue" between God and human creatures. God is "open" to receiving creaturely input. The course of history is not the product of divine or divine action alone but of humans' cooperating (or not) with God. God does not merely act but *reacts.* Indeed without genuine reaction on God's part, the integrity of the God-world relationship would be in serious jeopardy.

Clark Pinnock sounds familiar themes when he declares that his aim "is to do greater justice to mutuality and relationality in both the triune God and the God-human covenant."[61] For Pinnock, God is sovereign in the sense that he is free and able to create beings with free wills who are able to make a difference to his life. If God is no longer unconditioned, unaffected by everything outside himself, it is only because he has willed to be so. God, in other words, wills to be "open" to the effects of human history.[62]

It is difficult not to view the category of "openness" as just as much a part of a culturally informed hermeneutic as "substance" and "immutability" were categories of antiquity's interpretative framework. Indeed one could imagine the openness view as

---

[60]It is an open (!) question whether the so-called openness view of "relational theism" belongs with "theism" or "panentheism." While proponents of the open God are careful to distance themselves from process theologians, it is important to realize that not all panentheists (e.g., Moltmann) are process theologians. The position Philip Clayton sketches in his "Case for Christian Panentheism" (*Dialog* 37 [1998]: 201-8) strikes me as very similar to that of the openness theologians, especially in light of the "corrections" Clayton makes to panentheism to keep it genuinely Christian.

[61]Clark Pinnock, "Systematic Theology," in *The Openness of God: A Biblical Challenge to the Traditional Understanding of God,* by Pinnock et al. (Downers Grove, Ill.: InterVarsity Press, 1994), p. 101.

[62]In Pinnock's words: "God is unchanging in nature and essence but not in experience, knowledge and action" (p. 118)). "The open view of God stresses qualities of generosity, sensitivity and vulnerability more than power and control" (p. 125).

THE LOVE OF GOD

a species of "perfect being" theology with one important difference: in the context of contemporary thought and sensibility, "perfection" is now understood not in terms of unrelatedness but of "most-relatedness." For Charles Hartshorne, for example, God is the perfect being precisely because he is related to *everything* that is, whereas finite beings are related to—and hence able to influence for the good—only *some* things. It is not entirely clear, therefore, that panentheism or relational theism represents a recovery of the biblical teaching about God rather than a new development in the history of the concept of "perfect being." Is the panentheistic way—the open view— of thinking about the love of God a correction of philosophical notions in the light of the biblical witness, or an interpretation of the biblical witness in the light of contemporary thought forms? Is the open view a return to biblical sources or merely the substitution of one conceptuality of love for another?

Is it indeed necessary, with regard to classical theism, to abandon ship? John McIntyre was prompted to write *On the Love of God* in response to an overly exclusivistic understanding of the love of God (the book begins with an account of a Highland communion service in which only the "worthy"—a fraction of the congregation—dared partake). Some thirty years on, the cultural context has altered dramatically. Indeed the prime difficulty in giving full value to the concept of the love of God in the new paradigm may be its unduly narrow equation of the term not with an attribute but (to paraphrase McIntyre) with a *relation*. For the love of God is now seen as something thoroughly *inclusive* ("open"). There is now no fence around the Communion table: God's fellowship extends not only to faithful covenant servants but even to those in other religious traditions, faithful or not.[63]

The above review may lead us to conclude that it is inadvisable to define the love of God univocally. Like many other doctrines, the concept falls short of the narrative that generates it. If this is so, then perhaps McIntyre's method of combining six models is to be preferred to Brümmer's overarching relational model. It would seem that if we are to do justice to what Scripture says about God's love, we must say at least three things: that the love of God is something that God *has,* that the love of God is something that God *does,* and that the love of God is something that God *is.* And perhaps, in a manner that we cannot yet conceive, the love of God transcends the categories currently on offer in theism and panentheism alike.

God's Love: Communicative Action Oriented to Communion

For classical theism, God's love is a matter of his sovereign will, of *benevolence:* willing and acting for the other's good. Whereas the theist maintains that God's love is a

---

[63]The pressing pastoral problem, though it is beyond the scope of the present essay to evaluate it, has to do with the practical import of the new understanding of the love of God. To use Ellen Charry's phrase, is it "good for our souls" to believe that God suffers with us?

matter of his effective action (willing and doing), the panentheist suggests that God's love is more a matter of affective empathy ("I feel your pain").[64]

I stated at the outset that the opposite of love is indifference. Someone who is indifferent "turns a deaf ear," a phrase that strikingly depicts the futility of the speaker's communicative action. Silence, an utter lack of communicative initiative, is another indication of indifference. The God depicted in Scripture is hardly indifferent, either as speaker or as hearer. On the contrary, God is portrayed as engaging in dialogue with human persons—an active speaker and listener. God's presence is neither spatial nor substantive but *communicative*. It is the presence of personal address and response: "Come now, let us reason together" (Is 1:18). I therefore propose to focus on God's communicative action as the clue, and perhaps the key, to understanding the broader God-world relation.

A picture of God as causal agent holds classical theism captive. When God's willing the good is viewed in terms of causality, it is difficult to reconcile divine love with the notion of personal relation. Theists like Aquinas knew, of course, that God's lordly loving—his sovereign care for his creation—varies according to the nature of the creature. God wills the good for the inanimate world, but not in the same way he wills good for human beings. One way beyond the classical theism-panentheism impasse is, I suggest, to see God as a *communicative* agent. God's lordly loving of human persons largely takes the form, I believe, of communicative action.

On the one hand, communicative action is eminently personal. Human beings are never more human (personal) than when engaging in activities such as telling stories, making promises, asking and answering questions, sharing feelings, praying and praising. The last two forms of communicative action are particularly associated with the human person's relation to God. Yet God too relates to human persons by means of communicative acts such as promising, commanding, asking and answering. In short, God relates to the human world as speaker and hearer.[65]

Moreover, God's communicative action is perfect. According to Isaiah 55:11, God's speech is never empty but always accomplishes the purpose for which it was sent. Note too the immediate context of this affirmation concerning the efficacy of the divine word: Isaiah 55:8-9 contrasts the Lord's way with human ways, the Lord's thoughts with human thoughts. Like God's ways and God's thoughts, God's communicative action is "higher than" ours. Yet at the same time the very

---

[64]Cf. Edward Farley, *Divine Empathy: A Theology of God* (Minneapolis: Fortress, 1996), chap. 20.

[65]My focus in this chapter and the next is on a subset of the God-world relation: the relation between God and human beings. Accordingly my emphasis on God's communicative action should not be taken as a denial of God's causal agency, at least with regard to the nonhuman world.

purpose of communicative action is to *relate* to others.

The good God wills for human beings is communion: fellowship with one another and fellowship with God. The "openness" theists are entirely correct to call our attention to the centrality of the genuinely personal relation that God seeks with his people. This insight is hardly revolutionary, however, for even Aquinas envisioned a cosmic communion in which all things are drawn by God's love to participate in God's life.

What both classical and open theists need to acknowledge is the means by which God is bringing about his loving purpose. God's love is best viewed neither in terms of causality nor in terms of mutuality but rather in terms of communication and self-communication. From the vantage point of my communicative theism, God is transcendent not as an impersonal cause, the force behind what Jürgen Habermas terms "strategic" action, but rather as a properly communicative agent whose actions are efficacious in a way that is entirely appropriate to persons. To be sure, some postmoderns view language as a means for manipulating people, but this use of language goes against its divine "design plan," which is to be the means for communicative rather than instrumental action. What God brings about in communicative action is *understanding,* as well as its precondition, faith.[66]

Communicative action thus aims at understanding. Now understanding represents a specific type of communion, a meeting of minds, where the aims and intentions of one's action are recognized by another. Language is a sophisticated resource for performing simple and complex communicative acts, from issuing a greeting to constituting a government. Of course not all communicative action has to be verbal. Indeed it is possible to see not only the preaching of the gospel but the content of the gospel itself—the Word made flesh for us—as a divine communicative act: the bespeaking of a Word, Jesus Christ, that is received in the core of our being thanks to the "breath" (the energy, the power) or Holy Spirit which accompanies it. The purpose of this gospel act is nothing less than communion: union with God in Christ. Both faith and understanding come from the hearing of God's Word (Rom 10:17).

To communicate is to impart, to give something to another. In linguistics and communication studies (and very often systematic theology as well!), what gets communicated is *information.* In the context of the life and physical sciences, what gets communicated is *life* or *energy.* Interestingly, what God "communicates" through his Word and Spirit involves both information (truth) and energy (spirit). Human beings need both for salvation, that is, for participation in the divine life. This accords with the etymology of the term *communication:* "to make common."

---

[66]I argue for this more fully in chapter four in relation to Calvin's concept of the "effectual call."

The burden of the present section is to lay the groundwork for thinking of God's love, and hence of the God-world relation, in terms of communicative action proceeding from and leading to communion. The following chapter provides an in-depth analysis of one communicative act in particular in which God may be seen to be *both* loving *and* sovereign: the effectual call.

God is fully God in and of himself (and hence independent of the world). Father, Son and Spirit exist in a fellowship of communication and communion: "in the beginning was the Word." Or rather, in the beginning was the triune communicative agency and action of God. Communicative theism acknowledges God as the paradigm communicative agent, the One whose Word—eternally begotten, embodied, spoken or written—invariably accomplishes the purpose for which it is sent. In the mystery of his gracious love, God makes a communicative initiative and hence relates to what is other than ("outside") himself by sharing information, energy, life.

It is now time to return to our initial question: does God's love imply that he shares our pain, that he suffers with us, that what happens to us affects him in such a way that he could be said to "suffer change"? Surely my emphasis on God's love as communicative agency oriented toward communion suggests, with its stress on dialogue, that God is affected by what we say and do, that God's response will be conditioned by our own communicative acts, or lack thereof.

Let me briefly summarize my position. God loves his people largely by bringing about understanding (and faith) through his communicative action. This is not simply a matter of conveying information but of making promises, issuing commands and giving warnings, as well as comforting and consoling. The crucial point is that God brings about understanding (faith, hope, comfort and so on) not through manipulation but precisely in a manner that is appropriate for persons with reason, will, imagination and emotions. The question of God's "openness," in regard to communicative theism, is whether God's relation to his people can be genuinely loving if God is unaffected by the communicative acts of his human interlocutors.

As I shall argue in the next chapter, God's communicative acts are efficacious in a way that far surpasses their human counterparts. The relevant question at present, however, concerns the capacity of human communicative acts, no matter how efficacious, to affect God. Obviously certain human speech acts such as commanding or scolding are inappropriate when directed to God. It is a matter of present dispute whether *informing* is appropriate vis-à-vis God: can God learn new things? The nature of divine omniscience is complex and beyond the scope of this chapter. I will therefore confine my response to the question of God's openness to one subsidiary query: can there be real personal communion if what humans say or do does not influence or affect God?

It may come as something of a surprise that a position that gives pride of place to such "communal" notions as communication and communion would nevertheless wish to affirm the concept of divine impassibility, but such indeed is the case. Everything hinges on what divine impassibility means, however. I believe that a clue lies in a certain parallelism with Jesus' impeccability.

Jesus, the author of Hebrews tells us, was truly tempted as we are (Heb 2:18) though he remained sinless (Heb 4:15). There is no contradiction between Jesus' being "open" to temptation and it being certain that he would not sin. Though some have said that Jesus must not have felt the force of temptation, others contend that it is precisely the person who resists temptation who feels its full force. Or to use an image suggested by Augustus Strong: Jesus was sinless yet subject to real temptation in the same way that an invincible army is subject to attack. Something similar, I believe, may be said for divine impassibility.[67]

It is clear from Scripture that God is "open" to commiserating with his people. In a remarkable passage that depicts the tension between God's anger and compassion, we read, "My heart recoils within me" (Hos 11:8). God feels the force of his people's suffering: "I have seen the affliction of my people who are in Egypt, and have heard their cry because of their taskmasters; I know their sufferings" (Ex 3:7). Yet as Jesus feels the force of temptation without sinning, so God feels the force of the human experience without suffering change in his being, will or knowledge.

Impassibility means not that God is unfeeling but that God is never *overcome* or *overwhelmed* by passion. Though certain feelings may *befall* God, he will not be *subject* to them. In this strict sense, then, it is no contradiction to say that God experiences human sorrow yet is nevertheless apathetic (because this experience does not compromise his reason, will or wisdom). God genuinely relates to human persons via his communicative action, but nothing humans do conditions or affects God's communicative initiatives and God's communicative acts. Indeed it may well be the case that divine impassibility is a condition for divine freedom, if one defines freedom with Thomas Aquinas in terms of self-determination: "one's mastery over one's action" *(dominium sui actus)*.[68] If what God does is determined or influenced decisively by what humans say and do, then God is not free. The main point, however, is that God is a sovereign communicative agent who wills the good by bringing about certain communicative effects in his peo-

---

[67]Jesus' experience of sharing human weaknesses without sinning represents a kind of precedent for understanding divine impassibility. For the "ego" undergoing the experiences of the man Jesus was the divine person, the "I am." See the discussion of the "human" psychology of Jesus in Jacques Dupuis, *Who Do You Say That I Am? Introduction to Christology* (Maryknoll, N.Y.: Orbis, 1994), chap. 5.

[68]See Aquinas *Summa Contra Gentiles* 2.22.

ple, especially faith, understanding and consolation.

In sum: a Christian theology of the love of God requires us to speak both of the doctrine of the Trinity and of the concept of divine communicative action. I have argued elsewhere that these notions are linked: the Son and Spirit are means of the Father's communicative action.[69] Yet everything that God does is also loving. This is especially the case with God's communicative action. God is love; and God's Word—both the Word become flesh and the Word become verbal—is love's principal ongoing and outgoing work. To the extent that this is so, and to the extent that the notion of communicative action leading to communion eventually leads us to the doctrine of Scripture, then it would appear that the theme of God's love confronts us once more with a matter of "first theology."

Conclusion: Between Metaphor and Metaphysics

Brümmer and McFague agree that metaphors describe the way we relate to God, not the nature of God himself.[70] The model of love is no exception. Does not such an approach necessarily elide the distinction between the way we love God and the way God loves us? Does not thinking of God as "lover" or "mother" (or "father") risk confusing the way we love one another with the way God loves us? Anthropomorphism is an ever-present danger, even in theology according to the new paradigm.

If, however, the Word of God is the final criterion and control for God-talk, then Christian theology must attend to the biblical witness. Scripture consistently directs our attention to a God who pours himself out—in creation, in Jesus Christ, on the cross, through the Holy Spirit—on behalf of those who do not merit such attention. If this gospel, this story of salvation—a story of God's costly love for creation and above all for the covenant creature—is the control story for Christian life and thought, then we have a precious touchstone for what divine reality is like. Christian theologians must therefore be prepared to put their preconceived notions of perfect being—whether stemming from antiquity, modernity or postmodernity—to the critical test of the biblical text. Not just any model or metaphor will do.

Can we ever get beyond metaphor to metaphysics, beyond language to reality? Can love describe not merely the God-world relation but the being of God himself? I believe it can and does. As Janet Martin Soskice points out, scientific models and metaphors may refer to reality truly though not exhaustively. Religious metaphors are

---

[69]This is the burden of Kevin Vanhoozer, *Is There a Meaning in This Text? The Bible, the Reader and the Morality of Literary Knowledge* (Grand Rapids, Mich.: Zondervan, 1998), part 2. See also chapter six in the present work for an argument that the doctrine of the Trinity serves as the paradigm for understanding what is involved in communicative action.

[70]Brümmer states: "The metaphors and models employed in God-talk are primarily relational: they are intended to indicate the ways in which we are to relate to God" (*Model of Love*, p. 19).

THE LOVE OF GOD

similarly "reality depicting."[71] The metaphor of love adequately describes God's being, but only when biblical narrative—that is, the storied history of Jesus Christ—is allowed to regulate the use of the term *love*. When the narratives of the gospel of Jesus Christ do discipline theological thought, we may find ourselves cheering Richard of St. Victor's correction of Anselm's famous definition of God as the being "greater than which none can be conceived." Richard, focusing on the interpersonal, intratrinitarian relations, argued that such a God loves with a love "so great that nothing greater can exist and . . . of such a kind that nothing better can exist."[72]

What, then, is the place of the love of God in systematic theology? Will it serve as a linchpin to maintain the status quo, or will it provide critical leverage for a paradigm revolution? It is too soon to tell. Perhaps the moral of this chapter is that the love of God should occupy no one place in a theological system, but every place. Instead of trying to situate the love of God under one doctrinal locus, that is, the theologian's task is rather to witness to its inexhaustibility. To witness to the love of God is the Christian theologian's supreme privilege and supreme responsibility.

---

[71]Janet Martin Soskice, *Metaphor and Religious Language* (Oxford: Oxford University Press, 1984).

[72]Richard of St. Victor *On the Trinity* 3.2 (in *Richard of St. Victor,* trans. Grover A. Zinn [New York: Paulist, 1979], p. 375).

Four

Effectual Call
or Causal Effect?

Summons, Sovereignty &
Supervenient Grace

*A*ssumptions about the way God relates to the world lie behind every doctrine in systematic theology. The decision one makes as to how to conceive this relation is arguably the single most important factor in shaping one's theology. Paul Tillich spoke of two types of philosophy of religion to distinguish two ways of approaching God: by way of meeting a stranger and by way of overcoming estrangement.[1] The first, or cosmological, way conceives of God as a personal being who can interact (or not) with the world. The second, or ontological, way conceives of the world as always/already existing "in" God.

Christian theologians are today faced with a similar choice between "theism" and "panentheism." It may be only a slight exaggeration to say that we are in the midst of a paradigm revolution, but it is clear that the traditional doctrine of God—classical theism—is in crisis. Theologians of various denominational stripes, liberal and conservative, faced with the choice for or against classical theism, are increasingly abandoning ship.[2]

Such is the broad canvas to which I wish to apply some initial brushwork, though for the most part I shall confine my attention to a small corner only. While I am interested in these rival pictures of the God-world relation, my focus will be on saving

[1]Paul Tillich, "Two Types of Philosophy of Religion," in *Theology and Culture* (Oxford: Oxford University Press, 1959), pp. 10-29.
[2]It sometimes seems that the only people interested in classical theism these days are analytic philosophers of religion rather than systematicians.

grace. I shall therefore examine that Benjamin of theological concepts, the Reformed doctrine of the effectual call, keeping in mind the ways this doctrine is colored by, and perhaps itself affects, understandings of the broader God-world relation.

The Sovereign Stranger: Some Problems with Theistic Transcendence

Three criticisms are commonly applied to what Tillich describes as the first way of approaching God, the way of meeting a stranger: it is unbiblical; it is blasphemous; it is unscientific.

Clark Pinnock, for instance, claims that classical theism drank too deeply from the poisoned wells of Greek philosophy. Consequently its conception of God as immutable omnipotence is a far cry from the biblical picture of a dynamic, loving God.[3] Karl Barth renders a similarly harsh judgment on Reformed orthodoxy: "The dogmatics of these centuries had already been too closely bound up with a form not taken from the thing itself but from contemporary philosophies."[4] The fundamental problem with classical theism, Pinnock believes, is that it wrongly conceives the God-world relation in deterministic, impersonal terms.

Second, Tillich argues that theism, because it conceives of God as the supreme being, ends up in a kind of idolatry, identifying God as part of the furniture of the cosmos and believing that it can conceive God. That God is a "sovereign" being, whose decrees determine everything whatsoever that comes to pass, only complicates things. If God supernaturally intervenes in the world, then why is there suffering and evil? Feminist and process theologians similarly accuse theism's monarchical picture of God of providing a tacit endorsement of patriarchy and social oppression.

For many contemporary theologians, however, probably the most compelling reason to abandon the theistic paradigm is its apparent conflict with what modern science has taught us about our world. "It is probably safe to say that the whole of Christian doctrine as received from tradition is built on the assumption of supernatural causal intervention."[5] Yet few modern theologians are happy to construe the God-world relation in terms of divine intervention. Friedrich Schleiermacher influenced a whole theological tradition when he judged it a mistake to see God as overriding or supplementing natural causes, for to think of God in terms of exercising efficient causality is to think of God in terms appropriate to creatures: "It can never be necessary

---

[3]Clark Pinnock: "Above all, God is love, and therefore expresses his power, not by having to control everything like an oriental despot, but by giving humanity salvation and eternal life under the conditions of mutuality" (introduction to *The Grace of God, the Will of Man* [Grand Rapids, Mich.: Zondervan, 1989], pp. x-xi).

[4]Karl Barth, introduction to Heinrich Heppe, *Reformed Dogmatics* (Grand Rapids, Mich.: Baker, 1978), p. vi.

[5]Jeffrey Hopper, *Understanding Modern Theology*, vol. 2, *Reinterpreting Christian Faith for Changing Worlds* (Philadelphia: Fortress, 1987), p. 34.

in the interest of religion so to interpret a fact that its dependence on God absolutely excludes its being conditioned by the system of Nature."[6]

Summing up these three problems, we see that the main complaint against classic theism is that it pictures the God-world relation in terms of efficient causality. Indeed the theology of the so-called Reformed scholastics of the seventeenth century has been described as "causal analysis." Is it actually the case that the question "how do sinners get grace?" requires a causal explanation? This way of construing the God-world relation is today being challenged. Hence our problem: if God does not *intervene* in nature, then what are we to make of the effectual call?

Why the Effectual Call?

Why discuss the challenge to theism under the rubric of the effectual call? Why think that the effectual call affords us an interesting way into, and through, debates about the way to conceive the God-world relation?

First, because it represents a microcosm of the fundamental problem: the way God relates to the human world. As such, it affords an interesting test case by which to explore the respective merits of theism and panentheism.[7]

Second, because it focuses our attention on the particular problem of how divine grace brings about change in the world. In other words, it allows us to examine the Reformed picture of how God relates to the world at what many consider its most contentious, and most vulnerable, point: the relation of grace and human freedom.

And last, because it provides a vital clue to a better way forward for thinking of the God-world relation in general. For if we can understand how God can work in the human person without violating the laws of human nature, perhaps we will see better how God acts in the wider world without violating the laws of its nature. I believe that the notions of divine action in general and divine calling in particular may be mutually enriched when they are thought together.

Calling: The Nature of the Doctrine

Calvin. Calvin places his discussion of God's call in book three of the *Institutes,* "the way we receive the grace of Christ," immediately after his treatment of the doctrine of election. Indeed the call "confirms," "attests" and "makes manifest" God's election. Following Paul's order in Romans 8:29-30, Calvin insists that God first elects, then calls, then justifies: "And those whom he predestined he also called; and those whom he called he also justified" (Rom 8:30). Calvin makes the further point that "the man-

---

[6]Friedrich Schleiermacher, *The Christian Faith* (Edinburgh: T & T Clark, 1928), p. 178.
[7]Whereas D. M. Baillie saw the incarnation as the paradigm instance of how believers receive grace, I submit the effectual call as a better model. The effectual call is thus a microcosm of the paradox of grace.

ner of the call itself clearly indicates that it depends on grace alone" (3.24.2). What is this manner? For Calvin the call consists in the preaching of the Word *and* the illumination of the Spirit. This explains Calvin's later statement that there are two kinds of call: the general call associated with the "outward preaching" of the Word on the one hand, and on the other hand the special, inward call that is given to the elect only, which, thanks to the Spirit, "causes the preached Word to dwell in their hearts" (3.24.8). "Many are called, but few are chosen" (Mt 22:14).[8]

Seventeenth-century Reformed treatments. By the seventeenth century, the effectual call had gained privileged status in the *ordo salutis,* for the call effects one's union with Christ and is the beginning from which all other blessings flow. *Vocatio* "is the Act of God by which through the preaching of the Word and the power of the H. Spirit He brings man from the state of sin to the state of grace."[9] The effectual call takes place "over and above" the outward call by the inward power of the almighty Spirit. At the same time, the word by which the Spirit effects calling "is the same word by which God's call to grace is outwardly proclaimed."[10] The internal call is virtually indistinguishable from regeneration: "Calling is therefore the act of the H. Spirit, by which . . . He creates a new man. . . . The direct effect of such a calling is thus the regeneration of human nature."[11]

Twentieth-century Reformed treatments. Not much has changed in three centuries with regard to Reformed treatments of the effectual call. Three points in particular, however, deserve special mention.

1. *The effectual call is a divine act.* The call represents the temporal execution of God's eternal purpose.[12] Hence it is something that enters into human history.[13]

---

[8]Calvin adopts a biblical metaphor (calling) to guide his thinking about the way we receive grace. Yet he can also speak the language of the philosopher. Indeed he applies Aristotle's analysis of causation to the biblical teaching about salvation and argues that the efficient cause of our justification is the love of God the Father, the material cause the obedience of Christ, the instrumental cause the Spirit's illumination (faith) and the final cause the glory of God's generosity (*Institutes of the Christian Religion,* ed. John T. McNeil [Philadelphia: Westminster Press, 1960] 3.14.21).

[9]Heinrich Heppe, *Reformed Dogmatics* (Grand Rapids, Mich.: Baker, 1978), p. 510.

[10]Ibid., p. 518.

[11]Ibid.

[12]For a more extended treatment of biblical terms for calling, see Bruce Demarest, *The Cross and Salvation* (Wheaton, Ill.: Crossway, 1997), pp. 216-18. John Murray argues that most New Testament references to "call" and "calling" pertain not to the universal call of the gospel but to the effectual call that unites to Christ: "Calling is an act of God and God alone" (Murray, *Redemption Accomplished and Applied* [Grand Rapids, Mich.: Eerdmans, 1955], p. 89).

[13]To be precise, it is a sovereign act of God the Father, "who is the specific agent in the effectual call" (Murray, *Redemption Accomplished,* p. 89). Anthony A. Hoekema agrees, defining effectual calling as "that sovereign action of God through his Holy Spirit whereby he enables the hearer of the gospel call to respond to his summons with repentance, faith, and obedience" (*Saved by Grace* [Grand Rapids, Mich.: Eerdmans, 1989], p. 86).

2. *The effectual call is virtually indistinguishable from regeneration.*[14] The call is creative, or re-creative. "God's call to salvation is causative and effectual."[15] Only God can bring about the radical change needed to reorient and renew fallen persons dead in their sins to life in covenant fellowship with God. In his conversation with Nicodemus, Jesus states that no one can enter the kingdom of heaven unless he is "born of . . . the Spirit" (Jn 3:5).

3. *The effectual call is "grounded" in the evangelical call.* The internal call is an "act of divine power, mediated through the proclaimed Word."[16]

What follows in the later sections of this paper is an attempt to clarify the precise relation between the evangelical call—gospel preaching—and the effectual call.

A Causal Effect? Divine Sovereignty and Human Responsibility

Is the concept of causality an aid to Christian theology or a Trojan horse? Can we say of this concept what has been said of Aquinas's appropriation of Aristotle in general, that "the water of philosophy . . . has been changed into the wine of theology?"[17]

An objection: The effectual call is an impersonal cause. A cause is "an exertion of energy that produces a change."[18] The *kind* of causal effect wrought by the effectual call is nothing less than a "change of heart." If the human response is an effect of the call, does it not follow that God relates to human persons in an impersonal way? If the human being is both creature and person, dependent on God for his or her being yet able to make responsible decisions, why attribute the effectual call to God alone? Moreover, given the theistic understanding of divine transcendence, must not any divine action be an intervention from "outside" the spatiotemporal causal network?

Is it indeed fair to see the effectual call as a causal effect? *Is* God related to the world as a cause is related to its effect? Is saving grace an impersonal force? Aquinas applied Aristotle's conceptual apparatus, used in the *Physics* to examine natural processes, to the moral and psychological processes of human freedom. For Aquinas, an effect is simply a matter of the nature of its cause playing itself out: "No being can act beyond the limits of its specific nature, since the cause must always be of a higher

---

[14]So Augustus Strong, Herman Bavinck, Hoekema and most seventeenth-century Reformed theology. Louis Berkhof, however, prefers to say that effectual calling follows regeneration (*Systematic Theology* [Edinburgh: Banner of Truth Trust, 1958], p. 471) and Murray that effectual calling precedes regeneration (*Redemption,* pp. 115, 119-20).

[15]Demarest, *Cross and Salvation,* p. 217.

[16]Ibid., p. 221.

[17]Cited in Brian Davies, *The Thought of Thomas Aquinas* (Oxford: Clarendon, 1992), p. 11.

[18]Augustus Strong, *Systematic Theology* (Valley Forge, Penn.: Judson Press, 1907), p. 815.

potency than its effect."[19] Hence grace is "the work of God in human beings raising them above their human nature to the point where they become sharers in the divine nature."[20] Aquinas here invokes the Aristotelian doctrine of the Prime Mover. "It is in fact movement—change and instantiation—from which St. Thomas starts here in order to locate grace in a metaphysical pattern."[21] Grace is a supernatural cause, over and above human nature, that produces a supernatural effect.

Does grace *contravene* human freedom? No, grace enables human freedom to do what it otherwise could not. My actions are free if nothing *in the world* is acting on me so as to make me perform them. For Aquinas, to be free means "not to be under the influence of some other *creature,* it is to be independent of other *bits of the universe;* it is not and could not mean to be independent of God."[22] Aquinas, however, does speak of grace in terms of assistance as well.[23] In this case, grace acts on the soul "not in the manner of an efficient cause but in the manner of a formal cause; so whiteness makes something white and justice makes someone just."[24]

Reformed statements concerning saving grace continued to use the language and conceptuality of causality. They reclaimed the Augustinian theme of the irresistibility of saving grace in order to refute synergism, the suggestion that one's coming to saving faith is an event in which God and humans cooperate. Yet monergism suggests that God's will is both a necessary and a sufficient cause for moving the human will: "In itself calling is always effectual, although it is not so in those who are perishing, as the sun is effective by his light in itself, although it by no means illumines the blind."[25]

According to the Westminster Confession of Faith (10.2), effectual calling includes regeneration, a change in the "heart," in the very source of our motivation and dispositions. In Louis Berkhof's words: "There is a sense in which calling and regeneration are related as cause and effect."[26] Moreover, regeneration takes place "below consciousness"; Anthony Hoekema, for instance, locates one's change of heart in the subconscious.[27] This is problematic because it questions the necessity of the Word,

---

[19]Thomas Aquinas *Summa Theologiae* Ia2ae.112.1. Note: the newer scientific picture of the world as composed of hierarchical levels of ascending complexity contests this picture.
[20]Davies, *Thought of Thomas Aquinas,* p. 264.
[21]Cornelius Ernst, introduction to Aquinas *Summa Theologiae,* p. 30.
[22]So Herbert McCabe, cited in Davies, *Thought of Thomas Aquinas,* p. 177.
[23]Aquinas also views the grace of regeneration as an infusion of the theological virtues that transforms the source of one's actions—one's very being—and hence one's behavior.
[24]Aquinas *Summa Theologiae* Ia2ae.110.2.
[25]Heppe, *Reformed Dogmatics,* p. 517. The term *irresistible* is unfortunate, as even Reformed theologians have noted (e.g., A. A. Hodge, *Outlines of Theology* [Grand Rapids, Mich.: Zondervan, 1972], p. 452). Grace can be resisted, but ultimately God's call will be efficacious, that is, it accomplishes the purpose for which it has been sent (Is 55:11).
[26]Berkhof, *Systematic Theology,* p. 470.
[27]Hoekema, *Saved by Grace,* p. 104.

the external call, and casts doubt on whether grace works with human nature rather than against it.

If the human response were what made the call effectual, then the call would be no more than an invitation that lacked inherent efficacy. In order to ascribe salvation wholly to God, therefore, Reformed theologians insisted that faith is "not the 'cause' but the direct 'effect of regeneration'" and is "produced by effectual calling or regeneration."[28] Preaching is the instrumental cause of faith, but only when conjoined with the efficient causality of the Spirit. Indeed conversion involves two kinds of cause: moral and "physical."[29] By "physical" I think the dogmaticians meant to capture what, for instance, Acts 16:14 says about Lydia: "The Lord opened her heart to give heed to what was said by Paul." Bruce Demarest comments that "the opening of Lydia's heart by the power of God was the efficient cause of her coming to Christ."[30] Some of the language used in earlier dogmatics to describe the call does suggest a certain coercion, even violence—a *contravening* of human freedom. Martin Heidegger, for instance, says the Word not only opens but "attacks" hearts, irrevocably changing them in the process.

Other theologians reject the very idea of an effectual call as "sub-Christian." The authors of *The Openness of God,* for example, contend that the traditional picture of the God-world relation is deficient in several ways. "God's relation to the world . . . is one of mastery and control."[31] God remains "essentially unaffected" by cosmic events and human responses; hence there is no genuine dialogue between God and human beings.[32] It follows for these authors that a God who effectually calls cannot really love the world, for love is a matter, they say, of mutual, reciprocal and noncoercive relations. Theism's root metaphor of God as Prime Mover of the world and the will is ultimately incompatible with the biblical picture of a God who covenants with humanity. Emil Brunner's comment on Calvin's view of regeneration sums up the

---

[28]Heppe, *Reformed Dogmatics,* p. 527.
[29]Reformed theologians insist, against the Socinians, that conversion is more than a moral persuasion.
[30]Demarest, *Cross and Salvation,* p. 223.
[31]Richard Rice, "Biblical Support for a New Perspective," in *The Openness of God: A Biblical Challenge to the Traditional Understanding of God,* by Clark Pinnock et al. (Downers Grove, Ill.: InterVarsity Press, 1994), p. 11.
[32]Furthermore, the suggestion that grace is opposed to or separate from nature has been responsible for the loss of the sense of the divine in nature; supernaturalism, ironically, has led to secularization. So Jürgen Moltmann: "The more transcendent the conception of God became, the more immanent were the terms in which the world was interpreted. Through the monotheism of the absolute subject, God was increasingly stripped of his connection with the world, and the world was increasingly secularized" (*God in Creation* [San Francisco: Harper & Row, 1985], p. 1). I acknowledge that thinking of God in terms of causality may have done so, but I believe the emphasis on God as a communicative agent does not.

objection: *"The personal relation between God and Man became a causal relation: God the cause, faith the effect."*[33]

An alternative: A universal, potentially effectual call, or prevenient grace.
There is considerable dissent, even from evangelicals, regarding the notion of God's intervening grace and supernatural causality. How, then, do non-Reformed evangelicals and contemporary nonevangelical theologians understand the relation of God's grace to humanity?[34]

For so-called free-will theists who hold to the open view of God, God reacts and interacts with human beings in a way that respects creaturely autonomy.[35] For these theologians there is only one kind of grace, one kind of call and one kind of way in which God is related to the world. God exerts a constant attractive force on the soul—a kind of divine gravity. This universal call comes through a variety of media: the creation itself and conscience as well as proclamation about Christ. Grace is therefore "prevenient": that which "comes before" a person's ability to repent and believe.

On this view, God's call offers the possibility of salvation (salvation potential) to every human being.[36] Sufficient grace becomes efficient, then, only when the sinner cooperates with and improves it.[37] As one cooperates, the potential of salvation is actualized and becomes, for that person, a reality. In short, it is the human response—an exercise of free will—that makes the sufficient grace of God common to all efficient in the case of an individual. In Pinnock's words: "God's grace may be genuinely extended to people, but unless it meets the response of faith . . . it has no saving effect."[38] Of course to say that God's call is conditionally effectual is

---

[33]Emil Brunner, *Dogmatics,* vol. 1, *The Christian Doctrine of God,* trans. Olive Wyon (Philadelphia: Westminster Press, 1950), p. 315.

[34]I am aware that classical Arminians were also classical theists. It is possible, in other words, to be a theist and to hold to prevenient grace. However, I have not been able to do justice either to Aquinas or to classical Arminianism in the scope of this essay. My argument about the general trend in contemporary theology toward panentheism, however, is unaffected by this omission.

[35]See Pinnock, "From Augustine to Arminius: A Pilgrimage in Theology," in *Grace of God,* p. 27.

[36]The notion of universal prevenience signals the democratization of saving grace that is assumed by most non-Reformed theologians.

[37]"Grace may be judged to have of itself sufficient power to produce consent in the human will, but because this power is partial, it cannot go out in act without the cooperation of the free human will, and hence, that it may have its effect, it depends on free-will" (*Apol. Conf. Remonstr.,* cited in Hodge, *Outlines of Theology,* p. 455).

[38]Clark Pinnock, introduction to *Grace Unlimited,* ed. Clark Pinnock (Minneapolis: Bethany, 1975), p. 15. Note: the title signals the authors' belief that God's grace is unlimited in scope. It does *not,* however, appear to be unlimited in power. The only way to have grace unlimited both with regard to scope and with regard to power would be to opt for universalism, in which case all humans would be effectually called.

tantamount to saying that it is intrinsically *ineffectual*. To put the point more positively: God's grace is "non-manipulative and non-coercive."[39]

Was something like the above also the classical consensus of the ecumenical
councils and teachers of the first five centuries? To summarize Thomas Oden's reading of the ecumenical consensus: those who cooperate with the prevenient grace that
is always/already there will find that grace becomes effective. Grace cooperates with
human freedom, and God elects those who respond to the evangelical call.[40] "Grace
is working so as to elicit my energetic responsiveness, while my hard work is being
enabled by grace. . . . The ecumenical consensus has held closely together the freedom of the will and the efficacy of grace."[41]

If Oden is correct, we can squeeze even process theology into the ecumenical
consensus! Indeed process theologians have hardened the notion of the evangelical
call into a metaphysical principle. Here we return to the second of Tillich's two types,
to God as the ground of our being from whom, mysteriously, we have become alien-
ated.

Tillich, Schleiermacher and many other modern theologians agree that God is the
One to whom we are always/already related. Schleiermacher, for instance, thought of
God as that upon which humans feel themselves "absolutely dependent," though he
was wary of thinking of God's relation to the world in terms of supernatural causality. God is not a being alongside other beings but an energy that is constantly being
experienced to sustain us on our way, whether or not we are conscious of that fact:
"All divine grace is always prevenient."[42] For much modern theology, then, prevenient grace has become a matter of *ontology*.

Process theology represents what is perhaps the logical conclusion of the way
many non-Reformed theologians now construe the God-world relation. God is a creative participant in the course of world history, the leader of a cosmic community who
seeks to persuade beings to choose the good, namely, that which leads to greater self-
realization. Divine transcendence is understood as God's ability to relate to everything
that happens. God is not the ruler of the universe but its wooer, working not with
causal power but with the power of love and persuasion. The course of history thus

---

[39]Ibid. As Pinnock elsewhere puts it: "We believe that God not only acts but also reacts"
(*Grace of God*, p. x).

[40]Thomas Oden, *The Transforming Power of God's Grace* (Nashville: Abingdon, 1993). Oden
explains the difference between the many who are "called" and the few who are "chosen"
in terms of God's antecedent and consequent will: "The consequent will of God to save
offers the same divine grace as the antecedent. There is only one difference—God's
redemptive will is *consequent to, or follows upon* human responsiveness" (p. 89).

[41]Ibid., p. 97, 113. Oden writes: "That the synergy of grace and freedom became the consen-
sual teaching of the believing church is clear from the Third Ecumenical Council" (p. 98).

[42]Schleiermacher, *Christian Faith*, p. 485 n. 2.

takes the shape of a dialogue between God and the world. God and the world come together to converse, to "enjoy" one another.[43] The way God works with the world is by *convening* a cosmic conversation. Grace, we must say, is therefore *convenient*, achieving its effects not causally but, as it were, conversationally.[44]

Moltmann similarly takes issue with the traditional dualities.[45] If God is immanent to the world and if the world is immanent to God, then we "have to stop thinking in terms of causes at all."[46] We must no longer think in terms of one-way relationships such as "causing," "making" and "determining," but in terms of reciprocal relationships like "indwelling," "participating" and "accompanying."[47]

The Panentheistic Mind-Body Analogy and "Supervenient" Grace

Tillich, process theologians, Moltmann and others are all riding the panentheistic bandwagon. What is panentheism and why are so many people saying such nice things about it?

The theological concept of panentheism. Panentheism holds that the world is in some sense *in* God, though God exceeds the world. This is a novel solution to the problem of how to "make room" in the material world for God: by making room in God! To speak of God the Creator implies not a hard and fast distinction between God and the world but rather a recognition of "the presence of God *in* the world and the presence of the world *in* God."[48] Panentheism sits nicely with the notion of continuous creation—the idea that God has established processes in nature that bring about God's purposes over time. It is not as though God has to intervene in the world "from outside" the world, then, but rather that the "processes revealed by the sciences are themselves God acting as Creator."[49]

The philosophical concept of supervenience. Panentheism overturns not only

---

[43]See John Cobb Jr. and David Ray Griffin, *Process Theology: An Introductory Exposition* (Philadelphia: Westminster Press, 1976), p. 56.

[44]D. R. Griffin, "Relativism, Divine Causation and Biblical Theology," in *God's Activity in the World*, ed. O. C. Thomas (Chico, Calif.: Scholars Press, 1983), p. 132.

[45]For example, creation/redemption, natural/supernatural, and the dualistic principle on which they were constructed, that grace perfects nature. Moltmann proposes a new principle—grace prepares nature for eternal glory—and suggests that both Christ and the cosmos are moving toward a messianic goal in the power of the Spirit (*God in Creation*, p. 9).

[46]Ibid., p. 14.

[47]The God-world relation, in other words, reflects the trinitarian relationships of mutual interpenetration and perichoresis. Moltmann writes: "The Trinitarian concept of creation integrates the elements of truth in monotheism and pantheism. In the panentheistic view, God, having created the world, also dwells in it, and conversely the world which he has created exists in him" (ibid., p. 98). In the constructive portion of this article I attempt a trinitarian interpretation of the effectual call.

[48]Ibid., p. 13; cf. pp. 98, 103.

[49]Arthur Peacocke, *Theology for a Scientific Age*, 2nd ed. (Minneapolis: Fortress, 1993), p. 176.

the traditional God-world relation but also the way Reformed theology has conceived the relation of nature and grace. Can we reclaim and restate the doctrine of the effectual call, or ought we abandon it? I did not find much advance on seventeenth-century treatments of the doctrine in my literature review. However, in the rest of this paper I will explore two new things that might be said about the effectual call, in each case relying on a fairly recent philosophical concept: (1) the effectual call *supervenes* on the external call; (2) the effectual call is a *speech act* with a unique communicative force. The challenge, we may recall, is to avoid reducing God to a mere physical cause on the one hand, or to an ineffectual influence on the other.

"Interpretation," in the words of Paul Ricoeur, "is the work of concepts." As we have seen, classical theism pressed the concept of cause into theological service. Today there is an intriguing new concept that heralds a new chapter in the dialogue between theology and science. The term *supervene* appears in Samuel Johnson's *Dictionary* of 1775 with the meaning of "to come as an extraneous addition." The etymology of the term might lead one to suspect that supervenience—"coming from above"—is a fitting concept with which to explain God's supernatural agency. In fact the contemporary use of the term has nothing to do with coming from above.

Philosophers use the concept of supervenience to give naturalistic but nonreductionistic accounts of moral and mental phenomena.[50] The main idea involves a certain relation between two sets of properties that describe the same entity or event. R. M. Hare introduced supervenience into modern moral philosophy in 1952. Suppose that we say, "St. Francis was a good man." On this Hare writes: "It is logically impossible to say this and to maintain at the same time that there might have been another man placed exactly in the same circumstances as St. Francis, and who behaved in exactly the same way, but who differed from St. Francis in this respect only, that he was not a good man."[51] Supervenience is the relation between the "good," on the one hand, and certain patterns of behavior and character traits, on the other. Hare's point is that there is a necessary correlation between moral properties and nonmoral properties. This is the core idea of supervenience: "No differences in A properties without differences in B properties," where *A* stands for moral properties like goodness and *B* stands for nonmoral properties (e.g., actions like feeding animals or giving away money). St. Francis's goodness *depends on* his feeding animals and his poverty, but it cannot be *reduced* to these things. Being poor, after all, is not the same as being good.

Supervenience really comes into its own, however, in the philosophy of mind.

---

[50]See John Divers, "Recent Work: Supervenience," in *Philosophical Books* 39 (1998): 89-91; E. E. Savellos and U. D. Yançin, eds., *Supervenience: New Essays* (Cambridge: Cambridge University Press, 1995).

[51]R. M. Hare, *The Language of Morals* (Oxford: Clarendon, 1952).

Mental properties such as consciousness supervene on physical properties such as brain states. Thoughts *depend* on neural firings and other subvenient physical events, but they are not *identical* to these physical events, nor can they be explained in terms of brain states alone. Supervenient properties, that is, cannot be explained in terms of lower-level, subvenient properties.[52] It is this apparent *irreducibility* of the mental to the physical that distinguishes the supervenience relation from that, say, of causality. The relation between physical and mental events is not causal precisely because, as Aquinas rightly noted, an effect (consciousness) cannot be greater than its cause (neural firing). Supervenience is more like a part-whole relation, where the whole is greater than the sum of its parts.[53]

Jaegwon Kim, an analytic philosopher who has written on the concept more than anyone else, suggests that supervenience resembles the doctrine of emergence, popular among early twentieth-century supporters of evolution: "When basic physio-chemical processes achieve a certain level of complexity of an appropriate kind, genuinely novel characteristics, such as mentality, appear as 'emergent' qualities."[54]

The cell, for instance, is an emergent phenomenon, a distinct entity in the world with its own science (biochemistry), even though it is composed out of smaller atomic units. Yet one cannot explain the behavior of a cell in terms of the laws of physics. Similarly water, at the microphysical level, is composed of the basic particles and atoms of which matter is composed. At the molecular level of H_2O, however, we discover properties such as "wetness" and "power to dissolve sugar." At still higher levels, and under the appropriate conditions, we discover that water has the property of admitting one into the Christian church. Or to take an example from biblical scholarship (supervenience recognizes no disciplinary bounds!): the Christian canon emerges from (or supervenes on) the particular texts that make up the Old and New Testaments. And though canonical meaning depends on these texts, it cannot be reduced to or explained in terms of individual books. On the contrary, canonical criticism is a science of its own, with its own set of exegetical and explanatory tools.

---

[52]Jaegwon Kim, an analytic philosopher and one of the leading proponents of the concept, puts it this way: "Whether something exists, or what properties it has, is *dependent on,* or *determined by,* what other things exist and what kinds of things they are" ("Concepts of Supervenience," in *Supervenience and Mind* [Cambridge: Cambridge University Press, 1993)], p. 53).

[53]Note that supervenience is a topic-neutral concept that has applications in fields as diverse as morals and physics. An aesthetic example: the beauty of music supervenes on a sequence of sounds, yet we would be unwilling to identify or reduce aesthetics (and the notion of beauty) to physics and the level of sound waves.

[54]Kim, "Supervenience as a Philosophical Concept," in *Supervenience and Mind,* p. 134; Jaegwon Kim, "Downward Causation in Emergentism and Nonreductive Physicalism," in *Emergence or Reduction?* ed. Ansgar Berckermann, Hans Flohr and Jaegwon Kim (Berlin: De Gruyter, 1992).

God's call to the world and the causal joint: The mind-body analogy. How,
though, can the concept of supervenience help theologians conceive the God-world
relation? The "panentheistic analogy" asks us to think of God as a person like us, to
see a parallel between our action in our bodies and God's action in the world. In particular it asks us to think of the world as God's body and of God as the mind or soul
of the world.[55] As mental activity supervenes on physical processes, so divine action
supervenes on the processes of nature.

Interestingly, Heinrich Heppe compares the calling of the elect to the union of
soul and body.[56] There is thus orthodox precedent (of sorts) for my appeal to the
mind-body analogy. And there is of course *biblical* precedent in the picture of the
church as the "body" of Christ, conjoined to the "spirit" of Christ (1 Cor 12:13). And
as we have seen, the effectual call itself involves two sets of properties, the "external"
and the "internal": "There is strictly one calling, but its cause and medium is twofold:
instrumental, man preaching the word outwardly; principal, the H. Spirit writing it
inwardly in the heart."[57] Is it correct to construe *this* relation in terms of supervenience? Is the mind-body analogy the best way to conceive divine transcendence and
immanence?

The challenge is to conceive of what has been called the "causal joint" between
mind and body, between divine action (calling) and human action (response). Does
supervenience resolve or merely illustrate the problem? In particular, can one affirm
the supervenience of the mental on the physical *and* speak of the mind as initiating
mental and physical effects? In short, can one preserve the efficacy of the supervenient domain (the mind, God, the internal call) as opposed to that of the subvenient
(the body, world, the external call)? In the contemporary philosophical discussion,
the notion of a mental cause is a hotly disputed issue.

A brief typology of positions. The traditional position on the mind-body relation—Cartesian dualism—bears an uncanny resemblance to classical theism's view of
the God-world relation. What we have in both cases is a picture of two separate
realms composed of two kinds of reality that nevertheless interact. Both cases, that is,
present us with the problem of the so-called causal joint. Just what goes on in the

---

[55]According to Philip Clayton, "It now seems that this analogy represents one significant argument in favour of panentheism" (*God and Contemporary Science* [Edinburgh: Edinburgh
University Press, 1997], p. 242).

[56]Heppe, *Reformed Dogmatics,* p. 511. "By regeneration moreover new life is put into them
[the elect], as the result of gracious union with God and His Spirit. What soul is to the body,
God is to the soul" (p. 519).

[57]Ibid., p. 518. Demarest says that the single call of God to salvation "may be considered from
two perspectives": the external, evangelical call and the internal, effectual call (Demarest,
Cross and Salvation, p. 218). I shall later relate this to the position of "anomalous monism"
in the mind-body discussion.

pineal gland, the place where Descartes believed that mind and body meet? How is it that I form a decision to lift my finger and bring about the lifting of my finger? A similar problem holds for the relation of God and the world. Is there a theological equivalent to the pineal gland—the locus where the divine and human come into contact—perhaps the preaching of the Word or the administering of the sacraments (or alternately the incarnation)?

The point is that according to classical theism there is a fundamental dualism between Creator and creation, grace and nature. The causal joint must therefore span an *ontological* gap. To the extent that this is so, the effectual call resembles something of an intervention, where one kind of reality enters into another kind of reality to produce an effect that would otherwise not have come about. Saving grace, on this view, is necessarily *intervenient*.[58]

At the other extreme of the mind-body debate are the epiphenomenalists, who argue that mental causation is only apparent. The real causal work, they maintain, is carried out by material brain processes. Instead of supervenience relations, this position posits systematic identities between the mental and the physical. The net result is an ontological reductionism that recognizes the reality of the physical (or rather the microphysical) only.[59]

Modern science has been a major factor in how theologians and others have revised their conception of the God-world relation. How can we conceive of the God of the gaps when the gaps are few and far between? How can we prevent the notion of the "mighty acts" of God from sounding quaint or becoming outmoded? The theological counterpart of mind-body epiphenomenalism is a nonrealist position like Don Cupitt's. God just *is* what happens between loving people. God-talk, that is, can be reduced to talk about human beings. It is therefore inappropriate to speak of divine causality, as it would be inappropriate to await divine help. The effectual call would

---

[58]Under Cartesian dualism there can be no complete physical theory of physical phenomena, because the physical domain is open to influence from the mental. "We can say then that *Cartesian interactionism violates the causal closure of the physical domain*" (Kim, *Supervenience and Mind,* p. 336). Precisely the same complaint is directed against the idea of divine causality. Moltmann warns that when definitions are derived from separation rather than relation, the result is the domination of one term *(body)* by the other *(soul)*. Descartes describes the mind-body relation "as a one-sided relationship of domination and ownership" (Moltmann, *God in Creation,* p. 251). The tendency "to spiritualize the human subject and to instrumentalize the human body" parallels the tendency to see God as over the world, controlling it through causal interventions. Even Barth saw the ordered unity of the soul-body relation in terms of superordination and subordination (cf. supervenience and subvenience). Peacocke raises another problem with this picture: its view of nature as a closed mechanical system controlled by "laws of nature" is outdated. For Peacocke's criticisms of the concept of divine intervention, see his *Theology for a Scientific Age,* pp. 141-43.
[59]Reductivists argue that the way we normally speak of the mental (in terms of thoughts, decisions and intentions) will eventually be left behind, replaced by a successful brain science.

on this view be explained in terms of conscience or, more radically, in terms of the sociobiological urge, say, to belong. Whereas for Ludwig Feuerbach the secret of religion was atheism, for the epiphenomalist the secret of mind is physicalism.[60]

We come now to the panentheistic analogy, poised somewhere between the theistic and atheistic options we have just considered. On this third view it is not enough simply to affirm the causal joint—*that* God acts in the world, *that* the mind is distinct from the body. For without some plausible account of *how* God-mind might interact with the causal nexus of physical events, we cannot with integrity assert that there is such interaction.[61]

Panentheism is a holistic worldview in the sense "that it recognizes that whole systems and their parts mutually condition one another."[62] Each science analyzes not a different kind but a different *level* of reality, each with its own irreducible integrity. Theology is the science that deals with reality at its most all-encompassing level.[63] In the words of Nancey Murphy, theology is the supervenient discipline par excellence.[64]

With regard to the mind-body analogy, most of those who say that the mental supervenes on the physical are nonreductive physicalists. That is, they are naturalists who believe that nature is a hierarchy of complex systems whose higher levels are irreducible to lower ones.[65] Though nonreductive physicalists believe that the world is fundamentally physical (made up of physical entities and governed by physical laws), they reject reductive materialism for having an overly atomistic and mechanical view of these processes: "The ontological imagination was stultified at the start by [the picture] of microscopic billiard balls."[66]

---

[60]Kim notes that for Jonathan Edwards the situation is precisely reversed: God's creative activity is the real cause of things, and the causal relations obtaining between material bodies are cases of epiphenomenal causation. Fire does not cause smoke; rather, God causes the fire and then God causes the smoke (Kim, "Epiphenomenal and Supervenient Causation," in *Supervenience and Mind,* p. 92).

[61]Cf. Peacocke: "The mere assertion of the analogy to human action without any further explication of it, and so also analogically of divine action, leaves us still skeptical of the mere possibility of the latter" (*Theology for a Scientific Age,* p. 150).

[62]Nancey Murphy, *Beyond Liberalism and Fundamentalism: How Modern and Postmodern Philosophy Set the Theological Agenda* (Valley Forge, Penn.: Trinity Press International, 1996), p. 44.

[63]As Murphy explains, this is not necessarily to say that theology is merely the science of the whole cosmos but rather "that the behavior of the created universe cannot be explained apart from its relation to an additional kind of reality, namely, God" (ibid., p. 149).

[64]Murphy: "As a supervenient discipline, theology can answer questions that arise within science but cannot be answered by science alone" (ibid., p. 156).

[65]For a brief history of nonreductive physicalism, see Nancey Murphy, *Anglo-American Postmodernity: Philosophical Perspectives on Science, Religion and Ethics* (Boulder, Colo.: Westview, 1997), pp. 94-96.

[66]R. W. Sellers, quoted in ibid., p. 195. Interestingly, classical theism could perhaps be accused of something similar, at least with regard to its view of the world.

Nonreductive physicalism recognizes that something genuinely new is going on at the level of the mind that cannot be explained simply in terms of brain activity.[67] This is not quite proof for the existence of the soul. On the contrary, nonreductive physicalists would argue that there need be no spiritual "thing" (no *hypostasis*) that "has" mental properties. Nevertheless, some argue for the reality of the mental on the grounds that this yields greater explanatory power of the data than rival theories.[68]

Donald Davidson, in his much-discussed paper "Mental Events," claims that while mental events are identical to physical events, mental properties are dependent on the concepts we employ in describing those events. This is a subtle, but important, point: the nonreductive physicalist does not postulate a second kind of reality (the soul) as the subject of mental properties "but rather attributes mental and spiritual properties to the entire person, understood as a complex physical and social organism."[69] Neither the mental nor the spiritual is illusory; neither philosophizing nor praying can be reduced to brain matter in motion! Davidson further claims that there are no lawlike correlations between these mental concepts (e.g., intention, reason) and the concepts we use to describe physical events (e.g., mass, force). Science is unable to formulate laws that could explain the mental in terms of the physical. He is thus unwilling to reduce the mental to the physical, though at the same time, on the level of ontology, he rejects dualism. He chooses to call his hybrid position "anomalous monism."

The main objection to Davidson's argument is that it seems to make the mental causally inert. For it is one thing to describe an event with mental concepts, quite another to say that it is the mental aspect that is causally efficacious.[70]

---

[67]"For both the nonreductive physicalist and the emergentist, physical bases are by *themselves* sufficient for the appearance of the higher-level properties" (Kim, "The Nonreductivist's Trouble with Mental Causation," in *Supervenience and Mind*, p. 347).

[68]"Against the opponents of mental causation, I argue that *as long as* the explanatory power of idea-idea causation continues to be much greater than the neurophysiological account, we should straightforwardly assert its superiority and indispensability" (Clayton, *God and Contemporary Science*, p. 255).

[69]Murphy, *Beyond Liberalism*, p. 150.

[70]Fred Dretske gives an example of a soprano who sings meaningful words when she hits the glass-shattering high C. The meaning is irrelevant to the properties of the sound waves that cause the glass to shatter: "The fear concerning mental causation is that all content-properties [e.g., desires, beliefs] may be like those of the soprano's high C" (L. R. Baker, "Metaphysics and Mental Causation," in *Mental Causation*, ed. John Heil and Alfred R. Mele [Oxford: Clarendon, 1993], p. 76). The discussion in the journals is too technical to pursue much further here, other than to note a few salient points: Robert Audi helpfully proposes that we see mental causes as *sustaining causes* which, though they may not trigger events, dispose agents to act in certain ways. This puts an interesting new spin on being in a "state of grace."

There is an interesting parallel between anomalous monism and God's call: "Reformed theologians often speak of the gospel call and the effectual call as two aspects or sides of one calling."[71] The effectual call is dependent on the evangelical call but cannot be reduced to it. Does this mean that the effectual call *supervenes* on the external call, that God's Word supervenes on the human word? One difficulty with this suggestion is the covariation thesis: no A-differences without B-differences. If the required physical bases are present, the mental events that supervene on them must also be present. With regard to God's call, however, there is an obvious objection: Reformed theologians deny that the preached word works *ex opere operato*. To stipulate that God must always be salvifically at work wherever there is preaching is effectively to deny the freedom of God. We would then have to rewrite dominical wisdom: "many are called and *just that many* are chosen."[72]

Jaegwon Kim, whom I have already acknowledged as one of the leading specialists on the concept of supervenience, himself has serious doubts about the applicability of the concept to the notion of mental causation. Essentially, he believes that all instances of "macrocausation" are epiphenomenal, ultimately explicable in terms of microcausal, that is microphysical, relations.[73] Kim sees the claim that psychological properties are irreducible to their subvenient properties as the remnants of a dualist ideology. His verdict is: "Nonreductive physicalism, like Cartesianism, founders on the rock of mental causation."[74]

How can a nonphysical event (e.g., a thought, a call) causally influence the course of physical processes? Earlier generations assumed that causation was always bottom-up, that is, that the basic forces of nature were described by the Newtonian laws of physics. On this view, God had to be thought of as a mover, as a quasi-mechanical force that enters into the causal nexus from outside and initiates

---

[71]Hoekema, *Saved by Grace*, p. 88. Herman Bavinck writes: "It is one and the same word which God allows to be proclaimed through the external call and which he writes on the hearts of the hearers through the Holy Spirit in the internal call" (quoted in Hoekema, *Saved by Grace*, p. 89). The human person is now commonly seen as a psychosomatic unity with dual aspects.

[72]To escape Kim's reductionistic conclusions, some point out that mental properties are "multiply realizable." That is, the same mental property may be realized by or supervene on different physical events. Kim rebuts this move by arguing that in the absence of some physical realization, the mental property would not be there. He also defends the principle of "explanatory exclusion," which states that there can be no more than one complete and independent explanation for any single explanandum" (*Supervenience and Mind*, p. xiii).

[73]The trouble is that it is difficult to capture the dependence relation in a way that escapes the threat of reductionism. Since every property of every event supervenes on microphysical events and properties, it is hard to see how any macrophysical properties are causally relevant to anything.

[74]Kim, *Supervenience and Mind*, p. 339.

change.[75] Supervenience, at least in Kim's hands, continues to assume bottom-up causation. In Kim's universe, macro-causation reduces to micro-causation. However, what many of us want to say—what perhaps we have to say unless we wish to go mad—is that consciousness makes a real difference in the world. Indeed a number of thinkers believe that it is tantamount to intellectual suicide to deny the efficacy of macro-causation.[76] What is needed is a notion of nonreducible supervenient causation.[77]

If to be real is to have causal powers, what is the true causal story? What really moves the natural world, the human will? Human beings live on the level of macro-causation. True, many properties in chemistry and other sciences supervene on more basic properties. Yet who would deny that temperature, magnetism and the like have their own explanatory, even causal, power?[78] Why then should the same not go for mental and spiritual properties? Could we not say that "causes are the sorts of things that are cited in explanations of events"?[79] By and large we explain our own actions in terms of motives, desires and reasons rather than in terms of microphysics and brain chemistry. So does the biblical narrative, even when it invokes divine agency. As we have seen, however, others invoke the concept of supervenience to subvert the reality of macro-causation: "What midsized slow philosophers see is not always a key to the mysteries of ontology."[80] The same suspicion doubtless applies to midsized readers of the Bible.

Arthur Peacocke, a panentheist, suggests that the way God influences the world is analogous to the way the mind influences the body, which in turn is analogous to the way a whole influences its parts.[81] Peacocke contends that some systems have causal power over their component parts. Think, for instance, of the way an ecosys-

---

[75]Murphy herself believes that we should emphasize God's involvement at the quantum level, where we can conceive of divine action in terms that need not conflict with science. See her "Divine Action in the Natural Order: Buridan's Ass and Schrödinger's Cat," in *Chaos and Complexity: Scientific Perspectives on Divine Action,* ed. R. J. Russell and Arthur Peacocke (Vatican City: Vatican Observatory and Centre for Theology and the Natural Sciences, 1995), pp. 325-57. However, Clayton objects that such a conception of divine action is really a conception *from the very bottom-up,* which, while possible, is not very plausible: there neither is nor could be empirical evidence for it.

[76]Cf. L. R. Baker: "The conclusion that macro-properties lack causal efficacy is cognitively devastating" ("Metaphysics and Mental Causation," p. 90).

[77]See Berent Enç, "Nonreducible Supervenient Causation," in *Supervenience: New Essays,* ed. E. E. Savellos and U. D. Yançin (Cambridge: Cambridge University Press, 1995), pp. 169-86.

[78]According to Tyler Burge, "Outside our philosophical studies, we all know that epiphenomenalism is not true" ("Mind-Body Causation and Explanation," in *Mental Causation,* ed. John Heil and A. R. Mele [Oxford: Clarendon, 1993], p. 118).

[79]Baker, "Metaphysics and Mental Causation," p. 93.

[80]Cited in Enç, "Nonreducible Supervenient Causation," p. 175.

[81]Peacocke, *Theology for a Scientific Age,* p. 161.

tem influences an organism: an animal's environment, through natural selection, can over time affect a species' DNA. *Downward* causation (also called "top-down," "whole-part" or "supervenient" causation) opens the possibility of talking about divine action in noninterventionist terms, for on Peacocke's view, divine action is not like that of an object operating on the level of other objects, but rather at the level of the whole.

Peacocke helps us see why panentheism and supervenience are such compatible concepts. Panentheism says that the world is in God but God is greater than the world; supervenient or downward causation suggests that God acts on the world, but only at the level of the whole, as its overarching context: "If God interacts with the 'world' at this supervenient level of totality, then he could be causatively effective in a 'top-down' manner without abrogating the laws and regularities . . . that operate at the myriad sub-levels of existence."[82] In short, God's activity supervenes on the processes of nature themselves.

Brad Kallenberg suggests that God's action in the human world is similarly located at the level of the whole, the community of which individuals are parts.[83] And as with other levels of reality, "real properties emerge at this level of [social] complexity which cannot be accounted for by attention to phenomena concerning individual human beings in isolation."[84] Kallenberg's point is that the "mind of Christ" supervenes on the "body of Christ": "Those individuals who step outside the . . . 'church' miss those unique causal influences orchestrated by God within the Christian community."[85] Outside the church, one will not benefit from God's "mental causation."

What's wrong with downward causation? It is difficult to see how the mind could be dependent on the physical and yet at the same time exercise independent causal powers that affect the physical. Kim is reluctant to allow two distinct sufficient causes for the same event. To believe that the mind independently causes things is to espouse something like Austin Farrer's notion of double agency. For Kim's part, he believes that all higher-level processes are derivative from and grounded in funda-

---

[82]Ibid., p. 159. If the world is God's body, then the succession of the states of the world-as-a-whole is also a succession in the thought of God. On the other hand, Murphy locates the causal joint between God and the world at the level of quantum physics. At the quantum level, nature itself is indeterminate. In light of the butterfly effect, it is possible to think of God intervening at the microphysical level in order to bring about macrophysical changes (e.g., the parting of the Red Sea due to a kind of El Niño effect, or conversion due to the stimulation of neurons in the brain).

[83]Note that the community is one of the higher levels of reality which, like the others, has its own science and set of concepts (sociology, social theory, ideology, etc.).

[84]Brad J. Kallenberg, "Unstuck from Yale: Theological Method After Lindbeck," *Scottish Journal of Theology* 50 (1997): 210.

[85]Ibid., p. 214.

mental physical processes. To say otherwise is to introduce another kind of causality into the natural order and thus to breach the causal closure of the physical domain. If one is willing to embrace "higher powers" (e.g., psychic energies, souls, God), asks Kim, then why call yourselves a nonreductive physicalist? Why, for that matter, posit supervenience?

Does supervenience save the reality of mental causation? If not, it is difficult to see how the panentheist's mind-body analogy could illumine the nature of the God-world relation. We may need a concluding unscientific postscript on supervenience. Happily, something like this has recently been provided by Phillip Clayton. Clayton believes that theology indeed has a stake in arguing for the irreducibility of consciousness, but in the final analysis the theologian must assert that God's "mind" *transcends* the world and its processes. When it comes to the God-world relation, theological realists cannot be physicalists, even of the nonreductive variety.[86]

Must we conclude that theology contradicts science? Not necessarily, for Clayton rightly points out that the results of science *underdetermine* one's choice of metaphysical interpretations.[87] Science provides the exegetical data concerning the Book of Nature, we might say, but metaphysics (and theology!) supplies the hermeneutics. What Rudolf Bultmann said of biblical scholars applies equally to scientists: exegesis without presuppositions is impossible. Physicalism is a metaphysical, not a scientific, thesis. The question of the God-world relationship is similarly underdetermined by science.[88]

What of supervenience? Is it a scientific or a metaphysical concept? Its critics say that supervenience, failing a specific account of the dependence relation that underlies it, is "simply an empty sound expressing a faith that two levels of properties are somehow related."[89] While there does seem a sort of asymmetric relation between mind and body, why should the physical be thought of as more ontologically basic? Why should we accept the causal closure of the physical world?

Prevenient and Supervenient Grace: From Pinnock to Peacocke

Peacocke admits that his view allows for divine action only "on the world as a whole." This gets us no further than a "general call." Even Pinnock's emphasis on

---

[86]If this means that God's causality cannot be explained in terms of this-worldly processes, then how does one ultimately avoid falling into some kind of dualism? Clayton's answer to this query is not entirely clear.

[87]Clayton, *God and Contemporary Science*, p. 259.

[88]Note that for Clayton the theological supplementation of science "does bring panentheism more into the spirit of biblical theism" (ibid., p. 260). God is not simply an emergent set of divine properties but a being in his own right.

[89]Quoted in introduction to *Supervenience: New Essays*, p. 9.

prevenient grace gets us no further. According to the free-will theist, God is working behind the scenes with every individual entity to draw each one to himself; according to the panentheist, God is exercising systematic influence on the world as a whole. Both prevenient and supervenient grace, it would appear, have universal application, prompting us to speak of *continuous salvation*. What, then, is the role of the Spirit in applying salvation?

On the traditional view, the Spirit is the One who imparts grace to believers. The infusion of grace resembles a transfer of energy. The Spirit, then, is indeed like a physical force. Better, God, as love, acts on individuals like a force field, empowering humans freely to respond.

Peacocke prefers to see top-down causation in terms of a transfer of information (another kind of "glorious exchange") rather than in terms of energy.[90] God interacts with the world by inputting information—not by special revelation (too interventionist) but by "programming" natural processes, through their built-in propensities, progressively to realize his intentions.[91] God communicates his intentions through "patterns of meaning" within the evolutionary history of the natural world. Hence we are to see God's intentions manifested in, say, the emergence of human beings from lower forms of life. On this view the Spirit is more like the operating system, or software, of creation. In sum, God communicates to humanity through the fabric of the natural world.[92]

Peacocke's account of the incarnation, however, leads one to wonder whether supervenience ultimately fails to get us beyond a qualified deism. In the final analysis God acts only on "the world-as-a-whole."[93] The incarnation, for Peacocke, is not a matter of God's entering a closed nexus from the outside as a stranger but of certain divine properties *emerging* in the man Jesus from *within* the natural processes of cre-

---

[90]Peacocke attributes John Westerdale Bowker's *The Sense of God* (Oxford: Clarendon, 1973) with being the first work to see divine action in terms of "information input."

[91]Indeed the distinction between "natural" and "revealed" theology is too dualistic for Peacocke. He would prefer, I think, to say that revelation supervenes on universal history.

[92]Peacocke admits that it is difficult to say how God inputs information into the world-as-a-whole without an input of matter/energy: "This seems to me to be the ultimate level of the 'causal joint' conundrum" (*Theology for a Scientific Age*, p. 164). For a more explicitly trinitarian version of panentheism, see Moltmann's *God in Creation*. Many themes in Moltmann are relevant to the present essay, though beyond its scope. Moltmann views the world as a dynamic relation of open systems in which higher levels have higher capacities for communication (p. 204). In his view, "spirit" names the forms of organization and modes of communication in open systems (p. 263). Moltmann reconceives the body-soul relation in terms of his theology of trinitarian perichoresis (p. 259). Life is exchange: communication and communion. Life, or spirit, is what happens *between* individuals (p. 266). Though we cannot examine it here, it may be that for Moltmann the Holy Spirit supervenes on the Creator Spirit.

[93]Peacocke, *Theology for a Scientific Age*, p. 163.

ation.[94] Jesus, says Peacocke, was a totally God-informed man, the "ultimate emergent."[95] The incarnation therefore is not so much a miracle as it is a particularly pure case of how the information God inputs into creation results, through an evolutionary process, in the embodiment of God's intentions:

> The "Incarnation" in Jesus the Christ may, then, properly be said to be the consummation of the creative and creating evolutionary process. It would follow that, if Jesus the Christ is the self-expression of God's meaning, then the evoking in the world of *this* kind of person, with *these* values, just is the purpose of God in creation.[96]

Peacocke's mention of God's evoking brings us back to the notion of the effectual call: for him, God's call operates on the world as a whole to produce people like Jesus. The question is whether such a view is adequate for Christian faith. Is it possible to have a personal relation with One whose presence and activity is always only prevenient or supervenient?

Divine Communicative Action and "Advenient" Grace

Nicholas Wolterstorff, in his *Divine Discourse,* offers a stimulating series of philosophical reflections on the claim that "God speaks."[97] I propose to offer some theological reflections on this claim as well. The closing stage of this paper is hardly the place to propose a new picture of the God-world relationship, so what follows will necessarily be somewhat sketchy. In brief, I propose thinking of the God-world relation in terms of communicative rather than causal agency. The call exerts not brute but communicative force.

The challenge, we may recall, is to respond to the criticisms that theism is unbiblical, blasphemous and unscientific. A secondary challenge is to account for the peculiar efficacy of God's call. The concept of the speech act enables us, I believe, to unpack the nature of the effectual call, and of God's overall relation to the world, in terms of both energy and information. Moreover, speech act theory sheds new light on certain themes from our earlier discussion: (1) how the effectual call can be regenerative, (2) how the effectual call can be internal and external, and (3) how the illumination of the Spirit relates to the illumination of the Word.

---

[94]Peacocke understands incarnation "as exemplifying that emergence-from-continuity which characterises the whole process of God's creating" ("The Incarnation of the Informing Self-Expressive Word of God," in *Religion and Science: History, Method, Dialogue,* ed. W. M. Richardson and W. J. Wildman [New York: Routledge, 1996], p. 331). Note the similarity with Maurice Wiles's notion that creation is God's single "master act," with persons like Jesus Christ presumably being the culmination of the creative process.

[95]So Clayton, *God and Contemporary Science,* p. 225; cf. Peacocke, "Incarnation," p. 332.

[96]Peacocke, *Theology for a Scientific Age,* p. 334.

[97]Nicholas Wolterstorff, *Divine Discourse* (Cambridge: Cambridge University Press, 1995).

Summoning: A sovereign speech act. Speech acts belong to the twentieth-century philosophy of language. The main point is that in speaking we also *do* certain things. Words do not simply label; sentences do not merely state. Rather, in using language we do any number of things: question, command, warn, request, curse, bless and so forth. A speech act has two aspects: propositional content and illocutionary force, the "matter" and "energy" of communicative action.[98] The key notion is that of illocution, which has to do not simply with locuting or uttering words but with what we do *in* uttering words. We may distinguish, with Jürgen Habermas, speech acts from strategic acts; whereas the former aim to communicate, the latter aim only to manipulate. It is one thing to bring about a result in the world, quite another to bring about understanding. My claim is that God's effectual call is not a causal but a communicative act.

For Arminians, the New Testament language of calling is a matter of "naming" those who have believed. On the other hand John Murray, commenting on Romans 8:30, equates the effectual call with a summons: "Salvation in actual possession takes its start from an efficacious summons on the part of God and this summons, since it is God's summons, carries in its bosom all of the operative efficacy by which it is made effective."[99]

"Summoning" is a much stronger directive than "inviting." It is significant that Jesus did not invite the disciples to tea but rather said, "Follow me." Augustine found the idea of an effectual call in other biblical examples. Jesus commands, "Lazarus, come out" (Jn 11:43), a speech act that literally wakes the dead. For Augustine, something similar happens each time God summons a person to new life. Not everyone can issue a felicitous summons, however; certain truth conditions are assumed—for instance, that I have the authority to summon you. Only God, of course, has the right to say certain things, such as "I declare you righteous."[100]

The effectual call and the "communicative joint." Is the grace that changes one's heart a matter of energy or information? I believe it is both, and speech act theory lets us see how. God's call is effectual precisely in bringing about a certain kind of understanding in and through the Word. The Word that summons has both propositional content (matter) and illocutionary force (energy).

We have seen that some who champion the notion of supervenience assign an independent causality (and hence reality) to mental properties. Their main argument, again, is "that mental causation makes the best sense of the phenomena of human

---

[98] For a complete analysis, see John Searle, *Speech Acts: An Essay in the Philosophy of Language* (Cambridge: Cambridge University Press, 1969).

[99] Murray, *Redemption Accomplished and Applied*, p. 86.

[100] On my view, justification (the next doctrine in the *ordo salutis*) is very much a divine speech act too.

experience."[101] But what does mental causation really mean? How do ideas "cause" other ideas? Does the idea "2 + 2," say, cause the idea of "4"? Does Jesus' summoning his disciples *cause* them to follow?

Classical theism sees God as a mover. Causation is a transitive relation: x pushes, pulls, heats, freezes, saves y. Communication is a transitive relation too *(x addresses y)*, but is it causal? I have suggested that God is a communicative agent. While I agree with Kallenberg that language is an "emergent property," I think we can say more than he does about how God supervenes at the social level. Humans are indeed "ontologically constituted" by language, and this insight puts a wholly different spin on the question of how the effectual call works a change in the human heart. Moving beyond Kallenberg, why could we not see God as a member of the Christian linguistic community? After all, one of the most common biblical depictions of God is as a speaker. "We speak because he first spoke to us."

The doctrine of the effectual call prompts us to change pictures and think not of a causal but of a *communicative* joint and to identify the point at which communication takes place as *interpretation*. The effectual call thus provides the vital clue as to how God interacts with the human world. In my opinion, the Reformers were right to stress the connection between God's Word and God's work of grace.

Address and "advenient grace." If we are to make sense of the communicative joint, however, we must explain what happens when the Word of God enters the world. Speech act philosophy helpfully provides a set of concepts with which to think about *word* events. For it is indeed the Word that comes to the world and the Spirit that comes to the Word that informs and empowers—in a word, that is effectual. Perhaps the most adequate way to view the God-world relation is in terms of *advent*.

It is clear that when the Word of God comes, it brings about change. Acts 16:14 shows Lydia's regeneration taking place through Paul's gospel preaching. New human possibilities do indeed emerge, therefore, but not out of purely natural processes. Many emerge out of history, in particular out of communicative action, as Eberhard Jüngel recognizes: "The word is to be seen as the actual core of historical reality because it interrupts the natural context of existence in such a way that something like historical reality becomes possible."[102] The world, then, is not a hermetically closed system but one that is hermeneutically open.[103] And the way this system is put into motion is through God's communicative, and self-communicative, action.[104]

---

[101] Clayton, *God and Contemporary Science,* p. 256.

[102] Eberhard Jüngel, *God as the Mystery of the World* (Edinburgh: T & T Clark, 1983), p. 189.

[103] "It has to be understood as a system that is open—open for God and for his future" (Moltmann, *God in Creation,* p. 103).

[104] The philosopher G. H. von Wright argues that agency is the power to initiate change in a system. To affirm God as speaker is to assert that God puts language systems into motion (*Explanation and Understanding* [Ithaca, N.Y.: Cornell University Press, 1971]).

Yes, God "bends and determines" the will, but even the seventeenth-century theologians knew that God "moves the will to attend to the proof, truth and goodness of the word announced."[105] Divine communicative action is thus of a wholly different sort from instrumental action, the kind of action appropriate if one were working on wood or stone. God's work of grace is congruous with human nature.[106]

Jesus immediately qualifies his statement "No one can come to me unless the Father . . . draws him" with a quote from Isaiah 54:13: "And they shall all be taught by God." On this he provides the following gloss: "Every one who has heard and learned from the Father comes to me" (Jn 6:44-45). The Father's drawing, in other words, is not causal but communicative. The Word itself has a kind of force. One might say, then, with regard to grace, that the *message* is the medium.

I believe that certain concepts drawn from speech act philosophy help us better to understand what happens in a word event. Furthermore, I suspect that these same concepts may aid in the construction of a model for the broader God-world relation. What we have in gospel preaching is a *narrative* illocution. What does one do in narrating? One displays a world and commends a way of viewing and evaluating it.[107] One literary critic describes the illocutionary force of narrative as "ideological instruction."[108] Stories provide not only information but cultural formation as well; they give training in ways of being human. Even secular stories can sometimes prick our conscience or provoke a radical change of lifestyle. How much more the gospel narratives.

Jüngel observes that the event of addressing results in a concrete relation between the discourse, the subject of the discourse and the one being addressed. Something happens in and through talk about God in Christ. What happens is that God comes to speech: "God's humanity introduces itself into the world as a story to be told."[109] Only through narrative, says Jüngel, can we articulate, and then actualize, certain "emergent possibilities" for human beings. Jüngel construes the God-world relation, in other words, as a *story* that alters the course of history. "The hearer must be drawn existentially into this story through the word, precisely because it is also his story,

---

[105]Heppe, *Reformed Dogmatics*, p. 520.

[106]God's Spirit does not violate human nature but "acts in perfect consistency with the integrity of those laws of our free, rational, and moral nature, which he has himself constituted" (Hodge, *Outlines of Theology*, p. 452).

[107]See M. L. Pratt, *Towards a Speech Act Theory of Literary Discourse* (Bloomington: Indiana University Press, 1977).

[108]See S. S. Lanser, *The Narrative Act: Point of View in Prose Fiction* (Princeton, N.J.: Princeton University Press, 1981). I discuss narrative illocutions in Kevin Vanhoozer, *Is There a Meaning in This Text? The Bible, the Reader and the Morality of Literary Knowledge* (Grand Rapids, Mich.: Zondervan, 1998), p. 341.

[109]Jüngel, *God as the Mystery*, p. 302.

and this must happen before he can *do* what corresponds to this story."[110] For Jüngel, the gospel narrative effectually calls people to union with Christ by drawing them into the story of Jesus.

Does it follow that the effectual call supervenes on the preached word? No, for this proves too much. Not everyone who hears is automatically united to Christ. Though there is a connection between the external and internal calls, it is not supervenience.[111] As we saw earlier, anomalous monism holds that one can describe the same event with two sets of properties, but in the case of the effectual call the one (external) does not always entail the other (internal).

How then are we to understand the relation of the evangelical and the effectual calls? If God deals with us communicatively in a manner that befits our nature, what is it about certain communicative acts that renders them efficacious? Could it be not merely the message but *truth*? Charles Finney believed that the preacher and the Spirit alike can do nothing more than present the truth. Aquinas believes, on the contrary, that the truth carries its own persuasive force. Just as we cannot help but assent to logical truths once we have understood them, so we cannot but be drawn to what we see as good. On the other hand, the truth in and of itself often seems powerless to change us. Light alone does not enable the blind person to see. We need the illumination of the Spirit for that. Not for nothing has the Reformed tradition discussed the effectual call in terms of both Word and Spirit.

The Spirit's work is to illumine not the truth but the mind. One who has been illumined is both passive and active: being made to understand, one understands. "Here we perceive the link between the efficacy of God and the activity of man."[112] But we must press further: In what does the effectuality of the Spirit precisely consist? What, if anything, does the Spirit add to the Word?

There is a connection, I submit, between pneumatology and perlocutions. To return to speech act theory: a perlocution is what one brings about *by* one's speech act. Speech frequently presents an argument, but arguments are intended to produce assent. Perlocutions have to do with the effect on the hearer of a speech act.[113] Now, the primary role of the Holy Spirit, I believe, is to *minister the Word*. The application of salvation is first and foremost a matter of applying both the propositional content and the illocutionary force of the gospel in such a way as to bring about perlocutionary effects: effects that in this case include regeneration, understanding and union

---

[110]Ibid., p. 309.

[111]Or perhaps it is, if we follow Murphy and stipulate that the supervenience relation also depends on the surrounding circumstances, which could of course include the Spirit's presence.

[112]Strong, *Systematic Theology*, p. 822.

[113]The illocution—what the speaker has done—is the objective aspect of the speech act; the perlocution—the intended effect of the act—is the subjective aspect of the speech act.

with Christ. Not for nothing, then, does Paul describe the Word of God as the "sword of the Spirit" (Eph 6:17). It is not simply the impartation of information nor the transfer of mechanical energy but the impact of a total speech act (the message together with its communicative power) that is required for a summons to be efficacious. The Spirit, the "Lord of the hearing" according to Karl Barth, is nothing less than the subjective reality of God's sovereignty. The effectual call is best understood in terms of a conjunction of Word and Spirit, illocution and perlocution.

Does the Spirit, then, supervene on the Word? I can give no more than a qualified yes to this query, for while the Spirit's call depends on the external call and is irreducible to it, it is nevertheless possible to have gospel preaching without regeneration. *Advene* would therefore be a more accurate term. For the Spirit comes to the Word when and where God wills. The Spirit "advenes" on truth to make it efficacious.[114]

The best analogy to advenient grace I have yet come across comes from the autobiography of Helen Keller. Her problem—how someone blind and deaf could be brought to understand language—parallels that of the sinner, one whose mind is darkened and whose ears are closed to the call of God; and indeed Keller writes of her coming to understand in terms of a religious conversion.[115]

When her teacher first came, she spelled words into Helen's hand. Helen learned to imitate the finger movements that spelled various words, but she failed to understand that these movements were words. One day her teacher spelled the word *water* into one of Helen's hands as she held the other under a spout, and the mystery of language was revealed. Helen later wrote: "I knew then that 'w-a-t-e-r' meant the wonderful cool something that was flowing over my hand. The living word awakened my soul, gave it light, hope, joy, set it free!"[116] Here is no impersonal physical

---

[114]Representatives of the school of Samur held that the Spirit illumines the mind in such a way that the will cannot fail to follow practical reason. There is no direct operation of the Spirit on the human will; the Spirit works only through the mediation of the intellect. Mainstream Reformers typically deny this, arguing that the Spirit operates directly on the human will as well. Berkhof states that the influence of the Spirit is not the same as the influence of truth.

What we have here is a standoff between those who champion the "information" of the Word and those who privilege the "energy" of the Spirit. We can perhaps sidestep this criticism (that the Spirit's role is considered merely epistemic, that the Word is directed to the mind and not to the will) by observing (1) that speech acts involve more than propositional content and intellectual assent, (2) epistemology is itself indebted in various ways to ethics, and (3) that the speech act of summoning involves both propositional content and illocutionary force, that is, both Word and Spirit. For six arguments showing that there is an immediate influence of the Spirit on the soul, besides that which is exerted through the truth, see Hodge, *Outlines of Theology,* p. 451.

[115]The film of Helen Keller's life is entitled *The Miracle Worker,* a reference to her teacher, who I suppose is the counterpart of the Holy Spirit inasmuch as it was she who efficaciously ministered the word to Helen and brought about understanding.

force but a wonderful example of how communicative acts can achieve a liberating effect. Helen's teacher, a miracle worker like the Holy Spirit, ministered the word and brought about understanding.

Conclusion: Communicative Agency and the Sovereignty of God

God the speaker. What type of systematic theology am I advocating—the ontological, panentheistic type that views God as supervening on the world, or the cosmological, supernatural type that views God as a stranger to our world? In fact I have followed neither of these paths, preferring rather a communicative theism in which God is a sovereign speaker: locutor, illocution and perlocution. What God says makes a difference, but it would be perverse to describe this difference in terms of impersonal causation. If God's call must be described in terms of causality, it would have to be of a communicative kind, and hence personal. God comes to the world in, and as, Word. To be precise, God relates to the world with both "hands": Word and Spirit.

Sovereignty and supervenience. There is a prima facie tension between sovereignty and supervenience, best seen in the divergent ways theists and panentheists interpret saving grace. Supervenient grace is ultimately sacramental, for it is the cosmos rather than the Christian canon that mediates God, mediates whatever it is that makes Jesus "Christ."[117] A consistently panentheistic theology must assert that it is the world as a whole that represents God's general (though only partially effective) communicative intent.

For the theist, however, all of God's communicative actions originate from his free love. The Word of God is God's gracious communicative, and self-communicative, act. Nothing in the world, whether in its microphysical or its macrophysical dimension, can constrain God's Word or force God to speak. While perlocutions do "emerge" from illocutionary acts, they do not do so necessarily. To say that the internal call necessarily accompanies the external call would be to compromise God's freedom. In the strict or "strong" sense of supervenience, there is little scope for divine sovereignty. In sum, it is theologically incorrect to say that the effectual call supervenes on the evangelical call.

Classical and communicative theism. Finally, it must be asked: Have I relied, in my exposition of the effectual call, on "a form not taken from the thing itself but from contemporary philosophies" (Barth's worry about seventeenth-century theology)? No, for the "thing itself" (the effectual call, God's salvific relation to the world) takes the form of a communicative act: Jesus Christ, the Word of God made flesh.

---

[116]Helen Keller, *The Story of My Life* (New York: Signet, 1988), p. 18.

[117]So Peacocke, who sees the cosmos as a kind of sacrament (*Theology for a Scientific Age*, p. 192).

God's transcendence and immanence can be helpfully thought of in terms of communicative agency. God's transcendence is a matter of his being able to initiate and complete communicative action. Yet the distance between God and the world—from our side an infinite qualitative distance—can be traversed via communicative action. God's self-communication is "advenient." Jesus came to his own, though the world knew him not. It follows that the advent of God's Word is not a foreign intervention. On the contrary, if God is a stranger it is only because humanity has turned its back and made him so.

I have argued that the doctrine of the effectual call resists both the classical theistic picture of God's efficient causality and the contemporary panentheistic picture of God's supervenient causality. This doctrine rather leads us to rethink the God-world relation itself. I have suggested that one fruitful way forward for systematic theology is to conceive of God as a communicative agent. The effectual call (together with the incarnation) then becomes the paradigm for how God is related to the world more generally. The next step, and one that must be postponed for an occasion other than this, would then be to rethink other central Christian doctrines (e.g., creation, providence, justification, the Trinity) in terms of God's communicative action.[118]

---

[118]Ultimately what God wishes to communicate is himself. As we have seen, the effectual call ushers us into union with Christ, and thence into fellowship with the triune God.

Part Two

Scripture

Five

God's Mighty Speech Acts

The Doctrine of Scripture Today

And we also thank God constantly for this,
that when you received the word of God which you heard from us,
you accepted it not as the word of men but as what it really is,
the word of God, which is at work in you believers.
1 THESSALONIANS 2:13

What does a doctrine of Scripture hope to achieve? If the task of Christian theology is to show how Jesus is the "Christ," we may say that the task of a doctrine of Scripture is to show how the Bible is, or is related to, the "Word of God." A doctrine of Scripture tries to give an account of the relation of the words to the Word and of how this relation may legitimately be said to be "of God." A doctrine of Scripture seeks to show how biblical language and literature participate in the Word of God. All such attempts presuppose, therefore, some understanding of the meaning and locus of "Word of God."

Why a Doctrine of Scripture?

The "Scripture Principle." The so-called Scripture principle represents the historical orthodox view that the Bible is to be identified with the Word of God. Reformed confessions often expressed their concern for biblical authority by devoting a separate article to the doctrine of Scripture.[1] Calvin's statement is representative: "We have

---

[1] Cf. Karl Barth: "The Scripture principle is in fact expressed more or less sharply and explicitly at the head of all the more important confessional writings of the Reformed Church" (*Church Dogmatics* 1/2, trans. G. T. Thomson and Harold Knight [Edinburgh: T & T Clark, 1975], p. 547.)

to do with the Word which came forth from God's mouth and was given to us. . . . God's will is to speak to us by the mouths of the apostles and prophets. . . . Their mouths are to us as the mouth of the only true God."[2]

Various forms of biblical criticism since the Enlightenment have chipped away at such an identification of the Bible with divine revelation. The rootedness of the language and traditions of Scripture in human history became increasingly apparent, to the point that the Bible appeared to be a human-made rather than God-breathed product. In 1881 William Robertson Smith recommended the same methods of historical and literary analysis for the study of Scripture as those applied to other books, a suggestion that eventually led to his being put on trial in Scotland for heresy. In America during the following decade, the Presbyterian Church similarly charged Charles A. Briggs with heresy, largely because he rejected verbal inspiration. Briggs used both exegetical and historical arguments in his defense: neither the teaching nor the phenomena of Scripture supported the notion of verbal inspiration, nor did the notions of verbal inspiration or inerrancy reflect the views of the fathers and Reformers. The General Assembly of the Presbyterian Church in the United Church three times (in 1910, 1916 and 1923) declared, in response, that biblical inerrancy was an "essential doctrine" of the church.[3]

One of the major factors in the demise of the Scripture principle was the rise of historical criticism. What is perhaps less well documented is the extent to which the dispute about the Scripture principle was essentially theological. For what is at stake in debates about Scripture is ultimately one's doctrine of God.[4] In this article therefore I propose to deal more with theological than with exegetical or historical arguments against the Scripture principle.

Perhaps the single most important aspect of the doctrine of God which has a bearing on the doctrine of Scripture is divine providence. Indeed Pope Leo XIII entitled his 1893 encyclical on Scripture and scholarship *Providentissimus Deus*. The encyclical states: "All the books and the whole of each book which the Church receives as

---

[2]John Calvin, *Commentaries,* Library of Christian Classics, ed. Joseph Haroutunian (Philadelphia: Westminster Press, 1958), p. 83. Calvin is expounding 1 Peter 1:25: "'But the word of the Lord abides for ever.' That word is the good news which was preached to you."

[3]See George Marsden, *Reforming Fundamentalism: Fuller Seminary and the New Evangelicalism* (Grand Rapids, Mich.: Eerdmans, 1987), p. 112; Jack B. Rogers and Donald K. McKim, *The Authority and Interpretation of the Bible: An Historical Approach* (San Francisco: Harper & Row, 1979), pp. 348-61.

[4]Is it merely coincidence that biblical criticism arose, and flourished, when deism was increasingly in vogue? Or that classical views of revelation and inspiration presuppose theism? In our time theism appears to be giving way to various forms of panentheism (the idea that God is not "over" the world as Lord but rather that the world is "in" God, who serves as its inner ground). Work on how this broader theological context affects the doctrine of Scripture is urgently needed.

sacred and canonical were written at the dictation of the Holy Spirit."[5] Leo XIII was
simply repeating the simple identification of Scripture and revelation which characterized the confessions of the Protestant Reformation as well as the Council of Trent's
Counter-Reformation *Decree on Scripture and Tradition* (1546), from which Leo had
borrowed the phrase "at the dictation of the Holy Spirit." The fundamental issue in
the doctrine of Scripture concerns the manner of God's involvement in the words of
Scripture and thus the manner of God's activity in the world.

The nature of a "doctrine" of Scripture. Doctrine, according to Alister
McGrath, is an integrative concept with four essential elements: social, cognitive,
experiential and linguistic.[6] First, doctrine arises in response to threats to a community's self-understanding or identity. Clearly the doctrine of Scripture has indeed functioned as a means of social demarcation—and that with a vengeance!
Fundamentalism, evangelicalism, liberalism, postliberal, orthodox, neo-orthodox are
distinguished in large part on the basis of their respective stance toward Scripture.
Evangelicals of one school have a difficult time doing justice to other kinds of evangelicals. Gabriel Fackre's careful taxonomy of the various positions on biblical
authority even finds several species of inerrancy.[7] The situation today is comparable
to the christological controversies of the fifth and sixth centuries, which saw an
expansion in the vocabulary of Christology.

Second, doctrine arises in response to questions about the community's founding
narrative. Doctrine provides a "conceptual framework," suggested by the biblical narrative itself, for interpreting that narrative. There is a conceptual substructure to the biblical narrative that calls for thought—doctrine formulation. It is precisely this conceptual
substructure that is in dispute in debates over the doctrine of Scripture. One hundred
years ago B. B. Warfield wrote: "The subject of the Inspiration of the Bible is one which
has been much confused in recent discussion."[8] More recently Edward Farley and Peter
Hodgson write: "We do not believe that an adequate reformulation of the doctrine of
Scripture has yet been achieved by contemporary theology."[9] My thesis in what follows
is that the concept of divine speech acts may go some way in falsifying this judgment.

---

[5]Quoted in John Baillie, *The Idea of Revelation in Recent Thought* (New York: Columbia University Press, 1956), p. 31.
[6]Alister McGrath, *The Genesis of Doctrine: A Study in the Foundations of Doctrinal Criticism*
(Oxford: Blackwell, 1990), chap. 3.
[7]See Gabriel Fackre, *The Christian Story: A Pastoral Systematics* (Grand Rapids, Mich.: Eerdmans, 1987), 2:61-75.
[8]Benjamin B. Warfield, *The Inspiration and the Authority of the Bible* (Phillipsburg, N.J.: Presbyterian & Reformed, 1979), p. 105.
[9]Edward Farley and Peter Hodgson, "Scripture and Tradition," in *Christian Theology: An Introduction to Its Traditions and Tasks,* 2nd ed., ed. Peter Hodgson and Robert King (Philadelphia: Fortress, 1985), p. 81.

"Mighty speech acts." The doctrine of Scripture is intelligible only in the light of a whole network of other doctrines including revelation, providence and pneumatology. The concept of a speech act is, I believe, a helpful one with which to integrate and interpret the classical categories of revelation, inspiration and infallibility. Above all, it allows us to transcend the debilitating dichotomy between revelation as "God saying" and as "God doing." For the category *speech act* acknowledges that saying too is a doing, and that persons can do many things by "saying."

The biblical theology movement typically distinguished between God's acts and God's speaking. "The New Testament has no authority which is not the authority of Jesus and the authority of the mighty acts of God involving him."[10] Well and good—but disagreement arises over the nature of God's mighty acts. For many contemporary theologians, history is the arena of God's acts and consequently the proper category for understanding God's self-revelation. On this view the Bible is only a witness to revelation, not the revelation itself. According to G. E. Wright, when "the Word of God" is interpreted to mean "that the centre of the Bible is a series of divinely given teachings, then it is certainly a misconception."[11] This dichotomy turns up in other theologians too.

Whereas the biblical theology movement attended to the "act of God" in a salvation history *behind* the text, Barth argued that it is only through the singular history of Jesus Christ that God makes himself known. Wolfhart Pannenberg works yet another variation on the idea of revelation in history: because God is the "all-determining reality," *all* of history is revelatory of God. Because Jesus' resurrection anticipates the end of history, however, God may be said to be revealed in Christ. For Pannenberg the biblical texts are promissory, insofar as they anticipate the final shape of history and thus the nature and purpose of God. The Bible is a witness to (in the sense of anticipation of) the Word of God.

What these three approaches share is the conceptual distinction between Scripture and the mighty act(s) of God, located in a special, singular and universal history respectively. But just as the biblical theology movement earlier had difficulty articulating the notion of an "act of God," so today there is confusion over the nature of the "Word of God." For Bultmann the "Word of God" is a communicative act of address shrouded in the deep recesses of human subjectivity. In Barth's theology the Word similarly lacks definition, for the properly semantic moment of God's self-disclosure remains insufficiently analyzed. At the same time the emphasis on the Word's being a "mighty act" of God must not be lost. Instead God's Word and God's act must be thought together.

---

[10]Oliver O'Donovan, *On the Thirty-nine Articles: A Conversation with Tudor Christianity* (Exeter, U.K.: Paternoster, 1986), p. 51.

[11]G. E. Wright, "God Who Acts," in *God's Activity in the World,* ed. Owen C. Thomas (Chico, Calif.: Scholars Press, 1983), p. 25.

The notion of a divine speech act addresses both the problem of the nature of God's activity and the problem of the nature of biblical language. Specifically, it explains how God is involved with the production of Scripture and so overcomes the ruinous dichotomy between historical-actualist and verbal-conceptualist models of revelation, that is, the dualism between "God saying" and "God doing." Scripture is neither simply the recital of the acts of God nor merely a book of inert propositions. Scripture is rather composed of divine-human speech acts that, through what they say, accomplish several authoritative cognitive, spiritual and social functions.

A pathway. "That he may teach us his ways and we may walk in his paths" (Mic 4:2). Calvin's comment on this verse is instructive: "The church of God can be established only where the Word of God rules, where God shows by his voice the way of salvation."[12] The pathway into the doctrine of Holy Scripture is neither simple nor straightforward: it intersects with the doctrine of God—in particular the doctrine of providence—and with theories concerning the nature of language and literature. This is only as it should be, if indeed the task of a doctrine of Scripture is to explain how and why the Bible is the "Word" of "God." In what follows I first review the problems associated with the "received view" and some recent evangelical attempts to restate it. I then turn to consider the ways the doctrine of God is decisive for one's understanding of the doctrine of Scripture. Finally, I propose the model of communicative action for conceiving the Scriptures as the revelatory Word of God. The Bible, I shall argue, is a diverse collection of God's mighty speech acts which communicate the saving Word of God.

The pathway I am proposing leads to three theses and a corollary. First, one's view of Scripture is always correlated to one's view of God: no doctrine of Scripture without a doctrine of providence. Most theologians, I argue, gravitate toward a particular genre of Scripture in their construal of how God is involved with Scripture.

Second, I shall defend a version of the "identity thesis": Scripture is, in a sense yet to be defined, really the Word of God. Those who affirm biblical infallibility are often charged with holding a quasi-magical view of the Bible as a sort of talisman that reveals the secrets of the universe. The Scripture principle, it is true, can degenerate into a species of bibliolatry. However, I shall contend that identifying the Scriptures as the Word of God need not result in bibliolatry, so long as God's communicative acts are not mistaken for the divine being itself. The Word of God is God in communicative act, and there is no reason that some communicative acts cannot be verbal. This implies that the dichotomy between propositional and personal revelation is not as hard and fast as almost a century of debate has implied. We are not confronted with a stark choice of opting for the "system" or the "Savior" in Scripture. There are therefore

---

[12]Calvin, *Commentaries,* p. 79.

ecumenical possibilities for an evangelical view of Scripture that focuses on God's mighty speech acts. This chapter will have succeeded if it enables evangelicals of the left and of the right to discover a means for reconciling unnecessary differences.

Third, a number of theologians, prompted largely by Barth, see biblical authority in functional terms, as instrumental in leading us to Christ. Truth would on this view be a matter of faith and practice. The focus on God's mighty speech acts is a bit broader: the Bible is, to be sure, no science textbook, but neither is it restricted to serving only as a witness to Christ. Neither cosmo- nor christocentric, the Scriptures are rather centred on God's covenant. The covenant involves the cosmos, and Christ is at the center, but *covenantal efficacy* is the more comprehensive term to cover all the things that God does with and in and through the Scriptures. What we have in the Scriptures is therefore everything that God deemed necessary and sufficient for the doctrinal, moral and spiritual welfare of his covenant people.

We will find, finally, a corollary: why the doctrine of Scripture matters. Here it is perhaps more accurate to speak of a pathway *out of* the Scriptures: the Scripture principle matters because it is the norm of both dogmatics and ethics. The task of Christian dogmatics is nothing less than "the unfolding and presentation of the content of the Word of God."[13] Likewise the task of Christian ethics is nothing less than the unfolding and presentation of the content of the Word in individual and social practice. The doctrine of Scripture is far from being a theoretical abstraction. Those who "identify Scripture as God's Word, are deeply concerned to submit to its authority in their lives."[14]

The Doctrine of Scripture: Yesterday and Today
The Reformation understanding of Scripture has been variously interpreted. Some stress the elements of continuity with Protestant orthodoxy, others the discontinuity.[15] By "the received view" I am referring to Warfield's Princetonian doctrine of Scripture and its contemporary restatements.[16] I am more interested in the theological underpinnings of this position than in the historical question whether or to what extent this represents the view of the Reformers themselves. In any case, the received view was

---

[13]Barth, *Church Dogmatics* 1/2, p. 853.

[14]John Stott's definition of "evangelicals," in David Edwards and John Stott, *Evangelical Essentials: A Liberal-Evangelical Dialogue* (London: Hodder & Stoughton, 1988), p. 104.

[15]William J. Abraham, for example, claims that the Warfield-Packer view "involves substantial innovations in theology" (*The Divine Inspiration of Holy Scripture* [Oxford: Oxford University Press, 1981], p. 16), as do Rogers and McKim. For an opposing point of view see John Woodbridge, *Biblical Authority: A Critique of the Rogers/McKim Proposal* (Grand Rapids, Mich.: Zondervan, 1982), and Richard Muller, *Post-Reformation Reformed Dogmatics,* vol. 2, *Holy Scripture: The Cognitive Foundation of Theology* (Grand Rapids, Mich.: Baker, 1993).

[16]The received view was developed systematically by Warfield about one hundred years ago, and it was also a significant factor in the emergence of evangelicalism in America in the 1940s and in the founding of the Tyndale Fellowship in 1944.

the form that the doctrine of Scripture had assumed at the end of the nineteenth century, when it was attacked and defended with equal vigor. The story of the doctrine's
development in the twentieth century was, with few exceptions, one of hardening
nineteenth-century positions. One way or another, then, the received view continues
to function as the touchstone in debates about the doctrine of Scripture.[17] In this section I examine the development of the received view, problems with the received
view, and contemporary evangelical modifications and alternatives.

The "received view" stated. The components of the received view—propositional revelation, verbal inspiration and infallible authority—are doubtless familiar
and may be briefly sketched.[18] At its heart is an "identity thesis": the belief that Scripture *is* the Word of God.

1. *Propositional revelation.* Perhaps the most important, and contentious, claim is
that God reveals himself verbally in Scripture. The emphasis is on God's self-communication through the revealed truths formulated in the canon. Revelation is largely a
matter of doctrine or "sacred teaching." What makes the Bible authoritative is its cognitive content.

Of course one must be careful not to caricature the received view. Packer, for
instance, acknowledges that the Scripture principle is not self-standing: "When this
affirmation [that Scripture is revelation] is not related to God's saving work in history
and to the illumining and interpreting work of the Spirit, it too is theologically incomplete."[19]

2. *Verbal inspiration.* The Bible is the very Word of God itself. God so superin-
tended the process of composing the Scriptures that the end result manifests his
divine intention, and this without overriding the human authors and their intentions:
"The Bible is the Word of God in such a sense that its words, though written by men
and bearing indelibly impressed on them the marks of their human origin, were written, nevertheless, under such an influence of the Holy Ghost as to be also the words
of God, the adequate expression of His mind and will."[20] We might call this the
"direct identity thesis" (as opposed to Barth's "indirect identity thesis" and to James

---

[17]Just how pervasive the received view of revelation was may be illustrated by a comment
from John Baillie. Referring to the nineteenth-century Continental Protestant flight from the
doctrine of revelation, Baillie writes: "It is as if these thinkers felt revelation to be so universally understood as the verbal or conceptual communication of truth by divine authority that
only by abandoning the term itself could they effectively retreat from this wrong [sic] meaning" (*Idea of Revelation,* p. 15).

[18]For a comprehensive restatement of this position, see Carl F. H. Henry, *God, Revelation and
Authority,* vols. 1-3 (Waco, Tex.: Word, 1976-79). Cf. the articles on Packer and Warfield in
Walter Elwell, ed., *Handbook of Evangelical Theologians* (Grand Rapids, Mich.: Baker, 1993).

[19]J. I. Packer, "Scripture," in *New Dictionary of Theology,* ed. Sinclair Ferguson, D. F. Wright
and J. I. Packer (Leicester, U.K.: Inter-Varsity Press, 1988), p. 628.

[20]Warfield, *Inspiration and Authority,* p. 173.

Barr's "non-identity thesis"). It would be incorrect, however, to infer that a dictation theory necessarily follows from the identity thesis. Indeed Warfield makes two important qualifications to preempt just such a conclusion.

First, Warfield is cautious about drawing a Chalcedonian analogy to the doctrine of Scripture. "There is no hypostatic union between the Divine and the human in Scripture; we cannot parallel the 'inscripturation' of the Holy Spirit and the incarnation of the Son of God."[21] Warfield acknowledges a remote analogy only: though both involve a union of divine and human factors, in the one "they unite to constitute a Divine-human person, in the other they co-operate to perform a Divine-human work."[22] Second, Warfield is careful to affirm the reality of human agency in the writing of Scripture. His view entails a conception of concursus rather than mechanical dictation.[23]

3. *Infallible authority.* According to Packer, the Bible is the Word of God not only instrumentally (functionally) but intrinsically (materially). It follows that Scripture will be without error, for God cannot lie (Heb 6:18), nor is God ignorant (Heb 4:13). Gordon Lewis and Bruce Demarest claim that the human writers were kept from error by an "epistemological miracle" which they attribute to the Spirit. They see the Spirit's influence, however, not like that of an impersonal machine but rather like "worthy personal relationships."[24] Nevertheless, the tendency of this view is to see all parts of the Bible as forms of teaching whose purpose is to make true assertions about God and the world. "Hard" biblical authority claims the Scriptures speak truly on matters of history and science as well as on matters of faith.

Problems with the received view. The received view has been subjected to searching criticisms. I here focus only on criticisms that come from two opposing points of view: the neo-orthodoxy of Karl Barth and the neoliberalism of James Barr.

1. *Theological problems with "propositions."* According to Barth, to say "revelation" is to say "The Word became flesh."[25] The received view errs in elevating propositions about a person above a personal encounter. Revelation is a nonconceptual, personal encounter with Christ's person or with God's mighty acts. John Baillie: "God does not give us information by communication; He give us Himself in communion."[26] Or as he elsewhere puts it, revelation is always "from subject to subject."[27] The kind of knowledge that corresponds to divine revelation is therefore more like that of a per-

---

[21]Ibid., p. 162.
[22]Ibid.
[23]B. B. Warfield, "The Divine and Human in the Bible," in *Selected Shorter Writings,* ed. John E. Meeter (Nutley, N.J.: Presbyterian & Reformed, 1970, 1973), 2:547.
[24]Gordon Lewis and Bruce Demarest, *Integrative Theology* (Grand Rapids, Mich.: Zondervan, 1987), 1:162.
[25]Barth, *Church Dogmatics* 1/1, p. 119.
[26]Baillie, *Idea of Revelation,* p. 47.
[27]Ibid., p. 24.

sonal relation (knowledge by acquaintance) than like that of a particular kind of data (knowledge about).

According to George Hunsinger's reading, Barth holds that scriptural language refers to its revelatory subject matter (the Word of God) only by way of an analogy of grace. "The incapacity of human language in itself and as such is what separates Barth's view from literalism [which] tends to assume that human language is intrinsically capable of referring to God."[28] The worry, apparently, is that propositional revelation leads to a "natural theology," as it were, of biblical language. If the Bible is itself revelation, then this revelation is ascertainable by human reason and the truth of Christ can be procured by historical and scientific investigation. Barth's attitude toward the identity thesis and natural theology alike is briefly expressed: *Nein!*

From a wholly other perspective, James Barr believes that a perfectly good account of the Bible's status as Scripture can be given without appealing to the "Word of God" at all. For him the Bible is a record of the human attempt to understand and transmit the religious tradition of the people of God, not a movement from God to humankind.[29] Modern learning, with its rival descriptions of natural, social and historical processes, has dethroned the Bible as a document of propositional authority. Historical-critical study of Scripture has led scholars to believe that the Bible manifests the same kind of historical and cultural relativity as do other texts. Is the Bible a human response to divine revelation? "The real problem, as it seems to me, is that we have no access to, and no means of comprehending, a communication or revelation from God which is antecedent to the human tradition about him and which then goes on to generate that very tradition."[30]

The message is clear: where human language is, God is not (though Barth allows, as Barr does not, for the possibility of a miracle that would render human language the Word of God).

2. *Theological problems with the prophetic paradigm.* The Scripture principle is also thought to entail "a prophetic paradigm" of verbal inspiration. A number of contemporary scholars believe that this paradigm tends toward a docetic view of the Word which denies both the humanity and the spirituality of the Scriptures.

Barth objects to any "materializing" of inspiration which ties down what the Spirit can say to what the human words say. Against the received view of verbal inspiration, Barth posits a fundamental discontinuity between human speech and the Word of God. Barth acknowledges that the human authors were "inspired" in the sense that they were immediately related to the content of revelation, Jesus

---

[28]George Hunsinger, *How to Read Karl Barth: The Shape of His Theology* (Oxford: Oxford University Press, 1991), p. 43.
[29]James Barr, *The Bible in the Modern World* (London: SCM Press, 1973), p. 120.
[30]Ibid., p. 121.

Christ himself, as commissioned witnesses. Inspiration has more to do with the special content of the witness rather than its verbal forms.[31] The human witness becomes the Word of God only when the Spirit graciously appropriates the words for the purpose of self-revelation.

For Barr, the prophetic paradigm stands at the very center of evangelical thinking about inspiration: the authors speak not their own words but those given them by God.[32] An initial difficulty is that large portions of the Bible do not read as if they were composed in this fashion. The form of many biblical books "is that of a man-to-man communication."[33] John Barton observes that one cannot paste a prophetic imprimatur on every passage: "Samuel hewed Agog in pieces before the Lord in Gilgal: this is the Word of the Lord" creates an awkward moment in the liturgy.[34] Seriously to uphold the prophetic paradigm is, he argues, to subscribe to a dictation theory of inspiration. It is also to impose the same kind of truth claim on all parts of Scripture. But the Bible is manifestly composed of literature other than prophecy: wisdom, narrative, hymnody, apocalyptic, law and so forth: "Scripture contains genres which cannot be assimilated to the model of divine communication to men."[35] If one must characterize Scripture by a central genre, then Barton believes that wisdom literature, rather than prophecy, is the better candidate.[36] The Bible is people's reflection on their relationship with a God who is already known.

Barr's hesitations about verbal inspiration are closely related to his doctrine of God: "We do not have any idea of ways in which God might straight-forwardly communicate articulate thoughts or sentences to men; it just doesn't happen."[37] Inspiration means that God was "in contact" with his people and "present" in the formation of their tradition: "Today I think we believe, or have to believe, that God's communication with the men of the biblical period was not on any different terms from the mode of his communication with his people now."[38] This "soft" view of inspiration is like its poetic counterpart: as a result of some experience a writer's expression achieves sublimity and profundity, but not inerrancy or infallibility.

Must a doctrine of verbal inspiration presuppose the prophetic paradigm? I do not see that it must. After all, the primary purpose in stressing the verbal aspect of inspi-

---

[31]Barth, *Church Dogmatics* 1/2, pp. 520-21.

[32]James Barr, *Escaping from Fundamentalism* (London: SCM Press, 1984), chap. 3, "The Prophetic Paradigm."

[33]Barr, *Bible in the Modern World*, p. 123.

[34]Barton, *People of the Book: The Authority of the Bible in Christianity* (London: SPCK, 1988), p. 71.

[35]Ibid.

[36]Ibid., p. 36.

[37]Barr, *Bible in the Modern World*, p. 17.

[38]Ibid., pp. 17-18.

ration is to make a point about the final product, not the process, of inscripturation. The process may well involve free human agency, but the end result is what God intended. Indeed, Barton cited Austin Farrer's concept of double agency as the most satisfying account of how we should speak of Scripture if we did wish to claim that the scriptural writers convey divine revelation, though he fails to acknowledge that Warfield espouses a similar view.[39]

For all its valid caveats, Barr's understanding of the prophetic paradigm (and thus of verbal inspiration) remains something of a caricature. He points out that with regard to prophetic discourse God's judgments are not merely objective assessments but conditional on the people's response: "What is said by a prophet, then, is characteristically not an absolute. . . . The Lord does not through the prophets utter perfect, final, ultimate and unchangeable statements."[40] Yet the notion of verbal inspiration does not require that everything in Scripture be treated as an "absolute" assertion, only that what is said is taken to be divinely intended. To suggest that the prophetic paradigm implies that everything in Scripture must be an absolute truth is to overlook the semantics of biblical literature.[41]

3. *Theological problems with cognitive perfection.* Is the Spirit's "guidance" such that it overrides human fallibility, making the human authors mouthpieces of infallible communication? Bernard Ramm worries that the notion of propositional revelation "is but an alternate version of this Hegelian theory of pure conceptual language."[42] The divinity of Scripture is not a stable property that it permanently possesses. Verbal inspiration, says Barth, "does not mean the infallibility of the biblical word in its linguistic, historical and theological character as a human word. It means that the fallible and faulty human word is as such used by God and has to be received and heard in spite of its human fallibility."[43]

Many of the critics of the received view prefer to locate the Spirit at the point of the reception rather than production of the Scriptures. Ramm comments that if the Bible could transform lives without Christ and the Spirit, then its power would be

---

[39]Barton, *People of the Book*, p. 38. It is true, however, that Warfield sometimes speaks as though the human authors were only instrumental agents. For example: "The completely supernatural character of revelation is in no way lessened by the circumstance that it has been given through the instrumentality of men. . . . The Divine word delivered through men is the pure word of God, diluted with no human admixture whatsoever" (*Inspiration and Authority*, p. 86).

[40]Barr, *Escaping*, p. 24.

[41]See Kevin Vanhoozer, "The Semantics of Biblical Literature," in *Hermeneutics, Authority and Canon*, ed. D. A. Carson and John Woodbridge (Grand Rapids, Mich.: Zondervan, 1986), pp. 53-104.

[42]Bernard Ramm, *After Fundamentalism: The Future of Evangelical Theology* (San Francisco: Harper & Row, 1983), p. 90.

[43]Barth, *Church Dogmatics* 1/2, p. 533.

magical and not spiritual.[44] Scripture is a medium for knowing Christ. The Bible is
authoritative and infallible not for any purpose whatsoever, but only for the purpose
of witnessing to Christ. James D. G. Dunn wonders, "How *valid* is the proposition
that inerrancy is *the necessary implication* of scripture being God's word?" He
believes that historical exegesis must be open to the Spirit's prodding now. John
Baillie agrees: "The weakness of Protestant orthodoxy has been that it could show no
convincing reason for insisting on the plenary nature of the divine assistance to the
Scriptural authors while as firmly denying it to the mind of the Church in later days.[45]

For Barr, the Bible's authority is not ontological, a matter of what it is, but functional, a matter of what it does. Specifically, the basis of biblical authority "lies in its
efficacy in the faith-relation between man and God."[46] The Bible is the instrument of
faith, not its object. It is not properties but pragmatics that render the Bible authoritative: the Bible is Scripture only when it proves itself fruitful in the life of the believing
community.

What makes the Bible efficacious? Why should the Bible rather than some other
book function in this way? Does its functioning in this way have nothing to do with
the kind of work it is? It is not yet clear how the words of Scripture are related to the
Word of God. In a sense the christocentric understanding of infallibility is as reductive as the propositional. In both cases infallibility is reduced to a single kind of communicative function: in the one case asserting, and in the other witnessing.

Does the received view's affirmation of biblical infallibility deny the humanity of
the Scriptures? Must humanity entail errancy? I do not see that it does. Fallibility need
not entail actual fault. For example, it does not follow that just because a math textbook is written by a fallible human being, there must be mistakes in it! Of course
something more is being claimed for Scripture. Some—not all—defenders of the
received view draw a parallel with Chalcedonian Christology. To say that Jesus is sinless does not deny his humanity. Because of his real human nature, Jesus was
tempted. Because of his divine personality, Jesus did not sin. The debate about biblical infallibility mirrors that concerning Jesus' "impeccability."[47]

4. *Theological problems with the Bible as the "Word of God."* The words of Scripture are human words. For Barth, the Word of God is God in revelatory action.[48] Biblical statements must not therefore be directly equated with the revealed Word of

---

[44]Bernard Ramm, *Special Revelation and the Word of God* (Grand Rapids, Mich.: Eerdmans,
1961), p. 184.
[45]Baillie, *Idea of Revelation*, p. 112.
[46]James Barr, *Explorations in Theology* (London: SCM Press, 1980), 7:54.
[47]Some maintain that impeccability is inconsistent with Jesus' humanity. The issue turns on
how to define "humanity."
[48]See T. J. Gorringe, "In Defence of the Identification: Scripture as the Word of God," *Scottish
Journal of Theology* 32 (1979): 303-18.

God. Donald Bloesch here parts company with Packer: Scripture is not intrinsically revelation, "for its revelatory status does not reside in its wording as such but in the Spirit of God, who fills the word with meaning and power."[49] Similarly, the truthfulness of the Bible is not a property of the human words but of the Spirit who speaks through them.

The main problem with the identity thesis, according to its critics, is neither exegetical nor historical but theological: it falsely equates the human with the divine. Bibliolatry commits the most basic of theological errors: identifying God with what is not-God. Dunn worries that the heirs of the Princeton theology are in danger of bibliolatry, for by affirming the infallible authority of Scripture, they are according an authority proper only to the triune God.[50] Dunn rejects the Chalcedonian analogy between the divine and human in Christ (effecting impeccability) and the divine and human in Scripture (effecting inerrancy) and concludes that the Princeton doctrine is "theologically dangerous."

Whither an evangelical theology of the Word? As a consequence of the above-mentioned criticisms, many recent evangelical works on Scripture have given greater prominence both to the humanity and to the spirituality of the Bible.

1. *New emphasis on the dynamic relation between the Word of God and Scripture.* Bloesch sees three options: a rational evangelicalism that equates Scripture with revelation understood as propositional (principles or facts); an experiential liberalism that views the Bible as an illustration and intensification of human morality and spirituality; a spiritual evangelicalism that views the Bible as "the divinely prepared medium or channel of divine revelation rather than revelation itself."[51]

On the one hand are conservatives who swallow up the humanity of the biblical text in the notion of the Word of God and thus succumb to a kind of scriptural docetism. On the other hand are liberals who evacuate the biblical text of divinity, thus creating a parallel with the Ebionite heresy that denied the divinity of Christ. In the middle are "progressive" evangelicals, Barth included, who seek some kind of Chalcedonian analogy that would permit them to affirm, however paradoxically, that the Scriptures are at once "truly human" and "truly divine."

For Bloesch the answer is a recovery of the "paradoxical unity" of Word and Spirit. The Word must not be a dead letter but a living word. Bloesch espouses a sacramental model that sees revelation as God in action and Scripture as the means for encountering God. The Word of God must not be reduced to rational statements; it is rather God in action. The Word of God, to quote Calvin, is "the hand of

---

[49]Donald G. Bloesch, *Holy Scripture: Revelation, Inspiration and Interpretation* (Downers Grove, Ill.: InterVarsity Press, 1994), p. 27.
[50]James D. G. Dunn, *The Living Word* (Philadelphia: Fortress, 1988), p. 106.
[51]Bloesch, *Holy Scripture*, p. 18.

God stretching itself out to act powerfully through the apostle."[52]

Revelation is increasingly treated as bipolar. One cannot properly speak of revelation without speaking of someone's receiving revelation. Here we may note Ramm's comment that the discipline of communication studies may well be the next challenge for a theology of revelation. The divine message is received by an addressee only if the Spirit accompanies the signs: "The external letter must become an inner Word through the work of the Spirit."[53] The knowledge of God is always assimilated through the work of the Spirit. The Spirit uses the forms of the Word of God to minister its content: Christ the gospel of God. Ramm believes that fundamentalism loses this dynamic link between the Spirit and the Scriptures in its zeal to assert the authority of the letter.

2. *New emphasis on the humanity of Scriptures.* It is generally acknowledged that the received view "tended to ignore the human side" of Scripture.[54] What precisely is involved in such an admission? First, that the Bible may be read like any other book. The positive side to biblical criticism is that it serves as an antidote to a docetic interpretation of the Bible which reads it as if it had no human historical-cultural context. The Bible is a human text, with all the marks of human weakness. For instance, Pinnock says, its propositions "fall short of expressing exactly what a speaker would wish."[55] Moreover, the Bible is historically and scientifically "flawed." But God can use the "weak" things of this world to communicate his wisdom. Inspiration for Pinnock is a "dynamic" but "non-coercive" work of God whereby God communicates his message in such a way that the human authors "make full use of their own skills and vocabulary."[56]

William Abraham argues that the received view confuses divine inspiration with divine speaking, "as if it were some kind of complicated speech-act of God."[57] "Inspiring" is not one independent activity among others but something one does by doing other activities. A teacher, for example, inspires her pupils through her lectures, her questions, her eagerness and so forth. Abraham proposes that God inspired the authors of the Bible through his revelatory and saving acts. Inspiration is a consequence of these other acts rather than an act in its own right. Divine speaking is only one of the acts by which God inspired the biblical writers. Inspiration for Abraham is an effect (on the authors) of divine activity rather than a divine activity itself. (It is odd that Abraham is basing his theology of Scripture on an analysis of the ordinary usage of the term *inspiration.* In the received view *inspiration* operates as a technical term that refers to God's providential guidance of the authors in writing Scripture.

---

[52]Quoted in Bloesch, *Holy Scripture,* p. 49.
[53]Pinnock, *The Scripture Principle* (San Francisco: Harper & Row, 1984), p. 155.
[54]Ibid., p. 105.
[55]Ibid., p. 98.
[56]Ibid., p. 105.
[57]Abraham, *Divine Inspiration,* p. 37.

Abraham, like others who appeal to a poetic model of inspiration, may be guilty of a variant of the word-concept fallacy.)

Kern Robert Trembath, following Abraham, argues that biblical inspiration refers "to the enhancement of one's understanding of God brought about instrumentally through the Bible, rather than to the mysterious and non-repeatable process by which 'God got written what He wanted' in the Bible."[58] Inspiration on this view is something that happens to readers, not the authors, of Scripture. The recipient of inspiration is not a book but a believer. Such an understanding corresponds more or less with Barr's "soft" or "functionalist" revision of the doctrine of inspiration: *inspiration* refers to the Bible's capacity to mediate God's saving intention to the world.

3. *New emphasis on the spirituality of Scripture.* "Progressive" evangelicals tend to conceive of biblical authority in terms of the Bible's saving purpose. According to McKim: "For neo-evangelicals, the purpose of Scripture is to bring people to faith and salvation in Jesus Christ."[59] Note that this limits the various kinds of propositions and forms of literature in Scripture to one kind of authority: soteric. This is, in its own way, as restrictive as the "conservative" evangelical view, which tends to conceive of biblical authority in terms of the Bible's propositional perfection. Infallibility is something we confess after the fact. It is as much, or more, a statement about our experience as it is about some property of Scripture.

It is pointless to affirm Scripture as God's Word apart from a living faith in Christ. For G. C. Berkouwer it is the content of the Bible—Jesus Christ—that legitimates its authority. Inspiration is not an a priori formal principle so much as a material principle: Scripture is authoritative insofar as it witnesses to its subject matter, Jesus Christ.[60] Biblical authority, we might say, is a correlate of faith in Christ, not its foundation. One must first have a personal relationship with Christ before one can recognize the authority of the Scriptures.

The Centrality of the Doctrine of God

The doctrine of Scripture is not self-standing but depends on one's concept of God and of the way God interacts with his people.

"Construing" God. In his magisterial work *The Uses of Scripture in Recent Theology*[61] David H. Kelsey analyzes the diverse ways theologians use Scripture and concludes that every theologian "construes" (takes, interprets) the Bible *as* something

---

[58]Kern Robert Trembath, *Evangelical Theories of Inspiration: A Review and Proposal* (Oxford: Oxford University Press, 1987), p. 103.

[59]Donald K. McKim, *What Christians Believe About the Bible* (Nashville: Thomas Nelson, 1985), p. 91.

[60]G. C. Berkouwer states: "Every word about the God-breathed character of Scripture is meaningless if Holy Scripture is not understood as the witness concerning Christ" (*Holy Scripture* [Grand Rapids, Mich.: Eerdmans, 1975], p. 166).

[61]David H. Kelsey, *The Uses of Scripture in Recent Theology* (Philadelphia: Fortress, 1975).

or other (e.g., *as* history, *as* literature, *as* doctrine, *as* narrative). The nature of biblical authority is a function of one's construal of Scripture: doctrines have one kind of authority, history another, and narrative yet another. One's construal of Scripture, however, is determined not by the text but by the conjunction of two extratextual factors: the way Scripture is perceived to be used in the community and the way God is perceived to be present in the church.[62]

Darrell Jodock, following Kelsey, argues that our images of God's relation to the world are "logically extra-biblical," for all such images "assume a view of the world not found in the Bible itself."[63] Does the Bible have no say at all regarding how it is to be construed? Not according to Jodock: our picture of how God relates to the world "remains a theological judgment rather than a logical deduction from uniform biblical evidence."[64] Kelsey's view is more nuanced; he admits that the Bible provides patterns for judging Christian aptness. There are logical patterns (between doctrines), symbolic patterns, historical patterns (e.g., in salvation history) and literary patterns (e.g., type scenes). But the choice to make one pattern paradigmatic is, he insists, always an extrabiblical one. Neither historical nor literary criticism can tell us how to take Scripture today: only a study of how it functions in the church's life can do that.

Kelsey criticizes "God saying" as a comprehensive description for how God is related to Scripture. "God saying" is only one imaginative construal. The received view, in elevating the picture of "God saying," makes the Bible the source of theology and reduces theology to mere translation. God is not only "Revealer." To construe the Bible as "revelation" is to make the doctrinal aspect of Scripture the authoritative one. This fails to describe the way many theologians actually appeal to Scripture as authoritative, and so Kelsey rejects it. "God doing," according to Kelsey, more adequately grasps the diverse ways God uses the Scriptures to "shape Christian existence." Further, "shaping Christian existence" affirms God's presence with Scripture without specifying anything about the nature of Scripture itself. "Inspiration" pertains to a text's efficacious use, not its nature. Kelsey preserves a link between God and the Bible, but it is to God the sanctifying Holy Spirit rather than to God the revealing Word. Significantly, Kelsey suggests that the doctrine of Scripture should be discussed under the heading of ecclesiology rather than revelation. In so doing he gives voice to the spirit of postmodern philosophers and literary theorists who see knowledge and truth as a function of interpretive communities rather than of texts.[65]

Kelsey fails, however, to consider saying as a kind of doing. In omitting this possi-

---

[62]Kelsey calls the conjunction of these two factors the "discrimen."
[63]Darrell Jodock, *The Church's Bible: Its Contemporary Authority* (Minneapolis: Augsburg/Fortress, 1989), p. 66.
[64]Ibid.
[65]I am thinking here of thinkers such as Stanley Fish and Richard Rorty.

bility, I believe Kelsey overlooks a most fruitful pathway into an understanding of the nature of Scripture. He also overlooks the possibility that God may be doing different things in Scripture.

God and Scripture: A brief typology. My purpose in this section is to suggest, with Kelsey, that theologians do often work with a construal of God that affects their construal of Scripture (and vice versa). Specifically, I believe we can perceive a connection between one's construal of God and one's privileging a particular aspect, or literary genre, of Scripture.

1. *Classical theism.* Warfield formulated his doctrine of Scripture on the basis of classical theism as interpreted by the Reformed confessions. Scripture is God's Word because God is in control of history:

> When we give due place in our thoughts to the universality of the providential government of God, to the minuteness and completeness of its sway, and to its invariable efficacy, we may be inclined to ask what is needed beyond this mere providential government to secure the production of sacred books which should be in every detail absolutely accordant with the Divine will.[66]

Kelsey claims that God for Warfield is present in an "ideational" mode, that is, through the teaching of doctrine. This is a common description of Princeton theology. McKim describes fundamentalist theology as construing Scripture "as proposition" and Protestant scholastic theology as construing Scripture "as doctrine." There is some merit in this interpretation. Charles Hodge portrayed the Bible as the "storehouse of facts" for the theologian. God can be known because he has revealed himself in propositional form. Such a position tends to read Scripture as though everything were didactic literature, similar, say, to Paul's epistles. God thus becomes a rational communicator who is not self-revealing so much as revealing information about himself and his plan. Scripture, as a cognitive Word of God, is more like a rule of faith than a means of grace.

2. *Christocentric theism.* The situation is different in Barth, who reinterprets the sovereignty of God in terms of divine freedom. God's freedom entails that God's being is never merely a "natural" given, never "there" for the taking, but must be actively, "graciously" given. Barth worries that the identity thesis that equates the Bible with the Word of God leads to a natural theology—assuming a knowledge of God that could be had apart from God's free and gracious activity.

For Barth, God's being is in God's acts. God's being is revealed in the various acts that constitute the life and fate of Jesus Christ. Hunsinger calls this aspect of Barth's thought "actualism." Kelsey says that for Barth God is present in the mode of

---

[66]Warfield, *Inspiration and Authority,* p. 157. Jodock labels this the "supernaturalist" position because of its emphasis on the miraculous.

concrete actuality. The biblical genre that best corresponds to such actualism, as Hans Frei has shown, is narrative. Narrative is the preferred literary form for rendering an agent. We know who a person is by what the person does. If Jesus Christ is the Word of God, then narrative is the most adequate form of witness to him, insofar as narrative recounts what agents do and what people do to them.

3. *Process theism/panentheism.* The doctrine of God is somewhat underdeveloped in the thought of James Barr. In general, however, he seems to fit into the broad category of "liberal" theology, which McKim depicts as construing Scripture "as experience" and Lindbeck depicts as holding to an experiential-expressive view of doctrine. Jodock calls this the "ecclesial developmentalist" position, for it bases biblical authority "on an appeal to the historical continuity of the Christian community and the role played by the biblical documents in that history."[67] In the tradition of Schleiermacher, Barr and others, liberal theologians view both the Scriptures and theology itself as reflection on religious experience. God can be known only by his effects—through his "contact" with the believing community.

What biblical genre provides the paradigm for Barr's construal of Scripture as an inspiring record of religious experience? Is it historical narrative, with its emphasis on the development of religious traditions? Or is it, as Barton suggests, wisdom literature, with its emphasis on a people's reflection on their relationship with God?[68] In either case, the revelation or Word of God is what lies behind the Scriptures, not within it. The Bible is a historical record of human wisdom and human faith.

What doctrine of God funds this notion of a (functionally) authoritative history of tradition? Neither Barr nor Barton constructs a full-fledged systematic theology, nor do they show much interest in metaphysics. Neither would, as far as I am aware, claim to be a follower of Alfred North Whitehead or of process theology. However, by associating Protestant liberalism with process theism and panentheism, I wish to highlight the profound change in their understanding of divine activity from that of the received view. Whereas Warfield and Barth stress the transcendence of God, the liberal view we are now considering affirms an immanent God who is known through reflection on human experience. The God of process theology is not provident but only well-intentioned: his Word cannot rule, only woo. The process God is a dynamic, personal but noncoercive presence.

Such a doctrine of God seems to lie behind views of Scripture such as those of Barr and Barton. Revelation "is both an *identity*-forming presence . . . and a *community*-forming presence."[69] God is the shaper rather than the sovereign of Christian existence. God's active and purposive presence "synchronizes with the active, pur-

---

[67]Jodock, *Church's Bible,* p. 53.
[68]Barton, *People of the Book?* p. 56.
[69]Jodock, *Church's Bible,* pp. 93-94.

poseful response of human beings in a creative way."[70] The Spirit is the ongoing presence of God who participates in the community's "hunt for words" to articulate the divine presence. The Bible is authoritative only if, and to the extent to which, it actually reveals and inspires (mediates the presence of God).

What makes the biblical texts efficacious? How do we account for their salvific function? Jodock answers that they have the capacity to mediate God's identity-forming presence. But why do just these words have this capacity? The reason is unclear. For Barr, texts other than Scripture can also mediate God's presence. For if God is generally making himself available, his presence is confined neither to the canon nor to Christ. William Abraham correctly locates the weakness of this view: "The key point is this: Barr has not told us enough about God's present mode of contact with his people for us to be clear about the past mode of contact."[71]

Construing divine action and providence. "We cannot believe that God, having performed His mighty acts and having illumined the minds of prophet and apostle to understand their true import, left the prophetic and apostolic *testimony* to take care of itself. It were indeed a strange conception of the divine providential activity which would deny that the Biblical writers were divinely assisted in their attempt to communicate to the world the illumination which, for the world's sake, they had themselves received."[72]

1. *Sovereignty and Scripture.* Is it merely coincidence that at several key points in *People of the Book?* Barton appeals to divine providence? He acknowledges that his view of the Bible as human reflection on religious experience "entails some kind of theory about the providential character of the religion of Israel."[73] He affirms, with Irenaeus, that "we should not have these books without divine providence."[74] And yet when it comes to specifying why one should prefer his explanation of divine action to Warfield's, Barton is reduced to silence: "To untangle the relation of divine and human causality here is a task of the utmost intricacy—certainly not one for a biblical specialist to attempt."[75]

The main reason for the demise of the received view has been the decline of classical theism. Indeed Clark Pinnock's basic reproach of the Warfield position is that it relies on a Calvinistic theology of the sovereignty of God: "The theology of a Warfield or a Packer, which posits a firm divine control over everything that happens in the world, is very well suited to explain a verbally inspired Bible."[76] Pinnock himself prefers a "dynamic personal model" that upholds both the divine initiative and human

---

[70]Ibid., p. 97.
[71]Abraham, *Divine Inspiration,* p. 54.
[72]Baillie, *Idea of Revelation,* p. 111.
[73]Barton, *People of the Book?* p. 21.
[74]Ibid., p. 40.
[75]Ibid., p. 56.
[76]Pinnock, *Scripture Principle,* p. 101.

response. Can God achieve his will in the world? Pinnock opts, like process theologians, for a softer view of sovereignty: God may not have control over his charges, but he can outthink and outplay them. "God is present, not normally in the mode of control, but in the way of stimulation and guidance."[77]

Just how different is Pinnock's conception from that of Warfield? Warfield takes great pains to dissociate his position from a mechanical inspiration view: while it involves the Spirit's guidance, inspiration is a process "much more intimate than can be expressed by the term 'dictation.'"[78] However, at other times Warfield risks endorsing a quasi-dictation view when he suggests that providence only aids human capacities while inspiration imparts an immediate divine voice. "Inspiration" thus becomes a *donum superadditum* that enables human words to surpass human knowledge. Inspiration gives the biblical books a "superhuman" quality. Warfield comments: "It will not escape observation that thus 'inspiration' is made a mode of 'revelation.'"[79]

2. *The theological foundations of the "identity thesis": Farley's critique.* Perhaps the clearest recognition of how the doctrine of providence supports the Scripture principle comes from a theologian who seeks to overthrow it. Edward Farley's *Ecclesial Reflection: An Anatomy of Theological Method*[80] is the most incisive theological attack on the idea of the Scripture principle to date. Farley exposes the most basic presuppositions that undergird the attempt to identify the Bible with the Word of God.[81]

Salvation history, the first presupposition, expresses God's relationship to the world in a kingly or "royal" metaphor. The royal metaphor implies a "logic of sovereignty" that says God is able to accomplish his will through worldly means. "Salvation history" refers to those particular events that are under special divine control.

The second presupposition underlying the Scripture principle is the identity thesis itself. Farley asks, in light of the distinction between Creator and creature, how anything worldly can be called "divine"? How can we call the Scriptures "holy"? The principle of identity affirms an identity between what God wills to communicate and what is brought to language by a human individual or community. However, Farley correctly acknowledges (as other theologians do not) that what is in view is not an ontological but a *cognitive* identity. That is, the identity is between what God wants to communicate—the message—and the linguistic or literary expression of it. A creaturely medium

---

[77]Ibid., p. 104.

[78]Warfield, *Inspiration and Authority*, p. 153. Warfield sounds almost contemporary when he observes that the production of Scripture was a long process that involved varied divine activities (p. 156).

[79]Ibid., p. 160.

[80]Edward Farley, *Ecclesial Reflection: An Anatomy of Theological Method* (Philadelphia: Fortress, 1982).

[81]A shorter version of Farley's argument may be found in Farley and Hodgson, "Scripture and Tradition," pp. 61-87.

for God's communication is thus regarded as a substitute presence not for the divine being but for a divine *work*. This can only be brought about because of divine causal efficacy, hence the royal metaphor. "The principle of identity . . . is the basis for attributing infallibility and inerrancy to what appears to be human and creaturely."[82]

The temptation is to extend further these "identifications"—to a confession or a magisterium—and ensure the survival of the divine content. Farley points out that the later secondary representatives tend to become dominant (e.g., Chalcedonian Christology is now the framework for reading Scripture) and occasionally claim the same privileged status as the original (e.g., biblical and papal infallibility). The end result of this principle is that the divine will becomes inseparable from human interpretation (Scripture, doctrine). Farley worries that the divine-human identity is often claimed for the work of theology itself. Identifying human interpretation with the divine will mistakes vehicles of social duration for deposits of immutable truth. To identify Scripture and doctrine with the divine will violates the very essence of the church, whose role is to witness to revelation and redemption, not equate itself with them. Farley, like Barr, wants to locate the redemptive presence of Christ (the Word of God) in the continuing life of the church.[83]

The conjunction of these two presuppositions—the royal metaphor and the identity thesis—gives rise to what Farley takes to be an inescapable dilemma: either God controls or he does not control, and if he controls he controls something or everything. If we retain the royal metaphor (which salvation history does) and say that God controls only a section of history, then we must conclude that God wills a non-salvific presence in most of human history. If we retain the royal metaphor and say that God's will and action are universal, then the horrors of history have the same relation to God's causality as salvific events. Both of these options fail to meet the problem of evil: either God is involved with only part of the world in a loving way, or he determines all creation and is thus a determiner of good and evil.[84]

In short, salvation history—together with the Scripture principle that it supports—founders on theodicy: either God is King or God is love. In order to say that God is love, Farley abandons the logic of salvation history and the royal metaphor and thus deprives the Scripture principle of its foundation. In short, Farley would have us choose between the Scripture principle and a loving God: "To summarize, with the first alternative, salvation history, God's activity as heteronomous causality violates creaturely freedom and autonomy and therefore divine goodness and love are sacrificed. With the second alternative, these features are retained but salvation history goes. In my view there is really no choice."[85]

---

[82]Farley, *Ecclesial Reflection*, p. 39.
[83]Farley and Hodgson, "Scripture and Tradition," p. 65.
[84]Farley, *Ecclesial Reflection*, p. 156.
[85]Ibid., p. 157.

The three-stranded cord that binds together the doctrine of God, the nature of biblical authority and theological method in Farley's hands becomes a violent whip that has had its day. Farley prefers theological arguments that, like Scripture and divine activity itself, are persuasive rather than coercive. He ultimately rejects the Scripture principle because it relies on a picture of divine sovereignty that he can no longer accept: if God is in control of everything, why has he acted/spoken only *here*, in Scripture and the life of Jesus, not there?

A Way Forward: Divine Speech Acts

A contemporary doctrine of Scripture neglects the issues raised by the identity thesis and the royal metaphor only at its own peril. The former pertains to the nature and location of God's being or presence, the latter to the nature of and character of God's activity or providence. Both issues concern the relation between the Word of God and the human words of Scripture. This section briefly reviews the major problems and offers a pathway toward their resolution.

The identity thesis. By far the major obstacle to ecumenical agreement about the doctrine of Scripture is the identity thesis. I have argued that the task of a doctrine of Scripture is to explain how the church can confess that the Bible is the Word of God. It may be helpful at this point to heed McGrath's reminder about the nature of doctrine: doctrines should be recognized to be "perceptions, not total descriptions, pointing beyond themselves towards the greater mystery of God himself."[86] The question is: does the identity thesis, which locates the Word of God in Scripture, constitute an accurate, and adequate, perception about the nature of God's Word?

Both Barth and Barton argue that only Christ is truly the Word of God. Both decry what they take to be an idolatrous elevation of the canon over Christ: Scripture cannot save, but points to the One who can. The most they will admit is an *indirect* identity between Scripture and the Word of God.

Does this mean that the Word of God is not a verbal phenomenon? Does the "Word" of God have nothing to do with semantics (the study of verbal meaning)? Is it possible to articulate a biblically based, theologically sound and philosophically intelligible account of how the human words of Scripture can be or become the Word of God? What sense can it make to refer to Scripture as "God's Word written"?

It is not clear how, or even whether, Barth accounts for the properly semantic moment of God's self-disclosure. In the last resort, Barth's doctrine of Scripture moves to Christ *too fast*. Our challenge will be to reinterpret the identity thesis in such a way as to do full justice to the semantic as well as personal dimension of God's self-revelation. The way forward for the doctrine of Scripture must be, I

---

[86]McGrath, *Genesis of Doctrine,* p. 17.

believe, to overcome the dichotomy of personal-propositional revelation.

The royal metaphor. Throughout this chapter I have claimed that one's doctrine of Scripture depends on one's view of God and of God's activity. Farley assumes that we must choose: *either* God controls history and manifests his control through his secondary presence in Scripture-doctrine-church *or* humans are free and historically conditioned, in which case the Bible is only a human witness to antecedent revelation. Farley, Kelsey and Barr prefer a more "populist" metaphor: God is not over his people but among them. This personal-relational model of conceiving God's presence and activity is not, however, without its problems.

First, there seems to be a covert identity thesis at work here too, though the locus of God's presence is not the canon but the community. For Farley and Barr, the people of God have become the real authority for theological judgments. Farley and Barr assume that God is best reflected in the ecclesia. As I have suggested, such an emphasis on the authority of interpreting communities is well suited to the postmodern intellectual climate.

It is far from clear, however, by what means one can discern God's presence. The theological diversity within the Scriptures is nowhere near as pronounced as the theological diversity of the believing community. Indeed, just as many biblical scholars insist that we must speak of biblical theolog*ies,* so here we must speak of believing communit*ies.* In which community do we best see God's inspiring presence? Should we include the German Christians who supported Hitler? The main weaknesses in Barr's view, however, is that it does not correspond to what we see in Scripture. Even a casual reading of the Old Testament and New Testament discloses communities that are primarily *unbelieving* for much of their histories. What kind of authority can interpreting communities have if they misinterpret God?

God's communicative action. "It is my conviction that the next impetus to rethink our evangelical doctrines of inspiration and revelation is going to come from the modern communications theory."[87] I wish now to argue, in light of Ramm's suggestion, that the principal mode in which God is "with" his people is through speech acts. I find it difficult to conceive how one could discern God's presence or know anything whatsoever about God without communication on God's part. Mere "contact" is not enough. As Abraham observes: "Without His word, the alternative is not just a tentative, carefully qualified guessing at what God is doing, but a radical agnosticism."[88]

1. *The God who speaks.* As speech act philosophers J. L. Austin and John Searle have effectively shown, language is a productive force and a phenomenon of social

---

[87]Bernard Ramm, *The Evangelical Heritage: A Study in Historical Theology* (Grand Rapids, Mich.: Baker, 1979), p. 163.

[88]William Abraham, *Divine Revelation and the Limits of Historical Criticism* (Oxford: Oxford University Press, 1981), p. 23.

interaction. Scripture portrays God as a speech agent. Much of what God does—warning, commanding, promising, forgiving, informing, calling, comforting—he does by speaking. I know of no compelling philosophical or theological reason not to take Scripture's depiction of the speaking God seriously. If God is a personal, albeit transcendent, agent, and if God can do some things, then there is no prima facie reason that God could not speak as well. Indeed in the prophets the distinction between the one true God and false gods is precisely the criterion of speech: false gods are dumb.

The burden of proof lies with views that claim God, for some reason, cannot speak. I find it interesting that even theologians who eschew the notion of propositional revelation are often happy to talk about the promises of God and divine forgiveness. On my view, however, promising and forgiving are nothing if not speech acts. One can promise, for example, only by uttering a sentence that counts as a promise—by performing a speech act.

2. *A verbal Word?* Langdon Gilkey criticized the biblical theology movement for being only half orthodox and half modern. On the one hand it speaks of God's mighty acts in history, but on the other it affirms the modern assumption that God does not intervene in the natural-historical causal nexus. The "acts of God" of which the neo-orthodox theologians spoke seem to be visible only to the eyes of faith. There is an uncomfortable dualism between these mighty acts and actual history. This leaves the notion of an act of God empty or equivocal.

I have precisely the same problem, in regard to literature rather than history, with Barth's notion of the "Word" of God. On the one hand this Word is verbal, but on the other hand it is something that becomes verbal only when God freely and graciously decides that it does so. There is an uncomfortable dualism between the Word of God and the actual words of Scripture which threatens to render each equivocal. Barth apparently wants to have the Word both ways. On the one hand he identifies the Word of God with Jesus Christ—a personal, not propositional, communication. On the other hand he writes: "The personalizing of the concept of the Word of God, which we cannot avoid when we remember that Jesus Christ is the Word of God, does not mean its de-verbalizing."[89] At one point Barth actually calls revelation a divine "speech act" *(Rede-Tat)*.[90] And somewhat surprisingly, Barth says that "we have no reason for not taking the concept 'Word of God' in its primary and literal sense. 'God's word' means God speaks. 'Speaks' is not a symbol."[91]

What actually happens to the literal meaning of the human words when God graciously decides to disclose himself through Scripture in a miracle whereby the Bible "becomes" the Word of God? It would appear that the Word's "being," like the being of

---

[89]Barth, *Church Dogmatics* 1/1, p. 138.
[90]Ibid., p. 162.
[91]Ibid., p. 150.

God himself, is only in becoming. Barth fails to provide anything like a clear conceptual analysis of this event. Even Hunsinger's generally helpful guide to Barth fails to clarify matters here: "Although intrinsically incapable by nature, theological language has been made to correspond to its subject matter by grace."[92] God's Word for Barth is a semantic miracle. We may recall that for Barth what is at stake is ultimately God's freedom. God's being is not a natural "given," either in nature or in Scripture. While the human words are witnesses to the living Word, the Spirit is "Lord of the hearing." The phenomenon of a text that sometimes is and sometimes is not the Word of God prompts Pinnock to ask: "Is this Word of God . . . really the name for a personal experience?"[93]

Scripture, I suggest, is best viewed neither as a set of propositions nor as a sacramental story that mysteriously renders Christ, but rather as a set of human-divine communicative actions that do many different things. What one *does* by saying something is called an "illocutionary act." What the Bible does is not arbitrarily related to its nature but rather a function of its illocutionary acts. What Scripture does follows from what Scripture is.

The Bible as polygeneric. It is vital in this regard to see the various literary genres in Scripture as diverse kinds of illocutionary acts. Just here biblical criticism provides an indispensable service. Biblical criticism should "exercise its explanatory function in helping us to appreciate the letter of the biblical text in all its foreignness and complexity. It is to teach us to be close readers, straining to hear something other than our own voices."[94] Biblical criticism best fulfils this task when it becomes literary criticism and explores the nature of the biblical genres. The most spectacular and damaging interpretive errors are mistakes about genre. To misidentify a literary genre is to mistake the kind of illocutionary act a text performs.

1. *Speech genres.* Everything we say or write belongs to some speech or literary genre. Every communicative act belongs to a particular kind—warning, greeting, state-

---

[92]Hunsinger, *How to Read Karl Barth,* p. 44. Much has been said about the inadequacy of human words to speak of God. But in an important sense we can say what lies beyond our words. While we may not have nouns that "name" God, speaking is much more than a matter of "labeling" the world. Indeed the noun is not the basic unit of meaning in language. That privilege goes rather to the speech act. Moreover, the sentence has been described as the infinite use of finite means. Where individual words are unable to articulate the majesty and glory of God, sentences succeed in so doing.

I do not wish to be misunderstood. I am not suggesting that sentences transcribe the divine reality without remainder, but rather that some sentences themselves contain a "surplus of meaning" (Ricoeur) that is richer than any literal paraphrase.

[93]Clark Pinnock, *Tracking the Maze: Finding Our Way Through Modern Theology from an Evangelical Perspective* (San Francisco: Harper & Row, 1990), p. 56.

[94]Christopher E. Seitz, "Biblical Authority in the Late Twentieth Century: The Baltimore Declaration, Scripture-Reason-Tradition and the Canonical Approach," *Anglican Theological Review* 75 (1993): 484.

ment, question and the like. What are the implications for a doctrine of Scripture of seeing the Bible as composed of a variety of divine communicative acts? We may say, first of all, that there is no one kind of speech act that characterizes all of Scripture.

The limits of Kelsey's approach, or at least of the construals he studies, are here exposed for the reductions they are. Any attempt to catch up what is going on in Scripture in a synoptic judgment must be careful not to reduce the many communicative activities to a single function, be it doctrinal, narrative or experiential. Even Barth's construal of Scripture as "rendering an agent" is too narrow.

2. *Generic theology?* Theologians typically construe the diversity of God's Word in terms of one kind of genre. But any doctrine of Scripture that levels its generic diversity is bound to be inadequate. Such a reduction of generic multiplicity to generic uniformity represents both a literary and a theological mistake: literary, for one has misread the nature of a particular communicative act; theological, because one has mistaken the nature of God's involvement with the text.

Barton, we may recall, privileges the wisdom genre: "what is written in the Bible, with rare exceptions such as certain prophetic oracles, is presented as human words about God, not as words of God to man."[95] So too, I think, does Bultmann. For Bultmann theology is about the self-understanding of faith, which pertains more to existential possibilities that are always already present than to the significance of contingent historical events. Pannenberg, by according pride of place to anticipations of the end of history, makes the apocalyptic genre paradigmatic for Scripture and theology. And the list could go on. Kelsey himself opts for a broader vision of God "shaping Christian existence" through Scripture, but he overlooks how the Bible achieves this out of his concern to elevate "God doing" over "God saying."[96]

3. *Divine speech acts and the identity thesis.* What follows for the identity thesis from the model of God's Word as speech act? Does the Bible only become God's Word, or is it permanently God's Word? Does one's recognition of the Bible as God's

---

[95] Barton, *People of the Book?* p. 56. On the same page Barton acknowledges that revelation involves a complex relation between divine and human causality. Whereas Barton locates this relation behind the text, I wish to argue that the Bible itself suggests that this relation characterizes the scriptural texts themselves.

[96] Several scholars have now acknowledged the exegetical significance of the diverse literary genres in Scripture. Paul Ricoeur sees a theological significance as well and suggests that God is "named" or revealed differently in the various biblical genres. The Word of God, far from being monolithic, is rather mediated through a host of literary forms. Barton cites Ricoeur as one who has taken seriously "the need to make theological sense of the fact that Scripture contains genres which cannot be assimilated to the model of divine communication to men" (*People of the Book?* p. 71). What Barton means, of course, is that not all biblical genres correspond to the prophetic paradigm. True enough. But I have argued that God's communicative agency does not involve only statements about the past, or future, but includes questions, warnings, hymns, stories, letters and so on. God's Word written is not simply timelessly true propositions.

Word make it so, or is Scripture the Word of God even if no one accepts it? It is, of course, important not to lose sight of the personal reference of the Word of God to Jesus Christ. No one claims that the Bible is a part of the Godhead. What is being claimed is that the Bible is a "work" of God. While Christ is a fully human and fully divine agent, all we are claiming for Scripture is that it is a fully human and fully divine *act*.[97] Does bibliolatry still remain a possibility?

What sort of temptation is bibliolatry? What many theologians find objectionable in bibliolatry is its elevation of biblical statements to the status of absolute truths—a "paper pope." The worry is that the identity thesis leads to a view of the Bible as a textbook of timeless truths and inerrant propositions that could be "mastered" by students of divinity. Pinnock suggests that the appeal of such heaven-sent cognitive information is undeniable, for it offers "an apparently safe refuge from the relativising effects of history."[98]

But there are two problems with the argument that the identity thesis caters to a (perhaps sinful) desire for epistemological certainty. First, what absolute truths there are in Scripture still have to be interpreted. If they were to become a possession, it would be only after careful (and humble) exegetical work, whose outcome remains provisional. Second, and more important: the Word is not a collection of timeless truths that can be either withdrawn or left on deposit. Scripture is composed not only of assertions but of commands, warnings, promises and so forth. One does not "possess" a divine command; one obeys it. Insofar as the recurring theme of Scripture is good news, its content is to be shared with the world, not hoarded in the church.

4. *Divine speech acts and the royal metaphor.* A false view of "word" has held us captive: word as "literal" truth claim. Strictly speaking, letters (words, nouns) do not refer; only speech acts (and speakers) do that. God does many things with human language besides assert truths. Against Farley, we need not conclude that the identification of Scripture with God's Word leads to authoritarianism in theology. Not all speech acts assert timeless truths. One must first look to what is said/done in Scripture before equating "saying" with "making timeless truth claims." Theologians must recognize, and respect, the divine communicative action for what it is.

5. *Covenantal communication.* God's communicative action reaches its culmination in the Christ event. But this event needs to be interpreted. Even G. E. Wright

---

[97]Moreover, God's mighty speech acts work through and with the human speech acts of Scripture. God's action is communicative rather than coercive: "If we are looking for a way of picturing God's action which indicates what sort of efficacy it has, we should consider the spoken word. . . . Speech, too, is an action of sorts, but not the sort of action that can by itself deprive another of his freedom" (Robert King, *The Meaning of God* [London: SCM Press, 1974], p. 92).

[98]Pinnock, *Tracking the Maze,* p. 48.

acknowledges this principle: "By means of human agents God provides each event with an accompanying Word of interpretation, so that the latter is an integral part of the former."[99] God's diverse communicative action finds its unity in the end toward which it is variously directed: Jesus Christ, the supreme covenant blessing and crown of creation.

In his influential book which launched speech act philosophy, *How to Do Things with Words,*[100] J. L. Austin cites "making a covenant" as an example of a "commissive" speech act. God appears to his people as an agent who performs promissory speech acts which commit him to continuous activity. Without this commissive communicative act, how would we know of God's intentions? According to speech act philosophy, an agent signals an intention by invoking the appropriate linguistic or literary conventions. One's intending something is more than just randomly related to the meaning of one's sentence.

God is the agent who is true to his Word. "I will be your God and you will be my people"—such is the fundamental covenant promise. It is by keeping his word that God reveals himself to be who he is. The Bible is God's covenant "deed," in both senses of the term. It is an act and a testament: a performative promise wherein certain unilateral promises are spoken, and a written document that seals the promise. The canon is a collection of diverse speech acts that together "render" the covenantal God.

A trinitarian theology of holy Scripture. The Bible is the "Word" of God because it is the result of divine self-communicative action. I now want to show how God's being in speech act is trinitarian.

1. *God's being in speech act.* Barth arrived at the doctrine of the Trinity by analyzing God's self-revelation with the schema revealer-revelation-revealedness. Can we similarly unfold the notion of verbal revelation in the light of speech act theory? Such an attempt may contribute to that rethinking of revelation in terms of communication theory for which Ramm called more than ten years ago.

The Father's activity is locution. God the Father is the utterer, the begetter, the sustainer of words. He is the agent who *locutus est per prophetas* in former times, and who now speaks through the Son (Heb 1:1-2). God the Father's locution is the result of his providential involvement in the lives of the human authors of Scripture. God works in and through human intelligence and human imagination to produce a literary account that renders him a mighty speech agent.

The Logos corresponds to the speaker's act or illocution, to what one *does* in saying. The illocution has content (reference and predication) and a particular intent (a

---

[99]Wright, "God Who Acts," p. 26.
[100]J. L. Austin, *How to Do Things with Words,* 2nd ed. (Cambridge, Mass.: Harvard University Press, 1975).

force) that shows how the proposition is to be taken.[101] It is illocutionary force that makes a speech act *count* as, say, a promise. What illocutionary act is performed is determined by the speaker; its meaning is therefore objective.

The third aspect of a speech act is the perlocutionary. This refers to the effect an illocutionary act has on the actions or beliefs of the hearer. For example, by "arguing" (illocution) I may "persuade" (perlocution) someone.

The great benefit of this analysis is that it enables us clearly to relate the Spirit's relation to the Word of God. First, the Spirit illumines the reader and so enables the reader to grasp the illocutionary point, to recognize what the Scriptures may be doing. Second, the Spirit convicts the reader that the illocutionary point of the biblical text deserves the appropriate response: "But these are written that you may believe that Jesus is the Christ" (Jn 20:31).

The Spirit does not alter the semantics of biblical literature. Locution and illocution inscribed in Scripture remain unchanged. The Spirit's agency consists rather in bringing the illocutionary point home to the reader and so achieving the corresponding perlocutionary effect—whether belief, obedience, praise or some other. The testimony of the Spirit is nothing less than the effective presence of the illocutionary force. Thanks to the Spirit's testimony, these biblical words *deliver*. They convey illocutionary force and so liberate. Historical-critical scholarship alone cannot save the perlocutionary effect.

Is such a view similar to Barth's insistence that God the Spirit remains "Lord of the hearing" and that the Bible "becomes" the Word of God only when the Spirit illumines the reader? That depends on how one views communicative acts and on how one defines *Word*. Here evangelicals disagree:

☐ "People do not have to receive the Bible for it to become the Word of God. It *is* the Word of God objectively whether received as such or not."[102]

☐ "The presence of the living Word in the Holy Scripture is not an ontological necessity but a free decision of the God who acts and speaks."[103]

Speech act theory gives us a better purchase on Barth's trinitarian explication of divine revelation. According to the analysis I have just given, we may say that the Bible is divine-human communicative action: its locutions and illocutions are the result of double agency, what Austin Farrer calls the "causal joint." The warnings, promises, assertions, prophecies, songs and so forth in Scripture are divine as well as human communicative acts. God's Word is really written. However, whereas human discourse relies on rhetoric to achieve the intended perlocutionary effects, Scripture's

---

[101] See John Searle, *Speech Acts: An Essay in the Philosophy of Language* (Cambridge: Cambridge University Press, 1969), chap. 2.

[102] Lewis and Demarest, *Integrative Theology*, 1:168.

[103] Bloesch, *Holy Scripture*, p. 26.

perlocutionary effects depend on the Spirit's agency.

Is the Bible a divine communicative act, then, if a reader fails to respond to its illo-cutions? This is a subtle query. In the context of a trial, is the testimony of a witness true only if it is judged to be so? No, for a jury can err. Testimony can be true even though it is not accepted. The answer to my query depends on whether one includes the reader's response (the perlocutionary effect) in the definition of "communicative act." Interestingly, the Oxford English Dictionary includes both possibilities under its first entry: "communication" may be "the act of imparting propositions" or "the prop-osition communicated." Perhaps the solution is to affirm both that Scripture *is* the Word of God (in the sense of divine locution and illocution) and that Scripture may *become* the Word of God (in the sense of achieving its intended perlocutionary effects).

2. *Personal or propositional?* The doctrine of Scripture has been much damaged by an overestimation of the dichotomy between "God saying" and "God doing," between propositional and personal revelation. Paul Helm offers a salutary reminder: "There is no antithesis between believing a proposition and believing a person if the proposition is taken to be the assertion of some person."[104] Propositions need not always be taken as assertions. *Every* illocutionary act involves a proposition, but not all illocutions have the force of assertions. Promises have propositional content too (e.g., sense and reference) but are marked by commissive rather than assertive force.

Barr is therefore partly right and partly wrong when he suggests that the real issue in propositional revelation is genre and function.[105] He is right in saying that genre mistakes cause the wrong kind of truth values to be attached to biblical sentences; he is wrong in thinking that all propositional revelation must be assertive (and thus that some biblical sentences are false).

Against the dichotomy between personal and propositional revelation, I am inclined to say that *all* our encounters with persons are "propositional," in the sense of involving communicative action. Revelation, as Ramm puts it, is both a meeting and a knowing. An encounter with a person may be "propositional." Not all proposi-tions need to be characterized as "rationalistic." Not all propositions are put forward as claims of precise correspondence to reality. To suggest so is to caricature the notion of propositional revelation. Again: all illocutionary acts have a propositional element. The point to remember is that propositions may be taken, or given, in vari-ous ways (as assertions, questions, commands, etc.).

God identifies himself by his speech acts. Better: what God does with language reveals God's identity, just as our actions reveal who we are. The way we encounter

---

[104] Paul Helm, "Revealed Propositions and Timeless Truths," *Religious Studies* 8 (1972): 135-36.
[105] Barr, *Bible in the Modern World,* p. 125.

a person is largely through his or her speech acts, and one's identity is largely a function of whether, and how, one keeps one's word.[106] God identifies himself as the One who utters words on our behalf and as the One who keeps his words. God's Word is utterly reliable, whether that word is a command, a warning, a promise, forgiveness or, yes, even an assertion.

The neo-orthodox emphasis on the self-revelation of God is faulty only in its neglect of the semantic means by which this disclosure takes place. Scripture is itself a mighty speech act by which God reveals himself in his Son Jesus Christ. The Scriptures do not become a substitute for Christ but are the means by which the memory of Christ is given substance. God's personal identity is rendered in language and literature. Behavior without verbal interpretation is too ambiguous to reveal anything.

It is the fuzziness of the tie between illocutionary act and verbal meaning that ultimately makes Barth's account of the Word of God unsatisfactory. Is God so free that God's speech is exempt from the normal obligations that accrue to the uttering of a promise? It is difficult to see how Barth can talk about the divine promise if he were not prepared to acknowledge divine speech acts, such as promising, to which God holds himself accountable. As Austin put it: "Our word is our bond."[107] God too, therefore, is "tied" to these texts.

Conclusion: The Humility of the Word

Does God speak in Scripture? Calvin refers both to the majesty of God's Word and to the divine stammering. To say that God's word is "majestic" is to say that his illocutionary acts are mighty. It is to invoke, in explicit fashion, the royal metaphor. On the other hand, God's mighty speech acts are clothed in the form of human speech genres. In order to communicate with humanity, God has accommodated himself to creaturely media, to human language and literature, to human flesh and blood. God's Word, incarnate and inscripturate, is God in communicative action. The might of God's speech is hidden by the divine lisp as the might of God's saving act is hidden in Christ's cross. God's power is revealed in weakness; this applies to God's speech acts too.[108] A word of forgiveness can be ignored, or it can be accepted. The divine speech acts, though humbly clothed, are nevertheless powerful enough to liberate the captive, empower the weak, fill the empty and sustain the suffering.

The word that goes out from God's mouth will not return empty but will accom-

---

[106] See Paul Ricoeur, *Oneself as Another* (Chicago: University of Chicago Press, 1992), chaps. 5-6.
[107] Austin, *How to Do Things with Words*, p. 10.
[108] Need weakness, need *humanity* for that matter, imply fallibility, and beyond that, actual failure? Perhaps fallibility, but not actual fault. Many books—textbooks, phonebooks, cookbooks—contain no error. Fallibility means only "capable of making mistakes," not that mistakes have actually been made.

plish its purpose (Is 55:11). What is this purpose? I suggest it is *embodiment*. Jesus Christ is the unique and definitive embodiment of God's Word, the divine foundation and fulfillment of the covenant. The church, as the body of Christ, is a secondary and derivative embodiment—the human response to the covenant of grace. The written Word seeks, in the power of the Spirit, to be embodied in the life of the people of God. Scripture's warnings demand attention, its commands obedience, its promises faith. The Word must be continually "recontextualized"—"embodied in the lives, words and actions of contemporary human beings."[109] As literary style generates a corresponding lifestyle, so the biblical genres engender a culture—the kingdom of God.[110] To follow *these* words is to cultivate true freedom.

God is indeed involved in shaping Christian existence, through biblical law, wisdom, song, apocalyptic, prophecy, narrative and the other literary forms of Scripture. These are the ordained means of rendering, by the testimony of the Spirit, the meaning, the reality and the implications of God's act in Christ. The message of the Scriptures may be errant foolishness to some, but to those who are being saved it is the power of God (1 Cor 1:18). A doctrine of Scripture is therefore right to conceive of the Bible as God's mighty speech acts: "not merely as the record of the redemptive acts by which God is saving the world, but *as itself one of these redemptive acts,* having its own part to play in the great work of establishing and building up the kingdom of God."[111]

[109] Jodock, *Church's Bible,* p. 143.
[110] See chapter eleven in this volume.
[111] Warfield, *Inspiration and Authority,* p. 161 (emphasis mine).

Six

From Speech Acts to Scripture Acts

The Covenant of Discourse
& the Discourse of the Covenant

A word is dead
When it is said
Some say.
I say it just
Begins to live
That day.
EMILY DICKINSON

*K*now thyself." Socrates' demand that philosophers reflect on what it is to be human has been taken up by many in other disciplines as well. It is possible to study the functions of humans considered as biological organisms (physiology), emotional and mental dysfunctions (psychology), the actions of individuals in the past (history) as well as the behavior of various human groups (sociology). The study of human language is similarly interdisciplinary. It can be studied by linguists, cognitive psychologists, historians, logicians, philosophers and, yes, theologians. If the third-century theologian Tertullian was right to define a "person" as a being who speaks and acts (which is not so very far from what a philosopher, Peter Strawson, would say about individuals some seventeen hundred years later), then it may well be that we have to treat both topics—language and humanity—*together*.

To study language, then, is to touch on issues involving a whole world and life view. Some approaches to the study of language's origin and purpose presuppose that human existence and behavior are best explained in terms of Darwinian evolution. In a highly regarded work on linguistic relevance, for instance, Dan Sperber and Deirdre Wilson suggest that human cognition is a biological function whose mechanisms result from a process of natural selection: "Human beings are efficient information-process-ing devices."[1] For Sperber and Wilson, language is essentially a cognitive rather than communicative tool that enables an organism (or device) with memory to process information.[2] On the other hand, George Steiner claims, on the basis of his experience of transcendence in literature, that "God underwrites language."[3] Such disparate analy-ses should give philosophers pause. They also raise the question whether Christians should not approach the study of language from an explicitly Christian point of view. Such, however, is the intent of the present article: to reflect on language from out of the convictions of Christian faith.

Craig Bartholomew has called for those interested in the theological interpretation of Scripture to clarify just how the relation of philosophy to theology bears on bibli-cal study.[4] Here we probably do not want to follow Tertullian's suggestion, stated in the form of a rhetorical question, that Jerusalem (theology) has nothing to do with Athens (philosophy). We would do better to follow Alvin Plantinga's advice to Chris-tian philosophers not to let others—people with non-Christian worldviews—set the agenda, but to pursue their own research programs. What is needed, he says, is "less accommodation to current fashion and more Christian self-confidence."[5] Indeed, why should *Christian* faith be excluded from the search for understanding when other faiths—including modernity's faith in instrumental reason, empiricism and natural-ism—are not?

Christian theology takes faith in the revelation of Jesus Christ, attested in the Scrip-tures, as its ultimate criterion for judging what is true, good and beautiful. While not at all turning our back on the results, assured or not, of modern learning, it is impor-tant to acknowledge that all of us, Christians and non-Christians alike, come to the data with interpretive frameworks already in place. The present essay approaches the "data" concerning language and interpretation with an interpretive framework largely structured by theological concepts. Instead of excluding considerations of Christian doctrine from my inquiry, I intend to make explicit use of them. This is not to turn one's back on philosophy, but to let human reason be guided and corrected by Christian doctrine and by the language and literature of Scripture itself. Only by first conducting "theological investigations" of language and literature *in general* can we

---

[1]Dan Sperber and Deirdre Wilson, *Relevance: Communication and Cognition,* 2nd ed. (Oxford: Blackwell, 1995), p. 46.
[2]Ibid., p. 173.
[3]George Steiner, *Real Presences* (Chicago: University of Chicago Press, 1989).
[4]Craig Bartholomew, "Philosophy, Theology and the Crisis in Biblical Interpretation," in *Renewing Biblical Interpretation,* ed. Craig Bartholomew (Grand Rapids, Mich.: Zondervan, 2000).
[5]See his 1983 inaugural lecture to the John O'Brien Chair of Philosophy at Notre Dame, "Advice to Christian Philosophers."

come to discuss with philosophy the task of interpreting Scripture.

The most fruitful recent development for the dialogue between philosophy and theology about language is undoubtedly the emphasis on language as a species of human action: speech acts. Examining what people *do* with language represents a fascinating case study for the broader dialogue between philosophy and theology. Of course the idea that humans do things *in* speaking was well known to the very earliest biblical authors, even without the analytic concepts of speech act philosophy.

The present essay evaluates the extent to which speech act philosophy approximates and contributes to what theologians want to say about language. This is not to say that speech act categories will dominate the discussion. On the contrary, we will see that Christian convictions concerning, say, divine authorship, the canon and the covenant will lead us to both modify and intensify the typical speech act analysis. My goal is to let the "discourse of the covenant" (Scripture) inform and transform our understanding of the "covenant of discourse" (ordinary language and literature).

The first, and longer, part of the chapter explores what I shall call the "covenant of discourse": a philosophy *and* theology of communication. My hope is to achieve a certain consensus about language and understanding based on a strategic appropriation of certain philosophical concepts that will be amenable to Christian biblical scholars and theologians.

In the second part I turn to the "discourse of the covenant," that is, to a consideration of the Bible as written communication. Dealing with the canon—a complex, intertextual communicative act—will lead us to modify and develop our understanding of how biblical language works in ways that go beyond typical speech act theory. However, the benefit of using speech act categories to describe the divine discourse in Scripture will also become apparent. Throughout the essay I examine not only what speech acts are, but the implications for looking at language as a form of human action as well, particularly for the sake of interpretation. Here too the leading theme of covenant proves helpful, insofar as interpretation is largely a matter of fulfilling one's covenantal obligation toward the communicative agents, canonical or not, who address us.

The conclusion highlights what follows for biblical interpreters from this analysis. It is not insignificant that the leading categories for describing interpreters—witness, disciple—are drawn from the language of theology. For nothing less will do in describing our properly *theological* responsibility to hear, and to understand, what God and neighbor are saying/doing when they address us.

The series of theses running throughout the argument summarize the main claims and seek to provide the contours for the "mere communicative hermeneutic." My hope is that they begin to articulate an emerging consensus regarding the theological interpretation of Scripture.

The Covenant of Discourse: Speech Acts

> 'Tis writ, "In the beginning was the Word."
> I pause, to wonder what is here inferred.
> The Word I cannot set supremely high:
> A new translation I will try.
> I read, if by the spirit I am taught,
> This sense: "In the beginning was the Thought."
> This opening I need to weigh again,
> Or sense may suffer from a hasty pen.
> Does Thought create, and work, and rule the hour?
> 'Twere best: "In the beginning was the Power."
> Yet, while the pen is urged with willing fingers,
> A sense of doubt and hesitancy lingers.
> The Spirit comes to guide me in my need,
> I write, "In the beginning was the Deed."
> Johann Wolfgang von Goethe, *Faust*

Goethe, of course, did not have the advantage of having read Austin or Searle, or for that matter, me! We can therefore forgive him for not having Faust write something like the following:

> The mystery of the sign I now have cracked;
> "In the beginning was the *communicative act.*"

Much of what I wish to say about the significance of speech acts for contemporary interpretation in general, and of the Bible in particular, is implicit in these lines from Goethe's *Faust*. They also have the merit of directing our attention to Jesus Christ in such a way that Christ becomes, as Bartholomew puts it, "the clue to theology and philosophy . . . the clue to the whole creation."[6] Communicative action, as I understand it, indeed takes up and integrates the four possibilities for translating *logos* that Faust considers: word, thought, power, deed. For as we shall see, word-deeds involve both thought (propositional content) and power (illocutionary force).

To begin with, Goethe roots our thinking about speech acts in theology—trinitarian theology, to be exact. Faust is, after all, translating a text about the incarnation of the Logos. His successive tries at translating *logos,* taken together, suggest that the Word is God's-being-in-communicative-action. This approximates Karl Barth's trinitarian analysis of divine revelation in terms of revealer-revelation-revealedness.[7] God communicates himself—Father, Son and Spirit—to others. In terms of communication theory, the triune God is communicative agent (Father/author), communicative action

---

[6]Bartholomew, "Philosophy, Theology."
[7]Karl Barth, *Church Dogmatics* 1/1, trans. G. W. Bromiley (Edinburgh: T & T Clark, 1956).

(Son/Word) and communicative result (Spirit/power of reception). I shall suggest in due course that the canon too may be considered a species of divine communicative action.

Goethe in this passage also sets us thinking about the relation of God's speech act—the Logos—to the words of Scripture. Interestingly, John Macquarrie, in his own free rendering of John 1:1, suggests the following translation: "Fundamental to everything is meaning."[8] The question that needs to be asked here is whether the incarnation alone exhausts the divine speech or whether Scripture itself may be legitimately considered a divine speech act of sorts.

A new interdisciplinary consensus? For some fifteen years I have been exploring the potential of viewing language and literature in terms of speech acts.[9] I have been heartened by wayfarers from other disciplines who have since joined the pilgrimage toward the promised land of a communicative hermeneutic. In May 1998 participants representing five theological disciplines met in Cheltenham, England, to think together about how speech act philosophy might afford the conceptual resources with which to meet the contemporary crisis in biblical interpretation.[10] The discussion that follows attempts to set forth these conceptual resources, as well as their philosophical and theological basis.[11]

Why speech acts? First, because thinking in terms of speech acts approximates the way the Bible itself treats human speech. Moreover, as Nicholas Wolterstorff has demonstrated, speech act categories have the potential to help us appreciate what it means to call the Scriptures God's Word. For me, however, the most important contribution speech act philosophy makes is to help us to break free of the tendency either to reduce meaning to reference or to attend only to the propositional content of Scripture. Viewing texts as doing things other than representing states of affairs opens up possibilities for transformative reading that the modern obsession with informa-

---

[8]John Macquarrie, "God and the World: One Reality or Two?" *Theology* 75 (1972): 400.

[9]The earliest effort was "The Semantics of Biblical Literature," in *Hermeneutics, Canon and Authority,* ed. D. A. Carson and John Woodbridge (Grand Rapids, Mich.: Zondervan, 1986), pp. 49-104.

[10]The disciplines, and their representatives, were philosophy of religion (Nicholas Wolterstorff), Old Testament (Craig Bartholomew), New Testament (Anthony Thiselton), biblical theology (Francis Watson) and systematic theology (Kevin Vanhoozer).

[11]Some readers may want to know what, if any, advances the present essay makes on my *Is There a Meaning in This Text?* The new elements include a "missional" model of communication; a more consistent use of the concept of covenant and the concomitant notion of imputation; a reinvigorated, if not entirely new, defense of the priority of illocutions over perlocutions that incorporates William Alston's recent work on illocutionary acts; a new argument, based on an analysis of biblical covenants, for seeing a greater continuity between oral and written discourse than is often the case in contemporary philosophy and literary theory. Finally, and perhaps most surprisingly, there is an almost complete absence of the term *meaning!*

tion has eclipsed. Finally, speech act philosophy commends itself as perhaps the most effective antidote to certain deconstructive toxins that threaten the very project of textual interpretation and hermeneutics.

I am under no illusions about the difficulty of achieving such a consensus. Speech act theorists themselves are divided over, say, the relative importance of intentions (Paul Grice) over conventions (John Searle). The challenge is to specify the most important commonalities—the greatest common denominator, as it were—without diluting the remaining significant differences. So while we can agree on certain basic presuppositions and principles, some significant differences may persist.

Where do we agree? In my opinion there is considerable agreement about the following points: (1) We use language to do more than picture states of affairs. None of us believe that the sole point of language is reference or representation. We affirm that language is transformative as well as informative. Hence we are interested in the pragmatics as well as the semantics of language.[12] (2) We reject the idea, rampant among some postmoderns, that meaning and reference are radically indeterminate, as well as the related idea that the author is "dead" or irrelevant to the process of interpretation. (3) We agree that *action,* rather than representation, should be the operative concept, and that this entails certain *rights* and *responsibilities* on the part of authors and readers. In particular, we see the promise as the paradigm for what is involved in speech action (though in the present work I put forward *covenant* as an alternate). (4) We reject the idea, again rampant among some postmoderns, that readers are free to manufacture or to manipulate textual meaning in order to serve their own aims and interests.

Where do we differ? Two areas come to mind. First, some think that speech act analysis is most helpful in understanding particular parts of the Bible, for instance, Jesus' parables or Paul's preaching (Thiselton). Others use speech act theory to recover the notion of authorial discourse and to open up possibilities for reading the whole Bible as divine discourse (Wolterstorff). Still others, while not denying the pre-

---

[12]Anthony Thiselton misleadingly associates me with those who see meaning in terms of reference, largely because I used the phrase "single determinate meaning" (Thiselton, " 'Behind' and 'In Front of' the Text: Language, Reference and Indeterminancy," in *After Pentecost: Language and Biblical Interpretation,* ed. Craig Bartholomew, Colin Greene and Karl Möller [Grand Rapids, Mich.: Zondervan, 2001], p. 103 [published in the U.K. and Europe by Paternoster Press, Carlisle, U.K.]). Let me take this opportunity, then, to state that what I think is determinate is the whole communicative act. "Single" and "determinate" were intended to shore up the notion that what fixes the meaning of a text is what the author said/did, and that this does not change at the behest of the reader. "Single determinate meaning" is shorthand for the realist's intuition that the author's intentional action, however complex, is what it is and cannot be changed by interpreters at a later date. Moreover, determinate communicative acts often have presuppositions, entailments and implications that preclude our viewing interpretation in terms of "endlessly wooden replication" of a single propositional content.

ceding points, see speech act philosophy as contributing categories for a full-fledged interpretation theory that resonates well with properly theological themes (Vanhoozer). The continuing discussion thus concerns whether biblical interpreters should be concerned to develop specific strategies for reading Scripture in particular (special hermeneutics) as opposed to applying biblical and theological insights to interpretation theory in general (general hermeneutics).

Second, there is some difference over the role of the interpretive community's response and audience reception of a text. One symptom of this difference may be seen in the various ways we appreciate (or not) the potential contribution of Paul Ricoeur's hermeneutic philosophy.[13] Wolterstorff explicitly criticizes Ricoeur's theory of "textual sense" interpretation, whereas Thiselton explores Ricoeur's (and Hans Robert Jauss's) suggestion that the meaning of a literary work rests on the dialogical relation between the work and its audience in each age. The question this raises for biblical interpretation pertains to the mode and time of God's speaking: are God's speech acts in Scripture once for all, or does God speak anew in each present reading (and if this is so, does God say the same thing or something different on different occasions)?

My purpose in what follows is to develop some of the leading themes, philosophical and theological, of a hermeneutic of communicative action in order better to display what lies at the core of this emerging interdisciplinary approach. By no means is speech act philosophy the queen of the hermeneutic sciences, however. How could it be? It was developed to deal primarily with oral, not literary, discourse, and quite apart from any concern for a specifically Christian view of persons or language. So while speech act philosophy has formulated some key insights and concepts, I shall feel free to make use of other theories (e.g., relevance theory) and concepts (e.g., imputation) as well. The aim is to sketch a model—and it will be no more than a sketch—of what we might call, after C. S. Lewis, "mere hermeneutics."

Anatomy of communicative action. In order to succeed in some inquiry, says Aristotle, one must ask the right preliminary questions. If we seek to address, and resolve, the contemporary crisis in biblical interpretation, I believe the right preliminary questions concern language and communication. What is language? What is communication? These questions are philosophical inasmuch as they pertain to basic concepts—concepts that lie behind, and often govern, the actual practice of interpretation. My strategy in what follows is to explore what I take to be the best answers to such questions, where "best" is defined in terms of experiential and logical coherence, comprehensiveness and compellingness on the one hand and in

---

[13]I shall later cast this disagreement in terms of the distinction between illocutions and perlocutions and in terms of their relative roles in interpretation and understanding.

terms of "fittingness" with Scripture and Christian tradition on the other.

Language versus speech. Most theories of linguistic communication have been based on a "code" model, where language is the code and communication a matter of encoding and decoding messages. On this view, words are signs that represent thoughts: encoded thoughts. The main problem with this model is that it is descriptively inadequate, for several reasons: (1) some of the information conveyed is not actually encoded, (2) understanding involves more than decoding linguistic signals, and (3) words do more than convey information. The code theory leaves unexplained the gap between the code and the meaning that is actually communicated by the language. Mere mastery of a sign system is no guarantee of understanding.

Far more adequate are descriptions of language *use* or *discourse* (the technical term for language in use). Of course not just any use is in view. Repeating "The rain in Spain . . ." for the sake of improving one's English accent is not yet discursive. (For the same reason, standing on a hermeneutics textbook to reach the top shelf counts as a *use,* but not as an interpretation, of a text). Let us define *discourse* as "what someone sometime says to someone about something."

Ricoeur makes an important distinction between semiotics (the science of the sign) and semantics (the science of sentences). A sentence, or speech act, is not simply a larger sign but an entity of a completely different order.[14] A sentence is the smallest unit of language that can be used on a particular occasion to say something; it is more than the sum of its semiotic parts and requires a level of description all its own.[15] For Ricoeur, this distinction between semiotics and semantics "is the key to the whole problem of language."[16] The distinction thus deserves closer inspection.

A simple example shows how the linguistic meaning alone of a sentence-long discourse falls short of encoding what a speaker *S* means when she says, "Coffee would keep me awake." There is no problem breaking the code of this sentence. The language is clear and stands in good syntactical order. The information conveyed is that coffee, presumably the caffeinated kind, has an accelerating effect on the human nervous system. But what does the discourse—the use of the sentence on a given occasion—mean? Decoding the language is not enough. We need to know something about the circumstances of the discourse. Consider two different scenarios where *S* is asked "Would you like some coffee?" (1) *S* is studying for an exam late at night and is struggling to stay awake. (2) *S* has finished studying for an exam and would like to

---

[14]Paul Ricoeur, *Interpretation Theory: Discourse and the Surplus of Meaning* (Fort Worth: Texas Christian University Press, 1976), pp. 6-7.

[15]We may here note a parallel between the self and the sentence: each is what Peter Strawson calls a "basic particular," that is, an irreducible concept that cannot be explained by something more basic (see Vanhoozer, *Is There a Meaning?* p. 204).

[16]Ricoeur, *Interpretation Theory,* p. 8.

retire early in order to be fresh for the exam the following morning. In the first case the meaning of S's statement "Coffee would keep me awake" is "yes," in the second instance "no." What this example shows is that communication involves more than linguistic encoding; it involves, in ways that we have yet to specify, the broader, unencoded circumstances of someone's use of language.

Communication: The design plan of human language. Words alone have at best only meaning potential. Human languages should not be thought of as free-floating sign systems that enjoy an existence independent of their users. Even a dictionary simply reports the common usages associated with a given word. Hence to study a language apart from studying what language users do with it is a hopeless enterprise.

The philosopher William Alston advocates what he terms the "Use Principle": "An expression's having a certain meaning consists in its being usable to play a certain role (to do certain things) in communication."[17] A language, then, is a vehicle for communication. He claims that "interpersonal communication is the primary function of language; its other functions, for example, its use in the articulation of thought, are derivative from that."[18] By "speech act" or "discourse," then, I shall refer to language-in-communicative-use.

Using language to communicate is not an arbitrary happening. I have elsewhere argued that the "design plan" of language is to enable communication and understanding.[19] Here then is our first working thesis, a thesis that arises from a theological conviction.

---

1. Language has a "design plan" that is inherently covenantal.

Language is a divinely given human endowment and serves as a crucial medium for relating with God, oneself, others and the world. For the moment my focus is on interpersonal communication. My hope is that certain developments in recent philosophy will help us better to understand what we believe about language on the basis of our Christian theological convictions.

A missional model of communication (theology). The sender-receiver model is well known in communication studies. According to this model, a source (speaker, author) encodes a message into a linguistic signal (speech, text) that serves as the channel that conveys the message (through air, across time) to a destination (listener, reader) that receives the message by decoding the signal.[20] What light, if any, might

---

[17]William P. Alston, *Illocutionary Acts and Sentence Meaning* (Ithaca, N.Y.: Cornell University Press, 2000), p. 154.
[18]Ibid., p. 155.
[19]Cf. Vanhoozer, *Is There a Meaning?* pp. 204-7.
[20]Cf. Sperber and Wilson, *Relevance*, pp. 4-5.

theology have to shed on debates about the nature of language and communication? While I certainly do not think that everything in our world is a "vestige of the Trinity," I do think that in this case there is something more than an interesting analogy. The doctrine of the Trinity, I shall argue, stands not as an analogy but as a paradigm for human communication.

The triune God is an eternal communion of divine persons. Presumably, there is some "communication" between Father, Son and Spirit—the so-called immanent Trinity. Nevertheless, I propose to develop a theological understanding of communication on the basis of the "economic," not the immanent, Trinity. "The economic Trinity" is the technical term for the way the triune God progressively reveals himself in human history. The economic Trinity is the name for God in communicative (and self-communicative) action.

I can thus state a second thesis.

2. The paradigm for a Christian view of communication is the triune God in communicative action.

The so-called missions of the Son and Spirit, authorized by God the Father/Author, bear a certain resemblance to the economy of the "sender-receiver" model of communication. They represent God's attempt to reach out to human others in truth and love. The Son is God's "mission" to the world, as is indicated by the words of Jesus in John 17:18: "as thou didst send me into the world." Jesus' mission, at least in part, was to give to his disciples the words the Father had given him (Jn 17:8). At the core of Christian theology, then, is the theme of the *word sent*.

Irenaeus believed that the Father's work is two-handed: the Word provides form or shape (content), the Spirit provides animation and movement. "Sending," then, lies at the very heart of Christian thinking about the triune God. And in a biblical passage that largely accounts for my appreciation of speech act philosophy, we read God's declaring, through the prophet Isaiah, that his Word, like rain, is sent to nourish and enliven life on earth: "So shall my word be that goes forth from my mouth; it shall not return to me empty, but it shall accomplish that which I purpose, and prosper in the thing for which I sent it" (Is 55:11). If every piece of human discourse similarly aims at accomplishing *something,* then it follows that every statement is a "mission statement."

Does the notion of mission entail the code model of communication? That depends on whether the "Word," to return to Faust, is conceived exclusively as "thought" (information) or as "power" and "deed" as well. From the perspective of theology, the mission of the Son—God's "sending" his Word to earth—should be seen in terms of acting, not encoding. For the sending is not simply a conveying of information but a conveying of God's very person (a conveying of *communicative* as well as *informative* intentions). For what God purposed in sending the Son (and later the Holy Spirit) involved much more than conveying information. The purpose of the sending of God's Word was as much *transformative* as informative. Indeed the Gnostics (and others since then) erred precisely at this point, in thinking that salvation is only a matter of knowledge. If that were the case, then information alone could save us. But it is not the case. By communicative action, then, I have in mind the *many* kinds of missions on which verbal messages are sent.

Communication as intentional action. The missional model of communication, together with the design plan of language, encourages us to think of discourse in terms of intentional action. Humans typically conceptualize human behavior in intentional terms. Robert Gibbs, a cognitive psychologist, adopts the "cognitive intentionalist premise": "People's experiences of meaning are fundamentally structured by their inferences about the intentions of others."[21] Gibbs believes there is empirical evidence demonstrating that human beings are cognitively "hard-wired" to look for intentions in human linguistic, artistic and cultural products. Just as babies know to focus on their parents' faces and eyes, so listeners and readers attend to embodied intentions. "People use words to convey to each other first and foremost their communicative intentions, not the semantic meanings of the words or the unconscious causes that might underlie such intentions."[22]

Here again we see how one's view of language is conditioned by one's view of what it is to be human. From a Christian vantage point, human beings are neither mechanical automatons nor free spirits but embodied agents. Christian reject the modern picture of the sovereign subject who enjoys mastery over language and the postmodern picture of the victim of systemic socioeconomic or political forces who is more bespoken by than an active speaker of language.[23]

The subject of intentionality is far too complex to discuss thoroughly here. Yet it is far too important a subject to ignore. For what an agent does is ontologically and logically tied to the concept of what the agent intended. It follows that understanding is a matter of recognizing the agent's intention, for it is the intention that makes an act one thing rather than another. Whether a slap on the back is a greeting, an attempt to save someone from choking, a congratulatory gesture or an aggressive movement depends on the intent with which the act is performed. On my view, then, authorial

---

[21]Raymond W. Gibbs Jr., *Intentions in the Experience of Meaning* (Cambridge: Cambridge University Press, 1999), p. 326.

[22]Ibid., p. 42.

[23]For a fuller account of how human beings are communicative agents in covenantal relation, see Kevin Vanhoozer, "Human Being, Individual and Social," in *The Cambridge Companion to Christian Doctrine,* ed. Colin Gunton (Cambridge: Cambridge University Press, 1997), esp. pp. 175-83.

intention returns, not as a feature of psychology so much as an irreducible aspect of action. Intentions are embodied in a material medium, enacted via bodily movement or a verbal statement.

One popular though misleading view of intention involves identifying it with an agent's plans or desires ("I intend to be there on time"). What an agent *plans* to do and what an agent actually does are two different things. It is perhaps the failure to preserve this distinction, more than anything else, that accounts for the demise in current literary theory of the concept of authorial intention.

Only the concept of intention enables us to view actions as more than mere bodily movements. When we say that someone gives, or attacks, or borrows, or protects, we are describing not mere bodily movements but intentional actions. Similarly, only the concept of intention enables us to view words and texts as more than material marks. Only the concept of author's intention enables us to specify what the author is doing in using *(tending to)* just these words in just this way.

The so-called death of the author is actually a form of the worst sort of reductionism, where communicative acts and intentions are stripped away from the text, leaving an autonomous linguistic object. This is similar to reducing the wink—a communicative act in its own right—to the blink, that is, to a minor (and meaningless) bodily movement. If we ignore the intention—the factor that accounts for the unity of an action—we lose the act itself: no intention, no wink. Now, each stage of the physiological process of winking—the neural firings, the muscular contraction— could be described separately, but no one stage is the location of the intention, or the wink. "We murder to dissect." Failure to ascribe intentions thus results in "thin" descriptions. Descriptions are thin when they must rely on lower-level concepts like "neural firings" rather than higher-level, intentional categories like "flirting."

It is important to locate the cause of the text at the right level: not at the infrastructure (the sign system) nor at the level of the superstructure (the prevailing ideology) but at the level of the completed act, the level to which the author was attending. It is vitally important to resist "eliminative semiotics": the tendency to reduce meaning to morphemes in motion. Intention cannot be reduced to the nonintentional without losing the phenomenon of action itself.[24] The author's intention is the intrinsic factor that constitutes an act as what it is. A speech act, then, is the result of an enacted communicative intention.

Relevance. A relative newcomer to the scene of communications studies, rele-

---

[24]Gibbs prefers to think of a continuum rather than a stark contrast between the conscious and the unconscious. What people do, he argues, may be more or less intentional: "Any individual speech or artistic event actually reflects a hierarchy of intentions, with each level having a different relationship to consciousness" (*Intentions,* p. 33). I take Gibbs's point as a qualification rather than a contradiction of the position outlined here.

vance theory, has made several helpful contributions toward helping us understand communication in terms of intentional action. Dan Sperber and Deirdre Wilson write: "To communicate is to claim an individual's attention: hence to communicate is to imply that the information communicated is relevant."[25] According to Sperber and Wilson, communication is less a process of encoding than "a process of inferential recognition of the communicator's intentions."[26] Communication succeeds when the audience is able to infer the speaker's meaning from her utterance.

Relevance theory builds on insights into the dynamics of conversation associated with the philosopher Paul Grice. Grice's basic idea is that once a piece of behavior is identified as communicative, it becomes reasonable to assume that the communicator is trying to make herself understood. What a speaker says is evidence of the speaker's communicative intention. Hence the "cooperative principle": Make your conversational contribution such as is required for accomplishing its particular purpose in the particular situation in which it occurs. Be as informative as required, but not more so.

Relevance theory tries to answer three questions: What did S intend to say? What did S intend to imply? What was S's intended attitude toward what S expressed and implied? In many cases the linguistic meaning of a speech act by itself fails to communicate what the speaker means. Grice's cooperative principle, together with its four maxims, helps addressees make sense of a communicative act whose linguistic meaning appears irrelevant or ambiguous. The sentence "Coffee would keep me awake" appears on the surface—that is, with regard to its linguistic meaning only—to say something about the effect of caffeine on the human organism.[27] A literalist might reply, "I didn't ask you whether it would keep you awake, I asked if you wanted some." Such a reply fails to draw what Grice calls an *implicature* from the original speaker's answer.

Grice suggests that when hearers are confronted with a discourse that appears to be irrelevant or uninformative, and that therefore violates the cooperative principle, they must derive the intended message ("No thanks, I don't want any coffee") from their understanding of the broader situation in which the conversation takes place. An important question for biblical interpretation is whether there is a counterpart of the "cooperative principle" for *written* discourse.

According to Sperber and Wilson, communication concerns the conveying of relevant information. On their view, the purpose of communication is to alter the "cognitive environment"—the set of assumptions a person is capable of representing conceptually and accepts as probably true—of the addressee. To communicate

---

[25]Sperber and Wilson, *Relevance,* p. vii.
[26]Ibid., p. 9.
[27]For an extended analysis of this example, see ibid., pp. 11, 16, 34-35, 56.

successfully, they believe, we need some knowledge of the other's cognitive environment. As Raymond C. Van Leeuwen puts it, "Human communication presupposes existence in a *shared,* meaningful world . . . with encultured contexts of meaning that enable receivers of a language act (including book or text) to infer meaning that is relevant to their existence or situation."[28]

Every piece of discourse, merely by being expressed, makes a certain claim on our attention. By addressing us, a speaker manifests her intention to modify our cognitive environment in some way. Simply to say "Hi!" modifies the addressee's cognitive environment by making her aware of the speaker's presence. We assume that what is said is relevant and that we will benefit from the effort it takes to process the information. The "presumption of relevance" is that the level of cognitive effects—the communicative payoff, as it were—is never less than is needed to make the discourse worth processing. In other words, the cognitive *effort* of understanding must never outweigh the cognitive *effects* of understanding. We shall return to relevance theory in due course.[29]

Communicative action as locutionary, illocutionary and perlocutionary. On one level, speech act philosophy corresponds admirably with the missional model of communication as intentional action. Indeed the very title of J. L. Austin's seminal lectures *How to Do Things with Words* conveys his intention to move us beyond the picture of language as essentially a vehicle for transferring information (call it the FedEx model of communication). Speech acts, as Austin and others have pointed out, have other agendas than transmitting information.

This is not the place to develop a full-fledged theory of speech acts. There are many such accounts. Suffice it to say, by way of introduction, that most speech act theories distinguish three distinct aspects or dimensions of what we do with language. Consider the following utterance: "Jesus is Lord." Any of the following might be a correct report of what the speaker did in this utterance: (1) made vocal sounds, (2) spoke with a French accent, (3) said "Jesus is Lord," (4) confessed that Jesus is Lord, (5) told his neighbor that Jesus is Lord, (6) explained how her cancer had suddenly gone into remission, (7) made me feel unspiritual by comparison.

---

[28]Raymond C. Van Leeuwen, "On Bible Translation and Hermeneutics," in *After Pentecost: Language and Biblical Interpretation,* ed. Craig Bartholomew, Colin Greene and Karl Möller [Grand Rapids, Mich.: Zondervan, 2001], p. 286.

[29]Jürgen Habermas makes a similar point about what we might call the "presumption of rationality." Every competent speech act must meet three validity conditions: it must be true (it must represent something in the external world); it must be truthful (it must sincerely express the speaker's intentions or inner world); it must be right (it must fit appropriately into the context of the social world). These three conditions together make up the presumption of communicative rationality (Jürgen Habermas, *The Theory of Communicative Action,* trans. Thomas McCarthy [Boston: Beacon, 1984], 1:305-8).

To break down this example into speech act categories: 1-3 are *locutionary* (Austin, Searle) or *sentential* (Alston) acts. Nothing really communicative happens on this *locutionary* level. Statements 1 and 2 in particular are wholly indifferent to the *content* of the utterance. Each of the first three fails to describe the communicative intention of the speaker. This aspect—the essential aspect of the communicative act—is the *illocutionary* dimension. This was Austin's term for what one *does* in saying something. Statements 4 and 5 report the illocutionary act. Statement 6 is somewhat more complicated. It may be a legitimate implicature or entailment of the speech act, though only a consideration of the broader context of the communicative act could make that clear. Something altogether different, however, is happening in 7, which is a report on the *effect* or byproduct of the illocutionary act. Austin called this the *perlocution:* what effect is produced *by* the saying of something. As we shall see, the distinction between illocutions and perlocutions is absolutely fundamental to interpreting texts in terms of communicative intentions and communicative acts.

If analytic philosophy conducts an anatomy of communicative action, then the notion of illocution must be judged to be its heart. Interpretation is essentially a matter of identifying and specifying illocutionary acts: what speakers and authors have *done* in tending to their words as they have. Hence another principle emerges.

---

3. *"Meaning" is the result of communicative action, of what an author has done in tending to certain words at a particular time in a specific manner.*

Philosophy comes into its own as far as biblical interpretation is concerned when it trains its analytic sights on illocutionary acts. Accordingly I shall have recourse on more than one occasion to William Alston's work on illocutionary acts. I shall also try to deepen Alston's account by considering illocutions from the biblical-theological perspective of the covenant.

For the moment, suffice it to say that Alston has produced what is probably the single most complete apology for viewing meaning in terms of illocutionary acts. To be precise, he defines sentence meaning in terms of illocutionary act *potential*. A sentence's having a certain meaning consists in its being usable to play a certain role (to do certain things) in communication. The meaning of "Jesus is Lord" is that one can use it to confess that Jesus is Lord. It has this potential because of its propositional content, with *Jesus* as subject and *Lord* as predicate, and because its utterance enables the speaker to assume a certain stance toward that proposition—in this case an "assertive" stance.

Searle, Alston and Wolterstorff all take *promising* to be a, if not the, paradigmatic speech act. "My doing *A* in the future" is the content of my promise. Yet

FIRST THEOLOGY

identifying this concept does not exhaust what is *done* in promising. To promise is to lay an obligation on oneself with regard to some future action. Alston and Wolterstorff in particular emphasize the agent's assuming a normative stance toward the content of that promise. In other words, in uttering a promise the speaker assumes responsibility for the conditions for its satisfaction. Making a promise, then, alters one's normative stance; one is now responsible for doing something for which one was not responsible before making the promise. In Alston's words: "An utterance is most basically made into an illocutionary act of a certain type by virtue of a normative stance on the part of the speaker."[30] Assuming a normative stance means that one becomes liable to judgments of appropriateness and rightness. What a speech act *counts as* depends not only on the words used but on the intersubjective situation (the circumstances, conventions, rules, etc.) that render language usable.

Perhaps the purest examples of how people do things with language are what Searle terms "declaratives" and Alston "exercitives." This class of speech acts comprises "verbal exercises of authority, verbal ways of altering the 'social status' of something, an act that is made possible by one's social or institutional role or status."[31] The crucial fact here is that an utterance brings something about only if the utterer has the appropriate authority and makes his utterance in the appropriate circumstances. Examples of such "exercitive" speech acts would be "You're fired!" and "I now pronounce you man and wife." Another important example, examined by Ricoeur, is the pronouncement of a judicial sentence: "I sentence you to life imprisonment." "Sentencing" is, for Ricoeur, the place where the universality of law and the particularity of life situations meet and hopefully issue in wise and just judgment.[32] The point here is that these communicative actions involve much more than a linguistic code or the sheer meaning of words. They involve communicative agents taking responsibility for what they do with their words.

From communicative action to covenantal relation. Communicative action is essentially an interpersonal affair. There is thus a fourth, overarching dimension to communicative action: the *interlocutionary.* Let us call an interlocutor—either an agent or a recipient of communicative action—a *communicant.* Interestingly, even Austin, a philosopher, had an inkling of the covenantal dimension of illocutions, for

---

[30]Alston, *Illocutionary Acts,* p. 71.
[31]Ibid., p. 34.
[32]Ricoeur insists that the purpose of the judiciary is to ensure that words win out over violence, justice over vengeance (Paul Ricoeur, *The Just* [Chicago: University of Chicago Press, 2000], p. ix). Later in the same work he draws attention to a certain parallel between the trial and the process of textual interpretation. The analogy is apt, for as I argue below, interpreting the meaning of a text is essentially a matter of ascribing intentional action to a responsible agent.

he wrote, "Our word is our bond."[33] Thiselton has helpfully drawn attention to biblical material on the rights and obligations associated with human speech. Of course in
the context of Scripture, as he rightly points out, these "rights" do not attach to autonomous individuals, as in Enlightenment thinking, but appear in the context of covenants with others and with the other: "*Covenantal* obligations presuppose a network
of *relationality* which has a different basis from that of 'rights' for an isolated,
orphaned self who is not even 'the sojourner-guest within the gates.'"[34]

Whereas Thiselton pays special attention to covenantal promising, I tend to see *all*
communicative action in covenantal terms. Philosophers are generally more comfortable speaking of cultural and social conventions than of covenants. However, only if
we allow our theological convictions to deepen philosophy at this point by invoking
the design plan of language will a more adequate description of communication as a
species of *covenantal* action be possible. Communicative privileges and responsibilities are best seen in a covenantal framework. Language is a divinely appointed covenantal institution. Hermeneutics, as the discipline that aims to understand the
discourse of others, presupposes an interactive, interlocutionary self that exists only
in relation to others. What we need to see is that all discourse is a form of interpersonal, communicative—which is to say covenantal—action. The parties to the covenant of discourse, the communicants, are essentially two: speaker and hearer, or
alternately, author and reader.

The "who": Speaker/author. Deconstruction, it has been said, is the death of God
put into writing. The death of God is nothing less than the death of the Author of history. If there is no God, then ultimately history has no meaning, for the course of
events would no longer represent God's communicative action but a meaningless,
because impersonal, sequence of cause and effect. Similarly, if bereft of human
authors, texts would be radically indeterminate for the simple reason that we could
not identify what illocutionary act has been performed.[35] Texts without authors
would be mere entities, as devoid of meaning as the marks ocean waves leave upon
the sand. Why? Because meaning is the result of intentional (illocutionary) action, not
a natural event. There is verbal meaning only where someone means, or has meant,
something by using particular words in a specific context in a certain way.[36] The

---

[33]J. L. Austin, *How to Do Things with Words* (Oxford: Clarendon, 1962), p. 10.

[34]Anthony Thiselton, *The Promise of Hermeneutics* (Grand Rapids, Mich.: Eerdmans, 1999), p.
217. Thiselton also remarks that Cartesian individualism predisposes us to overlook the
interlocutionary dimension. For an illocution usually makes a claim not only of relevance
but of something else on the listener.

[35]For the sake of economy I shall refer to agents of communicative action, whether oral or
written discourse, as "authors."

[36]See Jorge J. E. Garcia's excellent article "Can There Be Texts Without Historical Authors?"
American Philosophical Quarterly 31 (1994): 245-53.

death of the author thus leads to hermeneutic nonrealism and to the suspicion that meaning, like God, is merely a projection on the part of the reader/believer. Neither hermeneutics nor theology can afford to follow Ludwig von Feuerbach's suggestion that what we find—God, meaning—is actually only a projection of ourselves.[37]

The theological response to deconstruction is to stress "the providence of God put into writing." The missions of the Son and Spirit, not to mention the mission of the Word of God spoken or written (Is 55:11), is an outworking of divine providence. Now human authorship is a (pale) reflection of divine authorship. Created in the image of God, humans have been given the "dignity of communicative agency." Humans are communicative agents in covenantal relation, creatures able to enter into dialogical relations with others and, to a certain extent, with the world. To be a communicative agent means that one has the ability to set a language system in motion and so bring about an act of discourse.

Think of the author as a historical agent whose action is fixed in the past. What one communicates or does with words depends both on the historical circumstances of the act and on the state of a particular language at a given place and time. In order to make sense of *p-a-i-n,* for instance, we need to know whether an author was doing something in English or in French. Unless we can associate texts with historical authors, they have potential meaning only.

The historical aspect does not exhaust the nature of the author's agency, however. The author is also an aesthetic agent who structures his or her text to make the communicative act effective. But we can go even further. The author is a moral agent who interacts with others in what he or she says and does. Authors of narrative, for instance, do not only tell stories but instruct people in right living, or give hope to the needy, or warn the unrighteous of the fate that awaits them. Finally, the author is a religious agent who in relating to words in a certain way ("let your yea be yea, and your nay, nay") either fulfils or fails his God-given responsibilities in the exercise of his tongue. In other words, the way we relate to our everyday discourse, as well as to the discourse of others, will prove us to be either faithful and true or untrustworthy liars. (The same religious quality pertains, as we shall see, to interpreters.)

We saw earlier that illocutionary acts involve authors' taking normative stances toward the content of their acts. To promise is to undertake to fulfill certain obligations and hence to make oneself responsible. I now want to generalize this point by suggesting that *the author is the one to whom certain illocutionary acts can be imputed.* Imputation is the operative concept, for it has to do both with the *capacity to act* and with the related notion of *responsibility for action.* It is also a notion that has an interesting pedigree, both in philosophy and in theology. Kant distinguished

---

[37]For a fuller analysis of this point, see Vanhoozer, *Is There a Meaning?* chap. 2.

persons and things precisely in terms of imputation: "A *person* is the subject whose actions can be *imputed* to him. . . . A *thing* is that to which nothing can be imputed."[38] *Imputation* names, in Ricoeur's words, "the idea that action can be assigned to the account of an agent taken to be its actual author."[39] The core of the concept of imputation is the attribution or ascription of an action to its author. The Latin *putare* implies calculation *(computare),* a kind of bookkeeping regarding who has done what. The metaphor of a balance book, at the limit the Book of Life (Rev 20:12), underlies the idea of "being accountable for."

Being an author, then, carries certain responsibilities. Yet every person who speaks is an author, that is, a communicative agent. Again we see the confluence of the themes of language and personhood. It is important to recognize, however, that authors are not only agents but *patients,* in the sense of those to whom something is done. For once the communicative act is complete, its author can do no more. We may here recall relevance theory's insistence that every speech act is a tacit request for someone's attention. Authors must "suffer" the reception of their works, including the possibilities that no one will pay attention or that some will pay the wrong kind of attention. What I have said about the author's agency needs to be balanced, then, by an acknowledgment of the author's passivity. The author is both an active agent and a passive "other"—a significant, signifying "other." The covenant of discourse works in both directions: the author is responsible for her action; the reader is responsible for her response to the other and the other's act.

The "what": Word, speech or text act. Up to this point I have compared language use with action. Speech is both a "doing" and a "deed." *Communication* can refer both to the process and to the product, both to the action of communication and to the completed act. The attempt to say just what a communicative act is may be helped by reversing the polarities in order to think of action as a form of speech. For actions have speech act attributes. In the first place, the doing of an action corresponds to the locution. Second, actions have propositional content (e.g., "S performs act y on the ball") and illocutionary force (e.g., kicking).[40] Finally, actions too may have perlocutionary effects ("S scores a goal").

Alston helpfully shows how illocutions "supervene" on locutions. One can perform

---

[38]Immanuel Kant, *The Metaphysics of Morals* (Cambridge: Cambridge University Press, 1996), p. 16.

[39]Ricoeur, *The Just,* p. xvi.

[40]Alston's analysis is slightly different. For him the "content" of an act includes object and performance: "kicking the ball." With regard to illocutionary acts, this means that for Alston the content of the act includes both its propositional component and its illocutionary force. For Searle (and usually me) "content" refers primarily to the propositional component of the illocutionary act. In my view the difference is largely terminological, though it ought to be kept in mind.

an illocutionary act only on the basis of locutions—words, sentences—though illocutions cannot be reduced to locutions. The same propositional content, say, "Jesus' walking on water," can be attended to in different ways, and these different ways—asserting, asking, advising—determine the "direction of fit" between our words and the world.

A text, then, is a communicative act with matter (propositional content) and energy (illocutionary force). Genuine interpretation, to stick with the analogy, conserves textual matter and energy; deconstruction lets it dissipate. It does not follow from the fact that a text is a determinate communicative action that there is only one correct way to describe it. Opinions as to what an author did may, and should, change as we come to a deeper understanding of the author's language and circumstances. But this is not to say that the author did something that she had not done before. At the same time, it is important to acknowledge that authors may intend to communicate complex, multilayered intentions.

There is an instructive dialogue in the opening pages of *The Hobbit*. The scene is Gandalf's first visit to Bilbo Baggins:

"Good morning!' said Bilbo, and he meant it. . . .
    "What do you mean?" he [Gandalf] said. "Do you wish me a good morning, or mean that it is a good morning whether I want it or not; or that you feel good this morning; or that it is a morning to be good on?"
    "All of them at once," said Bilbo. "And a very fine morning for a pipe of tobacco out of doors, into the bargain."

A bit later Bilbo uses the same locutionary act with a very different illocutionary intent:

"Good morning! We don't want any adventures here, thank you!"
    "What a lot of things you do use *Good morning* for!" said Gandalf. "Now you mean that you want to get rid of me, and that it won't be good till I move off."

Bilbo's first "Good morning" performs more than one illocutionary act. Well and good. I would say that in this case his single determinate meaning was, in fact, compound rather than simple. If need be, I would be prepared to abandon the term *single,* though I think it is still implied in the really important qualifying term *determinate.*

What is at stake in the foregoing is the status of the literal sense. The foregoing analysis suggests a definition that is also my fourth thesis.

---

4. The literal sense of an utterance or text is the sum total of those illocutionary acts performed by the author intentionally and with self-awareness.

There are many ways to study discourse, but not all are germane to the task of describing communicative action. Genuine interpretation is a matter of offering appropriately "thick descriptions" of communicative acts, to use Gilbert Ryle's fine phrase. A description is sufficiently thick when it allows us to appreciate everything the author is doing in a text—that is, its illocutions.

Typically, historical-critical commentaries describe either the history and process of a text's composition or "what actually happened." According to the traditional "picture theory" of meaning, the literal sense would be what a word or sentence *referred* to. On my view, however, the literal sense refers to the illocutionary act performed by the author. The important point is that the literal sense may require a fairly "thick" description in order to bring it to light. For Ryle, a thin description of, say, a wink would be one that offers a minimal account only ("rapid contraction of the eyelid"). The description is thin because it omits the intentional context that alone enables us to see what someone is doing. Much modern biblical scholarship, because of similar omissions, yields only "thin description." Text criticism gets bogged down on the locutionary level; historical criticism is obsessed with reference. The matter and energy of the Gospels is largely lost by historical-critical commentaries. The most important thing we need to know about a text, I submit, is what kind of communicative act(s) it performs and with what content.

The "wherefore" and "whereto": Reader. All speech acts, I declared, are mission statements, words on a mission: to accomplish the purpose for which they have been sent. That purpose, according to relevance theory, is to alter the addressee's cognitive environment in some way. The "whereto" of communicative action is the reader; the "wherefore" of communicative action is the reader's transformation (at a minimum, this means the reader will entertain a new thought).

Authors often wish to accomplish something by their discourse. The author of the Fourth Gospel, for instance, wants to elicit readers' belief that Jesus is the Christ by telling Jesus' story. The question is whether this extra effect—eliciting belief—should count as part of the author's communicative action. I think it should not. Alston is right: an illocutionary act may well produce perlocutionary effects, but it does not *consist* in such effects. The only effect that properly belongs to the author's illocutionary act is *understanding*—the recognition of an illocutionary act for what it is. Sperber and Wilson agree: "For us, the only purpose that a genuine communicator and a willing audience necessarily have in common is to achieve uptake: that is, to have the communicator's informative intention recognized by the audience."[41] In a neat reversal of Augustine's formula "Take up and read," we can say that understanding is a matter of reading and *taking up* (the illocution).

---

[41]Sperber and Wilson, *Relevance,* p. 161.

180

Philosopher of law R. A. Duff defines intention as "acting to bring about a result" and distinguishes it from both desire and foresight.[42] A desired consequence is like a perlocution; an unforeseen consequence is more like an accidental effect. Similarly, G. H. Von Wright uses the term *result* for results that are conceptually constitutive of an action and *consequence* for those further entailments that an action produces.[43] The distinction, then, is between what is intrinsic and extrinsic. A result is what occurs in the performance of an illocutionary act ("he *confessed* that Jesus is Lord"). A consequence, on the other hand, is an event that may or may not follow from the performance of an action ("he made me feel unspiritual"). The main point is that consequences are not intrinsic but extrinsic to actions.

Understanding is a matter of recognizing an author's illocutionary act for what it is. A communicative act succeeds in the illocutionary purpose for which it has been sent simply by virtue of its being recognized. Communication succeeds when the speaker's communicative intention becomes mutually known. The reader need not believe or obey what is said in order to understand it. The reader's role in the covenant of discourse is nothing less than to seek understanding. Our anatomy of communicative action has led us to a fifth thesis, a thesis of decisive importance for the task of biblical interpretation, as we shall see below.

5. Understanding consists in recognizing illocutionary acts and their results.

Communicative action, however, often produces consequences other than understanding. Strictly speaking, these are not part of the illocutionary act that I have argued is the true object of understanding. Of course there is nothing to stop a reader from inquiring into such unintended consequences. There *is* something that should stop us from calling such inquiries "interpretations," however, and that is our analysis of what communicative action just *is*.

Communicative action can be "overstood": readers can respond to texts other than by inferring illocutionary acts. There are often good reasons for overstanding. Gibbs, for example, cites the example of Jules Verne's *The Mysterious Island* from the U.S. Civil War era, often thought to be a pro-Union and pro-abolitionist novel. Yet many recent readers, sensitive to the ways ideologies can affect people at a deep level, detect lingering evidence of racism in Verne's work: "The book appears antiracist when read in terms of Verne's intentional meanings, yet racist when read from a

---

[42]R. A. Duff, *Intention, Agency and Criminal Liability: Philosophy of Action and the Criminal Law* (Oxford: Blackwell, 1990).
[43]See G. H. Von Wright, *Explanation and Understanding* (Ithaca, N.Y.: Cornell University Press, 1971).

more contemporary viewpoint."[44] Similar remarks have been made, of course, about the Bible with regard to sexism. While judgments of political correctness may be appropriate, however, it is important not to rush to judgment too quickly. The first step is to identify what has been done; only then is one in a position to evaluate the action. Indeed, *not* to identify what an author has done risks doing the author violence.

This underscores the importance of the reader, who is not merely a passive but an active recipient of an author's communication. To engage in communicative action— to make the communicative-covenantal presumption—is to hope that one will not fall prey to interpretive violence. This is simply the Golden Rule put into hermeneutics. "To be understood is in itself a source of joy, not to be understood a source of unhappiness."[45] Readers have an obligation to recognize an author's illocutionary act for what it is.

The citizen of language. Let us briefly gather up the results of this anatomy of communicative action before going on to discuss the implications for interpretation and for our understanding of the communicative action in Scripture.

Throughout this discussion I have assumed that the most interesting facts about language all pertain to how humans use it to perform certain actions. That our views of what language is are tied up with our views of what it is to be human should by now be taken as a given. It is no accident that Alston's analysis of illocutionary acts led him straight to the notion of speakers' rights and responsibilities. Inherent in the very notion of speech acts is the idea of a speaker to whom acts may be imputed. Examining language in philosophical perspective directs us to the topics of human action and responsibility; theology deepens the analysis by viewing human action and responsibility in covenantal terms. Authors have an obligation to fulfill the responsibilities that they inevitably assume in performing their illocutionary acts. Readers have an obligation to seek understanding: specifically, to recognize illocutionary acts for what they are.

A communicant—either author as active agent or reader as active recipient of communication—is necessarily a *participant* in the covenant of discourse. Communicants enjoy what we might call, after Pascal, the dignity—the privilege and the responsibility—of communicative action. Pascal himself marveled at the dignity of causality with which God has endowed the human race. Like God, we are able to bring about new things. Communicative action—the ability to transform the cognitive environment—is no less marvelous. The privilege of communicative action is that we have the capacity to take initiative in the world with our words

---

[44]Gibbs, *Intentions*, p. 267.

[45]Niels Thomassen, *Communicative Ethics in Theory and Practice,* trans. John Irons (London: Macmillan, 1992), p. 79.

and hence the capacity to make a difference.

The image of the covenant brings to light yet another dimension of the language-humanity relation: the social. Searle defines language as a rule-governed form of human behavior. I have been at pains to show that these rules are moral as well as simply grammatical. But there is a political dimension too. Speakers are neither sovereign subjects of language as a manipulable instrument (the modern error) nor slaves of language as an ideological system (the postmodern error), but rather citizens of language, with all the rights and responsibilities pertaining thereto.

According to Aristotle, human happiness is achieved not in solitude but in friendship, to which Ricoeur adds, "in the setting of the city."[46] We wish to live well with others in just institutions. One such institution is the "city" of language. *Citizenship* names the way an individual belongs to a *polis*. Citizens of language are communicants in the covenant of discourse. Indeed what I have called the covenant of discourse spells out *what it is to live justly in the institution of language (discourse)*. We now turn to consider what good citizenship in the city of language means when it comes to interpretation.

Interpretation and communicative action. The model of communication I have been sketching assumes not merely a cooperative (Grice) but a "covenantal principle" of discourse. What follows from our anatomy of communicative action for the practice of interpretation? Let the sixth thesis serve to anticipate the ensuing argument.

---

6. Interpretation is the process of inferring authorial intentions and of ascribing illocutionary acts.

Interpretation and illocutionary ascription. I agree with Alston that to understand a speaker "is to know what illocutionary act she was performing."[47] To interpret a text is thus to ascribe a particular illocutionary act, or set of acts, to its author. To interpret a text is to answer the question, what is the author doing in her text? Interpretation involves coming up with appropriately "thick" descriptions of what an author is doing that get beyond the locutionary level (e.g., "he uttered a sentence" or "he spoke with a French accent") to descriptions of relevant communicative, which is to say illocutionary, action ("he confessed Jesus is Lord").

Guessing what an author *wanted* or *planned* to do in a text is not yet interpretation. Such a guess in fact may have little or nothing to do with what an author has actually done. No, what needs to be described is what the author was actually

---

[46] Ricoeur, *The Just*, p. xv.
[47] Alston, *Illocutionary Acts*, p. 282.

attending to—performing intentionally, with the appropriate skill and with self-awareness—in doing things with words.

In the final analysis, interpretation is a matter of justice: of correctly ascribing or imputing to an author the illocutionary acts that have actually been performed. Interpretation is a matter of judging what an author has said/done in his or her words. The idea of inferring intentions from completed acts suggests a certain parallel between the process of textual interpretation and the judicial process of a court trial. The basis of the analogy should now be plain: both have to do with *imputing intentions to agents justly*. In the case of textual interpretation, of course, what are imputed are not criminal but communicative or, to be exact, *illocutionary* intentions.

Interpretation and illocutionary inference. The hard work of interpretation is largely a matter of inferring illocutionary intent from the evidence, which includes both the primary data (the text) and secondary considerations (context). For example, the information transmitted by the locution "Wet paint" is one thing; the illocution—"Do not touch"—is quite another. For simpler communicative acts like a "Wet paint" sign, we infer the illocution almost automatically, based on our appreciation of the situational context.

Relevance theory emphasizes the importance of inferring authorial intentions too: "According to the inferential model, communication is achieved by producing and interpreting evidence."[48] Interpretation is not simply a matter of decoding linguistic signs (locutions). Nor is it simply a matter of observing the effects of communicative action (perlocutions). No, interpretation must go on to determine which inferences regarding the speaker's communicative intention would confirm the communicator's presumption of relevance. Recall the statement "Coffee would keep me awake." What should be inferred about the communicative act that supervenes on this locution depends entirely on the nonlinguistic context of the utterance. It is not enough to know the dictionary meaning of the terms used in the sentence; one must know why just these words were used in just this way in just this circumstance. As Sperber and Wilson write: "The coded signal, even if it is unambiguous, is only a piece of evidence about the communicator's intentions, and has to be used inferentially and in a context."[49]

Speech act philosophy and relevance theory coincide at the point where the addressee has to *infer* what illocutionary act has been performed in a particular utterance. To return to the metaphor of the trial: one way to determine an agent's intent is to cross-examine her. Authors are not physically present, of course, to respond to our interrogations, but this need not prevent us from putting our questions to the text.

---

[48]Sperber and Wilson, *Relevance,* p. 2.
[49]Ibid., p. 170.

Normally these questions take the form of hypotheses; we ask ourselves whether an author *could have meant* this rather than that. Our hypotheses are put to the test precisely by being brought to the text. Those hypotheses that can account for more aspects or features of the communicative act have more explanatory power. Interpretation thus works through abduction, that is, by inference to the best explanation. An "explanation" is in fact a "thick description" of what an author has done. It "explains" insofar as it accounts for the relevance and coherence of the text as a completed communicative act.

Overinterpretation is a matter of drawing "unauthorized" inferences about what a speaker said/did. For example, one might take an insult as a compliment, thus ascribing the wrong illocutionary intent; conversely, one might take a compliment as an insult. The film *Being There* provides some particularly striking examples of overinterpretation. Almost every character in the film consistently reads into or infers excessively from what Chance, a lowly gardener, intended. These mistaken inferences lead in turn to *misinterpretations,* ascriptions of communicative intentions when others, or perhaps none, are present.[50]

Interpretation and perlocutionary effects. At this point readers may perhaps be forgiven for thinking that though the concept of the covenant of discourse has a certain attractiveness, we could perhaps jettison the ungainly analytic philosophical work on illocutions and the unduly weighty baggage of trinitarian theology to boot. I have anticipated these objections and tried to answer them by demonstrating the usefulness of the concept of illocution and the need for a distinctly theological account of the social institution of language. The practical payoff—the relevance!—of this extended discussion of illocutions comes to light in the contrast between interpreting for the sake of an ethical encounter with the other/author and using texts in ways that are less ethical than egocentric or ideological.[51]

Not all action is communicative. Many actions aim to effect a change in the environment merely by manipulating it. Such actions are causal, "instrumental" or manipulative—what Jürgen Habermas calls "strategic." Instead of saying "Please pass the salt," I can simply reach out and take it. In the same way, one can produce effects on other people through strategic rather than properly communicative action. After all, there are many ways to bring about change in an environment.

The success of *communicative* action wholly depends on bringing about this one

---

[50]The standard example of a mistaken inference when no communicative intention is present would be an interpreter's reading marks made by waves in the sand as conveying some message.

[51]By "ethical" in this context I have in mind Emmanuel Lévinas's insistence on recognizing the absolute priority of the "other." For an introduction to Lévinas's thought, see his *Ethics and Infinity* (Pittsburgh: Duquesne University Press, 1985).

effect: understanding. In contrast, the criterion for success in "strategic" action is simply bringing about an intended result, some change in the world, other than understanding. The intended result may be to produce an effect on a hearer or reader. Perlocutions—like the Holy Spirit, with whom I will associate this dimension of communicative action (see below)—remain largely on the margins of theories about discourse. Happily, Alston's discussion provides help, and not a little light, to considerations of the proper role for the reader's, or for that matter the interpretive community's, response to communicative action.

The real question is whether perlocutionary acts are essentially strategic rather than communicative. Actions that aim to produce an effect on the reader *other than understanding,* or *other than by means of understanding,* count as strategic, not communicative, actions. An emphasis on perlocutions can become pathological: (1) by aiming to produce effects on the reader independently of illocutions or (2) by defining illocutions in terms of the effect produced on the reader. Interpreters must bear in mind the following two mandates: (1) Do not think of communication in terms of perlocutions only. (2) Do not think of perlocutions as dissociated from illocutions. The danger lies in thinking about communication, and interpretation, in terms of effects produced on communicants. The seventh thesis puts perlocutions in their proper place.

7. *An action that aims to produce perlocutionary effects on readers other than by means of understanding counts as strategic, not communicative, action.*

Austin himself thought that "it is the distinction between illocutions and perlocutions which seems likeliest to give trouble."[52] Stated as simply as possible, Austin was not sure whether the (perlocutionary) effect should be deemed an essential part of the (illocutionary) act. In the current discussion of textual interpretation, we can see that Austin's initial confusion has grown exponentially; today there are many critics and theorists who think of meaning in terms of the effect a text has on a reader (the reader's response).[53]

For Alston the distinction is clear-cut. It is the difference between *having per-*

---

[52]Austin, *How to Do Things with Words,* p. 109.

[53]For example, Stanley Fish equates textual meaning with the reader's response. A similar confusion may lie behind the "functional equivalence" model of Bible translation that Van Leeuwen so competently interrogates and critiques. Philosophers who tend to define illocutions in terms of perlocutions include Paul Grice ("Meaning," *Philosophical Review* 66 [1957]: 377-88) and Stephen Schiffer (*Meaning* [Oxford: Clarendon, 1972]. For a fuller presentation of Alston's refutation of these views, see his *Illocutionary Acts,* chap. 2.

formed an action and *being understood to have performed that action.* What we have here is a variation on George Berkeley's idealism: not "to be is to be perceived" but "to act is to have been perceived to have acted." But perhaps the distinction is not so solid. For as communication theorists remind us, communication is not a one-way street. We do not know if we have communicated until we receive the appropriate feedback. To this Alston replies yes and no: if you didn't hear or understand my question, then yes, on one level my communicative purpose has been frustrated. But—and this is all-important—*it does not follow that I didn't ask you.*

Alston posits a hierarchy of supervenience in which the "higher" depends on but cannot be reduced to the "lower," and in which the "lower" cannot by itself do what is done at the "higher" level. Such hierarchical ordering is familiar to scientists: cells depend on atoms and electrons, but the properties and behavior of the cell cannot be reduced to or explained in terms of atoms and electrons. No, cells supervene on atoms and require their own set of explanatory concepts. Similarly, illocutions supervene on locutions. Requesting that someone pass the salt is something we do *in* doing something else (saying "Please pass the salt"). My *asking* depends on but cannot be reduced to my *uttering.*

Applying the same reasoning, Alston argues for an asymmetrical dependence of perlocutionary acts on illocutionary acts. To use the concepts just defined, this means that perlocutionary acts *supervene* on illocutionary acts. Acts are illocutionary when they pertain to what we are *doing in* speaking; acts are perlocutionary when they pertain to what we are *doing by* speaking. So perlocutionary acts can be based on illocutionary acts, but not vice versa. Now, communication can take place even where there are no perlocutionary effects; on the other hand, "if no IA [illocutionary act] is performed, there is no (linguistic) communication, whatever effects one brings about on another person."[54]

Humans relate to one another in various ways. It is possible to get people to do things other than by communicating with them. I can get a person to leave the room, for instance, by pushing him out the door. This brings about an effect on the "addressee" of my action, but it is not, strictly speaking, a perlocutionary one, for the simple reason that it does not supervene on an illocutionary act. The same effect would, however, be perlocutionary if the person left as a result of my saying, "Please leave." Less straightforward, but still easily handled, is the case of my using a mere locution to get someone to leave. The sheer physical quality of an utterance (e.g., "Boo!") may produce the desired effect. Clearly, however, this is an instance of strategic rather than communicative action.

Neither Alston nor I are indifferent to the effects produced on communicants.

---

[54]Alston, *Illocutionary Acts,* p. 170.

Indeed most of us communicate with one another not solely for the purpose of having our illocutionary acts recognized but for purposes that go beyond understanding. We want to modify cognitive environments to modify the natural or social environment. We say "Clean up your room" not because we want to be understood but because we want our addressee's room to be cleaner. Yet these ulterior effects are grounded in the content of our illocutionary acts. And our acts are what they are whether or not they produce perlocutionary effects. Though the distinction may still strike some as technical, the significance of maintaining it will perhaps come to light in my discussion below of the relation of Word and Spirit in interpreting the Christian canon.

Thiselton's work on 1 Corinthians is apt. He draws a contrast between Paul's apostolic ministry, which is largely illocutionary (testifying to Jesus Christ), and his Corinthian opponents, who wielded the instrumental (and ultimately manipulative) power of rhetoric: "I distinguish between *'illocutionary' speech acts*, which depend for their effectiveness *on a combination of situation and recognition,* and *'perlocutionary' speech acts,* which depend for their effectiveness on *sheer causal (psychological or rhetorical) persuasive power.*"[55] Here we may recall the importance of the author's assuming a normative stance. Many speech acts (e.g., marrying someone by saying "I do") depend on the identity and status of the speaker. Paul's proclamation of the cross—preaching the gospel—is directly tied to his status as an apostle, as "one sent" to perform a particular communicative action.

If all truth is only a species of rhetoric, as some postmoderns and apparently some first-century Corinthians believed, then all illocutions become perlocutions. Paul stakes his own apostolic ministry "on illocutionary promise, not on perlocutionary persuasion."[56] I take it that Thiselton is arguing that Paul's discourse transforms his readers not by manipulating them but rather by virtue of his testimony, which is as much to say by his *meaning* (illocutions), not by sheer manipulation (perlocutions).

Manipulative uses of language—by authors who employ deceitful rhetoric and by readers who impose their own interpretations alike—constitute a violation of the covenant of discourse.[57] I do not wish to be misunderstood on this point. There is nothing wrong with perlocutions, or with communicative acts' having a perlocutionary dimension. What I do resist is any attempt to produce effects on readers via language

---

[55]Anthony Thiselton, *First Epistle to the Corinthians,* New International Greek Theological Commentary (Grand Rapids, Mich.: Eerdmans, 2000), p. 51.

[56]Thiselton, *Promise of Hermeneutics,* p. 226.

[57]Thiselton forcefully argues that self-personhood is obscured, if not lost, by the postmodern assumption that all language use is essentially manipulative. The close correlation once again between one's view of language and one's sense of self should not be overlooked, See Anthony Thiselton, *Interpreting God and the Postmodern Self: On Meaning, Manipulation and Promise* (Edinburgh: T & T Clark, 1995), esp. pt. 1.

use that seeks to bypass the content of illocutionary acts.

The Discourse of the Covenant: Canonical Action

I have devoted the bulk of the present essay to thinking philosophically and theologically about language as communicative action, to general questions about language
rather than specific questions about biblical interpretation. This is not the place for a
full-scale treatment of biblical hermeneutics. However, I do want to suggest a few
ways my "mere communicative hermeneutic" may be stretched toward the theological interpretation of Scripture. To what extent does the model of the text as communicative action with communicative intent need to be modified when that text is the
Christian canon, the ensemble of texts that constitute the Old and New Testaments?

From "promise" and "sentence" to gospel and law. The promise is, as we
have seen, the paradigmatic speech act for philosophers such as Searle and Alston.
Thiselton has rightly called attention to its centrality in Scripture and in Christian theology as well. Fully to appreciate the discourse of the covenant, however, requires us
to deal with both *promising* and *sentencing*.

Communicating the covenant. Genesis recounts the beginnings of many human
institutions: marriage, the family, work. These are not merely social but *created* institutions, God-ordained orders intended to structure human experience every bit as
much as those other divine orders, space and time. For our purposes, however, perhaps the most important institution initiated by God is the covenant. In speaking,
God commits both himself and his addressees to certain obligations. In short, God
establishes a personal relationship with men and women by communicating covenants. Subsequent communicative acts of God also take the form of covenants: to
Noah (Gen 9:8), to Abraham (Gen 15:18), to David (2 Sam 7). Promising and sentencing are constitutive of the covenant Yahweh instituted with Israel as recounted in the
book of Deuteronomy.[58]

The *Shema* of Deuteronomy 6:4 ("Hear, O Israel") is a solemn summons to covenant fidelity.[59] What is called for is not just any readerly response but the specific
response of obedience. The promise that God will bless obedience is accompanied
by a divine sentence: "But if you will not obey the voice of the LORD your God or be
careful to do all his commandments and his statutes which I command you this day,
then all these curses shall come upon you and overtake you" (Deut 28:15). The "Deu-

---

[58]See J. Gordon McConville, "Metaphor, Symbol and the Interpretation of Deuteronomy," in
After Pentecost: Language and Biblical Interpretation, ed. Craig Bartholomew, Colin Greene
and Karl Möller (Grand Rapids, Mich.: Zondervan, 2001), especially the section on "Deuteronomy and Speech-Act Theory," pp. 342-46.

[59]Cf. Klyne Snodgrass, "Reading to Hear: A Hermeneutics of Hearing," in *Horizons in Biblical
Theology* (forthcoming), on the importance of a hermeneutics of hearing/doing.

teronomistic" history of Israel is largely the history of how Israel responds, or fails to respond, to the word of the Lord. The role of the prophets is largely that of "prosecutors" of the covenant. The prophets are the ones who bring the Lord's case against Israel for having violated the covenant document.

C. H. Dodd spoke of the "two-beat rhythm" of salvation history, composed alternately of judgment and grace, law and gospel—in short, the sentence and the promise. The two-beat rhythm reaches a crescendo, of course, in the cross and resurrection of Jesus Christ. For in Jesus Christ himself—God's Word made flesh—there is a yes and a no. The cross of Christ fulfills the sentence, the resurrection the promise. In this sense we could say that Jesus Christ is God's illocutionary act. We may note in passing that only God has the authority to assume the normative status of one who pronounces acquittal of sinners. "Justification"—the sentence of acquittal—is a divinely given institution and is (justifiably!) regarded by Protestants as one of the best divine illocutionary acts.

Oral or written covenant? From speech to Scripture acts. It is now time to consider a potentially fatal objection to the use of speech act categories in biblical interpretation. It amounts to the claim that, to quote Ricoeur, "with written discourse . . . the author's intention and the meaning of the text cease to coincide."[60] More radically, the objection is that the written text enjoys semantic autonomy both from its original author and from its original situation. The text, in other words, is independent—cut off—from the communicative agent who produced it and from the circumstances that provided the setting for the communicative action. Clearly if this objection can be sustained, we will need to revisit everything I have previously said about the centrality of illocutionary acts for interpretation.

What does philosophy have to say about the oral-written distinction? Interestingly, there is evidence in Ricoeur's own work that the distinction is not as hard and fast as the quotation above suggests. Most important, Ricoeur continues to see writing as a species of discourse: something said by someone to someone about something. To be precise, a text is "discourse fixed by writing." I see no reason why writing should lead us to omit the phrase "by someone." Ricoeur is happy to speak of meaningful human action as a text, so why can we not see texts as meaningful actions?[61] Indeed upon closer inspection it is clear that Ricoeur wishes to avoid both the intentional fallacy and the "fallacy of the absolute text": "the fallacy of hypostastizing the text as an authorless entity."[62] Often overlooked is Ricoeur's acknowledgment that discourse

---

[60]Paul Ricoeur, *Interpretation Theory: Discourse and the Surplus of Meaning* (Fort Worth, Tex.: Texas Christian University Press, 1976), p. 29.
[61]See Paul Ricoeur, "The Model of the Text: Meaningful Action Considered as a Text," in *Hermeneutics and the Human Sciences: Essays on Language, Action and Interpretation* (Cambridge: Cambridge University Press, 1981), pp. 197-221.

fixes not only the locutionary but the *illocutionary* act.[63] Ricoeur knows that one cannot cancel out this main characteristic of discourse—"said by someone"—without reducing texts to natural (nonintentional) objects like pebbles in the sand. It remains a mystery, however, how texts can be considered discourse if they are indeed "cut off" from their authors. Wolterstorff has amply demonstrated the incoherence of the notion of "textual sense" interpretation, so I need not pursue the point here.[64] Instead I wish to pursue a different, more properly theological argument in favor of conceiving texts as communicative acts.

Let us consider the book of Deuteronomy. All the illocutionary features of the covenant that God instituted orally with Abraham, Isaac, and Jacob are preserved in writing in the Book of the Covenant delivered by Moses and ratified by the whole nation of Israel. Gordon McConville makes the important point that the words that instituted the covenant at Horeb and then Moab are finally deposited in a book, the Book of the Law (Deut 28:58).[65] Others have argued that the very structure of Deuteronomy is patterned after ancient Near Eastern vassal treaties.[66] The significance of this parallel is that many Hittite treaties included a provision for the treaty's inscription. The fact that the Tables of the Law are written on stone signals their author's insistence on the permanence of the discourse.

According to Deuteronomy, the Book of the Covenant, precisely as written discourse—text—functions as a standing witness against the nation of Israel (Deut 31:26). The law was placed alongside the ark of the covenant, and it was to be written on stone at the threshold of the Promised Land as a permanent reminder of the blessings and curses associated with the covenant (Deut 27). As such, the text of Deuteronomy calls not for "wooden repetition" but rather for continual decision, for or against its illocutions. Directives (laws) must be obeyed; commissives (promises) must be trusted.

The covenant as a written document continued to have potency, but only when the people attended to it. Time and again the kings of Israel neglected to read and obey it. The notable exception is King Josiah, during whose reign the book of the law was found. Josiah's reader response was immediate and drastic: he tore his clothes (2 Kings 22:11), not because this was the intended perlocutionary effect but because Josiah realized that the law was a divine directive that had been disobeyed. A similar response, this time on the part of a whole community, is recorded in

---

[62]Ricoeur, *Interpretation Theory*, p. 30.
[63]"To the extent that the illocutionary act can be exteriorized thanks to grammatical paradigms and procedures expressive of its 'force,' it too can be inscribed" (ibid., p. 27).
[64]See Wolterstorff, *Divine Discourse*, chap. 8.
[65]McConville, "Metaphor, Symbol," p. 345.
[66]See Meredith Kline, *Treaty of the Great King: The Covenant Structure of Deuteronomy—Studies and Commentary* (Grand Rapids, Mich.: Eerdmans, 1963).

Nehemiah 8: mass weeping. These passages attest to the determinate content and the binding force of the written covenant. We may therefore conclude that *written texts preserve the same illocutionary act potential as oral discourse*. If we can take this point as settled, we may now turn to consider whether the biblical canon has features that distinguish it from other types of written discourse.

Anatomy of canonical action. Do the categories of speech act philosophy apply to the task of biblical interpretation? While sentences are the basic tools for performing illocutionary acts, they can become part of something more complex, just as other basic actions (hammering, sawing, drilling) can become ingredients in a more complex act (building a bookcase). Texts are communicative acts of a higher order. The question now becomes: are there specific illocutionary acts that emerge only on the level of the text, and perhaps on that of the canon? And if there are, should they be seen as instances of *God's* authorial discourse? Before turning to the level of the canon, however, let us examine what takes place at the level of the individual books of Scripture, at the level of the literary whole. We can then proceed to examine what might emerge at the higher levels of "testament" and "canon."

Consider how one might describe some of the acts that constitute writing a Gospel:

☐ he gripped the pen and moved it in straight and circular motions
☐ he formed Greek characters
☐ he wrote the word *theos*
☐ he said "a virgin shall conceive"
☐ he quoted from Isaiah 7:14
☐ he said Jesus' birth fulfilled Old Testament prophecy
☐ he narrated the events surrounding Jesus' birth
☐ he confessed Jesus as the Christ

Some of these descriptions pertain to illocutionary acts; some do not. We need not rehearse those distinctions here. The claim I am now making is that some of Matthew's illocutions can be inferred from his discourse only when it is *taken as a literary whole*.

Ascribing generic illocutions. "Every piece of writing is a kind of something."[67] Each literary genre does something distinct and is hence able to affect one's cognitive environment in a different way. Specifically, each major genre enables a distinct way of engaging reality and of interacting with others. The Russian literary theorist Mikhail Bakhtin views genre not merely as a medium of communication but as a medium of cognition. Different literary genres, he contends, offer distinct ways of thinking about

---

[67]John B. Gabel and Charles B. Wheeler, *The Bible as Literature: An Introduction* (Oxford: Oxford University Press, 1986), p. 16.

or experiencing the world.[68] In this respect, forms of literature function like metaphors—they are models, indispensable cognitive instruments for saying and seeing things that perhaps could not be seen or said in other ways. The point is that some illocutionary acts may be associated with texts rather than sentences. Accordingly we need a supplement to Austin: "How to Do Things with Literature."

Let us test out Bakhtin's hypothesis on narrative. What do narratives do that other kinds of literature do not and perhaps cannot? Mary Louise Pratt argues compellingly that narratives perform the unique act of *displaying a world*.[69] In narrative, the place of propositional content is taken by the plot. Susan Lanser's *The Narrative Act* appeals to speech act theory as providing a valuable aim in studying point of view, that is, the author's perspective on the world displayed in the text.[70] What Wolterstorff and Alston have shown to be the case with speech acts thus applies to text acts too: authors do not simply display worlds but in displaying also take up some normative stance toward these worlds (e.g., praising, commending, condemning). In Lanser's words: "Much like the biblical parable, the novel's basic illocutionary activity is ideological instruction; its basic plea: hear my word, believe and understand."[71]

What we may term a generic act—an illocutionary act performed on the level of a literary whole—is the unifying act that orders all the other acts that constitute authoring a piece of written discourse. Take the book of Jonah. It is only when we consider the text as a unified whole that we can discuss what is going on at the literary level. What is the author doing besides "telling a story"? At the level of the literary whole, it is harder to maintain that the author of Jonah was primarily making truth claims about certain forms of sea life that swim in the Mediterranean. Interpretations that never rise above the level of reported events are not thick enough. Genuine interpretation involves ascribing illocutionary acts to authors. I believe the author to be satirizing religious complacency and criticizing ethnocentrism.[72] The illocutionary act of "satirizing" emerges only at the literary level, that is, at the level of the text considered as a completed communicative act. Note that to describe this generic illocution is to describe the communicative act that structures the whole text.

---

[68]Mikhail Bakhtin, *Speech Genres and Other Late Essays* (Austin: University of Texas Press, 1986).

[69]Mary Louise Pratt, *Towards a Speech Act Theory of Literary Discourse* (Bloomington: Indiana University Press, 1977).

[70]Susan Snaider Lanser, *The Narrative Act: Point of View in Prose Fiction* (Princeton, N.J.: Princeton University Press, 1981).

[71]Ibid., p. 293.

[72]It is striking that by the end of the book everyone has repented—the king of Nineveh, the people of Nineveh, even the beasts of Nineveh—save one, Jonah. Jonah stands for those Israelites who had become complacent about their covenant privileges and responsibilities. Indeed Jonah goes so far as to accuse God of being excessively merciful! As for Jonah himself, he is portrayed as feeling more concern for a plant than for a people (see Jon 4).

The example of satire in Jonah illustrates my thesis: some things that authors do come to light only at the level of the text considered as a whole. To identify a text's literary genre is the first step to determining what the author was doing. We simply would not appreciate what Jonah is doing—ridiculing religious ethnocentrism—apart from considering the text as a whole. Note that the literal sense of Jonah is the sense of his literary act: satire. The moral should be clear. Biblical interpreters would do well to ascertain what kind of literature—what literary genre—they happen to be interpreting. Literary genres are relatively stable institutions, and this stability creates the possibility of a shared context between author and reader—a shared *literary* context.

The main point is that some of the author's illocutionary intentions come to light only at the level of the literary whole. Going beyond Alston's analysis, then, I maintain that we should recognize *generic* illocutions: the narrative act, the parabolic act, the apocalyptic act, the historical act, the prophetic act and so on. In other words, each of the major forms of biblical literature has its own characteristic illocutionary forces: wisdom ("commending a way"), apocalyptic ("encouraging endurance"), prophecy ("recalling covenant promises and obligations") and so on. To describe and ascribe generic illocutionary acts, then, is to say what an author is doing in his text considered as a whole.[73]

Canonic illocutions? So much for the diversity of canonical acts. What communicative act, if any, unifies the canon as a whole? Is a "testament" a genre? Should we think of the canon as a genre unto itself or as a space wherein the diverse literary genres, like elements of a Hittite treaty, interact and affect one another? Or are there new illocutionary acts that emerge only at the canonical level? The question is whether there is perhaps not an even higher level of illocutionary action at the canonical level.

I agree with the literary critic Charles Altieri that "texts are best viewed as actions performed on a variety of levels for our contemplation."[74] Take the many things done in making a covenant:

☐ the Lord of the covenant identifies himself ("I am Yahweh")

☐ the Lord recounts the history of what he has does for his vassals ("who brought you out of Egypt")

☐ the Lord stipulates what he will do for the people and what they will do for him ("I will be your God, and you will be my people")

☐ the Lord lists blessings and curses for obedience and disobedience ("You will keep possession of the promised land"; "You will lose possession of the land")

---

[73]Note that generic illocutions supervene on illocutions at the sentence and paragraph level.
[74]Charles Altieri, *Act and Quality: A Theory of Literary Meaning and Humanistic Understanding* (Amherst: University of Massachusetts Press, 1981), p. 10.

☐ the Lord makes provisions for passing on the covenant to the next generation (through its inscription)

Each of these illocutionary acts is performed throughout Scripture; yet all are also ingredients of a larger, testamental, illocutionary act: *covenanting*.[75]

Brevard Childs argues that the canon was intentionally shaped so that it would function authoritatively for future generations in the believing community. The unity of the whole follows, Childs thinks, from its consistent witness of Jesus Christ. I welcome his emphasis on reading each part of Scripture in its larger canonical context, but I doubt that Childs has given a sufficient warrant for the practice. I agree with Paul Noble, who argues that what Childs's approach tacitly depends on and actually requires is an explicit affirmation of divine authorship. Indeed Childs's claim that the meaning of biblical texts can be arrived at only in the context of the canon as a whole "is formally equivalent to believing that the Bible is so inspired as to be ultimately the work of a single Author."[76]

This brings us closer to Wolterstorff's proposal about dual-author discourse. I propose to take such a view as a given and to move on to a consideration of how the divine authorial intent in Scripture may be discerned. The concept of divine authorship is, of course, miles away from the notion of the "death of the author." This is as it should be. A Christian view of language and literature will have nothing to do with "the death of God put into writing" and everything to do with "the providence of God put into writing." The main claim to be advanced here is that *God is doing providential things in his Scripture acts*. The divine intention does not contravene but supervenes on the intentions of the human authors.

---

8. To describe a generic (or canonic) illocution is to describe the communicative act that structures the text considered as a unified whole.

There are two complementary senses in which I wish to affirm the canon as God's illocutionary act.[77] First, there is divine appropriation of the illocutions of the human authors, particularly at the generic level but not exclusively there. For example, God still uses the book of Jonah to satirize religious ethnocentrism. (Indeed the message of Jonah is as relevant today as ever.) Yet God may be doing new things with Jonah and other biblical texts too by virtue of their being gathered together in the canon.

---

[75]Interestingly, Austin included "making a covenant" in his original list of illocutionary acts.
[76]Paul R. Noble, *The Canonical Approach: A Critical Reconstruction of the Hermeneutics of Brevard S. Childs* (Leiden, Netherlands: E. J. Brill, 1995), p. 340.
[77]I am happy to consider the locutions too as a product of divine discourse, as traditional theories of inspiration maintain, but this is not the focus of the present essay.

Could it be that certain illocutions come to light only when we describe what God is doing at the canonical level? More work needs to be done in this area, but for the moment let me offer the following as possible candidates for the divine canonical illocutions: instructing the believing community, testifying to Christ, and perhaps most obviously, covenanting.

Scripture acts: Transforming cognitive (and spiritual) environments. God's Word will not fail to accomplish the purpose for which it was sent (Is 55:11). Just what kind of purpose did Isaiah have in mind, illocutionary or perlocutionary? Is the Bible really a divine communicative act if readers fail to respond to its illocutions and perlocutions? Is the Bible the Word of God written, or does it only *become* the Word of God when God takes up the human words and does something with them? Opinions differ. Everything hinges on whether we wish to include the reader's response (illocutionary uptake, perlocutionary effect) in the definition of communicative action.

Karl Barth appealed to the Holy Spirit as the "Lord of the hearing" and suggested that it is only when God freely and graciously takes up the human words that the Bible becomes the Word of God for a given hearer. Is the Bible God's Word? Barth and evangelicals have been at loggerheads on this issue for decades: "is," "is not." Can our anatomy of communicative action move us beyond the impasse? I think so.

On my view, Barth is partly right and partly wrong. He is wrong if he means to deny that God performs illocutionary acts in Scripture. He is right if one incorporates the reader's reception of the message into one's definition of "communicative act." Communication, we may recall, can connote both senses: the act of communicating or the completed communication, including its reception. Human authors of course lack the ability to make their readers understand, much less to guarantee the intended perlocutionary effects. There is nothing human authors can do to make sure their recipients "get it." God, however, has no such limits: the Spirit is the "Lord of the hearing." The Spirit is the energy that enables the Word to complete its mission. My proposal, then, is to say both the Bible *is* the Word of God (in the sense of its illocutionary acts) and to say that the Bible *becomes* the Word of God (in the sense of achieving its perlocutionary effects).

Does not my proposal tie God down to the texts? Does it not compromise God's freedom? No, for God's freedom is the freedom to initiate communicative action and to keep his word. Once God makes a promise, however, he is obliged to keep it, not from some external force but because God's word is God's bond. Neither is it any part of my suggestion that just because God's discourse is fixed in writing we can somehow "possess" God's Word or master it. On the contrary, one does not "possess" or "master" warnings, promises, commands and so forth. We are rather in the situation of Ezra: in reading Scripture we are confronted with a word that seeks to transform, indeed to master, us.

A final objection. Does not this identification of Scripture with God's illocutionary acts demean Christ as God's Word? Again, no, because what Scripture is doing—particularly at the canonical level of communicative action—is pointing to Christ, offering appropriately "thick descriptions" of his meaning and significance for Israel and the church. Is this not what Luke implies: "And beginning with Moses and all the prophets, he [Jesus] interpreted to them in all the scriptures the things concerning himself" (Lk 24:27)? It is precisely through responding to the various illocutions of Scripture—belief in its assertions, obedience to its commands, faith in its promises—that we become "thickly" related to Christ. Indeed we cannot have the intended effect—union with Christ—apart from the content of Scripture's illocutionary acts (e.g., telling a story, making a promise, pronouncing pardon).

Sperber and Wilson define relevance as the property that makes information worth processing. On these terms, must we not conclude that of all words that can be heard, the gospel is the most relevant? Information is relevant, we may recall, when it modifies one's cognitive environment. Well, the gospel does this and much more. In the first place, instead of making manifest a set of assumptions (so Sperber and Wilson), Scripture manifests Christ, the revelation of God and the hope of glory. Just as significant is the fact that the gospel modifies cognitive and spiritual environments alike. It is not only that Scripture gives new information but that it radically transforms the very way we process information. What ultimately gets communicated through the canon is the way, the truth and the life.

Biblical interpretation and canonical action: Whose action is it? Perhaps the most important question we can ask of the canon is: *whose* act is it? If interpretation is a matter of ascribing and inferring communicative intentions, to whom do we ascribe the illocutions?

Interpretation after Pentecost: Which voice? whose tongue? Just what difference, if any, does Pentecost make for biblical interpretation? What is the Holy Spirit's role in God's triune communicative action? Many Christian traditions affirm the "inspiration" of the Scriptures. The Westminster Confession of Faith, for instance, accords supreme authority to "the Holy Spirit speaking in the Scripture." Much depends on how we parse this phrase: "the Spirit speaking." There are, at present, two approaches to interpretation that risk confusing divine communicative action—the Word of God—with the communicative action of the interpretive community: (1) performance interpretation, where the reader assumes the role of the author, and (2) perlocutionary interpretation, where the illocutionary act is bypassed or eclipsed in favor of achieving a predetermined effect other than understanding. Of interest here is how each approach has been brought to bear on biblical interpretation and how each makes a tacit appeal to the work of the Holy Spirit.

Ricoeur, as we have seen, announces the semantic autonomy of the text from its original author. Yet the text remains discourse. So whose discourse is it? Jorge Luis Borges's story "Pierre Menard" wonderfully illustrates the problem I have in mind. The story is about a twentieth-century French critic, Pierre Menard, who has written, word for word, several chapters of Cervantes's *Don Quixote*. On the locutionary level, Menard has simply replicated Cervantes's act. Yet Menard does not want to merely repeat the seventeenth-century meaning (what Cervantes had in mind), for that is too easy. Instead he wants to produce the same text but with an entirely different meaning. This is an excellent example of what Wolterstorff calls "performance interpretation." The basic idea is this: in performance interpretation, we read the text as if *we* had written it. There is no law against doing that, of course, if one fancies conducting that kind of experiment (what would I have meant if I had authored *Ulysses,* or *The Lord of the Rings,* or 1 Corinthians?).

There is no law against such performance interpretation, but neither is there any understanding. For once the attempt to infer the communicative intentions of the author is abandoned, so is the means for a meaningful encounter with the "other." This is deeply to be regretted; it is difficult to learn or grow or be transformed when one is in dialogue only with oneself.

Stanley Grenz works an intriguing variation of the above. He suggests that "the Spirit speaking in Scripture" refers to the *Spirit's* illocutions, but these are not identical with those of the human authors'. The performance interpretation that now counts is that of the Spirit. Grenz views the Bible as the instrumentality or vehicle *through* which the Spirit speaks. He is clear that the authority of Scripture "does not ultimately rest with any quality that inheres within it as such (for example, its divine authorship or inspired character)."[78] So the Spirit's speaking is not to be equated with the Spirit's authorship of Scripture. What then does it mean to say "the Spirit speaks"? Grenz answers: "Obviously, when we acknowledge that the Spirit speaks through the Bible, we are referring to an illocutionary, and not a locutionary, act."[79] He considers Wolterstorff's account of authorial discourse, only to reject it. The Spirit does not appropriate the authorial discourse, says Grenz, but rather "the biblical text itself."[80] What kind of illocution does the Spirit perform? Exegesis alone, while relevant, cannot answer this question. At this point Grenz's analysis shifts somewhat awkwardly, from a grudging concession that the original meaning of the text is not wholly eclipsed to what he is clearly more interested in: the Spirit's perlocutionary act of creating a world.

Because Grenz abandons the authorial discourse model and embraces Ricoeur's premise that the text takes on a life of its own, he has difficulty specifying just what

---

[78]Stanley Grenz, "The Spirit and the Word," *Theology Today* 57 (2000): 358.
[79]Ibid., p. 361.
[80]Ibid.

illocutionary acts the Spirit performs. Indeed the only *illocutionary* act Grenz actually ascribes to the Spirit is speaking: "The Spirit performs the perlocutionary act of creating a world through the illocutionary act of speaking . . . by appropriating the biblical text as the instrumentality of the divine speaking."[81] Speaking, however, is not an illocutionary act! So it is not at all clear how "speaking" *simpliciter* can produce perlocutionary effects.[82]

The Spirit can, of course, work through many diverse means to accomplish his sanctifying work (creating the new world "in Christ"). The crucial question, however, is whether the Spirit performs this work independently of Scripture's illocutionary acts. Grenz's account fails to explain how we can infer what illocutionary acts have been performed and to whom we should ascribe them. Consequently he leaves unanswered the fundamental question of how Scripture's actual *content* is related to the Spirit's accomplishing his further, perlocutionary, effects.

There is much to admire in Grenz's article. I agree with his overall vision that the Spirit leads people to reconceive their identity and worldview by means of the interpretive framework found *in* Scripture that recounts the eschatological event of Jesus Christ. I even agree with his fundamental premise that the Spirit's perlocutionary act is to "create a world" (though I explain it theologically in terms of the Spirit's ministry of the Word, and philosophically in terms of perlocutions supervening on illocutions). Yet at the same time I am troubled by his analysis, for both philosophical and theological reasons.

First, the philosophy of speech acts. As we have just seen, Grenz mistakenly identifies the Spirit's illocutionary act as "speaking through Scripture." But "speaking" per se is not an illocutionary act. Illocutionary acts have to do with what is done *in* speaking.[83] Moreover, it is the peculiar role of narratives to display a world. This is an illocutionary, not a perlocutionary, act. It is, to quote Susan Snaider, the distinctive *narrative* act. Second, as regards theology. The Spirit does indeed perform perlocutionary acts—no disagreement here. Yet the Spirit does so only on the basis of the concrete textual illocutions—the content!—of Scripture. The Spirit's creating a world, then, is not a new illocutionary act but rather the perlocutionary act of enabling readers to appropriate the illocutionary acts already inscribed in the biblical text, especially the narrative act of "displaying a world."

---

[81]Ibid., p. 365.

[82]It may be that Grenz does intend to say that the Spirit performs specific illocutionary acts, but if so, it is not clear how these acts are related to the actual propositional content and illocutionary force of the appropriated human discourse.

[83]In Alston's words: "The issuing of an utterance with a certain content can itself have effects, and so the production of those effects can supervene on that content presentation. But a content cannot attach to the production of an effect by an utterance, so as to make that effect production what carries that content" (Alston, *Illocutionary Acts,* p. 31).

The eclipse of biblical illocutions: Reading for formation. There is a second contemporary approach to biblical interpretation that fails to see the importance of illocutionary acts. This approach focuses on a particular perlocutionary purpose of
Scripture, namely spiritual formation: "The aim of reading Scripture, to build up
Christian faith and practice, should always order decisions about which methods and
approaches to adopt."[84] This is a laudable aim, and essential to the piety of the
church. But is it an *interpretive* aim? I do not dispute the aim of spiritual formation.
However, I do resist letting this intended perlocutionary effect run roughshod over
Scripture's communicative action.[85] Spiritual formation can be the aim, but not the
norm, of biblical interpretation. The norm must remain the author's illocutionary
intent. Once again, the problem arises from the confusion between illocutionary acts
and perlocutionary effects. To proceed too quickly to perlocutionary effects is to run
the risk of making the illocutionary content hermeneutically dispensable.

It is of course important that Christians read the Scriptures for the sake of spiritual
formation and edification. Yet this aim, while absolutely vital, must not displace the
prior aim of coming to understand the text. The thrust of the present argument is that
just as perlocutions can never precede but must always *proceed* from illocutions, so
spiritual formation can never precede but must always proceed from the ministry of the
Word—that *thought, power, deed* whose mission it is to transform those who receive it.

Ministering the discourse of the covenant: Of pneumatology and perlocutions. "The
Spirit speaks." Yes, but the Spirit "will not speak on his own authority, but whatever
he hears he will speak" (Jn 16:13). Here is a case where speech act categories make
perfect sense. Insofar as Scripture is inspired or "God-breathed," we may say that
even the locutions of Scripture are divinely authored. But Jesus' point in John is that
the Spirit confines his communicative activity to speaking only what he receives. The
Spirit *ministers* Christ, not himself. The Spirit, to use Gordon Fee's fine phrase, is
God's—God the Son's—empowering presence.

We are now in a position to understand how God's Word accomplishes the purpose for which it has been sent. It is because the Spirit accompanies it, speaking not
another word but ministering the word that was previously spoken. The Spirit is
nothing less than the *efficacy* of the Word. In short, the Spirit renders the word effective by achieving its intended perlocutionary effects. The point that must not be
missed, however, is that the Spirit accomplishes these effects not independently of
the words and illocutions but precisely *by, with* and *through* them. Hence my ninth
and penultimate thesis, directed primarily, though by no means exclusively, to the
task of biblical interpretation.

---

[84]Lewis Ayres and Stephen E. Fowl, "(Mis)reading the Face of God: The Interpretation of the
Bible in the Church," *Theological Studies* 60 (1999): 528.
[85]See chapter ten of the present volume.

9. The Spirit speaks in and through Scripture precisely by rendering its illocutions at the sentential, generic and canonic levels perlocutionarily efficacious.

Here then, where we might least expect it, we see a certain convergence between philosophy and theology with regard to language and the word. The asymmetrical dependence of perlocutionary on illocutionary acts defended by Alston has a theological counterpart in the idea that the Holy Spirit proceeds from the Father *and the Son—* the celebrated *Filioque* ("and from the Son"). Perlocutions "proceed" from locutions and illocutions, but not vice versa. Uttering a content can have effects, but a content cannot attach itself to the production of effects. Though Alston does not use the term, I think it is fair to say that he believes in the *illocutioque* ("and from the illocution").[86]

This surprising convergence of *illocutioque* and *Filioque* does not prove anything. It is inadvisable to draw general conclusions about the philosophy of language from trinitarian theology, nor should one formulate one's understanding of the three Persons on the basis of an analysis of speech acts. Such has not been my intent. Instead I have sought to reinforce insights gained from one discipline with insights gained in another, all the while looking for places where philosophy might approximate our theology and where theology might adjust our philosophy. Alston's insistence that perlocutions depend on illocutions does support my contention that biblical interpreters should seek to infer illocutionary content before seeking to achieve perlocutionary effects. This is also, I believe, how the Holy Spirit works through biblical interpretation to form the people of God: not by producing effects unrelated to the text's communicative action but precisely by ministering the divine communicative action, in all its canonical unity and variety.

10. What God does with Scripture is covenant with humanity by testifying to Jesus Christ (illocution) and by bringing about the reader's mutual indwelling with Christ (perlocution) through the Spirit's rendering Scripture efficacious.

Conclusion: The Covenant Community

Theories about language affect human practice, communication and interpretation alike. What we say about language affects what we think about ourselves. Through-

---

[86]My argument does not depend on a particular version of the *Filioque*. The analogy with illocutions and perlocutions will work equally well if one adopts alternative suggestions such as "from the Father *through* the Son."

out this essay I have assumed that using language is a covenantal affair. I have
adopted what we might call the *presumption of covenantal relation*. This goes
beyond the presumption of relevance. The latter states that implied in every speech
act is the claim that it is relevant. The covenantal presumption states that implied in
every speech act is a certain covenantal relation—a tacit plea, or demand, to understand. Language itself cannot make this demand on us. Language, considered in the
abstract, holds no rights. No, the presumption of covenantal relation stems from the
fact that we are obliged to do justice to the words of a communicative agent in order
to do that *person* justice. Here we may invoke Emmanuel Lévinas's notion that the
face "speaks." The "face" says "Do not kill," and stands for the infinite obligation we
have toward our neighbor. Similarly, the "voice" in the text says "Hear me," and
stands for the obligation we have toward our neighbor, as good citizens of language,
to understand what that person is saying and what that person is doing in her saying.
Interlocutors therefore "always share at least one common goal, that of understanding and being understood."[87]

The church is an interpretive community, a people of the book. As such, it is a
covenant community in both of the senses employed in this essay. The church is first
of all a community oriented to the discourse of the covenant, the Christian Scriptures.
Yet the church should also be a community that cares about the covenant of discourse in general. For as I argued at the outset, language is a divinely ordained institution with its own divine design plan.

In conclusion, let me highlight three features that I believe should characterize
members of the covenant community.

Covenant keepers. We must keep the covenant of discourse, the bonds that language forges between two persons, between person and world, and between human
persons and God. We must be promise keepers and truth tellers. But we must also be
active listeners. For this is the only way to be peacekeepers in the covenant of discourse. There are many forms of violence, but readers must especially be wary of
interpretive violence. We must resist imposing our own interpretations on the discourse of others. We must resist ascribing intentions to authors where there is no evidence of that intent, and we must be honest enough to recognize authorial intentions
where there is adequate evidence of such. We must cultivate what I call elsewhere
the "interpretive virtues": those dispositions of the heart and mind that arise from the
motivation for understanding.

Witnesses. "Do not bear false witness." To me this is the categorical imperative of
hermeneutics. To bear false witness—to say that an author is doing something in a
text that he or she did not do—is to subject the author to a form of violence. Reduc-

[87]Sperber and Wilson, *Relevance,* p. 268.

tionist approaches—thin descriptions—are similarly distorting because they fail adequately to attend to what the author was in fact doing in a text. Theirs is the sin of
omission, of not telling the whole truth. Willful misinterpretation is a violation of the
other. Those who participate in the covenant of discourse are thus obliged to bear
true witness. Indeed this is essentially what interpretation is: bearing witness to the
meaning of the authorial intentions enacted in the text. This is why it is important to
attend to the history of interpretation. God has spoken to previous generations
through his Word, and we need to hear what God said to them as well as the original
readers. It may be, in fact, that God speaks to us in Scripture by way of the tradition
of its interpretation. This would be the case, however, only if previous generations
had rightly discerned God's canonical action in Scripture.

Disciples. Let us not forget Goethe's cautionary tale. Faust's error was to think
that interpretation is something confined to one's study, that interpretation is a matter
of knowledge only, quite separate from virtue and spirituality. Yet every text contains
not merely information but an implicit call: "Follow me." The vocation of the interpreter is to respond to that call and to follow at least to the point of reaching understanding, and perhaps farther. Just as we indicate our understanding by saying "I
follow you," so we indicate our understanding of Scripture when we start to follow in
its way. The privilege of biblical interpretation—the Protestant insistence on the
priesthood of all believers—finally leads to the responsibility of hermeneutics: the
call to become not masters but "martyrs" on behalf of meaning, not only hearers but
doers, and perhaps sufferers, of the Word.

"In language man dwells." Well, Heidegger was almost right. The true end of the
covenant of discourse and the discourse of the covenant is indeed a kind of dwelling
or, better, a mutual indwelling. The Bible simply calls it *communion:* we in Christ,
Christ in us. I am referring of course to the supreme covenant blessing: life with God.
Perhaps this blessing will one day be realized without benefit of language. Until then,
however, humans are embodied persons who have to walk and talk with one
another to have fellowship. It is noteworthy that God is depicted as walking and talking with human beings in the garden—before Babel, and before Pentecost. For language is not only a medium of communicative action; it is arguably the most elastic,
variegated and powerful medium of interpersonal communion as well. "In the beginning was the Word, and the Word . . . dwelt among us."

Summary of Theses

1. Language has a "design plan" that is inherently covenantal.

2. The paradigm for a Christian view of communication is the triune God in communicative action.

3. "Meaning" is the result of communicative action, of what an author has done in

tending to certain words at a particular time in a specific manner.

4. The literal sense of an utterance or text is the sum total of those illocutionary acts performed by the author intentionally and with self-awareness.

5. Understanding consists in recognizing illocutionary acts and their results.

6. Interpretation is the process of inferring authorial intentions and of ascribing illocutionary acts.

7. An action that aims to produce perlocutionary effects on readers other than by means of *understanding* counts as strategic, not communicative, action.

8. To describe a generic (or canonic) illocution is to describe the communicative act that structures the text considered as a unified whole.

9. The Spirit speaks in and through Scripture precisely by rendering its illocutions at the sentential, generic and canonic levels perlocutionarily efficacious.

10. What God does with Scripture is covenant with humanity by testifying to Jesus Christ (illocution) and by bringing about the reader's mutual indwelling with Christ (perlocution) through the Spirit's rendering Scripture efficacious.

Part Three

Hermeneutics

Seven

The Spirit of Understanding

Special Revelation &
General Hermeneutics

What Christianity gives the world is hermeneutics." Martin Buber's remark is both provocative and ambiguous. Is he saying that Christianity gives the world a *special* hermeneutic, that is, a method for interpreting the Bible in particular, or is he suggesting that *general* hermeneutics is somehow beholden to Christian faith?[1] My object is not to make a judgment as to what Buber actually intended but to use his statement as a starting point for reflection. When Philip asked the Ethiopian eunuch if he understood what he was reading (Isaiah 53), the answer was "How can I, unless someone guides me?" (Acts 8:31). What exactly is the nature of this guidance, this extra help that goes beyond the reading of the words? Is it the guidance of tradition, community participation, the canonical context, or is it, in a sense yet to be determined, the guidance of the Spirit (Jn 16:13)?[2]

For more than a thousand years, Augustine, not Philip, provided would-be readers with guidance. His *On Christian Doctrine* provided rules for biblical interpretation that served as the foundation of medieval culture. Despite its rich Christian parentage, however, hermeneutics has of late been squandering its inheritance. The prodigal

---

[1]Hermeneutics is the "critical reflection on the practice of interpretation—its aims, conditions, and criteria" (Charles Wood, *The Formation of Christian Understanding: An Essay in Theological Hermeneutics* [Philadelphia: Westminster Press, 1981], p. 9). "General hermeneutics" refers to the principles that govern the study of literary meaning as such. "Special hermeneutics" refers to the additional rules or principles that govern certain kinds of texts.

[2]Both Philip with the eunuch and Jesus with the travelers to Emmaus interpret Scripture with Scripture. G. C. Berkouwer comments: "Understanding is not achieved by putting Scripture aside" (*Holy Scripture*, trans. and ed. Jack Rogers [Grand Rapids, Mich.: Eerdmans, 1975], p. 112).

interpreter has quit the house of authority in pursuit of Enlightenment autonomy. In the desert of criticism his means of sustenance were eventually exhausted; famished for meaning, he wished to be called again. Now, giddy with freedom and hunger, he reads riotously, feeding off texts with no taste in a Dionysian deconstructive carnival.

Carnival comes from the Latin (*carne valere,* literally "to put away flesh [as food]") and refers to the custom of partying before the Lenten fast. The etymology is instructive, and the analogy with deconstruction is apt: the deconstructive carnival puts away the matter, the meat, of the text. It denies the presence of the Logos in the letter. Accordingly it refuses nourishment from the text and remains in a state of perpetual fast; the feast—communion with the meat and matter of the text—is endlessly deferred. "Carnival" describes hermeneutics gone into the far country, where it has abandoned itself to deconstructive dissolution.

My strategy in what follows is twofold: I want to answer the question about how we read the Bible, whether with general or special hermeneutics, by looking at the debate between the Yale and Chicago schools, and to do so in the light of postmodern literary theory. By looking at one debate in particular, I hope to show hermeneutics in general the way back to its Christian home.

Theology undergirds our theories of language and interpretation. The Bible should be interpreted "like any other book," but every other book should be interpreted with norms that we have derived from a reflection on how to read Scripture. I stake my claim that the Bible should be read like any other book, and that every other book should be read like the Bible, within a Christian worldview. Where does the Spirit fit into the process of faith seeking understanding?[3] Only the Spirit of understanding can convict us of hermeneutic sin—interpretive violence that distorts the text—and illumine our eyes so that we see the Logos that is "really present" in the letter. In the valley of the shadow of deconstruction, the best general hermeneutics may prove to be a *trinitarian* hermeneutics. It remains to be seen, however, why I think the Spirit of understanding must be the Holy, rather than a secular, Spirit.

Theology and Literary Theory: Beyond Secular Hermeneutics

David Tracy is undoubtedly correct when he notes the pervasive influence of literary theory on theology.[4] I believe the reverse also to be the case: literary theory is bound

---

[3]The idea that biblical meaning is something that can be recovered by understanding simply by reading relegates the doctrine of the Holy Spirit to the theological margins (so Francis Watson, referring to Richard Hooker, in Francis Watson, *Text, Church and World: Biblical Interpretation in Theological Perspective* [Edinburgh: T & T Clark, 1994], p. 295 n. 5).

[4]"The influence of literary criticism and literary theory on Christian theologies has become a major factor in any reasonable interpretation or assessment of theology today" (David Tracy, "Literary Theory and Return of the Forms for Naming and Thinking God in Theology," *Journal of Religion* 74 [1994]: 302).

up with the modification or the rejection of orthodox Christian positions. Secular literary theories are theologies or antitheologies in disguise.[5] There is good reason then to consider the hermeneutical character of theology as well as the theological character of hermeneutics.

In the first place, what is hermeneutical about theology? Theology is hermeneutical "since it deals with a tradition mediated in no small measure by written texts and their interpretation."[6] Here, however, the consensus ends.

Should we read the Bible "like any other book"? This is precisely what Benjamin Jowett contends, in his famous essay "On the Interpretation of Scripture" (1860). One of his primary concerns for reading the Bible critically was "to combat the obscuring of the true meaning of biblical texts through traditional interpretations being forced upon them."[7] Reading the Bible "like any other book" is the "master principle" for biblical interpretation. Two corollaries follow: one must pay attention to the historical context, and a text has only a single meaning, the meaning it had for the original author.

Jowett spoke of the "diffusion of a critical spirit" in his time that inspired the interpreter to rise above theological and denominational controversies: "His object is to read Scripture like any other book, with a real interest and not merely a conventional one. He wants to be able to open his eyes and see . . . things as they truly are."[8] Critical interpretation would lift the fog of dogmas and controversies that had obscured the literal sense. The critical spirit, in recovering the original meaning, will cast out the "seven other" meanings that had taken up their abode in the text. The alternative to critical truth is ideology and illusion: "Where there is no critical interpretation of Scripture, there will be a mystical or rhetorical one. If words have more than one meaning, they may have any meaning."[9]

Stanley Hauerwas disagrees: "The Bible is not and should not be accessible to merely anyone, but rather it should only be made available to those who have undergone the hard discipline of existing as part of God's people." Fundamentalist literalists

[5]The allusions to John Milbank are intentional. Milbank argues that secular social theory is constituted in its secularity by its "heretical" relation to orthodox Christianity [John Milbank, *Theology and Social Theory: Beyond Secular Reason* (Oxford: Blackwell, 1990], pp. 1-3). I want to say the same of secular literary theory.

[6]Werner G. Jeanrond, "Theological Hermeneutics: Development and Significance," in *Studies in Literature and Religion*, ed. David Jasper (London: Macmillan, 1991), p. 9.

[7]Paul R. Noble, "The Sensus Literalis: Jowett, Childs and Barr," *Journal of Theological Studies* (1993): 3.

[8]Ibid., p. 7.

[9]Benjamin Jowett, "On the Interpretation of Scripture," in *The Interpretation of Scripture and Other Essays* (London: George Routledge & Sons, n.d.), p. 31. Jowett's essay has occasioned a lengthy debate between James Barr and Brevard Childs about what Jowett means by "like any other book." See James Barr, "Jowett and the Reading of the Bible 'Like Any Other Book,'" *Horizons of Biblical Theology* 4 (1985): 1-44.

and liberal critics alike are "but two sides of the same coin, insofar as each assumes that the text should be accessible to anyone without the necessary mediation of the Church."[10] Jowett mistakenly believed that if interpreters only used the right tools they could attain the objective meaning and truth of Scripture. What is needed, says Hauerwas, are not scholarly tools but saintly practices: in order to read the Bible correctly we must be trained in Christian virtue.

Hauerwas challenges the "two dogmas of criticism"—that biblical scholarship is objective and that biblical scholarship is apolitical. First, against objectivity, Hauerwas argues that we cannot understand Scripture simply by picking it up and reading it "like any other book." Facts are not just "there." What we see depends on where we stand. The presumption that the Bible can be read "scientifically," with common and critical sense, leads to the second dogma, that individuals can interpret and understand the Bible by themselves. Fundamentalists and biblical critics alike, says Hauerwas, "fail to acknowledge the *political* character of their account of the Bible. . . . They want to disguise how their 'interpretations' underwrite the privileges of the constituency that they serve." Truth cannot be known "without initiation into a community that requires transformation of the self."[11] Contrast Hauerwas's manifesto with Jowett's equally uncompromising position: "It is better to close the book than to read it under conditions of thought which are imposed from without."[12]

Hauerwas maintains that the whole endeavor to interpret the Bible "on its own terms" is vain nonsense. There is no such thing as the "real meaning" of Paul's letters to the Corinthians once we understand that they are not Paul's letters but the church's Scripture. It is the "sin of the Reformation," we are told, to assert *sola Scriptura,* for this exposes Scripture to subjective and arbitrary interpretation. *Sola Scriptura* is a heresy because it assumes "that the text of the Scripture makes sense separate from a Church that gives it sense."[13]

"Meaning" for Hauerwas is a matter of the use to which one puts the texts for the edification of the church. The obvious question, of course, is how the church knows what God is saying though the Scriptures if what God is saying does not coincide with the verbal meaning. Hauerwas here invokes the Spirit: "the Church, through the guidance of the Holy Spirit, tests contemporary readings of Scripture against the tradition."[14] A theological issue therefore lies at the heart of hermeneutical debate: how

---

[10]Stanley Hauerwas, *Unleashing the Scripture: Freeing the Bible from Captivity to America* (Nashville: Abingdon, 1993), pp. 9, 17.
[11]Ibid., p. 35.
[12]Jowett, "On the Interpretation," p. 11.
[13]Hauerwas, *Unleashing Scripture,* p. 155 n. 7, pp. 25, 27.
[14]Ibid., p. 27.

does the Spirit lead the church into all truth? For Stanley Fish, a literary critic on whom Hauerwas depends, it is the reading practice of the interpretive community that produces the meaning. There is no such thing as the literal meaning for Fish. Similarly, for Hauerwas, the meaning that interests the church is not "the meaning of the text" but rather "how the Spirit that is found in the Eucharist is also to be seen in Scripture."[15]

What is theological about hermeneutics? The answer comes into view when we trace the development of the so-called three ages of literary criticism. We can view their unfolding in terms of a downward spiral into a theological abyss, though there are signs that hermeneutics may now be returning from the far country.[16]

The crisis in contemporary literary theory seems to be a direct consequence of Nietzsche's announcement concerning the "death of God." According to Mark Taylor, "the death of God was the disappearance of the Author who had inscribed absolute truth and univocal meaning in world history and human experience."[17] For Roland Barthes, the disappearance of God leads to the death of the human author. The author's absence means that there is nothing that fixes or stabilizes meaning. The death of the Father-Author "thus liberates an activity we may call counter-theological . . . for to refuse to halt meaning is finally to refuse God."[18] As George Steiner puts it: "God the Father of meaning, in His authorial guise, is gone from the game."[19]

Interpretation is theological if it is based on the belief that there is something that "transcends" the play of language in writing. Barthes and Jacques Derrida are *countertheologians:* there is nothing outside the play of writing, nothing that guarantees that our words refer to the world. The loss of a transcendent signifier—Logos—thus follows hard upon the death of the author. The result is a textual gnosticism that refuses to locate determinate meaning in the literal sense. Every truth claim is dissolved in a sea of indeterminacy. Hermeneutics has become the prodigal discipline, rejecting both the authority of the Father and the rationality of the Logos, squandering its heritage in riotous and rebellious reading.

With the death of the author and the rejection of the autonomous text, the reader is born.[20] Meaning is not discovered but made, by the reader's rediscovered Nietzschean will to power. The text "has no rights" and "can be used in whatever

---

[15]Ibid., p. 23.
[16]As I shall argue below, there are hints of a new turn to "Spirit."
[17]Mark Taylor, "Deconstructing Theology," in *AAR Studies in Religion* 28 (Chico, Calif.: Scholars Press, 1982), p. 90.
[18]Roland Barthes, "Death of the Author," in *The Rustle of Language,* trans. Richard Howard (New York: Hill & Wang, 1986), p. 54.
[19]George Steiner, *Real Presences* (Chicago: University of Chicago Press, 1989), p. 127.
[20]Some critics have spoken of a "Readers' Liberation Movement."

ways readers or interpreters choose."[21] With the birth of the reader, the divine has been relocated: the postmodern era is more comfortable thinking of God not as the transcendent Author but as the immanent Spirit.[22] The Shekinah cloud has settled on the interpreting community.

Ironically, it is largely nontheologians who have been calling, in current critical debates, for theological hermeneutics.[23] One of the most eloquent of these calls comes from a literary critic, George Steiner: "Any coherent account of the capacity of human speech to communicate meaning and feeling is, in the final analysis, underwritten by the assumption of God's presence."[24] Steiner makes a wager on transcendence; he has faith that what we encounter in language and literature transcends the mere play of signifiers. Logocentrism, for Steiner, is the basis for the covenant between word and world, the conviction that reality is "sayable." Steiner believes that the reader encounters an "otherness" that calls the reader to respond. There is a Word in the words, to which the reader is responsible. Of course the sense of an other's "presence" in language may be only "a rhetorical flourish," as the deconstructionists say, rather than "a piece of theology."[25] If the appearance of presence turns out to be false, the result is a "deconstructionist and postmodernist counter-theology of absence."[26]

For Steiner, then, reading for the "other," for transcendence, is a theological activity. Interestingly, deconstruction also positions itself as defender of the other. Indeed in Derrida's more recent works, the theme of ethics—by which he means responsibility to otherness—has come to the fore. Steiner and Derrida represent therefore two very different ways—the one theological, the other countertheological—of doing justice to the "alterity" or otherness of the text.[27]

---

[21]John Barton and Robert Morgan, *Biblical Interpretation* (Oxford: Oxford University Press, 1988), p. 7. Ronald L. Hall suggests that "the spirit of writing for Derrida is a demonic perversion of spirit. The spirit of writing is . . . a perpetual breaking, a perpetual sundering, a perpetual hovering, a perpetual play of signs. The spirit of writing is essentially disembodied, essentially a break with the world" (Ronald L. Hall, *Word and Spirit: A Kierkegaardian Critique of the Modern Age* [Bloomington: Indiana University Press, 1993], p. 178).

[22]In his essay "Towards a Concept of Postmodernism," Ihab Hassan puts "God the Father" in the column of "modernity" and "Holy Spirit" under the category of the postmodern (Ihab Hassan, "Towards a Concept of Postmodernism," in *Postmodernism: A Reader*, ed. Thomas Docherty [London: Wheatsheaf, 1993], p. 152).

[23]Umberto Eco worries about "overinterpretation"—the exaggeration of the rights of the reader over the rights of the text (*Interpretation and Overinterpretation*, ed. Stefan Collini [Cambridge: Cambridge University Press, 1992], p. 23).

[24]Steiner, *Real Presences*, p. 3.

[25]See Graham Ward, "George Steiner and the Theology of Culture," *New Blackfriars*, February 1993, pp. 98-105. See the essays in Nathan A. Scott Jr. and Ronald A. Sharp, eds., *Reading George Steiner* (Baltimore: Johns Hopkins University Press, 1994).

[26]Steiner, *Real Presences*, p. 122.

[27]More recently several studies have suggested that Derrida is more appropriately associated with the tradition of negative theology.

Which interpretive paradigm—which "theology" of interpretation—best guards
the otherness of the text, its ability to say something that would confront and address
us rather than reflect our own interests? Neither hermeneutics nor theology can afford
to follow Ludwig von Feuerbach's suggestion that what we find—God, meaning—is
only a projection of ourselves. The hermeneutical equivalent to Feuerbach's suggestion that theology is really only anthropology is the view that exegesis is really only
eisegesis. Such a strategy stifles transcendence and reduces the scriptural "other" to
the cultural "same."[28] Deconstructive reading—insofar as it undoes determinate textual meaning—is violent. Instead of protecting the textual other, it tears it asunder by
a kind of close reading that sometimes resembles harmless play but at others textual
vivisection.[29] Only a hermeneutic that has cut its teeth on Scripture will be able to
read for an understanding of the other. In what is to come, I shall defend the following thesis: the best general hermeneutics is a *theological* hermeneutics.

Yale and Chicago Revisited: Spirit and Letter
The discussion to this point has set a broad stage on which to rehearse the important
debate between theologians at Yale and Chicago over biblical narrative. If we speak

---

[28]Cf. Kevin Vanhoozer, "From Canon to Concept: 'Same' and 'Other' in the Relation of Biblical
and Systematic Theology," *Scottish Bulletin of Evangelical Theology* 12 (1994): 96-124. Some
have tried to counter deconstruction by reasserting the authority of the divine author. For
Richard Lints, the Bible cannot be read like any other book, not only because it functions as
Scripture but because it has God as its author: "Certainly evangelicals can share with Jowett
a concern for the original authorial intention in Scripture, but they must take care not to lose
sight of the other half of the dual authorship or they will surely lose sight of the meaning"
(Richard Lints, *The Fabric of Theology: A Prolegomenon to Evangelical Theology* [Grand Rapids, Mich.: Eerdmans, 1993], p. 75). What does divine authorship add? For Lints, it means that
we should read each portion of Scripture in the context of the canon as a whole, for this is
the appropriate context in which to consider the Bible as God's writing. Let me also note
Lints's belief that while God's meaning is never unrelated to the plain sense, neither it is limited to the plain sense (ibid., p. 77). Charles Wood agrees: the claim that the Bible is the
Word of God has functioned as a hermeneutical principle that instructs us to read the text as
a unity. To read the Bible as Scripture, he claims, is to read the Bible *as if* it were a whole,
and *as if* the author of the whole were God. See Wood, *Formation of Christian Understanding*, p. 70.

[29]John Milbank believes that modern secularity is linked to an "ontology of violence," a worldview that assumes the priority of force and tells how this force (desire, energy, language,
ideology, etc.) is best managed and confined—by secular reason. Christian theology, however, does not recognize chaos and violence as first principles. Only Christian theology is
able to overcome nihilism. There is another way to think difference: not in terms of repres-
sion but of reconciliation, of a peace that surpasses any totalizing reason. Christianity, says
Milbank, "exposes the non-necessity of supposing, like the Nietzscheans, that difference . . .
and indeterminacy of meaning necessarily imply arbitrariness and violence" (*Theology and
Social Theory*, p. 5). I shall develop these ideas in terms of hermeneutics in my reflections
on the Spirit of understanding as a Spirit of peace.

of the "return" of hermeneutics to Christianity, to what home does it return? Where one locates biblical hermeneutics, whether nearer New Haven or Chicago, depends on how one answers the following question: Should we read the Bible like any other book? If we should not, can we approach Scripture with a special hermeneutics without falling prey to fideism or relativism? The fate of the literal sense will serve as our litmus test as we attempt to deal with these questions.

For Hans Frei and the Yale theologians, the crucial issue is whether Christian theology and the biblical text are instances of a larger class—religion, text—and thus to be subsumed under general criteria of intelligibility and truth. Orthodoxy ultimately stands or falls on whether we can say that the Gospels are about the irreducible man Jesus Christ or whether the texts are really about moral or religious truths of which Jesus is merely an illustration. Hermeneutics is inextricably linked to Christology. To put it baldly, nonliteral interpretation takes Jesus off the cross. The passion becomes something else than the story of Jesus.

For David Tracy, on the other hand, the crucial issue is whether we can read for the literal sense in a way that is both faithful to the tradition and intelligible to people today. Whereas Frei bows the knee to the criterion of "Christian appropriateness," Tracy worships in the spirit of "contemporary intelligibility." In Chicago the literal sense converses with the "lived sense" of human existence today.

Which of these two theological options best contains the resources with which, first, to do justice to the literal sense of the biblical text and, second, to withstand the onslaughts of deconstruction? This particular debate about the literal sense in biblical hermeneutics may serve to illumine the hermeneutical situation in general.

Like many other contemporary theologians, Tracy, one of the foremost representatives of the Chicago tradition, wants to make the Christian faith intelligible in a pluralistic world. His strategy is to explain religion, the less well-known phenomenon, in terms of our experience of art, the more familiar. Works of art are true, not as accurate representations of the world but rather as disclosures of some deeper truth about the world and ourselves. Both artistic and religious classics have the power to disclose certain existential possibilities, ways of seeing and being in the world. Aesthetic experience becomes a general model in the light of which Tracy can declare: the Gospels are *like that*. Indeed he can even claim that the truth claims of art and religion stand or fall together. Biblical interpretation is therefore a species of a much larger class.

How does the approach to theology and interpretation just sketched affect the literal sense? Like Rudolf Bultmann, Tracy believes that the literal sense objectifies God. God does not literally have arms and eyes. No, the real referent of the biblical narratives—human existence—is metaphorical. What distinguishes the Bible from other poetic texts is not the way we read it but the kind of possibility we find therein. For Chicago, religious truth is a matter of disclosing existential possibilities that can transform the life of the reader.

Frei, on the other hand, ranks criteria of Christian appropriateness higher than criteria of contemporary intelligibility. The prime directive of theology is to approach the object of its study—God's revelation and redemption in Christ—in an appropriate way. We must resist the "temptation of all theology" (Barth) to try to set out in advance the conditions for meaningful and true talk about God (natural theology) or about the biblical narratives (hermeneutics).[30] What good are universal criteria of rationality if one is trying to describe something as utterly and absolutely unique as the Christ event?

Historical critics like Jowett approached the texts with their own standards of intelligibility and truth. The natural world was more real to them than the world of the biblical text. In order to "save" the text, they had to interpret it in such a way that they could accept it: as a source for determining what actually happened. The critic did not trust the text as it now stands and so interpreted it to mean something other than what lay on the surface. Frei has brilliantly described how both conservatives and liberals eclipsed the biblical narrative. "Fundamentalism identified the grammatical and literary sense of a text with what the text's words ostensibly referred to."[31] They shared with biblical critics the urge to turn the literal sense into "a detective's clue to the discovery of [the historical] referent."[32] Some critics mistook the meaning for the historical referents behind the story; others mistook the meaning for the eternal truths above the story. In each case, however, the meaning becomes separable from the narrative itself. Biblical interpretation became "a matter of fitting the biblical story into another world . . . rather than incorporating that world into the biblical story."[33]

Frei looks to Karl Barth as a model of how to read the biblical narrative literally: "The universal role of interpretation is that a text can be read and understood and expounded only with reference to and in the light of its theme."[34] Form and matter are inseparable. What the text says is what the text is about. Its meaning, in other

---

[30]Karl Barth, *Church Dogmatics* 1/2, ed. G. W. Bromiley and T. F. Torrance, trans. G. T. Thomson and Harold Knight (Edinburgh: T & T Clark, 1956), p. 4.

[31]Hans Frei, *Types of Christian Theology*, ed. George Hunsinger and William C. Placher (New Haven, Conn.: Yale University Press, 1992), p. 158.

[32]Hans Frei, "'Narrative' in Christian and Modern Reading," in *Theology and Dialogue: Essays in Conversation with George Lindbeck*, ed. Bruce D. Marshall (Notre Dame, Ind.: University of Notre Dame Press, 1990), p. 152.

[33]Hans Frei, *The Eclipse of Biblical Narrative: A Study in Eighteenth and Nineteenth Century Hermeneutics* (New Haven, Conn.: Yale University Press, 1975), p. 130.

[34]Barth, *Church Dogmatics* 1/2, p. 493. Theological reading "is the reading of the text, and not the reading of a source, which is how historians read it" (Frei, *Types of Christian Theology*, p. 11). Understanding the text is an ability, a capacity "to follow an implicit set of rules unintelligible except in the examples of text . . . in which they are exhibited" (Hans Frei, "Theology and the Interpretation of Narrative: Some Hermeneutical Considerations," in *Theology and Narrative: Selected Essays*, ed. George Hunsinger and William C. Placher (Oxford: Oxford University Press, 1993), p. 101.

words, is not "behind" it in history, "above" it in myth or allegory, or "in front of" it in the experience or world of the reader. In George Lindbeck's celebrated formula, "it is the text, so to speak, which absorbs the world, rather than the world the text."[35] With regard to realistic narrative, we have the reality only under the narrative description.[36] We cannot go around or behind or over or under the narratives to get to their subject matter; we have to go through them. Jesus is the literal subject of the Gospel narratives; the story is about him, not someone or something else.[37]

Tracy recognizes Frei's contribution in specifying the criterion of Christian appropriateness, the literal sense of biblical narrative, with greater precision. However, he cautions against privileging any one literary form of Scripture. We need to do justice to the plurality of biblical genres.

On Tracy's view, Christian tradition must be correlated with independent human experience in the world.[38] Frei's claim to self-referentiality is artificial; it disconnects the text from the extratextual world and from the process of reading.[39] In Francis Watson's words, "To regard the church as a self-sufficient sphere closed off from the world is ecclesiological docetism." Insights originating in the secular world can have a positive role in assisting the community to understand Scripture. The broader canonical context "suggests that the Spirit dwells within the created and human world as well as within the church, in which case truth may proceed from the world to the church as well as from the church to the world."[40]

These diverse criticisms raise the same fundamental query: Is intratextuality ade-

---

[35]George Lindbeck, *The Nature of Doctrine: Religion and Theology in a Postliberal Age* (Philadelphia: Westminster Press, 1984), p. 118.

[36]Frei, *Types of Christian Theology*, p. 139.

[37]The realistic literal sense of the resurrection narratives, for example, is that the resurrection is a predicate of Jesus, not of the disciples. Bultmann is wrong to say that the resurrection stories are really about the disciples' coming to faith. Yet Carl Henry is wrong too if he implies that the resurrection is a kind of scientific fact. The notion of "fact" is as extratextual as Bultmann's category of "myth." The resurrection for Barth is neither myth nor history; the risen Jesus is neither a historical nor an ideal referent. What is the relation of the risen Christ in the text to history? Neither Frei nor Barth can specify the way the text refers to reality. The literal sense is a textual, not a historical, sense. To put it another way, one can read the texts literally "and at the same time leave the referential status of what was described in them indeterminate" (Frei, *Types of Christian Theology*, p. 138).

[38]Tracy is not as pessimistic about the utility of general hermeneutics as is Frei. Tracy's own interpretation of the Gospels is correlated with, but not founded on, his general hermeneutical analysis of the religious classic (David Tracy, "On Reading the Scriptures Theologically," in *Theology and Dialogue*, ed. Bruce Marshall [New Haven, Conn.: Yale University Press, 1992], p. 59 n. 16).

[39]Frei was later to make this criticism of his own position. See Frei, "The 'Literal Reading' of Biblical Narrative: Does It Stretch or Will It Break?" in *Theology and Narrative: Selected Essays*, ed. George Hunsinger and William C. Placher (Oxford: Oxford University Press, 1993), p. 141.

[40]Watson, *Text, Church and World*, pp. 236-37.

quate for the full range of theology's task—for the church's mission to the world? The Yale school's strength is its clarification of the criteria of Christian appropriateness.[41] But that is only half of theology's job description. We need to engage the world in conversation about our theories rather than trying to hide behind our ecclesial skirts. Criteria of intelligibility are also necessary. Yet Yale remains suspicious of the terms of this conversation: general theories are Trojan horses. Existentialism may have made Paul's anthropology intelligible to certain twentieth-century thinkers, but in the end it chokes the gospel within its own categories—a perfect illustration of philosophy capturing Christian thought (Col 2:8).

What think ye of Christ? The Tracy of *The Analogical Imagination* might reply, "He is the manifestation of an always already possibility of an agapic mode of being-in-the-world." The literal sense is, on this view, dispensable. This is neither hermeneutically nor theologically appropriate to Christian faith, for the incarnation and resurrection are decidedly not members of a general class! Like Barth, Frei believes that we must begin with the particular. To begin with general categories is to risk swallowing up the act or the Word of God in a human conception of what was or was not possible. There simply is no nontextual access to the reality of Jesus Christ.

Yale has questions with regard to the suitability of Chicago's criteria of intelligibility as well. The community in which we stand does affect the way we read. We hear the Word when we participate in the form of life within which alone it makes sense. Furthermore, the reasons one gives for preferring the literal sense of the gospel as one's basic explanatory framework are internal to the Christian tradition. So are *all* reasons that commend one's tradition, including the tradition of the Enlightenment. The only honest position to take in a rational conversation is to say "Here I stand." Tracy, however, tries to have it both ways: "Here I stand . . . and *there*."

Tracy and Frei have qualified their respective positions in the wake of their confrontations in the early 1980s. Tracy has become less inclined to use a single conceptual scheme to interpret the Gospels; Frei became reluctant to define the literal sense in terms of realistic narrative. We might characterize the emerging position that has resulted from these peace talks as *canonical conversation in correlation with community context*. What new mutation of the literal sense does such a development represent?

In a 1994 article Tracy agrees with Frei that all Christian theologians should acknowledge the plain sense as normative.[42] But Frei's emphasis on a unified coher-

---

[41]"No theologian should deny that one major task of all responsible theology is to show how it is the tradition itself that is being interpreted and not interpreted away or invented" (David Tracy, "Lindbeck's New Program for Theology," *The Thomist* 49 [1985]: 468).

[42]"Surely Hans Frei . . . [was] not wrong to insist that God's identity is Christianly established in and through the passion narrative's rendering of the identity of and presence of Jesus as the Christ" (Tracy, "Literary Theory," p. 310).

ent narrative overlooks the plurality and ambiguity within the canon itself. What theology needs is the full spectrum of forms in the Bible itself, with Jesus Christ as the supreme "form" that informs all Christian understanding of God.[43] Neither modernity nor a united narrative provides a general framework within which one can correlate religion and rationality. Tracy continues to believe that the project of correlation is indispensable. Conversation is the form rationality must take in the postmodern era. The interpreter converses with the ambiguous text and with the plural traditions of interpretation. Postmodernism calls for an ethics of resistance to all monologues, to all *isms,* that seek to close the conversation prematurely. Postmodern mystic readings identify God "as positive Incomprehensibility"; postmodern prophetic readings identify God as the one who acts in the cross of the oppressed and marginalized.[44] By identifying God as positive Incomprehensibility and as the one who is in solidarity with the suffering of the oppressed, Tracy seeks to preserve the literal sense of the passion narratives while at the same time going beyond it.

In his later work Frei adopted a different strategy for preserving the particularity of biblical narrative from the hegemony of general theory. He focused on how the Gospels have been read by the church.[45] The proper context for determining the literal sense, he came to believe, is no longer literary but sociolinguistic.[46] Literal sense is less a quality of the text than a function of community practice.[47] In short: "The

---

[43]David Tracy, "Theology and the Many Faces of Postmodernity," *Theology Today* 51 (1994): 111. Frei apparently conceded that Tracy might better fit into the third of his five types of theology. On this view, though Tracy would still wish to correlate the specificity of Christian faith with general criteria that would be culturally intelligible, he would do so in an ad hoc or piecemeal rather than systematic fashion. See Frei, *Types of Christian Theology,* p. x, for the suggestion that Frei became "fond" of Tracy, and p. 71 for a description of type 3.

[44]The principal biblical forms of naming God are the prophetic and the mystical. These are the two basic kinds of "further readings" of the plain sense (Tracy, "Literary Theory," p. 316).

[45]The literal sense, Frei observes, is not one thing. See Frei, *Types of Christian Theology,* pp. 14-15. Just as its fortunes changed in the eighteenth century when it no longer meant "the sense of the text" but rather "the referent of the text," so it underwent a far-reaching (and fateful) change in his own work. Frei apparently dissociated himself from his earlier view on realistic narrative, even referring to it in the third person.

[46]Not all of Frei's followers support him in this move (see Placher's comment). This may prove to be a significant breakup of a Yale consensus.

[47]Frei began to speak of the "literal reading" rather than the "literal sense." He was influenced in part by his colleague David Kelsey's functional definitions of "Scripture" and by George Lindbeck's idea that the way religious language is used in the community is its normative meaning. For Kelsey, to say that a text is "Scripture" is not to predicate some property of the text but to say something about the way the text functions in community. According to Lindbeck, Christianity is a language game and form of life with its own logic. The meaning of a term, or of a text, is a matter of participating in the Christian form of life. That is, neither words nor texts mean "in general" but only in specific contexts when used for specific purposes. Sentences do not correspond to reality in and of themselves but only as "a function

plain sense is a consensus reading."[48] The inspiration for this approach is Ludwig von Wittgenstein, who urges us to look not for "the meaning" but to the use of a word or phrase. Frei applies this insight to the gospel as a whole. The community consensus on Scripture thus becomes the stabilizing force for the notion of the literal sense. Frei finds that throughout the history of the church there has been broad agreement on two important matters: first, to take Jesus Christ as the ascriptive subject of the biblical narratives, and second, not to deny the unity of the Old and New Testaments. Any readings that do not violate these two conventions are permissible.[49]

Two consequences attend this new definition. First, the literal sense is no longer a feature of the "text in itself" but rather the product of the community's interpretive practice.[50] It follows that there is no longer "any absolute distinction between the text's 'proper' sense and the contributions of an interpretive tradition."[51] No conflict between letter and spirit here: it is spirit, or community reading conventions, all the way down. Has Frei exchanged his hermeneutical birthright for a mess of pottage, or rather Fish-stew? It was Fish, Hauerwas's muse, who first suggested that meaning is a product of the way it is read. It is the community, ultimately, that enjoys interpretive authority. Must all hermeneutic roads lead to Rome?

The second consequence of Frei's redefinition is a certain optimism with regard to the believing community. Interpretive might makes right. One may well question the grounds of such optimism: the believing community is all too often portrayed in Scripture as unbelieving or confused, and subsequent church history has not been reassuring either. If the literal sense is a function of community conventions, if there is no text in itself, how can we guard against the possible misuse of Scripture?

Tracy too now prefers to speak of "Scripture in tradition." The literal sense is the plain *ecclesial* sense. So long as the church gives priority to the plain sense of the passion narratives, other readings are permissible. Liberation and feminist theologians, Tracy assures us, have their own ways of maintaining "fidelity to the plain

---

of their role in constituting a form of life . . . which itself corresponds to the . . . Ultimately Real" (Lindbeck, *Nature of Doctrine,* p. 65). The correspondence that counts is not that between mind and thing, but self-in-action and God. The context that determines the meaning of Scripture is the church.

[48]Kathryn Tanner, "Theology and the Plain Sense," in *Scriptural Authority and Narrative Interpretation,* ed. Garrett Green (Philadelphia: Fortress, 1987), p. 63.

[49]The consensus covers the meaning of the stories about Jesus in an ascriptive mode, but not the reality status of the ascriptive subject Jesus. To put it simply, the consensus in Western Christian tradition concerns the literal sense rather than the literal reference of the Gospels (Frei, *Types of Christian Theology,* p. 143).

[50]Frei remarks that the "plain sense"—the consensus reading of Christian tradition—could well have been the "allegorical" rather than the "literal-ascriptive." That the plain sense happens to be the literal sense is a matter of an apparently arbitrary community convention.

[51]Tanner, "Theology and the Plain Sense," p. 64.

sense of the passion narratives." Even a "controlled allegorical exegesis" need not deprive the literal sense of its priority.[52] But what exactly does it mean to give "priority" to the literal sense, if this does not rule out multiple meanings, and especially if a pluralist like Tracy can now pledge his troth to the literal reading too? What are the criteria for going beyond the letter? In ascribing authority to the interpreting community, both Tracy and Frei are relying on a theology, largely implicit, of the Holy Spirit.

What Reformed Theology Has to Say to New Haven and Chicago

I turn now to an explicit theological reflection on these two species of hermeneutical theology. What does Edinburgh—my location, my particularity, home of the Scottish Reformation and entry point of Barth into the English-speaking world—have to say to New Haven and Chicago? We can recast contemporary figures in Reformation roles: Tracy could play Erasmus; Frei, Luther; Jowett could stand in for Socinus; Lindbeck and Hauerwas could compete for the part of Menno Simons—and I shall take the part of Calvin. We can even cast Derrida, perhaps as a Ranter, or alternately as representing the Reformers' untempered iconoclastic zeal. For what deconstruction does best is expose the sociopolitical and ideological interests surreptitiously at work in interpretation. At its best, deconstruction "calls me to be on guard against reinscribing the other in my image for my purposes."[53]

Truth: Sola Scriptura. In recalling Reformation debates, two themes are especially pertinent. First is *sola Scriptura*. New Haven's insistence that "the text absorbs the world" seems to represent a "second coming" of the doctrine of *sola Scriptura*. Absorbing the world into the text means ascribing primary truth to the literal sense of the biblical text and interpreting all other experience in terms of that. New Haven has often been misinterpreted here. To say that the text absorbs the world is not necessarily to retreat into canon and commitment; it is rather a means by which the church can make public truth claims without first having to buy into some general conceptual scheme.[54]

Truth is textually mediated. Frei was right to insist that the concern for intelligibility can skew one's reading of the plain sense of the passion narratives. Bultmann, for

---

[52]Tracy, "On Reading the Scriptures Theologically," pp. 49, 65 n. 64.

[53]Gary A. Phillips, "The Ethics of Reading Deconstructively, or Speaking Face-to-Face: The Samaritan Woman Meets Derrida at the Well," in *The New Literary Criticism and the New Testament,* ed. Elizabeth Struthers Malbon and Edgar V. McKnight (Sheffield, U.K.: Sheffield Academic Press, 1994), p. 317.

[54]Frei is willing to speak of reference and truth, but in each case "it must be the notion of truth or reference that must be re-shaped . . . not the reading of the literal text" (Hans Frei, "Conflicts in Interpretation," in *Theology and Narrative: Selected Essays,* ed. George Hunsinger and William C. Placher (Oxford: Oxford University Press, 1993), p. 164.

instance, had great difficulty satisfying simultaneously the criterion of Christian appropriateness and that of contemporary intelligibility. Indeed his allegiance to both criteria generated the so-called structural inconsistency that debilitated his theology—no one can serve two masters.[55]

We can applaud Frei's dogged insistence that we have no independent access to the subject matter of the Gospels without thereby sliding down the slippery slope of self-referentiality into Derrida's arms and the conclusion that there is nothing outside of the text. Frei's point is *not* that there is nothing outside of the text but rather that there is no way we can provide an independent description of its subject matter. The referent of the Gospels is Jesus, "not as someone to whom we may gain independent unmediated access but insofar as that historical person is mediated to us in and through the text."[56]

Sola Scriptura means that Christians will view meaning and truth in a particularistic way. According to the philosopher Donald Davidson, interpreters seek to maximize the number of true sentences among a speaker's sentences in order to discover what they mean.[57] This is his so-called Principle of Charity: interpret in such a way so as the bulk of the speaker's sentences can be considered true. In the seventeenth and eighteenth centuries, biblical critics began to ascribe centrality to another set of narratives in deciding about truth: modernity's naturalistic account of human history and religion. Accordingly they interpreted the Bible in such a way as to make its sentences compatible with their new secular canon. Decisions about what is generally true thus shaped decisions about what the biblical text could possibly mean. Bultmann's demythologizing is the logical outcome of such "charity." In order to absorb the world into the text, however, we must ascribe primacy to the

---

[55]On the notion of a "structural inconsistency" in Bultmann, see Schubert Ogden, *Christ Without Myth: A Study Based on the Theology of Rudolf Bultmann* (New York: Harper, 1961), p. 96, and Roger A. Johnson, *The Origins of Demythologizing: Philosophy and Historiography in the Theology of Rudolf Bultmann* (Leiden, Netherlands: E. J. Brill, 1974), pp. 15-18.

[56]Watson speaks of Frei's "intratextual realism": the Bible refers beyond itself to extratextual reality, while at the same time regarding that reality as accessible to us only under the textual description (Watson, *Text, Church and World*, pp. 224-25). The truth, then, is textually mediated, but it *is* a claim to truth. If we believe that the biblical narratives—our spectacles of faith—are the primary interpretive framework with which to interpret reality, then we must be prepared to meet challenges from other views. While we acknowledge that we see the truth from within and through the stories, we must continue to claim that it is the truth that we see. A retreat into narrative is not an option for a missionary faith.

[57]Bruce Marshall believes that Donald Davidson's "truth-dependent" account of meaning provides a help to what Frei and Lindbeck are trying to say. See esp. Bruce D. Marshall, "Meaning and Truth in Narrative Interpretation: A Reply to George Schner," *Modern Theology* 8 (1992): 173-79. For an application of Davidson's theories to general hermeneutics, see Reed Way Dasenbrock, ed., *Literary Theory After Davidson* (University Park: Pennsylvania State University Press, 1993).

biblical narratives in deciding about truth and goodness.[58]

Perhaps the main function of *sola Scriptura,* as Gerhard Ebeling observed, is that it preserves intact the distinction between text and interpretation.[59] Can New Haven and Chicago continue to do so? There is a real danger in tying the fate of the literal sense too closely to community consensus. Deconstructionists like nothing better than to dismantle dominant interpretations. To speak of a seventeen-hundred-year-long consensus on reading conventions is virtually to beg to be "undone." Yale and Chicago now agree that what is normative for theology is "Scripture in tradition." Each affirms the priority of the literal sense, but Chicago wants to correlate it with what is intelligible in the contemporary context and Yale with what is appropriate in the context of the Christian community. Given their emphases on the uses of Scripture in Christian tradition, can they preserve the literal sense from corruption by the community on the one hand and from deconstruction on the other?

The Yale school uses broadly Wittgensteinian arguments for locating meaning in community use rather than in some alleged reference. Let us assume that this account of meaning is broadly correct. Does it follow that what theologians should describe is the use of Scripture *today* rather than the use to which words and sentences were put by those responsible for the final form of the biblical text? To replace *sola Scriptura* with "Scripture in tradition"—which is to say, with community conventions—is to use the wrong strategy at the worst time. We live in an age when deconstruction is exposing and exploding social conventions. The masters of hermeneutic suspicion excel in showing that what is mistakenly thought to be "natural" is merely "conventional"; this goes for the plain, "natural" sense of Scripture too. Furthermore, we interpret in an environment strewn with cognitive pollution and subject to ideological pressures. Alvin Plantinga argues that human cognitive capacities have a design plan that specifies their proper functions, and he rightly observes that there is a difference between *normal* functioning and *proper* func-

---

[58]Marshall observes, however, that according epistemic primacy to biblical narrative does not entail that Christians can never revise their beliefs in light of secular learning. The community's various reasons for holding beliefs true are not incompatible with the function of Scripture to serve as the primary criterion for truth. "Dialogue with the adherents of other views of the world can give the Christian community compelling reasons to change its own established beliefs, without requiring it to surrender its identity by epistemically decentralizing the gospel narratives" (Bruce D. Marshall, "Truth Claims and the Possibility of Jewish-Christian Dialogue," *Modern Theology* 8 [1992]: 235). To take one example: the discovery of the Dead Sea scrolls may lead Christians to revise their interpretation of certain biblical passages. To do so is not to make one's allegiance to the literal sense of Scripture secondary, but rather to express one's allegiance to the text rather than to the tradition of one's interpretation of it.

[59]Gerhard Ebeling, *The Word of God and Tradition: Historical Studies Interpreting the Divisions of Christianity,* trans. S. H. Hooke (Philadelphia: Fortress, 1968), p. 136.

tioning.[60] I see no reason that cognitive malfunction could not be corporate as well as individual.

The interpreter has, it is true, an elder brother, the Christian tradition.[61] Individuals always read in some interpretive community. Perhaps the wisdom of the tradition exercises a moderating effect on readers today? Yet elder brothers, as everyone knows, can occasionally be bullies. The Council of Trent used 2 Peter 1:20 ("no prophecy of scripture is a matter of one's own interpretation") to justify the church's right "to judge regarding the true sense and interpretation of holy Scriptures."[62] The Spirit of understanding is shut up here in a hierarchical interpretive institution.

The suggestion that community convention is of hermeneutic significance goes back further than Yale or even Wittgenstein. It has at least one Reformation precedent. John Yoder draws attention to the novelty of the Anabaptist idea that "the text is best understood in a congregation." He points out that Ulrich Zwingli appealed to 1 Corinthians 14:29 to make the point: "the Spirit is an interpreter of what a text is about only when Christians are gathered in readiness to hear it speak."[63] This is not the general Wittgensteinian point about meaning as use but rather the Pauline point about understanding as discipleship. The Anabaptist hopes for something like Habermas's ideal speech situation, in which all those engaged in dialogue about what the text means now in concrete terms would, without coercion, discover unanimity. The final outcome of the conflict of interpretations would be reconciliation: "It seemed good to the Holy Spirit and to us."[64]

Can the church, empowered by the Spirit who leads us into all truth, ever go beyond *sola Scriptura*? Some Anabaptists, like Thomas Müntzer, went too far in their pneumatic exegesis, claiming that the Spirit of understanding goes beyond what the written Word says. Does Frei's emphasis on community consensus similarly bypass the letter? Can the community ever "correct" the canon, say, for its position on women or slavery? Can readers resist the literal meaning if it is oppressive? On the new view from Yale, "whether a text is experienced as contrary to the gospel is determined not only by its objective content but also by the way it is understood in the community."[65] But is it

---

[60]Proper function is a matter of our design plan; normal functioning is a matter of statistics. Alvin Plantinga, *Warrant and Proper Function* (Oxford: Oxford University Press, 1993), pp. 199ff.

[61]I borrow this analogy from Karl Barth.

[62]Quoted in Berkouwer, *Holy Scripture*, p. 115. Calvin, in his commentary on 2 Peter, takes this verse as a warning against arbitrary interpretation. Nothing in the context suggests that the point was to draw a contrast between individual and community.

[63]John Yoder, "The Hermeneutics of Anabaptists," in *Essays on Biblical Interpretation: Anabaptist-Mennonite Perspectives*, ed. Williard M. Swartley (Elkhart, Ind.: Institute of Mennonite Studies, 1984), p. 21.

[64]Quoted in ibid., p. 24.

[65]Watson, *Text, Church and World*, p. 235.

the interpretation or the text that is oppressive? My worry about defining the literal sense in terms of community practice is that we risk losing precisely this distinction between literal sense and community reading.[66]

Kathryn Tanner, a second-generation Yale theologian, has tried to reconcile the traditional emphasis on the integrity of the "plain sense" with Frei's emphasis on habits of reading. Tanner defines the plain sense as what an individual would naturally take the text to be saying "insofar as he or she has been socialized in a community's conventions for reading that text as scripture."[67] Textual sense is not "plain" in and of itself, but only to those who have learned specific habits of reading. But these habits are not themselves the plain sense. The community usually identifies the plain sense with "the verbal sense" or "the sense God intended." Community consensus, in Tanner's scheme, is only the formal, not the material, principle of the plain sense. Our ability to distinguish between text and interpretation, between the literal sense and the way it is conventionally read, ultimately hinges on this fragile conceptual distinction. Tanner insists that this distinction derives not from general hermeneutics but from a particular convention of community practice. Thus the formal principle of the literal sense—the one that gives the text priority over subsequent interpretation—is grounded in a community habit and the material sense, which specifies the nature of the literal sense by decrying the bad reading habits into which critics had fallen at the Enlightenment. To tie the literal sense to community habits seems particularly inappropriate in an age when consensus is an endangered species and when many readers have fallen into bad habits.

Of course, what I am calling "social conventions" could be described by New Haven as the Spirit's guidance. It remains unclear whether the Spirit may lead the church into new interpretations that go beyond the letter.

Trinitarian Hermeneutics: Word and Spirit. "He will guide you into all the truth" (Jn 16:13). How then does the Spirit relate to the literal sense?[68] This question lies at the heart not only of the skirmish between Yale and Chicago but also of the larger cultural

---

[66]Barth is the paradigm for the claim that coherence with Scripture is the primary criterion of truth for Christian theology. According to Marshall, "Scripture is rightly used as a test for truth only when it is read in a certain way" (Marshall, "Truth Claims and the Possibility," p. 235). However, Marshall notes that for Barth the right way is the way that accords with the text. It appears that while the Yale school continues to follow Barth's view of theology as a form of Christian self-description, they have departed from Barth insofar as what is described is a habit of reading rather than the text itself.

[67]Tanner, "Theology and the Plain Sense," p. 63.

[68]A number of studies have begun to explore the hermeneutical significance of the Holy Spirit. An early statement of this interest comes from A. J. MacDonald: "The Spirit's func-

wars that blight the late modern era. The Reformers' notion of the relation between Word and Spirit clarifies the nature of the literal sense as well as Steiner's notion that there is a "real presence" in the text. Only a trinitarian hermeneutic will meet the challenge put to interpretation by the massive atheology of contemporary literary theory.[69]

First, to whom does the Spirit bear witness? Unlike traditional Roman Catholicism on the one hand, where the Spirit is endowed to the church, and enthusiasm on the other, where the Spirit is independent of both Word and church, Protestants affirm the Spirit's witness to individuals and community alike.[70] The apostle Paul writes that "those who are unspiritual do not receive the gifts of God's Spirit" (see 1 Cor 2:14).[71] Gordon Fee comments that the Spirit is thus "the key to everything"—to Paul's preaching, to the Corinthians' conversion "and especially their understanding of the content of his preaching to be the true wisdom of God."[72] This view of the Spirit's work gives a theological underpinning to Yale's emphasis on community practice. Frei concurs: "When Christians speak of the Spirit as the indirect presence now of Jesus Christ . . . they refer to the church."[73] Pneumatology becomes the crucial doctrine in determining whether special revelation needs a special hermeneutic. It also lies behind the Yale-Chicago debate over the possibility of correlation. Must we limit the Spirit of understanding only to the community of faith?

Tracy argues that general human experience is a proper test of Christian tradition insofar as God is present, as Spirit, in creation as well as in the community of the redeemed. True, some passages indicate that the Spirit was not "given" until Jesus was glorified (Jn 7:39) and that the world "neither sees him nor knows him" (Jn 14:17); yet the broader canonical context may suggest "that the Spirit dwells

---

tion is to teach, remind, guide, witness, glorify—surely all functions of a sustained process of interpretation whereby that which has been revealed by the Word . . . is made plain to men" (A. J. MacDonald, *The Interpreter Spirit and Human Life* [London: SPCK, 1944], p. 118).

[69] A complete response is beyond the limits of this present discussion. Elsewhere I have developed Barth's threefold analysis of divine revelation in terms of communicative action. God, the Author-Father, is the agent of the act; God, the Logos-Word, is the communicative act; God, the Spirit-Hearer, is the communication of the Author's Word. Only some such trinitarian analysis can respond, I believe, to the death of the author and the loss of determinate meaning—the "counter-theology" of Barthes and Derrida. My chapter five contains a fuller presentation of these ideas.

[70] See George S. Hendry, *The Holy Spirit in Christian Theology* (London: SCM Press, 1957), chap. 3.

[71] According to Gordon Fee, what only Spirit-filled people understand is the gospel—God's salvation through the crucified One, the wisdom of God. See Fee, *God's Empowering Presence: The Holy Spirit in the Letters of Paul* (Peabody, Mass.: Hendrickson, 1994), pp. 102-3.

[72] Ibid., p. 104.

[73] Hans Frei, *The Identity of Jesus Christ: The Hermeneutical Bases of Dogmatic Theology* (New Haven, Conn.: Yale University Press, 1974), p. 157. Fee similarly observes that the Spirit is the Spirit of the whole body of Christ. Fee, *God's Empowering Presence*, chap. 15.

within the created and human world as well as within the church."[74] Is there perhaps a general as well as a specific witness of the Spirit? For Tracy, the Spirit is less a consequence of the historical work of Christ than a universal of creation.[75]

Does New Haven unnecessarily confine the Spirit to the church by making the Spirit's work a function of community reading practices?[76] According to Stephen Stell, in an article that tries to move beyond Yale and Chicago, the identity of Jesus Christ is defined not only by the narrative framework of the Gospels "but also by particular experiences in our current existence."[77] Jesus' story does not end with resurrection but with Pentecost, the birth of the church. The authoritative story that identifies Jesus as the Christ is thus the one that is continued by the church, in the power of the Spirit.[78] Because the story is ongoing, Stell argues that the tradition, the community's use of Scripture and thus the literal sense are all alike open to creative transformation. Theological interpretation requires three elements working in cooperation: common human experience founded on God's work in creation, the Christian tradition grounded on God's covenant faithfulness, and creative insight into the divine life drawn from the guiding of the Holy Spirit. Biblical interpretation that is intelligible, appropriate and inspired demands the cooperation of all three factors. Experience must be creatively interpreted and challenged by tradition; tradition must be creatively interpreted and challenged by human experience; creative insight must be challenged and interpreted

---

[74]Watson, *Text, Church and World,* p. 237. Watson also appeals to John Owen's claim that the Spirit works "in things natural, civil, moral, political, and artificial" (quoted on p. 239).

[75]David Tracy, *The Analogical Imagination: Christian Theology and the Culture of Pluralism* (New York: Crossroad, 1981), p. 386. Stephen L. Stell says that in Tracy's account "the specificity of God's historical work in Jesus Christ is compromised by its transposition into the universal interpretive framework of created existence. And consequently, the work of the Spirit in revealing the proper interrelationships of the triune God . . . and the proper interconnections of God's activity among humanity . . . is effectively precluded" (Stephen L. Stell, "Hermeneutics in the Theology and the Theology of Hermeneutics: Beyond Lindbeck and Tracy," *Journal of the American Academy of Religion* 61 [1993]: 691). I made a similar criticism of Paul Ricoeur, arguing that Ricoeur systematically excludes the Spirit from his hermeneutics by consigning the power of appropriating and applying the text to the human imagination. See Kevin Vanhoozer, *Biblical Narrative in the Philosophy of Paul Ricoeur: A Study in Hermeneutics and Theology* (Cambridge: Cambridge University Press, 1990), chap. 9, esp. pp. 248-57.

[76]According to Lindbeck, the internal witness of the Spirit is restricted to "a capacity for hearing and accepting . . . the true external word" (Lindbeck, *Nature of Doctrine,* p. 34). Stell notes the oddity of this position, maintaining uneasily as it does both that the Spirit has meaning only *within* the cultural-linguistic framework of the church and that the Spirit's work is *outside of* the church insofar as it consists in encountering and enabling those who are outside of the church to "hear" (Stell, "Hermeneutics in the Theology," pp. 691-92).

[77]Stell, "Hermeneutics in the Theology," p. 695.

[78]Milbank, *Theology and Social Theory,* p. 387. Stell believes that the hermeneutical deficiencies of both New Haven and Chicago are rooted in a theologically deficient understanding of the Holy Spirit (Stell, "Hermeneutics in the Theology," p. 697).

by experience and tradition. This is a powerful trinitarian model.

But is Stell right in associating the work of the Spirit with the creative imagination? And what, in his correlation of tradition, experience and imagination, has happened to the text and its literal sense?

Discerning the Spirits: Hearing the Word of the Author

To each of us the Spirit is a sword which cleaves open the stubborn and obscure passages, illumines the chambers of the mind so that dark and uncertain thoughts and conclusions become clear and effective, and supplies us with practical interpretation.[79]

I propose a different trinitarian model, based on the notion of revelation as communicative action. The Westminster Shorter Catechism states: "The Spirit of God maketh the reading, but especially the preaching, of the Word an effectual means of convincing and converting sinners." The Bible will be heard as God's Word (and thus interpreted as a coherent unity) only if we are enabled to hear it as such by the Holy Spirit. The Spirit, says Barth, is the Lord of the hearing.

Does it follow that the Spirit's witness changes the meaning of the text, alters the literal sense? The witness of the Spirit is connected with the effectual use of the Scriptures. Whose use? Not the variable use by the community of readers, but the normative use of the author. The creed says, after all, that it was God the Father who spoke by the prophets.

Let us consider Scripture as a species of divine communicative action, consisting of three aspects. First, the Father's "locution"[80]: the words are the authorized words of the Father/Author. Second, the "illocutionary" dimension: what God *does* in Scripture is testify, in various ways, to Christ.[81] Finally, to return to the catechism, we may best view the Holy Spirit's work as God's "perlocution," that is, as what happens as a *result* of speaking. For example, by stating something (an illocution), I may persuade someone (a perlocution). The Bible includes many types of communicative acts and calls for a variety of responses and appropriation. While a good "general" hermeneutical rule might be "Read for and respect the illocutionary point," this is not the end of understanding. For understanding includes a moment of appropriation. Either the Spirit of Christ absorbs our world into the text, or the spirit of the age absorbs the text into our world. The *Filioque* thus has an important hermeneutic parallel: as the Spirit

---

[79]MacDonald, *Interpreter Spirit and Human Life,* p. 157.

[80]God the Father is the one who *est locutus per prophetas* in former times and who now speaks through the Son (Heb 1:1-2).

[81]*Illocution* is a term in speech act philosophy that pertains to what one does in speaking: we can warn, promise, forgive, command and so forth. The illocution is what makes a communication count as a particular kind of action. For further discussion see chapter six.

proceeds from the Father and the Son, so we might say that the perlocution—the efficacy of the speech act—follows from the speaking and the illocution. Or to put it yet
another way: application must be governed by explication; a text's literal sense—its
extended meaning. This is, I believe, how Calvin and the Reformers understood the
Spirit's illumination: the Spirit convicts us that the Bible contains God's illocutions and
enables us to respond to them as we ought. The Spirit is the effective presence of the
Word or, on my terms, the power of Scripture's efficacious perlocution.

What, then, is it to understand the Bible? As the Yale school has pointed out, there
are many "spirits" of understanding—historical, literary, sociological. The Christian
understanding, however, is the one that *follows* the Word. "Following" has at least
two senses. We can follow an argument, or an explanation, or directions, or a story.
But the other sense of following is the kind Jesus wanted when he said, "Follow me."
The difference is, I think, the same as between explanation and application. The
Christian is not a hearer only but a doer of the Word. We can follow an argument yet
disagree with its issue. All too often, interpreters never reach the stage of application.
The meaning of the Bible's promises, warnings, commands and so forth "lies plain
before their eyes," but they are suppressed in unrighteousness. The most profound
kind of understanding, however, has to do with cultivation of the ability to follow the
Word of God, not just in our reading but in personal response to what we have read.
"One who understands a text will be able to make use of the text in ways that demonstrate—and in some sense constitute—understanding."[82] Understanding is our ability to follow the Word.

Understanding is theological because we are enabled to follow the issue of the
text only by the Holy Spirit. The role of the Spirit is to enable us to take the biblical
texts in the sense that they were intended, and to apply or follow that sense in the
way we live. To use Fee's fine phrase, we might say that the Spirit is the "empowering presence" of the Word in the written words. The Spirit of understanding enlivens
the church only when it is a church of the Word, and the Spirit enlivens the Word
only when it is a Word in the church.

How shall we respond to the French Revolution in literary theory? Edmund
Burke's *Reflections on the French Revolution,* two centuries old, proves surprisingly
relevant and provides us with some starters. Like the French Revolution, deconstruction is rife with the rhetoric of *liberté* and *égalité*. Burke spoke of the "confused jargon of their Babylonian pulpits" and warned that "learning will be cast into the mire,
and trodden down under the hoofs of a swinish multitude." What moral might my
mediation of New Haven and Chicago have for the hermeneutic revolution coming
out of Paris?

---

[82]Wood, *Formation of Christian Understanding,* p. 17.

Approaching the Other: Understanding as Privilege and Responsibility

"Logocentric commentary . . . is docetic; it favors the spirit at the expense of the body of the text."[83]

Because interpreters are also sinners who suppress the Logos in unrighteousness, a certain amount of suspicion can be healthy. A *little* deconstruction may not be a dangerous thing. However, when deconstruction seeks to undo not only oppressive interpretations but the texts themselves, when it pries apart textual coherence for the sake of a repressed otherness, here I cannot follow. Deconstruction, far from protecting the text as an other, licenses interpretive violence.

Deconstruction contradicts two basic principles of a Christian worldview: first, the "realism principle" (we can adequately know the world and are responsible for doing so); second, the "bias principle" (we never know the world apart from biases that influence our perception of reality).[84] Now apply these two principles to hermeneutics. First, the realism principle: we can adequately understand texts; second, the bias principle: we can never understand texts apart from biases that affect our understanding. The Spirit of understanding progressively convicts us of our biases and conforms us to reality.

Language does not bar us from reality, though reality comes mediated by language. Neither language nor finitude justifies interpretive sloth. Being indifferent to the text is not a way of doing justice to its otherness. While we must be as honest as possible about our biases, they do not constitute an excuse not to interpret. Language, a gift of God, is adequate for the purposes for which it was created.[85] Babel is not a license for interpretive anarchy, neither does it warrant a despair of language. The biblical text, taken literally, is an adequate testimony to Jesus Christ.

If the hermeneutics of conviction declares, "Here I stand," the hermeneutics of humility asks, "How does it look from where *you* stand?" The false humility of deconstruction degenerates into a despair of language and of our ability to interpret. True hermeneutic humility, on the other hand, is willing to receive something from the other, from the text and from other interpreters.

Does humility before the text rule out a critical moment in which the reader assesses its content? Am I advocating hermeneutic fideism: "Love God, and read as

---

[83]Phillips, "Ethics of Reading Deconstructively," p. 289.

[84]I am borrowing from Lints, *Fabric of Theology,* p. 20.

[85]Dallas Willard attributes to me the view that language is necessarily distorting. In fact, I am not in despair about language so much as about willful interpreters. I am not a framework-relativist. The problem is not finitude but fallenness. The interpretive difficulties my discussion raises concern neither the social nor cultural positions of interpreters, but rather their moral and spiritual *dispositions*. The Spirit of understanding does not circumvent our finitude but renews, restores and perfects our interpretive capacities.

you please"? No, for understanding must be tested. Christian interpreters must endure every test that critics care to throw at them. Testing and enduring: these are signs of rationality and humility alike. Interpreters should never idolize their interpretations. I am seeking a degree of interpretive confidence somewhere between pride and sloth—the humble conviction that stands firm, even while acknowledging that it is rooted on earth rather than looking down from heaven. We do not yet have absolute knowledge. Yet we do have adequate knowledge, enough to respond to the overtures of the Word. Our first reflex upon being addressed should be trust. We must at least be willing to hear the other rather than drown out its voice, even when its message is a potential threat to our way of being in the world.

General or Special Hermeneutics?

Karl Barth and Paul Ricoeur are the two influential figures behind the Yale and Chicago schools respectively. Each has tried, in different ways, to reverse the hermeneutical reversal by making general hermeneutics a subset of biblical hermeneutics. We might paraphrase their strategies as follows: "Read any other book like the Bible"—a thought that neatly turns Jowett's maxim on its head. It is from just such an inverted position that we can, I believe, respond to deconstruction.

There is no such thing, for Barth, as special biblical hermeneutics. Nor is there an adequate general hermeneutics apart from biblical hermeneutics: "It is from the word of man in the Bible that we must learn what has to be learned concerning the word of man in general."[86] General hermeneutics is therefore a "predicate" of biblical hermeneutics. We begin with biblical interpretation and learn how to interpret texts in general. "Is it not the case that whatever is said to us by men obviously wants . . . to make itself said and heard? It wants in this way to become to us a subject matter."[87] What all speakers want, however, only the Spirit, as Lord of the hearing, can actually achieve. Buber's remark—"What Christianity gives the world is hermeneutics"—is not only a past fact but also a promise.

Just what is the role of the interpreter in understanding? Barth accepts the bias principle: "There has never yet been an expositor who has allowed only Scripture alone to speak." We must not think that any one interpretive scheme is particularly suited to apprehend the Word of God: "there is no essential reason for preferring one of these schemes to another." Barth then draws an astonishing conclusion: those schooled in biblical interpretation are best able to do justice to textual otherness. "Even from a human point of view, it is possible to regard scriptural exposition as the best and perhaps the only school of truly free human thinking—freed, that is, from

---

[86]Barth, *Church Dogmatics* 1/2, p. 466.
[87]For his view of the literal sense, see ibid., chap. 3, esp. pp. 464-72, 492-95, 715-36.

all the conflicts and tyranny of systems in favor of this object."[88] Ricoeur agrees, insisting that understanding the other requires the reader to put oneself into question and to be ready to abandon one's self-understanding.[89]

This leads me to the following thesis: *All hermeneutics, not simply the special hermeneutics of Scripture, is "theological."* Does special revelation need a special hermeneutic? On the contrary, I am advocating a trinitarian hermeneutic for all interpretation; better, I am arguing that general hermeneutics is inescapably theological. Our polluted cognitive and spiritual environment darkens understanding of *all* texts. Derrida is right to expose the many sources of coercion and distortion in the process of communication. Often we do not wish to understand the other, perhaps because the other has a claim on us, perhaps because we might have to change. Self-love can pervert the course of interpretation as it does every other human activity. It is the Spirit who enables us to transfer attention away from ourselves and our interests to the text and its subject matter. Understanding—of the Bible or of any other text—is a matter of ethics, indeed of spirituality.

Interpretation ultimately depends upon the theological virtues of faith, hope and love. *Faith* that there is a real presence, a voice, a meaning in the text; *hope* that the interpretive community can, in the power of the Spirit, attain an adequate, not absolute, understanding; *love,* a mutual relation of self-giving between text and reader. Abraham Kuyper contrasts our darkened understanding with love, the "sympathy of existence": "A lover of animals understands the life of the animal. In order to study nature in its material operations, you must love her. Without this inclination and this desire toward the object of your study, you do not advance an inch."[90] Kuyper's "principle of charity" is far removed from Davidson's, where we "love" the other by making it conform to what we think is true.

---

[88]Ibid., pp. 728, 733, 735.

[89]Like Barth, Ricoeur argues that biblical interpretation, which is prima facie an instance of regional or special hermeneutics, in fact overturns the very relation between general and special hermeneutics. The object of hermeneutics in general is to "unfold" the world of the text (Paul Ricoeur, "Philosophical Hermeneutics and Theological Hermeneutics," *Studies in Religion* 5 [1975-1976]: 25). The Bible is special because its world reveals my world in a new way, which forces me to abandon my old self-understanding. For Ricoeur, such revelation is experienced as a nonviolent appeal to the imagination. Theological hermeneutics thus qualifies general hermeneutics: all readings of poetic texts, insofar as they have the capacity to transform my existence, are potentially "revelatory." Ricoeur depicts a general hermeneutics that has been transformed by biblical hermeneutics. Note, however, that sacred hermeneutics has been secularized: the power of appropriating the world of the biblical text is attributed to the creative imagination, not to the Holy Spirit. See Vanhoozer, *Biblical Narrative,* chap. 9.

[90]Abraham Kuyper, *Principles of Sacred Theology,* trans. J. Hendrick De Vries (Grand Rapids, Mich.: Baker, 1980), p. 111. I am indebted to Nicholas Wolterstorff for this point. See Wolterstorff, "What New Haven and Grand Rapids Have to Say to Each Other," in *The Stob Lectures* (Grand Rapids, Mich.: Calvin College and Theological Seminary, 1992-1993), pp. 28-30.

Non-Christian hermeneutics wreaks interpretive violence on the other of the text.[91] Deconstruction claims to be ethically responsible in reading for the other, for all those things that do not neatly fit into our systems. Deconstruction, according to Gary Phillips, "calls me to be on guard against reinscribing the other in my image for my purposes."[92] I do not agree. Deconstruction does not serve the other. The message of the text is not allowed to "be"; the sense of the text is undone, doomed to wander like a shade through the rubble of signifiers that signify nothing. Deconstruction is a denial of the literal sense, a hermeneutic gnosticism that claims to "know" the absence of the Logos.

The prodigal interpreter has need of theological virtues.[93] Faith, hope and love alone enable us to avoid doing interpretive violence to the text. The fruit of the Spirit of understanding is peace—a letting be, a welcome reception of the other.

The mention of peace and justice recalls the Anabaptists, who emphasized the role of discipleship and obedience in biblical interpretation. That we are able to surrender our self-interests and extend the "sympathy of existence" toward the text is a fruit of the Spirit.[94] In addition, the Anabaptists acknowledged a link between obedience and knowledge: "The readiness to obey Christ's words is prerequisite to understanding them."[95]

If understanding involves obedience, it is easy to see how deconstruction could

---

[91]This is essentially John Milbank's thesis about social theory transferred to the realm of *literary* theory. See Milbank, *Theology and Social Theory*, pt. 4.

[92]Phillips, "Ethics of Reading Deconstructively," p. 317.

[93]Dallas Willard wonders whether I have worked a hermeneutical variant of "occasionalism," a philosophical theory (largely discredited and associated with Malebranche) about the mind-body problem that maintains that mental intentions are coordinated with bodily movements only with divine assistance. In other words, it is God who puts together my intention to raise my arm and my arm's actual movement. Is it my position that the interpreter's understanding is coordinated with the text only thanks to divine assistance, that understanding a text is like raising my arm? The answer depends on what one means by "understanding." I agree that readers often can recognize illocutionary points without divine assistance. Humans are, I believe, created with the capacity to understand discourse. However, I also believe that this cognitive equipment has been affected by sin. It is often in the sinner's interest willfully to misunderstand, or at least not to respond to what has been understood. If understanding involves a movement of personal appropriation, that is, if understanding includes the perlocutionary effect, then we can agree with Barth that the Spirit is the "Lord of the hearing." There are indeed some things we cannot do without divine assistance. We may be able to raise our arms, but we are able to raise our arms in praise to God only thanks to the prompting of the Holy Spirit.

[94]Henry Poettecker, "Menno Simons' Encounter with the Bible," in *Essays on Biblical Interpretation: Anabaptist-Mennonite Perspectives,* ed. Williard M. Swartley (Elkhart, Ind.: Institute of Mennonite Studies, 1984), pp. 62-76.

[95]Walter Klassen, "Anabaptist Hermeneutics: Presuppositions, Principles and Practice," in *Essays on Biblical Interpretation: Anabaptist-Mennonite Perspectives,* ed. Williard M. Swartley (Elkhart, Ind.: Institute of Mennonite Studies, 1984), p. 6.

quench the spirit of understanding. According to Derrida, there is nothing "there" in the text to which we can respond. Deconstruction's vaunted ethics, which supposedly guards the otherness of the text from being swallowed up by dominant interpretations, ultimately founders in the absence of something determinate to which the reader can responsibly respond. There can be no genuine encounter if the interpretive community's practice creates the text. If the world of the text is the reader's projection, interpretation is only the repetition of the self-same and the same self. Contrast that vain repetition with C. S. Lewis's "taste for the other": Lewis read to enlarge his being and to transcend himself. For the deconstructive critic who lacks the spirit of understanding the other, however, to read a thousand books is still to be alone with oneself.[96]

The Spirit of the Letter

To sum up: the Spirit of understanding is not Jowett's critical spirit, nor Tracy's spirit of the age, nor Lindbeck's community spirit, nor the rebellious spirit of deconstruction. I have argued that the Spirit of understanding is the Holy Spirit, the Spirit of Christ. The Spirit may blow where, but not *what,* he wills. The Spirit is subordinate to the Word. Perlocutions "proceed from" illocutions.

The other spirits are ultimately false spirits insofar as they devalue the letter—the Word of God written. They devalue the letter by emptying it of determinate meaning, depriving the text of any independent integrity and of ability to resist the projections that critics foist upon it. I have argued that the Spirit witnesses to what is other than himself—to meaning "accomplished"–and that the Spirit enables readers to respond to this textual other, to meaning "applied." For the sake of clarity, we can distinguish three aspects of the Spirit's role in the process of interpretation.

First, the Spirit *convicts* us that the Bible is indeed the locution of God that bears authoritative witness to the living Word (and thus that we should view it as a unity).[97] Even this aspect of biblical hermeneutics has its secular counterpart, insofar as ethical interpretation means reading for the intent of the author.

Second, the Spirit *illumines* the letter by impressing upon us the full force of its communicative action, its illocutions. The Spirit does not alter biblical meaning. Rather, "the spiritual sense is the literal sense correctly understood."[98] The distinction between "letter" and "spirit" is just that between reading the words and grasping what one reads. Likewise, the difference between a "natural" and an "illumined"

---

[96]The original quote from C. S. Lewis reads: "In reading great literature I become a thousand men and yet remain myself" (C. S. Lewis, *An Experiment in Criticism* [Cambridge: Cambridge University Press, 1961], p. 141).

[97]This is a restatement of the traditional Reformed notion of the "internal witness."

[98]Charles Wood, commenting on Luther, in Wood, *Finding the Life of a Text,* p. 102.

understanding is that between head and heart knowledge, between having an opinion and having a "deep sense of its truth, goodness, and beauty."[99] Illumination has to do with the quality and the force of our appreciation of the literal sense.

Third, the Spirit *sanctifies* us and so helps us to accept what is in the text instead of preferring our own interpretations. The Spirit progressively disabuses us of ideological or idolatrous prejudices that prevent us from receiving the message. (This aspect of the Spirit's work is relevant for general hermeneutics too). In so doing, the Spirit renders the Word *effective*. To read in the Spirit does not mean to import some new sense to the text but rather to let the letter be, or better, to apply the letter rightly to one's life. The Spirit of understanding is the efficacy of the Word, its perlocutionary power. According to John Owen, the Spirit is the "primary efficient cause" of our understanding of Scripture. Yet the Spirit's illumining work is not independent of our own efforts to understand. "It is the Spirit's activity, effected through our own labor in exegesis, analysis, and application, of showing us what the text means for us."[100]

Two unresolved questions remain. First, we have seen that the relation between God's universal work in creation and God's particular work in the church is of no little hermeneutical significance. Is there some relation between human beings (as spirits) and God, other than that established in Christ?[101] In what measure is the Spirit of understanding outside of the church? Is biblical interpretation a work perhaps of common grace? The point to note is that all of these hermeneutical questions are properly theological as well.

Second, how can we recognize the Spirit of understanding? I must offer at least the outline of an answer to such an important query. We recognize the Spirit in those who confess that Jesus—the Logos—came in the flesh. Similarly, we recognize the Spirit of understanding in those who respond to the literal sense—to the commands, the promises, the warnings, the narratives—in a hermeneutically and Christianly appropriate manner. In short, we recognize the Spirit of understanding in those who "follow," that is, in those who hear and do the Word. "Those who would live under the authority of the Spirit must bow before the Word as the Spirit's textbook. . . . Those who would live under the authority of Scripture must seek the Spirit as its interpreter."[102]

---

[99]Fred H. Klooster comments, "The aim of Spirit-illumined interpretation should be heart-understanding," by which he means the worship and service of God (Fred H. Klooster, "The Role of the Holy Spirit in the Hermeneutic Process," in *Hermeneutics, Inerrancy and the Bible*, ed. Earl D. Radmacher and Robert D. Preus (Grand Rapids, Mich.: Zondervan, 1984), p. 468.

[100]J. I. Packer, *Keep in Step with the Spirit* (Leicester, U.K.: Inter-Varsity Press, 1984), p. 239.

[101]Hendrey, *Holy Spirit in Christian Theology,* chap. 5.

[102]Packer, *Keep in Step,* p. 240.

The Homecoming of Hermeneutics

If hermeneutics were to return home to Christianity, this would indeed be cause for rejoicing. In anticipation of this homecoming of the prodigal, then, I wish to conclude with the image of a feast. We must remember to conjoin Word with sacrament as well as Spirit. The eating of Christ's flesh is a tangible reminder that an Easter feast follows our Lenten fast. Christians conduct this feast not in the spirit of carnival but in the spirit of communion: with Christ and with one another. We may likewise celebrate the feast of interpretation. The Spirit of Pentecost overcomes the cultural and ideological biases that distort communication and so restores language as a medium of communion. Thanks to the Spirit of understanding, the letter of the text becomes an enlivening and nourishing presence. Not only do we enjoy the first fruits of understanding, but we look forward to that day when we will understand as we have been understood. *Veni spiritus interpres!* Come interpreter Spirit!

Eight

The Reader
at the Well

Responding to John 4

A chapter that treats the reader in New Testament study may appear, at first sight, to be singularly inappropriate in a volume devoted to God and Scripture. However, there are many today who contend that theology begins with the reader—with the reader's social location, gender and politics. Does not the reader figure prominently in every approach to biblical interpretation insofar as it is the reader who chooses a particular method—be it historical criticism, structuralism, feminism or another—and puts it into practice on specific texts? Such has it been from the beginning of biblical interpretation: "The reader you have with you always."

Recently, however, the reader has come to the forefront in discussion of literary theory and biblical interpretation alike. Indeed some critics speak of a readers' liberation movement. What is it that readers have hitherto not been free to do? The answer of an increasing number of literary theorists is "Make meaning." Reading is not merely a matter or perception but also of production; the reader does not discover so much as create meaning. At the very best, there would be no meaning at all if there were no readers reading. What is in the text is only the potential for meaning. Meaning is actualized not by the author at the point of the text's conception but by the reader at the point of the text's reception.

If we compare the text to a well, to what should we liken meaning: to the water in the well, to the ways the water is drawn or to the drinking of the water? In this chapter I will examine a number of contemporary approaches to interpretation that accord a privileged role to the reader's "response." I first examine the reasons, both literary and philosophical, for the reader's newfound fame and freedom.

Reading as Theory-Laden: The Philosophical Explanation

The philosophical roots for reader-response criticism ultimately go back to Kant's "Copernican revolution." Whereas Descartes had defined knowledge in terms of a "mind" apprehending an "object," Kant argued that the knower contributes something to the object of knowledge. The mind does not simply mirror but constructs its object, processing sensations outside the mind with the mind's own concepts. As Copernicus suggested that the sun does not revolve around the earth but the earth around the sun, so Kant suggested that the mind does not correspond to the world but the world to the mind. The mind actively participates in the construction of knowledge. This was the essence of Kant's critique of metaphysics, that search for the true description—the single correct conceptual interpretation—of ultimate reality. But whereas Kant believed that all human beings interpret the world with the same set of categories, today most philosophers hold there is no one conceptual framework that yields absolute truth or a God's-eye view of the world. What one draws from the well of the world depends on the type of bucket one uses.

The analogy with literary interpretation is exact: we do not perceive the text as it is in itself, but only the text as construed and constructed by the human mind. Kant's critique has been directed by literary theorists against the "metaphysics" of meaning. Hermeneutical realism—the notion that there is something that precedes reading to which reading must correspond—has become increasingly difficult to defend. Thomas Kuhn, a philosopher of science, argues that all observation is theory-laden. Every scientist belongs to some community or other whose research is oriented by a particular "paradigm" or interpretive framework. For Kuhn, the scientist's context in a particular community influences the kinds of questions that will be asked.[1] The hermeneutical antirealist insists that there are many equally valid sets of interpretive categories with which to process texts and produce meaning. If all reading is historically conditioned and theory-laden, then no reading is objective and the reader becomes, almost by default, the determining factor in interpretation.

The Three Ages of Criticism: The Literary Explanation

Of course it was not always so. Literary criticism has only gradually perceived the significance of these philosophical and scientific revolutions. The traditional reader, more Cartesian than Kantian in inclination, believed that objectivity in interpretation

---

[1]Thomas S. Kuhn, *The Structure of Scientific Revolutions* (Chicago: University of Chicago Press, 1970).

was possible. David J. A. Clines comments that the end of Cartesian thinking is only now beginning to be felt in biblical studies: "Most active scholars appear to write as if they were still engaged in a quest for objectively determinate meanings."[2] What was the mind-independent or reader-independent something to which good reading had to correspond? Most biblical commentators from the Reformation on held that it was the author's intention. It was the author's will to mean this rather than that, with such and such a verbal sequence in such and such a historical context, that was considered the determining factor of textual meaning and the object of the interpreter's quest. In short, determinate textual meaning—that is, meaning that is anchored and fixed—was a function of authorial activity. Consequently this "first age" of criticism belonged to the author.

Kant's Copernican revolution complicated this quest. So did the subsequent realization that humans are historical beings. We are, as readers, distant from the author, both temporally and in our ability to know. And there is yet a third element that comes between the reader and the author: language.

These three elements—the mind, time, language—constitute, for many, an impenetrable screen. But it is a screen on which readers "project" their image or construction of what they think the author (and his or her intention) is like. According to Roland Barthes, the "author" is a convenient fiction that provides the illusion of a stable sense and a determinate meaning. Instead of cause, the author is for Barthes an *effect* of the text.

An illusory author is, however, no better than no author at all. Barthes thus pronounces the author "dead," echoing Nietzsche's earlier declaration of the death of God. Indeed the two deaths are related, insofar as they are both variations on the theme of antirealism. Feuerbach argued that "God" was merely the projection of human thought; Barthes, similarly, argues that "the author's intention" is a projection of reading. It was Nietzsche who saw the implications of this antirealism most clearly: if we cannot discover the nature of reality, we must invent it. Barthes agrees: "Once the Author is removed, the claim to decipher a text becomes quite futile. . . . The birth of the reader must be at the cost of the death of the Author."[3]

What now functions as the norm of interpretation after the author's demise? Is meaning really there, somehow "in" the text? Is there anything independent of the process of reading that can now hold the reader responsible? Does truth lie at the bottom of the well, or is it interpretation all the way down? Is there still a way, after the author, to judge interpretations bad or good? Or, to paraphrase Dostoyevsky, if

[2]David J. A. Clines, "Possibilities and Priorities of Biblical Interpretation: An International Perspective," *Biblical Interpretation* 1 (1993): 75.
[3]Roland Barthes, "Death of the Author," in *The Rustle of Language* (New York: Hill & Wang, 1986), pp. 53-55.

there is no Author, is everything (in interpretation) permitted? Beginning with the New Criticism in the 1940s and continuing through structuralism in the 1960s, literary critics have attempted to find a principle for determinate meaning based of the text alone, considered as an entity autonomous from its author. Since the late 1960s, however, attention has focused on the reader's role in decoding and using the text. In the 1970s Hans Robert Jauss argued that literary historians should turn their attention away from authors and their works to study the reader and the expectations and interests the reader brings to texts. We cannot study the text as it is in itself, but only the history of how readers have received it.[4] If meaning is not somehow "in" texts, then reading is like "dropping buckets into empty wells" (Cowper). With this thought, Kant's Copernican revolution is complete.

What Is the Role of the Reader?

Readers and reading: Some presuppositions. Philosophical developments have served as midwife to the birth of the reader. What exactly has been born? Why do readers read, and what do they do beyond moving their eyes from left to right across the page? The traditional answer is that we read in order to understand—to grasp the author's meaning. Reader-response criticism, on the other hand, relates meaning to the ways texts are received by readers: meaning is not simply reproduced but produced.

The place of the reader: Who? When? Where? The reader is neither a detached Cartesian mind nor a *tabula rasa*. It was Rudolf Bultmann who first alerted New Testament interpreters to the importance of the "place" of the reader by arguing that exegesis without presuppositions is not possible.[5] For Bultmann, the most pressing question readers have concerns their own temporal existence and its meaning. His suggestion that the reader's ontological context is the decisive context has not been accepted, but what has proved to be of more lasting significance is his notion of the reader's "horizon," the set of interests and expectations that affects what the reader looks for, and finds, in the New Testament texts. Hans-Georg Gadamer views the process of understanding as an encounter between the text and reader, an encounter that he describes as a "fusion" of two horizons.[6]

On the traditional author-oriented view, understanding meant occupying the same place and perspective as the author. Objective interpretation required the interpreter to leave his or her prejudices behind. The death of the author, however, deregulates interpretation. Readers need no longer apologize either for their location or for their

---

[4]Hans Robert Jauss, "Literary History as a Challenge to Literary Theory," *New Literary History* 2 (1970): 7-37.

[5]Rudolf Bultmann, "Is Exegesis Without Presupposition Possible?" in *Existence and Faith,* ed. Schubert M. Ogden (New York: Living Age, 1960), pp. 289-96.

[6]Hans-Georg Gadamer, *Truth and Method* (New York: Seabury, 1975), pp. 269-74.

interests. Indeed, according to John Barton and Robert Morgan, the text has no aims or interests.[7] There is no one thing that readers must do with texts. Readers will have any number of interests, depending on their place and context. Some readers may show interest in a text's formal structure, others in the events that lay behind the text or gave rise to its production, still others in the relevance of the text in the light of contemporary social questions. On this view, the most important context for interpretation is thus not the original historical context of the text but the present context of the reader. The traditional goal of disinterested reading has given way to "interested" readings. The birth of the reader accounts for the current plethora of interpretive schools (feminist, Marxist, Freudian, liberation, etc.), each derived from a dominant interest. The place where the reader stands, far from being considered an obstacle to interpretation, has today become holy ground.

The indeterminacy of meaning. If the place of the reader determines what he or she gets out of a text, then meaning is indeterminate. However, one can understand indeterminacy of meaning in two different ways. Some reader-response critics point to certain "gaps" in the text that call for filling in by the reader. On this view, indeterminacy refers to an unfinished meaning that the reader completes by following authorial instructions and textual indications. Indeterminacy also has a more radical sense, according to which the reader determines what to make of the text. On this view, texts do not have a fixed "meaning." Reading is so theory-laden that what we claim to discover in texts and then dignify by calling it "the meaning" is actually the result of a certain way of reading.

Jeffrey Stout proposes that we drop the term *meaning* altogether and speak rather of what readers wish to do with texts. Some readers, it is true, try to reconstruct the author's intention, but other readers have other interests. Why, asks Stout, should we equate only the interest of the first group with "the meaning" of the text? The "goodness" of an interpretation depends on the interpreter's aim and interest. Talk of interpretive aims thus replaces talk of actual meaning. The interests of the reader drive the process of interpretation. The text thus assumes the character of a wishing well, from which readers may draw what they like. Stout rejects the idea of a hermeneutical equivalent of Kant's moral imperative, a single duty or rule that should govern all reading. There is no one thing that makes a reading "good." On the contrary: "Good commentary is whatever serves our interests and purposes."[8] Clines agrees, noting the importance of the reader's context: "There is no one authentic meaning that we must all try to discover, no matter who we are or where we happen to be standing."[9]

---

[7]Robert Morgan and John Barton, *Biblical Interpretation* (New York: Oxford University Press, 1988), p. 7.
[8]Jeffrey Stout, "What Is the Meaning of a Text?" *New Literary History* 14 (1982): 6.
[9]Clines, "Possibilities and Priorities," p. 78.

The myth of objectivity dies hard, however. Stephen Moore states the challenge now facing biblical interpreters: "Today, it is not our biblical texts that need demythologizing so much as our ways of reading them."[10]

The nature of interpretation: Two types of reader response. At the heart of the contemporary debate in the third age of criticism is the question whether there are normative aims for reading. If there are no norms, as Stout contends, does it follow that there can be no such thing as a misinterpretation? Reader-response critics are currently divided over how to respond to such questions. Umberto Eco distinguishes between "closed" texts, which evoke a predetermined, calculated response, and "open" texts, which invite the reader's participation in the production of meaning.[11] In order to make sense of the role of the reader in contemporary New Testament interpretation, we must make a similar distinction between readings that attempt to *reproduce* a meaning that is in some sense already "there" and readings that attempt to *produce* a meaning *ex libris*.

Early reader-response critics tended to be "conservative," acknowledging the role of the reader in the process of making meaning but focusing on the dynamics and direction of the text, the various ways the rhetorical strategies of the text itself invite the reader to participate in the production of meaning. As early as the 1920s, I. A. Richards's *Principles of Literary Criticism* stressed the power of poetry to evoke feelings and affect the reader. The emphasis in this view is on uncovering the rhetorical mechanisms by which the text induces and produces these effects in the reader. "Understanding" is still the end of the interpretive process, though the means to that end involve active reader participation. Reading is on this view essentially an *obedient* activity. Its aim is to let the author and the text manipulate the reader so that he or she gradually comes to experience and adopt the ideology (the worldview) of the text. Again, the emphasis is squarely on understanding, on discovering and embracing the ideology of the text.

"Radical" reader-response critics, on the other hand, privilege the ideology or position of the reader rather than that of the text. The text becomes the opportunity for the reader to pursue his or her own interests and agenda. Such readers do more than respond: they react. Reactionary readers lobby for their respective causes and points of view. Since nothing is really "there" in the text, they try to undo traditional interpretations by claiming that they reflect the interests of some institutional authority—a state, a church or a school.

In some cases, where the text itself displays an unwelcome ideology (such as

---

[10]Stephen D. Moore, *Literary Criticism and the Gospels* (New Haven, Conn.: Yale University Press, 1989), p. 66.

[11]Umberto Eco, *The Role of the Reader: Explorations in the Semantics of Texts* (Bloomington: Indiana University Press, 1979).

patriarchy), reactive readers must read against the text: poisoned wells must be politically purified. At other times reactive reading goes against the history of a text's
interpretation. We could here speak of reader rejection rather than reader reception
of a text, and of "strong-willed" readers who unapologetically impose their own ideologies onto that of the text. They are more interested in "overstanding"—pursuing
their own aims and interests and questions—than in understanding a text. Literary
criticism here moves beyond describing a text and its ideology to an outright critique
of it.

Given the increasing number of contexts in which the Bible is being read, what
should the interpreter do? Clines espouses a "market philosophy of interpretation." In
recognition of the pluralistic intellectual marketplace, he believes interpreters should
"devote themselves to producing interpretation they can sell."[12] In the absence of
absolute meanings, the interpreter can still hope to produce *attractive* readings.

Given the ideologically divided and market-driven situation in literary theory at
present, it is hardly surprising that the issue of the ethics of interpretation has come
to the fore. In the wake of authorial antirealism and interpretive relativism, the
reader's interests become the determining factors in interpretation. There is no innocent reading; rather, all reading is interested, and to the extent that these are vested
interests, all reading is ideological. Our choice of interpretive aim is ultimately a political decision. How could it be otherwise, if there is no such thing as a "disinterested"
reading?

Making meaning: The procedures. Reader-response critics "make" meaning in
two very different ways.

Conservative reader response: Reader respect. According to Wolfgang Iser, texts are
unfinished objects whose "gaps" and indeterminacies call out for completion by the
reader. What, for instance, should one "make" of the silence of the women at the end
of the Gospel of Mark (16:8)? Only the "act" of reading produces patterns and realizes
meaning. Reading is the process of filling in the blanks, of making connections. Iser
draws an analogy between two readers and two stargazers "who may both be looking at the same collection of stars, but one will see the image of a plough, and the
other will make out a dipper. . . . The 'stars' in a literary text are fixed; the lines that
join them are variable."[13]

It is unclear to many, however, whether Iser wishes to give the reader the right to
connect the dots as he or she may see fit, or whether he regards the text as giving
instructions for the reader's actualizations. According to his detractors, the reader to
whom Iser gives birth is underdeveloped. Though Iser studies the reader's response,

---

[12]Clines, "Possibilities and Priorities," p. 80.
[13]Wolfgang Iser, *The Implied Reader: Patterns of Communication in Prose Fiction from Bunyan to Beckett* (Baltimore: Johns Hopkins University Press, 1974), p. 282.

he construes this response as an effect of the text. The implied reader "embodies all those predispositions necessary for a literary work to exercise its effect."[14] The implied reader is thus not only an effect of the text but an unchanging textual property. Consequently, though real readers are active, their activity is limited to performing a prescripted role laid down in the text—so much so that Werner Jeanrond worries that Iser's "act of reading" may turn into a "slavery to the text."[15]

Paul Ricoeur also stresses the importance of the reader's "realizing" textual meaning. Interpretation is short-circuited, he believes, if the text is only "explained." As written discourse, texts are unfulfilled until they are appropriated or applied by readers; discourse ("someone saying something about something *to* someone") is incomplete without a recipient. What the reader receives according to Ricoeur is not the author's intention but the "world of the text"—that is, a proposed way of being-in-the-world. Reading is the process by which the world of the text intersects with the world of the reader. Interpretation is fulfilled only when the "world" is appropriated through the words. The act of reading is thus a war of the worlds: "Reading is, first and foremost, a struggle with the text."[16]

The text is inert until reactivated by the reader. As Ricoeur puts it, "reading is like the execution of a musical score; it marks the realization, the enactment, of the semantic possibilities of the text."[17] The analogy with music is apt: like musicians performing a musical score, readers perform texts. Interpretations differ as a result of the different interactions between the text's proposals and the reader's responses. No one interpretation or performance exhausts a text's interpretive possibilities.

Must we then speak of textual "worlds without end"? Is reading arbitrary? In reply, Ricoeur affirms the importance of textual constraints on interpretation as well as textual openness. Reading is a balancing act between believing that each text has only one correct interpretation and projecting ourselves into the text. "Perhaps we should say that a text is a finite space of interpretation: there is not just one interpretation, but, on the other hand, there is not an infinite number of them."[18]

Ricoeur ultimately privileges the world of the text over that of the reader. He agrees with Marcel Proust that in interpreting texts, the reader "reads" himself or herself. That is, texts are for Ricoeur occasions to understand ourselves in a new light.

---

[14]Wolfgang Iser, *The Act of Reading: A Theory of Aesthetic Response* (Baltimore: Johns Hopkins University Presss, 1978), p. 34.

[15]Werner G. Jeanrond, *Text and Interpretation as Categories of Theological Thinking* (New York: Crossroad, 1988), p. 110.

[16]Paul Ricoeur, "World of the Text, World of the Reader," in *A Ricoeur Reader: Reflection and Imagination,* ed. Mario J. Valdes (New York: Harvester Wheatsheaf, 1991), p. 494.

[17]Paul Ricoeur, *Hermeneutics and the Human Sciences,* ed. John B. Thompson (Cambridge: Cambridge University Press, 1981), p. 159.

[18]Ricoeur, "World of the Text," p. 496.

The reader is active, but the reader's activity is oriented to receiving the text. In appropriating the text's world, the reader gives up (at least temporarily) his or her own self-understanding. Reading exposes the reader to new worlds and in so doing enlarges his or her sense of self. Appropriation is not a matter of making the text one's own but of surrendering oneself to the text. Insofar as interpretation thus "enlarges" human beings, Ricoeur can say with Francis Bacon: "Reading maketh a full man."

Radical reader response: Reader resistance. Radical reader-response critics resist any claim—either textual or interpretive—that pretends to be authoritative, exclusive and absolute. They see all attempts to fix "the meaning" of texts as covert attempts to impose an authoritarian rule on the reader. Interpretation that claims to be theoretically "correct" is judged politically incorrect. Determinate meaning threatens the freedom of the reader. There are two main varieties of reader resistance: poststructuralist and neo-pragmatist.

Roland Barthes likens the reader to a playful producer rather than a dutiful consumer of meaning. Interpretation is a matter not of recognizing the single correct meaning of a text but of perceiving a plurality of meanings. For the consumer, reading is a safe, comfortable activity that treats the text "like a cupboard where meanings are shelved, stacked, safeguarded."[19] A creative reading, on the other hand, is a productive contribution to the economy of interpretation.

"Writerly texts" are those works that call attention to their status as complex sign-systems capable of various decodings—linguistic labyrinths. The text is "a multidimensional space in which are married and contested several writings, none of which is original; the text is a fabric of quotations, resulting from a thousand sources of culture."[20] Indeed the pleasure of the text for Barthes consists in its serpentine paths: its codes generate many levels on which the text may be traversed. The impossibility of completing or closing the process of interpretation is for him no reason for dismay; on the contrary such texts produce an ecstatic bliss insofar as they induce the thrill of losing oneself—and thus the possibility of finding oneself somewhere else.

Barthes proclaims both the death of the Author (previously thought to be the "owner" of the text and the "authority" over interpretation) and the birth of the Reader. Because reading is a production of meaning, the class distinction dividing author and reader appears vague and arbitrary. The author simply supplies the reader with a complex code that calls for and enables multiple readings/meanings. Barthes does not hesitate to draw the conclusion: the ultimate aim in liberating the reader from bondage to "the author's intention" is to make the reader into a writer. Com-

---

[19]Roland Barthes, *S/Z* (New York: Hill & Wang, 1974), pp. 200-201.
[20]Barthes, "Death of the Author," p. 53.

mentary becomes as authoritative and creative as the "original" text: "Just as Einsteinian science compels us to include within the object studied the *relativity of reference points,* so the combined action of Marxism, Freudianism, and structuralism compels us, in literature, to relativize the relations of *scriptor,* reader, and observer (critic)."[21]

Many contemporary forms of biblical criticism unapologetically advance their own ideology, their own minority and marginal interest. These "users" abandon any pretense of neutrality. Richard Rorty, the patron philosophical saint of interpretive neo-pragmatism, argues that the texts do not have "natures," only "uses." No one use should be equated with the "right" way of reading. Instead of trying to "get it right," the neo-pragmatist interpreter simply wants to produce a useful or interesting reading.

It would be misleading to infer that the readers' liberation movement endorses interpretive anarchy. But where do the criteria for interpretation come from? Where is the locus of interpretive authority? Stanley Fish claims that authority belongs to the "interpretive community." Every reader belongs to some community in which certain interpretive interests and procedures are shared. What a reader discovers in a text is thus the function of the community to which he or she belongs. Interpretation is thus not arbitrary, but neither is it dependent on the "myth" that meaning is "in" the text. Meaning is rather a function of the reading strategy brought to a text. As Fish puts it: "The interpretation constrains the facts rather than the other way around and also constrains the kinds of meaning that one can assign to those facts."[22] It is the community, not the canon, that constrains the reader.

Both Barthes and Fish have in different ways obliterated the traditional distinction between text and reader, meaning and commentary. With radical reader-response theories, Kant's Copernican revolution reaches its apotheosis: readers do not discover but construct meaning. The roles of text and reader have not only been revolutionized but reversed: "Texts, like dead men and women, have no rights, no aims, no interests. They can be used in whatever way readers or interpreters choose."[23]

Reader Response in Relation to Other Approaches
Historical-critical approaches. Critical readers since the Enlightenment have indeed been active: subjecting textual testimonies to critical assessment, taking texts apart and putting them back together in more "accurate" form, reconstructing the history that lies behind the text and the history of the text's own composition. The reader assumed in much historical criticism was a disinterested, objective, apolitical

---

[21]Barthes, "From Work to Text," in *The Rustle of Language,* p. 57.
[22]Stanley Fish, *Is There a Text in This Class? The Authority of Interpretive Communities* (Cambridge, Mass.: Harvard University Press, 1980), p. 293.
[23]Morgan and Barton, *Biblical Interpretation,* p. 7.

scholar—in short, a myth. Bultmann's recognition that exegesis without presuppositions was impossible was simply an aftershock of the Kantian epistemological earthquake. All that we have access to as readers is textual phenomena; the historical "noumenon"—the thing-in-itself (the original situation, context and reference of the text)—is unavailable. History—that is, the history we tell—is always interpreted, a product of the readerly activity, of selection and "emplotment."[24]

Literary-critical approaches. Many of the same points could be make with reference to literary-critical approaches. The turn to the text (instead of its author or the history it recounts) is not yet a turn to the reading subject. The reader is often a figure in the background. Literary-critical techniques attend to the text's conventions and formal features and the processes by which it conveys sense. This would be true of structuralist, rhetorical, narrative and canonical approaches to the biblical text, for instance. These approaches, however, continue to eclipse the role of the reader in making meaning. Structuralists continue to trade on the model of objective knowledge, insisting that their approach is a "science" of the text.

Ideological approaches. Elisabeth Schüssler Fiorenza argues that readers must ethically evaluate the text as well as respond to its initiatives.[25] The principal aim of Marxist or "materialist" readers, for instance, is to examine the relation between a text and the sociopolitical forces associated with its production and reception. Both texts and readers are viewed as sociopolitical products. Biblical stories are read with an interest in discovering something about the struggles of various classes or groups. Equally important, the contemporary reader is also situated in a class-based economic and political system. Readers are the first to be liberated by liberation theology. The assumption that only scholars in First World universities can discover the "proper" meaning of the Bible is exploded. For Carlos Mesters, the experience of poverty and oppression is just as important a "text" as Scripture itself. The place of the poor affords them special insight into the biblical message.[26] The context of the reader is just as important as the context of the text.

Ideological readers try to make the text conform to their devices and desires. Reading is a form of power. Not only what we read but how we read is ultimately a matter of politics. If meaning is a matter of the reader's construction, then disagree-

---

[24]So Hayden White, *Metahistory* (Baltimore: Johns Hopkins University Press, 1974); and Ben Meyer, "The Challenge of Text and Reader to the Historical-Critical Method," in *The Bible and Its Readers,* ed. W. A. M. Beuken, Concilium (London: SCM Press/Philadelphia: Trinity, 1991), pp. 3-12.

[25]Elisabeth Schüssler Fiorenza, "The Ethics of Biblical Interpretation: Decentering Biblical Scholarship," *Journal of Biblical Literature* 107 (1988): 3-17.

[26]Carlos Mesters, "The Use of the Bible in Christian Communities of the Common People," in *The Bible and Liberation: Political and Social Hermeneutics,* ed. Norman Gottwald (Maryknoll, N.Y.: Orbis, 1983), pp. 119-33.

ments over readings—the conflict of interpretations—are really conflicts of ideologies. But if reading is in the eye of a community of beholders (Fish), what can possibly arbitrate interpretive disputes among "believing" communities?

Deconstructive approaches. Deconstruction is not a method of interpretation but a method for *undoing* interpretations, for exposing readings as functions of various ideological forces. Every textual structure has to repress those elements that threaten to undo it: patriarchy suppresses women, racism suppresses ethnic minorities, conventional morality suppresses gays. The point of the deconstructionist critique is that every structure is, like language itself, arbitrary and conventional. No structure, no sense, is "natural." Frank Kermode writes, with reference to the parable of the good Samaritan: "My way of reading . . . seems to me natural; but that is only my way of authenticating, or claiming as universal, a habit of thought that is cultural and arbitrary. My reading would certainly not have seemed 'natural' to the church Fathers."[27] The realm of culture and interpretation is a human construct, where power is pitted against power. What deconstruction ultimately deconstructs is the accumulation of power in interpretation.[28] To deconstruct is to take issue with the text as it is constructed by the reader.

Deconstructive reading mercilessly exposes the reader's interests by undoing interpretation and by exposing the rhetoric, not logic, behind interpretation. It detoxifies the poisoned well and is the ever-vigilant attempt to keep the act of reading from coming to rest in a settled interpretation, for of the making of many meanings there is no end. I agree with Jeanrond's assessment: "One of Derrida's main contributions to hermeneutics lies precisely in his powerful warning against any form of absolutist or authoritarian reading of texts."[29] Of course the deconstructionists' quasi-Reformation cry—"always rewriting"—can itself become an excuse *not* to respond to what is "there" in the text. Insofar as deconstruction renders meaning undecidable it drains away both the authority and the otherness of texts. But if nothing determinate is in the text, how can the reader respond and read responsibly?

Critical Remarks

Readers are indeed active in the interpretive process. The key question concerns the nature of this activity of the reader's response. Will the reader, confronted with a text's initiatives and invitations, respect or suspect them, obey them or rebel against

---

[27]Frank Kermode, *The Genesis of Secrecy: On the Interpretation of Narrative* (Cambridge, Mass.: Harvard University Press, 1979), p. 35.

[28]David Jobling, "Writing the Wrongs of the World: The Deconstruction of the Biblical Text in the Context of Liberation Theologies," *Semeia* 51 (1990): 81-118, here 102.

[29]Werner G. Jeanrond, *Theological Hermeneutics: Development and Significance* (London: Macmillan, 1991), p. 104.

them? To what extent does reader response infect (or enable) the interpretive stages of explication, understanding and application?

Criticism, using and interpreting. In the past, *criticism* referred to obtaining knowledge of a text. Today, however, *criticism* denotes the reader's claim to enjoy a privileged perspective from which the text may be used or evaluated. It follows that "criticism" loses its disinterested, scholarly allure. What used to pass as "objective" description is now viewed as "subjective" or intersubjective ideological evaluation. But need it follow that we can no longer distinguish "using" from "interpreting" texts? Is "getting it right" strictly equivalent to "making it useful," as Rorty implies? To put it another way: are all interpretive interests and critical perspectives equally valid?

Readers must not only respond but respond *responsibly*. There are, I believe, normative aims that readers ought to have as they approach the biblical text. One would be to seek understanding before "overstanding." That is, readers should seek to ascertain the nature of the text's communicative intent (its genre and sense) before seeking to use or evaluate it. What is the text trying to do and how is it doing it? This question must be answered with honesty and integrity. To treat a text justly is to respect it for the kind of thing it is, that is, to entertain its perspective and to heed its voice.

Of course readers inhabit their own worlds, and their interests may be different from those of the text. Readers who seek answers to their questions "overstand" the text. We might say that understanding seeks the "meaning" and overstanding the "significance" of the text. But it is crucial that readers evaluate a text's significance only after they have understood its sense. It may be that once having grasped the text's intended sense, the reader will recoil in disgust. While some texts may give a taste of heaven, others hold horrors. But the point is that the reader's first reflex should be charitable: understanding precedes criticism as interpretation precedes use. George Steiner goes so far as to treat critics and readers as two different species altogether: Critics function at a distance from the text, of which they are judge and master. The reader, however, "serves" the text and is its shepherd.[30]

Misreading and other misdemeanors. Is there such a thing as a poor reading? a false one? If the reader both creates and discovers meaning, how can we maintain distinctions between exegesis, text and commentary, meaning and significance, description and evaluation, the ideology of the text and the ideology of the reader? Eco, a believer in the reader's indispensable role, worries that the rights of readers have recently been exaggerated over the rights of the text.[31] Though Eco is willing to speak of a legitimate interpretive pluralism, he also speaks of the fundamental duty

---

[30]George Steiner, "Critic/Reader," *New Literary History* 10 (1979): 423-52.
[31]Umberto Eco, *Interpretation and Overinterpretation* (Cambridge: Cambridge University Press, 1992), p. 23.

of protecting texts before "opening" them. There is a difference between disagreeing about what one thinks the text is trying to say and deliberately misreading the text. "Misreaders" ask neither author nor text about their intentions but beat the text into a shape that will suit their purposes. Interpretation, on the other hand, means reading a text "in order to discover, along with our reactions to it, something about its nature."[32]

Humpty-Dumpty thought meaning was a matter of who was going to be the master, the words or the one using them: "When *I* use a word . . . it means just what I choose it to mean—nothing more, nothing less."[33] Contemporary poststructuralists and pragmatists have given Nietzsche's will to power to the reader. The Nietzschean counterpart to Humpty-Dumpty is even more hard-boiled. For the willful misreader there is no such thing as absolute meaning or a text-as-it-is-in-itself; every interpretation is the result of our aims and practices. Such strong-willed reading raises the question of interpretive violence. In the words of one American deconstructionist theologian: "Interpretation is a hostile act in which interpreter victimizes text."[34]

The ethics of reading. The violence of radical reader-response criticism is a function of its basic philosophical presuppositions. Its unsatisfactory ethical implications are symptomatic of its inadequate view of the nature of meaning and interpretation. Insofar as it denies that meaning is "there" in the text, radical reader-response criticism is a form of antirealism, the philosophical view that reality is not independent but at the behest of our theories about it. While it is true that even scientists approach the world with interpretive schemes, it is not the case that our theories are hermetically sealed off from the world. On the contrary, the world does "kick back," challenging and often falsifying our ideas about it.

Similarly, there must be a realism in the realm of meaning or else anything goes in interpretation. *Gulliver's Travels* remains political satire even though some readers might mistake it for a mere children's story. If it did not continue to be so, if texts became whatever we made of them, then there would be no way in which to judge a reading false. Or, as Jeanrond says, "a reading which claims to have interpreted the *text,* yet in reality has either only interpreted a section of a text outside of its textual context or used the text or fragments of it in order to promote the reader's own thoughts, must be considered fraudulent."[35]

If meaning were not in some sense "there" in the text, how could texts ever challenge, inform or transform their readers? How could texts ever criticize a dominant

---

[32]Umberto Eco, *The Limits of Interpretation,* (Bloomington: Indiana University Press, 1990), p. 57.

[33]Lewis Carroll, *Through the Looking-Glass,* in *The Philosopher's Alice,* ed. Peter Heath (New York: St. Martin's, 1971), p. 193.

[34]Mark C. Taylor, "Text as Victim," in *Deconstruction and Theology,* ed. T. Altizer (New York: Crossroad, 1982), p. 65.

[35]Jeanrond, *Text and Interpretation,* p. 116.

ideology? Without a certain "realism of reading," where meaning is independent of the interpretive process, reading would cease to be a dangerous, world-shattering prospect. One would then have not to celebrate the birth of the reader but to mourn the stillborn reader.

If the text is at the mercy of the reader, what should readers do with it? First and foremost, readers should *let it be*—not in the sense of leaving it alone but in the sense of allowing the text to fulfill its communicative aim. What the ethical reader gives to the text is, in the first instance, attention. Only then can the text give something back. Steiner depicts the ideal reader as shepherd of the text's "being." Michael LaFargue similarly sees the reader as the text's protector: "The role of the biblical scholar, as scholar, is to be a servant of the biblical text, to guard its otherness, to help make its substantive content something modern people can in some way experience and understand, in its particularity and in its otherness."[36] The prime interpretive interest should be to let the text have its say, that is, to heed and hearken to the text with attention, humility and respect.

We may well have a responsibility to assess and criticize a text, or to disagree with its theological or political implications. But we can do so with integrity only if we have first made the intellectual and ethical effort to receive the text on its own terms: "Whoever has ears to hear, let that person hear." The Golden Rule—for Christian ethics and interpretation alike—is "Do unto others as you would have them do unto you."

Reader Response in Practice
What do readers do when they interpret John 4? This question demands a twofold answer, in keeping with my distinction between conservative and radical reader-response critics.

Conservative examples: Reader reception. Conservative reader-response critics believe there is something in the text prior to the act of reading—gaps, indeterminacies, instructions, flags and signals, for example—that calls for and governs their response. The reader follows invitations; like a polite guest being shown the narrative sights, the reader obliges the author by catching cues and looking in the right direction. R. Alan Culpepper observes that by the time readers reach John 4 they should know something (on the basis of the information recorded in John 1—3) about Jesus and his mission. For instance, the reader of John 4 would already know that Jesus will be rejected by his own and believed in by some. The reader of the well story is a privileged onlooker, a guest of a reliable voice—of the "omniscient"

---

[36]Michael LaFargue, "Are Texts Determinate? Derrida, Barth and the Role of the Biblical Scholars," *Harvard Theological Review* 81 (1988): 355.

narrator—who gives the reader just enough information to make the right evaluation of the characters and the action in the story.[37]

Following John. John 4 offers three examples of the way textual stimuli guide the reader's response. First, the text recalls a familiar type-scene from the Old Testament, the man-meets-woman-at-the-well device. There are several recurring elements. The future bridegroom (or his surrogate) journeys to a foreign land, he meets a maiden at a well, someone draws water from the well, the maiden rushes home to bring news of the stranger, and a betrothal is arranged. The characters are of course unaware that they are playing out a familiar plot; the type-scene is a textual strategy for guiding the reader's understanding of what is happening in the story. In John 4, however, instead of going to a betrothal meal Jesus tells his disciples, "My food is to do the will of him who sent me" (Jn 4:34). Only the reader can appreciate this unexpected twist.[38] Such differences are the keys to understanding how this author is manipulating not only a literary convention but also the reader's response.

Second, Lyle Eslinger claims that the reader will recognize a number of double entendres in the conversation, all of which have sexual overtones. This ambiguity prompts the reader to wonder whether one should attribute a carnal or spiritual meaning to the dialogue. Does Jesus ask for a drink because his disciples are unavailable "or because he and the woman are alone and he can make free with her without damaging her reputation?"[39] The woman, of course, lacks the knowledge of John 1—3. As far as she is concerned, Jesus is being friendly, even forward. According to Eslinger, readers are invited to give a sexual connotation to Jesus' "living water" on the basis of such texts as Jeremiah 2:13 and Proverbs 5:15. The reader feels the force of the woman's interpretation but cannot identify completely with it, being privy to additional information about Jesus' identity.

Third, though the reader has the advantage of the prologue, which identifies Jesus with the Logos, John 4 is designed in such a way as to give the reader the same sense of confusion as to who Jesus is and what he is about. What is Jesus' motive in asking the woman for a drink? The woman "responds" to his request by hinting that he is

---

[37]J. Eugene Botha argues that the text may also "wrongfoot" readers, for example, by leading them to associate John 4 with similar man-meets-woman-at-well scenes of the Old Testament, only to dash their expectations as the story progresses and no betrothal takes place (*Jesus and the Samaritan Woman: A Speech Act Reading of John 4:1-42* [Leiden, Netherlands: Brill, 1991], p. 191). Jeffrey Lloyd Stanley speaks of the "victimization" of the implied reader by the implied author, who turns the familiar scene into "a brilliant parody of the patriarchal betrothal scenes" (*The Print's First Kiss: A Rhetorical Investigation of the Implied Reader in the Fourth Gospel* [Atlanta: Scholars Press, 1988], p. 99).

[38]Lyle Eslinger, "The Wooing of the Woman at the Well: Jesus, the Reader and Reader-Response Criticism," in *The Gospel of John as Literature: Twentieth Century Perspectives,* ed. Mark W. G. Stibbe (Leiden, Netherlands: Brill, 1993), pp. 165-79.

[39]Ibid., p. 176.

being rather forward: Jesus is a Jew, she a Samaritan; Jesus is a man, she a woman. Eslinger believes that the text encourages the reader to share in the woman's "carnal" interpretation of Jesus' words. To have "dealings with" (Jn 4:9) has sexual overtones, he claims, as does "living water."[40] The reader's privileged knowledge of who Jesus is (Jn 1) and what "the gift of God" is (Jn 3:16) prevents the reader from giving free rein to the carnal interpretation: "His privilege puts him in a quandary, the experience of which gives him a direct perception of the basic problem in the gospel of John, man's misconception of Jesus and misunderstanding of what Jesus says."[41] The reader temporarily loses the omniscient narrator in the maze of the dialogue, forcing the reader to occupy the fallible human perspective of the woman at the well. "In chapter 4 the reading experience becomes an actual experience of the communication gap that the reader has already observed several times between the human characters in the story and Jesus."[42] The reader not only reads about but undergoes the experience of misunderstanding Jesus.

Following irony. Misinterpreting Jesus is one of the themes of the Fourth Gospel. Culpepper notes that the misunderstandings and mistaken identities that pervade the Fourth Gospel function to teach readers how to read the Gospel correctly: "As we read, watching the encounters and forming judgments on each character, the narrator shapes the response we think we are making on our own and wins our confidence by elevating us above the characters to his position."[43] To follow the Fourth Gospel, then, the reader must be able to recognize irony.

According to Gail R. O'Day, Bultmann failed to see the dynamics of the revelatory process in the Fourth Gospel because he focused on the sheer fact of Jesus as revealer rather than on how the narrative shapes and communicates the revelation.[44] The reader must follow John's textual strategy, especially irony, in order to participate in the revelation. Irony is a form of speech in which the reader is asked to hold two meanings in tension and, as a result of moving through the tension, to arrive at what the author intends to express:

> Irony reveals by asking the reader to make judgments and decisions about the relative value of stated and intended meanings, drawing the reader into its vision of truth, so that when the reader finally understands, he or she becomes a member of the community that shares that vision, constituted by those who have also followed the author's lead.[45]

---

[40]Ibid., p. 178.
[41]Ibid., p. 179.
[42]Ibid., p. 173.
[43]R. Alan Culpepper, *Anatomy of the Fourth Gospel: A Study in Literary Design* (Philadelphia: Fortress, 1983), p. 234.
[44]See Gail R. O'Day, "Narrative Mode and Theological Claim: A Study in the Fourth Gospel," *Journal of Biblical Literature* 105 (1986): 657-68.
[45]Ibid., p. 664.

The reader becomes the woman at the well to the extent that he or she is asked to sort through the double meanings and to move from one level of meaning to another. In John 4:10 Jesus says that if the woman knew who was asking her for a drink she, in a complete role reversal, would be asking him for "water." But the woman will not be able to interpret "living water" correctly until she recognizes the identity of the one who is speaking. Jesus' clue to his true identity "is an invitation both to the woman and to the reader to grasp both levels of the conversation . . . and to move through the woman's level to Jesus'."[46] By following the text's irony, there-fore, the reader participates in Jesus' revelation. "Irony is an excellent example of this participation because of the type of reader response it embodies. To follow irony, one must participate and engage creatively in the text."[47] The Fourth Gospel is not just a report of Jesus as revealer but an opportunity for the reader to experience Jesus' revelation for himself or herself.

Radical examples: Reader rejection? Real readers, as opposed to ideal read-ers, may be less than sympathetic to the text's prompts. Accordingly there is a history not only of text reception but also of text rejection.

Resisting John. Culpepper comments that readers "dance" with the author whether they want to or not, and in the process they adopt the author's perspective on the story. But not all readers are so compliant as Culpepper believes; some prefer to lead rather than follow. Willi Braun observes that some readers do not trust the implied author. Many resist being drawn into the narrator's ideology and point of view. Braun sets forth a strategy of "resistant" reading that seeks to read the Fourth Gospel from the vantage point of those who may be marginalized by the text—Jews, for instance. These implied victims of John's irony have become real victims of Christian anti-Semitism. There is thus an "enormous incentive" to dissent from the Johannine ideol-ogy. Reading may spring not only from the will to power but also from "the will to clear space for oneself over against a menacingly 'strong' text."[48]

Imploding Johannine irony. Stephen D. Moore questions the text's ability to lead readers through complications and deferrals to understanding. He claims that his reading, which is deconstructive-feminist, is "closer" than that of conservative reader-response critics. His reading is both suspicious and scrupulous inasmuch as it seeks rigorously to examine every resistance to understanding. Deconstructive reading is particularly attentive to everything that threatens the text, or interpretation, with inco-herence. A hermeneutics of suspicion seeks thereby to "poison the well" and so to caution would-be readers against swallowing everything the text appears to offer.

---

[46]Ibid., p. 667.
[47]Ibid., p. 668.
[48]Willi Braun, "Resisting John: Ambivalent Redactor and Defensive Reader of the Fourth Gos-pel," *Studies in Religion* 19 (1990): 64.

Moore acknowledges that the text's apparent irony trades on the woman's failure to distinguish the literal and material from the figural and spiritual (Jn 4:15). The woman is oblivious of the meaning (and the water) "from above." She is discoursing, and drawing water, "from below." As we have seen, conservative reader-response critics believe that the text's strategy is to lead the reader through irony from the lower to the "higher" meaning. Deconstruction is the dismantling of privileged hierarchical oppositions, such as male and female, spiritual and physical, figurative and literal. It is just such oppositions of higher and lower that make the woman at the well a "victim" of Jesus' irony. Moore wants his reading to overturn the text's oppositions and to show that the Samaritan woman's insight is superior to that of Jesus.

Moore notes that the complete meaning of "living water" is not given in John 4. Jesus speaks of thirst and living water again in John 7:38: "He who believes in me, as the scripture has said, 'Out of his heart shall flow rivers of living water.'" The narrator, in an aside, informs the reader that Jesus said this "about the Spirit, which those who believed in him were to receive" (Jn 7:39). The reader is thus in a superior position to Jesus' audience, knowing something that they do not know. But Moore points out that there is a second deferral of meaning. "The figure of living water being imbibed is interpreted as the receiving of the Spirit, but its narrative representation is postponed until later: 'as yet the Spirit had not been given, because Jesus was not yet glorified' (7:39)."[49] The themes of thirsting and drinking occur once again at the scene of the crucifixion in a way that for Moore "strangely echoes" their first occurrence in John 4. In John 19:28, however, it is Jesus who says "I thirst"—and this apparently for literal earthly, not living, water! "Expectations have been steadily raised and redirected from 4:10ff from the mundane to the supramundane. Jesus, source of the figural water, is now thrust into the very condition of the literal thirst that his discourse has led the audience to transcend."[50]

The waters become even muddier for Moore when after the satiation of Jesus' physical thirst (itself a fulfillment of Scripture—Jn 19:28), Jesus says, "It is finished," and yields up–what? his spirit? the Spirit? Moore comments: "The satiation of Jesus' physical thirst in 19:30 is an arrestingly strange precondition for the symbolic yielding up of that which is designed to satiate the supra-physical thirst of the believer."[51] Not only strange but contradictory, since the very order of the spiritual and the physical appears to have been inverted.

The literal, material, earthly level, hierarchically superseded in John 4:7-14 and

---

[49]Moore, *Literary Criticism,* p. 160. See also Stephen D. Moore, "Are There Impurities in the Living Water That the Johannine Jesus Dispenses? Deconstruction, Feminism and the Samaritan Woman," *Biblical Interpretation* 1 (1993): 207-27.
[50]Moore, *Literary Criticism,* p. 161.
[51]Ibid.

shifted into the background, is reinstated in John 19:28-30 as the very condition (physical thirst, physical death) that enables the Spirit itself, emblem and token of the supramundane order (cf. 14:17) to effectively come into being.[52]

The opposition between the spiritual and physical on which the irony of John 4 depends is thus overthrown from within the text—imploded. The ostensibly superior term—living water, the Spirit—is shown to depend for its existence on the inferior term, literal water.

Jesus' death is followed by the return of the "repressed"—physical water—when the soldiers pierce Jesus' side. Upon Jesus' death, therefore, the Spirit (living water) is yielded up and material water flows from Jesus' side. What shall we make of this last flow? Moore suggests that we are left "with a symbol (the flow of water) of a meta-phor (living water) for the Spirit."[53] The water that flows from Jesus' side is neither simply material nor simply spiritual; rather, it is *both* literal and figurative.

And what of the Samaritan woman? On Moore's analysis, she is closer to the truth about the water, and about Jesus, than Jesus himself. Whereas Jesus presupposes a dichotomy (and hierarchy) between the literal and figurative, physical and spiritual, the woman resists such oppositions. For her the water in the well is more than merely physical; it is water from a well dug by Jacob that has lasted centuries—it is symbolic. Far from being the victim of irony, therefore, the woman at the well has correctly recognized that all such ironies built on hierarchical oppositions eventually implode. Insofar as the woman resists the opposition between literal and figurative, she outstrips her male teacher. Such a reading is not what the text intended, but it is buried in the text's "structural unconscious." Moore argues that Jesus, insofar as he mistakenly thinks that the spiritual is "higher" than the physical, is the main ironic casualty of this undoing of the traditional interpretation of John 4. The woman at the well, far from being a victim of the author's irony, turns out to be the first deconstruc-tive-feminist critic!

Conclusion: The Reader as Disciple

We are left with two opposed models for reading. Which follows the text more closely: the one that rejects or the one that respects the author's intentions and the textual strategies that embody them? Following a text means understanding the nature of its communicative activity. Following irony is not the same as following an argument, but both are forms of reader response to textual strategies. Margaret Davies says that competent readers of the Fourth Gospel need to know the Scrip-tures and the story of Jesus and must be part of a confessional community living out

---

[52]Ibid.
[53]Ibid., p. 162.

(following) the Gospel insights. "The ideal readers of this narrative are those who can play the role of the narratees in believing that Jesus is the Christ."[54]

Finally, with regard to meaning: do readers find it or make it? Albert Schweitzer concluded his classic *The Quest for the Historical Jesus* with a memorable image about a well: when investigators peered down into the well of Jesus' history, they managed to see only the reflection of their own faces in the water below. The reader at the literary well will come away with as great a thirst as ever if, in search of the textual Jesus, she similarly discovers only herself. Readers who feed only on themselves are likely to emerge from the process of interpretation unfulfilled. It is one thing to study well water, to smell it and analyze its chemical composition, and quite another thing to drink. One who continually suspects well water of contamination and never drinks will never quench his or her thirst.

The reader at the well, in order to be nourished, must draw from and drink of the text. To "drink" here means to accept and to appropriate. The reader has a responsibility to receive the text according to its nature and intention. Steiner describes good reading as responsive to its source, resulting in a creative echo to the text.[55] One can do many things with water from a well; but in the desert of criticism, a drink should be received with eagerness and thanks.

---

[54]Margaret Davies, *Rhetoric and Reference in the Fourth Gospel* (Sheffield, U.K.: JSOT, 1992), p. 373.
[55]George Steiner, "Narcissus and Echo: A Note on Current Arts of Reading," *American Journal of Semiotics* 1 (1981): 14.

Nine

The Hermeneutics of I-Witness Testimony
John 21:20-24 & the Death of the Author

*These are not memoirs about myself. These are memoirs
about other people. Others will write about us. . . . One must speak the
truth about the past or not at all. It's very hard
to reminisce and it's worth doing only in the name of truth. . . .
I was an eyewitness to many events and they were important events. . . .
This will be the testimony of an eyewitness.*
DIMITRI SHOSTAKOVICH

John 21:20-24 calls not only for interpretation but for reflection on the interpretive process itself. Its subject, the Beloved Disciple, is presented as at once an interpreter par excellence and the victim of a misinterpretation, the rumor that he would not die. The attempt to understand this text thus leads us to think about the aims and methods of textual understanding in general. Exegesis passes naturally into hermeneutics. For John 21:20-24 raises several crucial and absorbing hermeneutical issues concerning the author, text and reader. These issues all center on the figure of the Beloved Disciple, who is mentioned six times in the Fourth Gospel (Jn 13:23-30; 19:25-27; 20:2-10; 21:7; 21:20-23; 21:24), usually in passages emphasizing eyewitness testimony. John 21:24, the last of these references, serves as touchstone and structuring principle for our inquiry with its threefold reference to the Beloved Disciple: he is (1) the author "who has written these things," (2) the witness "who is bearing witness to these things" and (3) the model disciple for the reader, for "his testimony is true."

The Beloved Disciple is a controversial figure in Johannine scholarship. Not only his identity but his very existence and historicity are subjects of some dispute. While some commentators find the disclosure of the author's identity as the

Beloved Disciple to be the climax of the Gospel, others maintain that John 21:24 is a later editorial addition. In this essay I wish to explore the extent to which the question of authorship becomes a properly hermeneutical as opposed to historical problem. To what extent does the question of authorship affect the interpretation of texts and the activity of interpretation? And to what extent ought it to do so?

If such a question holds center stage, it is because the rumor of the "death of the author" is being spread not only in the wings and on the margins of biblical scholarship but increasingly "among the brethren." I intend to show that this latter rumor, distinctly lacking in dominical authority, has serious implications for the way we interpret biblical testimony. Just as the death, actual or contemplated, of the Beloved Disciple raised the problem of a continuing authoritative witness in the original believing community, so the death of the author raises for us the problem of how to preserve and do justice to the authoritative textual witness of the other.

Though Jesus never promised immortality to the Beloved Disciple, he probably did not envisage the way that the Beloved Disciple would be killed off, at least as an author, in modern and postmodern biblical scholarship. Much historical-critical work on the Fourth Gospel has taken the form of a quest for the historical author. But all too often the question of historical authorship has shaded into a discussion of the historical reliability of the Johannine tradition. The result: conservative and liberal commentators alike have treated authorship as a matter of apologetics rather than interpretation. With some exceptions, most historical critics have concluded that the Fourth Gospel in its present form could not have been written by the Beloved Disciple. Why? Because John 21:23, together with a complicated theory concerning the composition of the Gospel, implies that he had probably died before the Gospel was published.

Of late, however, scholars have begun to read the Fourth Gospel with literary-critical aims and interests. A book-length review of Johannine scholarship between 1970 and 1990 concludes with this thought: "The most contemporary development, perhaps, is the reading of John as the kind of literary product it is, a narrative or story, independently of historical consideration such as authorship and time, or circumstances of composition."[1] Such approaches have convincingly demonstrated the Evangelist's literary artistry and rhetorical strategies while neatly sidestepping the vexed question of historical authorship. While agreeing that the "how" and the "what" of discourse are legitimate objects of textual study, one may nevertheless wonder what has happened to the "about what" of discourse, that is, the question of reference to historical reality.

Deconstruction takes the literary approach to an extreme, not only killing but burying the author, effectively extinguishing all signs of his presence. The idea of the author is ultimately, as Roland Barthes correctly observes, a theological

---

[1]G. S. Sloyan, *What Are They Saying About John?* (New York: Paulist, 1991), p. 948.

notion.[2] The Author is the origin of meaning, the place where words and world come together, the guarantee that talk corresponds to reality. The presence of the Author thus assures the objectivity of meaning. *Logocentrism* is Derrida's term for the confidence that language refers to the real. For Derrida, however, logocentrism is a myth; the author is absent, not present. Signs refer not to reality but only to other signs. Of the writing that is Text there is no end: "The necessity of commentary . . . is the very form of exiled speech. In the beginning is hermeneutics."[3]

Perhaps no text is more conspicuously logocentric than the Fourth Gospel, the book of signs and testimonies that point to an incarnate Logos who is Truth. And of the many logocentric texts in the Fourth Gospel, John 21:24 is doubtless one of the more offensive to deconstructionist sensibilities. "We know that his testimony is true" is the supreme manifesto for logocentric hermeneutics.

To what extent is authorship of hermeneutical importance? Should biblical interpreters resist or celebrate the death of the author? The purpose of this essay is not to answer that general query but rather to examine the consequences of the death of the author for the interpretation of one kind of text in particular: "I-Witness" testimony (I use the pronoun rather than the name of the bodily part in order to stress the fact that the witness is a human person). I shall argue that testimony, of all literary forms, is least welcoming to deconstruction and radical reader-response criticism. For the reader either to impose his own meaning or to affirm indeterminate multiple meanings is to deny the very nature of testimony; it is to subject testimony to interpretive violence. Deconstruction castrates the text; bereft of its true voice, must not the text necessarily speak falsetto? Radical reader-response criticism therefore risks excluding the very idea of testimony, the voice of the other. Rightly to receive testimony, I shall argue, means to attend to and respect the voice of the author. Testimony may indeed lead to the death of the author, but not in the way suggested by deconstruction. It is precisely because the witness articulates the voice of an unwanted other that the author is killed. Testimony challenges us to respect the alterity of the other and to resist the temptation to reduce the voice of the other to our own.

The Voice of the Other and Authorial Rights

"Who has written these things . . ." (Jn 21:24).

"The question of the authorship of the book is tantalizing" and confronts us "with the problem of interpretation."[4] Indeed, and not only so for historical-critical scholar-

---

[2]Roland Barthes, "The Death of the Author," in *The Rustle of Language* (New York: Hill & Wang, 1986), p. 54.

[3]Jacques Derrida, *Writing and Difference*, trans. Alan Bass (Chicago: University of Chicago Press, 1978), p. 67.

[4]C. K. Barrett, *The Gospel According to St. John*, 2nd ed. (London: SPCK, 1978), pp. 3-4.

ship, as a riddle to be solved, but also for hermeneutics, as a problem with which to reckon. But what exactly is the question of authorship? For historical criticism, the question is "Who?" For hermeneutics, the question is "What?"

The salient facts with regard to the question of the identity of the author of the Fourth Gospel are quickly summarized; not so the multifarious theories which they have spawned. The earliest external evidence is virtually unanimous in attributing the Fourth Gospel to John the son of Zebedee, though much of this evidence can be traced back to the testimony of Irenaeus: "Afterwards John, the disciple of the Lord, who also reclined on his bosom, published his gospel, while staying at Ephesus in Asia" (*Adversus Haereses* 3.1.1). The earliest known manuscripts are headed *kata Ioannēn,* and significantly, they all include 21:24, which identifies the author as an "I-witness."

Of course the text itself constitutes the bulk of the relevant data, and the internal evidence is the subject of wildly divergent assessments. What does John 21:24 say and when did it say it?

When was 21:24 added to the Fourth Gospel? Bultmann believes that the Evangelist used four sources to compose the bulk of the narrative, which was reshaped by a later editor who also added John 21, and he is largely followed by Raymond Brown, who agrees that the evangelist cannot be the Beloved Disciple.[5]

But what exactly does 21:24 say? "This is the disciple . . . who has written these things." Does this verse make the claim that the Beloved Disciple is the author of the Fourth Gospel? There are two parts to this question. First, what is the scope of "these things"? Is this a reference to the anecdote immediately preceding about the rumor concerning the Beloved Disciple,[6] or a reference to the whole of John 21, or is it a reference to the entire Gospel?[7] Again, the case must rest entirely on internal evidence, that is, on interpretation. But second, and more important for our purposes, what is the meaning of "who has written" *(grapsas)?* At one extreme is the suggestion that the author wrote in his own hand. Others take the term in a causative sense: "had these things written" (by dictating or supervising the account). At the other extreme, Gottlob Schrenk suggests that *grapsas* indicates a much more remote conception of authorship: the Beloved Disciple's recollections were only the basis or the occasion for the composition of the Fourth Gospel.[8] D. Moody Smith gives a succinct

[5]Raymond E. Brown, *The Gospel According to St. John 13-21,* Anchor Bible 29 (New York: Doubleday, 1970), pp. 1078-82.
[6]C. H. Dodd, "Note on John 21,24," *Journal of Theological Studies* 4 (1953): 212-13; Margaret Davies, *Rhetoric and Reference in the Fourth Gospel, Journal for the Study of the New Testament* Supplement Series 69 (Sheffield, U.K.: JSOT, 1992).
[7]Paul S. Minear, "The Original Functions of John 21," *JBL* 102 (1983): 85-98.
[8]Gottlob Schrenk, "γράφω," in *Theological Dictionary of the New Testament,* ed. Gerhard Kittel and Gerhard Friedrich (Grand Rapids, Mich.: Eerdmans, 1964), 1:743.

picture of the critical consensus, such as it is:

> The Johannine community conceived of itself as linked directly to Jesus and the original
> circle of disciples through the Beloved Disciple, however that linkage may have been
> understood and whatever may be its validity as a historical claim. One finds a wide con-
> sensus on this point, a narrower one on whether the Beloved Disciple was an eyewit-
> ness, and a small but articulate minority willing to identify him with John the Son of
> Zebedee in accord with the ancient church tradition.[9]

Can we say anything more about the nature of this "link" between the Beloved
Disciple and the Fourth Gospel? C. K. Barrett thinks that *grapsas* "means no more
than that the disciple was the ultimate and responsible authority for 'these things.'"[10]
Similarly, Stephen Smalley believes that the Beloved Disciple handed on to a disciple
or a group of disciples an oral account of the deeds and sayings of Jesus. The disciples then wrote a first draft, and after the death of the Beloved Disciple the church
published an edited version. Brown locates the Beloved Disciple's involvement in the
first stage alone of the five stages of the Gospel's composition. The question "Who?"
leads therefore to the more fundamental query: "*What* is an author?" There is little
evidence in ancient literature of *grapsas* referring to such a notion of remote authorship, to authorship at a distance of four compositional stages.[11] What is at stake here
is not merely the fact but the very meaning of authorship.

Smalley concludes that the Beloved Disciple's witness lies behind the Gospel
though others were responsible for its composition and writing.[12] But on such a
reconstruction, does the Beloved Disciple meet Barrett's definition of an author: "the
man (or group) who would accept responsibility for the book as we read it in the
ancient MSS"?[13] Does it make sense to say that it is the Beloved Disciple "who has
written" or even "had these things written" if he is only a source? And even if he were
the prime or only source, can we really say, with Schrenk, that the Beloved Disciple
is "spiritually responsible" for the contents of the Gospel? Is this not a bit like saying
that Paganini was "responsible" for Rachmaninov's variations and modifications of his
theme? Surely the mind and spirit behind "Rhapsody on a Theme of Paganini" is distinctly Rachmaninov's. Paganini did not author or compose the "Rhapsody," nor
could he have.

Historical critics, in their zeal to solve one riddle about authorship, have created a

---

[9]D. M. Smith, "Johannine Studies," in *The New Testament and Its Modern Interpreters,* ed. E. J.
Epp and G. W. McRae (Atlanta: Scholars Press, 1989), p. 285.

[10]C. K. Barrett, *The Gospel According to St. John,* 2nd ed. (Philadelphia: Westminster Press,
1978), p. 587.

[11]F. R. M. Hitchcock, "The Use of *graphein,*" *Journal of Theological Studies* 31 (1930): 271-75.

[12]Stephen Smalley, *John: Evangelist and Interpreter* (Exeter, U.K.: Paternoster, 1978), p. 121.

[13]Barrett, *Gospel According to St. John,* p. 5.

new one: how can a distant source be responsible for a text over which he had no final control? Dennis Nineham insists that eyewitness testimony had little impact on the process of Gospel composition.[14] The Fourth Gospel, however, is a finely tuned work, dependent on subtleties of structure, irony and so forth to achieve its effect. It is difficult to see how the substance of the witness could be preserved if the Beloved Disciple were not also responsible for its form. But if he is responsible for its form and substance, would he then not be the sole author?

Literary critics, as one might expect, take a different approach to the question of the meaning of authorship. R. Alan Culpepper is more interested in the author as an implication of the text than he is in a historical figure. The "implied author" is the presence whose values and vision shape the work and response of the reader. As such, the implied author is "an ideal, literary, created version of the real man; he is the sum of his own choices."[15] "The Beloved Disciple may be just another character through whom the author's point of view is communicated, or he may be an ideal- ized representation of the author (hence a dramatic approximation of the implied author)."[16] In an ironic reversal, the "author" moves from being the cause of the text to being one of its rhetorical effects.

One of the great services of rhetorical criticism has been to call to our attention the vast array of techniques an author employs to inform, engage and guide the reader. Now one of the principal means of persuading the reader to accept the world of the text is to create a sense of the author's presence, intelligence and moral sensi- bility. Aristotle in his *Rhetoric* recognized that this sense of the personal character or "ethos" of the speaker itself functions as a means of persuasion. The equivalent of ethos in a narrative is the voice of the implied author.

The ethos of the Fourth Gospel largely depends on the identification of the author with the Beloved Disciple. The Beloved Disciple enjoys, says Brown, the "authority of a witness."[17] According to Calvin, the author reveals his identity as the Beloved Disciple in John 21:24 "so that the greater weight may be attached to an eye-witness who had fully known all that he writes about."[18] "A witness is someone who has seen and/or heard something and then testifies to others in order to persuade them of its truth."[19] Bearing witness is thus the Evangelist's function and peculiar authority. The

---

[14]Dennis E. Nineham, "Eye-Witness Testimony and the Gospel Tradition, Part 1," *Journal of Theological Studies* 9 (1958): 13.

[15]W. C. Booth, *The Rhetoric of Fiction* (Chicago: University of Chicago Press, 1961), pp. 74-75.

[16]R. Alan Culpepper, *Anatomy of the Fourth Gospel: A Study in Literary Design* (Philadelphia: Fortress, 1983), p. 44.

[17]Brown, *John,* p. 1121.

[18]John Calvin, *The Gospel According to St. John 11-21,* trans. T. H. L. Parker (Edinburgh: Oliver & Boyd, 1961), 1:226.

[19]John Ashton, *Understanding the Fourth Gospel* (Oxford: Clarendon, 1991), p. 523.

Beloved Disciple is depicted in each of his appearances as having either privileged access to the meaning of Jesus' ministry and death (in Jn 13:23-26 he enjoys the intimacy of Jesus' bosom; in Jn 19:25-27 he stands at the foot of the cross; in Jn 20:2-5 he is the first to the empty tomb) or privileged insight into the identity of Jesus (in Jn 20:8 he believes in the risen Jesus; in Jn 21:7 he recognizes the risen Jesus; in Jn 21:24 he bears true testimony to Jesus). Evidently the Beloved Disciple was hermeneutically gifted: "he has no misunderstandings."[20]

Authorship is a hermeneutical as well as historical category insofar as it relates to the ethos of the work, particularly a work of "I-witness" testimony. In testimony the questions "Who?" and "What" converge, for if the text is "I-witness" testimony then the integrity of the "I" makes all the difference. For the authority of testimony depends not only on the correctness of the reports but on the competence or ethos of the witness. As Martin Warner observes, rhetorical criticism here subverts the historical-critical tendency to focus on the history of the text's composition and the history of the community that composed it. To say that the narrative is an invention is to destroy the ethos of the work and "to evacuate the rhetoric of its persuasive power."[21] To the author(s) of John 21:24, if different from the Beloved Disciple, we must say, "The Beloved Disciple we know, but who are you?"

The death of the author. It is well known that the Fourth Gospel uses its characters' misunderstandings as a foil to clarify important points. The rumor concerning the Beloved Disciple, later identified as the author, is a case in point. It is the climax of a series of gentle contrasts between Peter and the Beloved Disciple, who, according to Augustine, represent two states of the Christian life: active faith (Peter) and eternal contemplation (the Beloved Disciple).[22] More recent scholarship correlates the contrast between the two disciples with the historical situation of the Johannine community: Peter stands for a pastoral, John for a prophetic ministry.[23]

According to Bultmann, however, the purpose of John 21:15-23 is to show that Peter's ecclesiastical authority has been transferred after his death to the Beloved Disciple, and thus to the Gospel.[24] Bultmann finds it incredible that an author could pass himself off as the Beloved Disciple and at the same time attest to his own death. Here

---

[20]Culpepper, *Anatomy,* p. 121.

[21]Martin Warner, "The Fourth Gospel's Art of Rational Persuasion," in *The Bible as Rhetoric: Studies in Biblical Persuasion and Credibility,* Warwick Studies in Philosophy and Literature, ed. Martin Warner (London: Routledge & Kegan Paul, 1990), p. 176.

[22]Augustine, "Homilies on the Gospel of John," in *Nicene and Post-Nicene Fathers of the Christian Church,* ed. Phillip Schaff (Grand Rapids, Mich.: Eerdmans, 1956), 7:450-51.

[23]Barrett, *John,* p. 583; Charles Talbert, *Reading John: A Literary and Theological Commentary on the Fourth Gospel and the Johannine Epistles* (London: SPCK, 1992), pp. 262-63.

[24]Rudolf Bultmann, *The Gospel of John: A Commentary,* trans. George R. Beasley-Murray (Oxford: Blackwell, 1971), p. 717.

Bultmann displays a surprising lack of sensitivity: one would have expected a former student of Heidegger to be open to the possibility that it is not his actual death but his being-toward-death, his mortality, that is here acknowledged. For Bultmann, however, the story of the fates of Peter and the Beloved Disciple is just a prop for the claim that the Fourth Gospel enjoys apostolic authority.

Similarly, Brown suggests that the saying about Peter's death is merely a means of getting to the real point—the death of the Beloved Disciple. For Brown, the rumor about the Beloved Disciple's not dying was false because he had in all probability already died. The episode is included because the community "was disturbed by the death of their great master since they had expected him not to die."[25] The anecdote about his respective task and fate is intended to reassure the Johannine community that his testimony would survive in the Gospel. John Ashton suggests that the Fare-well Discourse was also intended to help the community confront not only the departure of Jesus but that of the Beloved Disciple too.[26]

These interpretations make the figure of the Beloved Disciple a "device" in an ideological struggle. The Johannine community claims apostolic authority for its Gospel even though the apostle (whoever he was) stands at a distance from the finished product. If the Beloved Disciple has died, then it is certainly not his voice we hear in the text. Whose voice, then, is it? This literal deconstruction of the author plays into the hands of the literary deconstructionists who contend that the very idea of an "author" is an ideological construct.

"The anonymity of the biblical writers chimes in nicely with the 'death of the author' approach to literature of certain post-war French writers. . . . For Barthes 'writing is the destruction of every voice, of every point of origin.'"[27] The anonymity of biblical writings wonderfully facilitates poststructuralist readings. The death of the author liberates the reader from the bondage of having to discover authorial inten-tions and from having to decipher the text. For Michel Foucault, the idea of the author serves to give a false sense of textual unity and coherence: "The author is therefore the ideological figure by which one masks the manner in which we fear the proliferation of meaning."[28]

What is at stake in the death of the author, and the death of this author, the Beloved Disciple, in particular, is the integrity and authority of the text. Is there an independent voice or source of knowledge in this text, or are all voices merely pre-

---

[25]Brown, *John*, p. 1119.
[25]Brown, *John*, p. 1119.
[26]Ashton, *Understanding*, pp. 441, 478.
[27]R. P. Carroll, "Authorship," in *A Dictionary of Biblical Interpretation*, ed. R. J. Coggins and J. L. Houlden (London: SCM Press, 1990), p. 74.
[28]Michel Foucault, "What Is an Author," in *Textual Strategies: Perspectives in Post-structuralist Criticism*, ed. J. V. Harari (Ithaca, N.Y.: Cornell University Press, 1979), p. 159.

tenders, ideological constructs and rhetorical effects? Such a question strikes at the very heart of the nature of discourse that claims to be true testimony.

Authorial rights. Is the figure of the Beloved Disciple merely a rhetorical or ideological product of an anonymous later redactor, or is it possible that the Beloved Disciple is in some real sense the author? Barrett says, "The balance of probability is that a man would not so refer to himself."[29] What other explanation is there for this curious epithet? Augustine attributes it to authorial modesty: "For it was a custom with those who have supplied us with the sacred writings, that when any of them was relating the divine history, and come to something affecting himself, he spoke as if it were about another."[30] B. F. Westcott proposes a similar explanation: "It is quite intelligible that an Apostle . . . should separate himself as the witness from his imme- diate position as the writer."[31] It is worth noting that these hypotheses are not incom- mensurable with what was established earlier with regard to the ethos of the implied author. The Beloved Disciple indeed functions as a rhetorical device, but rhetoric may be enlisted to serve the interests of truth as well as power.[32]

In John 20:2 the Beloved Disciple is referred to as "the other disciple." Brown believes that this was perhaps a self-designation whereas "Beloved Disciple" was the title given him by his disciples to indicate his elevated status. What is intriguing, how- ever, is the restraint with which this figure is depicted. There is no hint that he is superior to Peter, just different. Moreover, it has been widely noticed that though the Beloved Disciple has inside knowledge, he does not share it: "he understands but does not bear witness until later."[33] Of course the modesty of the laconic "other disci- ple" who figures in the narrative is more than compensated for by the profound wit- ness of the loquacious Beloved Disciple in his capacity as writer of the Fourth Gospel.

What we appear to have in the Fourth Gospel is the voice of the "other disciple." The hermeneutic question with regard to authorship is simply this: should interpret- ers seek to recover the voice of the author, the voice of the other? Robert Morgan and John Barton have suggested that "texts, like dead men and women, have no rights, no aims, no interests."[34] Writers, they go on to say, have some short-term moral right to be understood as they intended, but "that right dies with them or with the occa- sions for which the utterance was intended."[35] Not only has the author died; he has

---

[29]Barrett, *John,* p. 117.
[30]Augustine, "Homilies," p. 311.
[31]B. F. Westcott, *The Gospel According to St. John* (Grand Rapids, Mich.: Baker, 1980), p. lv.
[32]Warner, "Art," p. 8.
[33]Culpepper, *Anatomy,* p. 44.
[34]Robert Morgan and John Barton, *Biblical Interpretation,* Oxford Bible Series (Oxford: Oxford University Press, 1988), p. 7.
[35]Ibid., p. 270.

died intestate. Such a condition is especially troubling when the text in question is testimony. Indeed one of the main points of John 21 is to provide (possibly in advance) for the departure of the I-witness. The testament is precisely that which survives its author.

In an era when animals and plants, even bacteria, are increasingly accorded certain rights (at least the right to survive), it strikes even the politically incorrect interpreter as a bit odd that Barton and Morgan deny to texts and authors the same courtesy. Do we not owe a debt to the past, an obligation never to forget, say, the Shoah testimony of those who endured the Holocaust, as well as the unspoken testimony of those who did not? In an age when minorities and other marginal groups are being granted a hearing, it remains something of a scandal that the author's voice remains on the margins of biblical scholarship. The other's testimony to Christ has been displaced by theories about the Gospel's composition that make the Fourth Gospel answer questions about the history of the Johannine community. Is it not the time to campaign for the rights of the author—the author's right to be heard and understood?

To return to the definition of the author: I shall understand by "author" the person(s) responsible for the final form of the text. The author of the Fourth Gospel, as other, is an I-witness. Attending to the ethos of his testimony may persuade us that he is an eyewitness as well. I-witness testimony insists that it be taken for what it is: the voice of the other. Of all literary forms, testimony most vigorously resists an interpreter's reading something into it.

Radical reader response excludes the very possibility of true testimony, the voice of the other. But as a significant and signifying other, the author has an initial right (it may be forfeited; one could be a compulsive liar) to have his or her primary communicative intent attended to and respected. As I hope now to show, authors have a right to be considered innocent (truthful) until proven guilty.

Testimony: Trying the Text
"He is bearing witness to these things . . ."

With regard to the author I asked: are there any rights? Turning to the text, let us now ask, are there any wrongs? That is, are false interpretations possible? John 21:23 treats one instance of misinterpretation in an interesting manner. It is but one of several instances in the Fourth Gospel in which the logos is fulfilled unexpectedly. In the case of 21:23, however, we are not given the correct interpretation. Rather, we are redirected to Jesus' words. The disciples had failed to give sufficient attention to Jesus' words.

Readers of the Fourth Gospel would do well to take this cautionary example to heart. The words matter. Logos is a form of rhetoric too, a means of persuading by means of the apparent proof of the speech itself. Testimony has to do not only with the ethos of the one who bears witness but with the content or logos of the witness too.

But why should we trust the witness's testimony? If we must believe in order to understand, are we not caught in a vicious variation of the hermeneutical circle? For if we deem a witness trustworthy, is it not because we trust the testimony? and do we not often trust one's testimony because we trust the one giving it?

Hermeneutics of suspicion. In light of the above dilemma, modern critics have opted out of the hermeneutical circle altogether. A hermeneutics of suspicion casts its pall over the history of much modern biblical criticism. Gabriel Josipovici, commenting on John 21:24, defines the trial of testimony: "Unfortunately such assertions remain nothing but words, and the rule of the game seems to be that the more an author asserts the truth of what he is saying the less likely we are to believe him."[36] Multiplying the number of witnesses, as the Fourth Gospel does, "will only reinforce our sense of the author behind the scenes, manipulating things."[37]

A distrust of appearances is the reflex of biblical critics who profess the new morality of historical knowledge. According to D. E. Nineham, whereas ancient historians regarded testimony as "the bed-rock truth below which he cannot dig," their modern counterparts question testimony: "His very integrity and autonomy as an historian prevent his taking his 'sources' at face value."[38] Nineham approves of R. G. Collingwood's reluctance to accept eyewitness testimony, for doing so implies that the historian is "allowing someone else to do for him what, if he is a scientific thinker, he can only do for himself."[39] Justification by one's own (academic) works is apparently the only way to achieve epistemological virtue. For John Locke, faith is the assent to propositions made on the basis not of sufficient reason but the credit of the proposer—which is as much to say, on no basis at all. Or as W. K. Clifford put it in his celebrated essay "The Ethics of Belief": "it is wrong always, everywhere, and for anyone, to believe anything upon insufficient evidence."[40]

The hermeneutics of suspicion is taken to the limit in deconstruction, which denies the very possibility of knowledge as justified true belief. For deconstruction, justification is always rationalization. Judgment is never impartial or evenhanded; we might as well speak of the amorality of literary knowledge. For deconstruction, the author's

---

[36]Gabriel Josipovici, *The Book of God: A Response to the Bible* (New Haven, Conn.: Yale University Press, 1988), p. 213.

[37]Ibid., p. 216.

[38]D. E. Nineham, "Eye Witness Testimony and the Gospel Tradition, Part 3," *Journal of Theological Studies* 11 (1960): 258.

[39]Ibid.

[40]W. K. Clifford, "The Ethics of Belief," in *Lectures and Essays* (London: Macmillan, 1886), p. 346.

voice is both undecidable and indecipherable. Texts have no determinate meaning, and texts with no determinate meaning cannot witness, report or confess. Honest readers must resist the seduction of the text: like Venus flytraps, texts lure the unsuspecting readers with the promise of representation and the scent of reality, only to close their jaws, entrapping them in an unending, self-referring labyrinth of language and textuality. Shed of its naiveté, interpretation becomes "a *hostile* act in which interpreter victimizes the text."[41] Because there is no text-in-itself that subsists apart from interpretation, the text exists only as victim. To be a text is to submit to interpretive violence. After the indignities of being prodded and examined by historical critics, the deconstructed text now suffers the ultimate humiliation—interpretive rape.

Hermeneutics of belief. "Beyond the wastelands of critical thought, we wish to be challenged anew."[42] Is there any way to recover the voice of the other, and once it has been recovered, can we again heed its call and believe?

Authorship has largely been treated by scholars of the left and right as an apologetical or historical rather than a hermeneutical or theological problem. Most scholars today consider the evidence with regard to the Fourth Gospel to be inconclusive. Does this legitimate our withholding belief? For Brevard Childs, historical-critical theories about origin and purpose try to give to the text "an historical concreteness which it simply does not have."[43] Childs says that the witness of the Beloved Disciple (Jn 21:24) is not historically verified but is rather taken up into the living voice of the believing community. "The crucial methodological issue at stake is doing justice to the theological function of the book's witness to authorship without converting the question immediately into one of historicity."[44] Thanks to the ending (Jn 21:24), the text is capable of addressing future generations of readers.

Childs is right, I think, to remind us that the problems of meaning cannot be reduced to the domain of historical reference. But it is also possible that Childs exaggerates the canonical function. Where the historical critics immediately convert the question of meaning into questions concerning the original situation, Childs converts the question into one that addresses the church's future situation. Texts have an interest in being recognized for what they are, rather than for what they were or might become. Childs moves to canon too fast. Before proceeding to canonical function, one must take the necessary detour of analyzing the various literary genres, in this case testimony.

---

[41]M. C. Taylor, "Text as Victim," in *Deconstruction and Theology*, ed. T. J. J. Altizer (New York: Crossroad, 1982), p. 65.

[42]Paul Ricoeur, *The Conflict of Interpretations* (Evanston, Ill.: Northwestern University Press, 1974), p. 28.

[43]Brevard S. Childs, *The New Testament as Canon: An Introduction* (London: SCM Press, 1984), p. 124.

[44]Ibid., p. 130.

A number of recent approaches to the Fourth Gospel agree with Childs that historical-critical readings that look for some data behind the testimonies are misguided. "It
is inappropriate to focus on anything other than the final form of the text of John."[45]
But neither is it appropriate to assign to the Fourth Gospel the same canonical function as texts of very different genres may perform. No, the canonical role of the
Fourth Gospel must be a function of the kind of thing, the kind of logos, it is. What is
the Fourth Gospel? It is an I-witness testimony that claims to be eyewitness testimony
as well: "The witness . . . makes a report of the event. . . . This first trait anchors all
the other meanings in a quasi-empirical sphere. It consequently transfers things seen
to the level of things said."[46] Testimony is neither simply rhetorical nor simply
rational, but both together, it is "caught in the network of proof and persuasion."[47]
Testimony is a literary form that aims to persuade rationally through reliable report-
age (both investigative and interpretative) and through the quality of the character of
the witness.

Because literary form and content are inseparable, attempts to verify the witness
by going beyond it is doomed to failure. This is especially the case with testimony, a
genre that attempts to convey the fact and meaning of singular events of absolute significance. Testimony is a speech act in which the witness's very act of stating p is
offered as evidence "that p," it being assumed that the witness has the relevant competence or credentials to state truly "that p."[48] With many if not most cases in the
Fourth Gospel, the testimony is the only access we have to the events in question.
Francis Fiorenza draws the obvious implication: "The attempt to get behind these testimonies does not enable us to say more but to say less than they do."[49]

For too long now a picture of responsible scholarship has held us captive. The
hermeneutics of suspicion is not misguided, only misplaced. Distrust should never be
the first hermeneutical reflex, especially not with testimony. It is time to unmask the
historical critic's vaunted autonomy for what it is: a species of ethical individualism
and intellectual pride. Much of the suspicion and skepticism surrounding the interpretation of John 21:20-24 is unwarranted. The epistemological foundationalism
grounding the historical-critical enterprise has itself been severely shaken of late. In a
philosophical monograph C. A. J. Coady argues "that our trust in the word of others
is fundamental to the very idea of serious cognitive activity."[50] Trusting the word of

---

[45]Talbert, *Reading John*, pp. 63-64.
[46]Paul Ricoeur, "The Hermeneutics of Testimony," in *Essays on Biblical Interpretation*, ed.
  Lewis Mudge (Philadelphia: Fortress, 1980), p. 123.
[47]Ibid., p. 127.
[48]C. A. J. Coady, *Testimony: A Philosophical Study* (Oxford: Clarendon, 1992), chap. 2.
[49]Francis S. Fiorenza, *Foundational Theology: Jesus and the Church* (New York: Crossroad,
  1986), p. 41.
[50]Coady, *Testimony*, p. vii.

others is a necessary and inescapable dimension of human intellectual activity: what passes for autonomous knowledge is actually underpinned by a covert reliance on what others tell us.

For Nineham and Clifford, on the other hand, eyewitness testimony is reliable only if it is *mine*. Testimony is trustworthy only if I have confirmed the account, or at least the character of the witness. Anything less is an abdication of cognitive autonomy. This means, however, that the autonomous scholar will not believe anything that he or she does not observe firsthand. If this is the sole criterion for reliable knowledge, then historical critics are skating on thin ice in a very small pond indeed. Coady offers a caustic verdict: the tendency to privilege perception over testimony is really "a hankering after a primacy for my perception."[51] But it should be evident that by the very nature of the case, modern critics are at a distinct disadvantage when it comes to the subject matter of the Fourth Gospel.

Testimony is as basic a means of knowledge as are perception and memory. Just as we do not *infer* that an object is blue from our perception of it, so we believe someone's testimony that the object is blue. We do not have to infer it. A person's stating it is, under normal circumstances, reason enough. We have little choice but to believe what we are told unless there is good reason for doubting it. The witness is thus considered epistemically innocent until proven guilty.

This principle is, I believe, of the utmost importance for the interpretation of the Fourth Gospel. Testimony is a legitimate mechanism for producing beliefs. There need be no contradiction between the rhetoric and the rationality of the Fourth Gospel, nor is there need to make some further inference about the reliability (or identity?) of the Beloved Disciple before taking his word for it. To repeat: testimony is as reliable a means of knowing as perception and memory. Indeed testimony makes the past and present perceptions of others available to those who could or did not perceive for themselves.

None of this, of course, means that the witness of the Fourth Gospel is true. As the writers of the Scriptures well knew, false testimony unfortunately abounds. But which attitude—suspicion or belief—is hermeneutically more fruitful when it comes to interpreting testimony? The skeptic, at best, enjoys greater safety from error, but runs the risk of ignoring a narrative framework with greater explanatory power than the alternatives and of losing a number of beliefs that may be true. The believer runs the risk of acquiring false beliefs, but is open to receiving a greater number of true beliefs and an interpretive framework for understanding the life and fate of Jesus. The "believer" is not necessarily a fideist, however: "We may have 'no reason to doubt' another's communication even where there is no question of our being gull-

---

[51]Ibid., p. 148.

ible; we may simply recognize that the standard warning signs of deceit, confusion, or mistake are not present."[52] With the notion of the reader as a believer we now move from the morality of knowledge to the ethics of interpretation.

Reader Response and Reader Responsibility: The Trial of Reading

"His testimony is true."

To this point we have assessed the Beloved Disciple's role as author and witness. But the Beloved Disciple plays yet another role in the Fourth Gospel: that of model disciple. By the end of the Fourth Gospel, the disciple who has witnessed the significance of Jesus' life and fate begins to give testimony. Indeed the whole point in contrasting the fates of the Beloved Disciple and Peter is to show that the ministry of the Beloved Disciple will take the form of a "martyrdom of life"[53] rather than death. The Beloved Disciple follows Jesus by "remaining"—remaining, that is, to give constant witness.

Accordingly the Beloved Disciple prefigures the role of the ideal reader, one who receives testimony and believes it. The Beloved Disciple shows how the reader should be affected by the narrative testimony of the Fourth Gospel. As ideal reader, the Beloved Disciple now stands under Aristotle's third rhetorical sign, that of pathos. Pathos has to do with the way readers respond to or appropriate discourse. Interpretations that fall short of this moment of appropriation remain incomplete, short-circuited. If discourse is someone's saying something to someone, then discourse is unfulfilled until the addressee receives the message. The Beloved Disciple is a model reader who not only follows testimony in the sense of understanding it but follows out its implications to the point where his or her own life becomes a life of testimony.

The aim of the author is to make the reader a disciple. This is perhaps the deepest irony of the Fourth Gospel: ostensibly an account of Jesus' trial, the narrative ends up trying the reader.

Responsibility to the other. What obligation, if any, does the reader have vis-à-vis the text? Barton and Morgan imply that just as authors have no rights, so readers have no universal responsibilities. What a reader does with a text is a function of the reader's aims and interests.[54] As a description of what readers actually do with texts, it is hard to fault this statement. But is there nothing else to be said? Is every reader lord of his or her own hermeneutic fiefdom? Or, following Emmanuel Lévinas rather than Clifford, does the individual's uniqueness lie not in autonomy but rather in responsibility to the other?[55]

---

[52]Ibid., p. 47.
[53]Westcott, *John*, p. 374.
[54]Morgan and Barton, *Interpretation*, p. 270.
[55]Emmanuel Lévinas, *The Lévinas Reader*, ed. Sean Hand (Oxford: Blackwell, 1989), p. 202.

Ricoeur has argued repeatedly that humans are not self-constituting but rather progressively appropriate a self through interpreting texts that mediate traditions, cultures and worlds.[56] The self is summoned to responsibility by the other, particularly by the suffering other. By "suffering" Ricoeur means "the reduction, even the destruction, of the capacity for acting, of being-able-to-act, experienced as a violation of self-integrity."[57] On the basis of this definition, we can speak of the text's suffering too, and of the witness as a suffering servant. The text "suffers" in the sense that it is unable to take the initiative in interpretation; that privilege belongs to the reader. The witness is a suffering servant in the sense that he or she labors to repay an obligation to the past and to others not to forget. The witness is under obligation to the other to testify. One must read Dmitri Shostakovich's *Testimony,* not to mention the works of Alexander Solzhenitsyn, bearing this in mind. The witness becomes a martyr because his or her testimony is a dangerous memory. Shostakovich's testimony was a condemnation of Soviet society that was smuggled out of the country and published only after his death. But the memories embodied in the Forth Gospel are no less dangerous to the powers of this world—especially to the world of the reader.

If the text is indeed at the mercy of the reader, what should the reader do? The answer is *to let it be*—not in the sense of leaving it alone but in the sense of letting it fulfill its aim as a work of written discourse. If the initiative belongs to the reader, the reader should lend an ear and receive this discourse of the other with courtesy and respect. What the ethical reader gives to the text is, in the first place, attention. The text, thus restored to life, is able to give something back in turn. Indeed in testimony the text gives something to the reader that the reader is capable only of receiving, not achieving: the narrative confession of the ministry and fate of Jesus Christ. "In true sympathy, the self, whose power of acting is at the start greater than that of its other, finds itself affected by all that the suffering other offers to it in return."[58]

Anselmian hermeneutics. What does it mean to give respect and attention to a text? What is the appropriate way for a reader to approach testimony? The ideal reader knows how to respond to the rhetorical strategies of the text. "The implied reader of the Fourth Gospel is encouraged by its rhetoric to accept its view of Jesus' significance and to lead a life characterized by a love like Jesus'."[59] Readers can come to a correct understanding only "by accepting the role of the narratives, by understanding Jesus from the perspective of belief."[60]

---

[56]Kevin J. Vanhoozer, *Biblical Narrative in the Philosophy of Paul Ricoeur: A Study in Hermeneutics and Theology* (Cambridge: Cambridge University Press, 1990), pp. 249-66.

[57]Paul Ricoeur, *Oneself as Another,* trans. Kathleen Blamey (Chicago: University of Chicago Press, 1990), p. 190.

[58]Ibid., p. 191.

[59]Davies, *Rhetoric,* p. 367.

[60]Ibid., p. 368.

For the ideal reader, therefore, the moment of understanding is also the moment of belief. We here encounter Anselm's famous *credo ut intelligam:* I believe in order to understand. Barth read Anselm as saying that the truly scientific or critical approach to an object lets the object dictate the manner in which it is known or appropriated. Such an approach might be called, when applied to literary objects, "Anselmian hermeneutics."

Hans Frei has shown how this hermeneutics works when applied to the Synoptic Gospels. As realistic narratives, they literally mean what they say (cf. Jn 21:23). There is no way to get at their subject matter without going through the story. To read those narratives correctly, says Frei, is to see that they identify Jesus as the One who now lives. Their rhetoric escapes the level of textuality and makes an extratextual reference to the risen Lord. Frei observes, "To know who he is in connection with what took place is to know that he is."[61]

Something similarly Anselmian happens when we interpret the Fourth Gospel as testimony. To understand this text—testimony-narration to the life and fate of Jesus—is to receive and believe it. To understand this testimony is to believe that it is true. The hermeneutics of I-witness testimony is twice Anselmian. First, it recognizes that testimony can be received only on its own terms. Testimony may not be reduced to metaphysical symbols of the human condition nor to moral examples. Second, the testimony of the Fourth Gospel is such that it is not understood if it is not believed. If you are not reading with belief, then you must not be reading with understanding. As with Anselm's God, which must exist if one correctly thinks it (as the being than which nothing greater can be conceived), so with the Beloved Disciple's testimony: if one is reading it properly one will see that it is trustworthy and true. "Those who cannot play this role, even for the duration of their reading, are unlikely to continue the task the text sets them."[62]

Discipl(in)ing the reader. Ideal readers, however, will continue the task the text sets before them. This may well involve a certain degree of self-discipline. For though the text calls the reader to respond, some responses are less helpful than others. Some readers may wish to play with texts in order to experience an autoerotic pleasure, but such self-centered indulgences are unlikely to advance the cause of textual understanding. Willfully to go one's own way as a reader is to abdicate the responsibility to attend to and understand the other.

Testimony calls us, as it did the one who wrote it, to bear witness. Testimony calls us to trust the voice of the other, to follow its call. This is what we find the Beloved Disciple doing at the conclusion of the Fourth Gospel. Jesus' last words, after his

---

[61]Hans Frei, *The Identity of Jesus Christ: The Hermeneutical Bases of Dogmatic Theology* (Philadelphia: Fortress, 1974), p. 145.

[62]Davies, *Rhetoric,* p. 373.

cryptic remarks about the Beloved Disciple's remaining, are "Follow me." But the Beloved Disciple was already following (Jn 21:20). Moreover, he had been following Jesus' story from the moment he was introduced. And John 21:24, which identifies the Beloved Disciple with the author of the Fourth Gospel, shows what form his following now takes. He has taken Jesus' story up; he is bearing it by bearing witness to it. As the Father sends the Son, so the Son sends his disciples. Why? To bear witness.

For the reader to respond as does the Beloved Disciple, he or she must accept the truth of his testimony. Accepting the truth of his testimony means becoming a witness oneself. Such is the "martyrdom of life." "The Gospel's rhetoric encourages fidelity but supposes that only the Paraclete can create it."[63] Jesus prayed not only for those who have seen and bear witness but for those who believe in him through their word (Jn 17:20) Thanks to the ministry of the Paraclete, the reader is assured of being able to respond—of being able to be responsible—to the call of the text.

As we have seen, it is part of the logic of testimony that the witness himself or herself becomes a premise for the truth of the testimony. The I-witness testimony of the Beloved Disciple is prima facie evidence for his claim concerning God's presence in Christ. If the Beloved Disciple is indeed the model reader, can the good reader today likewise becomes a witness?

Jesus' words to Peter could well be redirected to historical and literary critics who become preoccupied with the identity of the witness to the point of losing its content. They too must desist from wild speculation about the fate of the Beloved Disciple and get on with attending to the words and following the Word: "For indeed that is John's object in creating this character in the first place. . . . It is his hope that each reader will be so drawn by the Gospel to believe in Jesus and to follow him, that he will discover himself in the true discipleship of the Beloved Disciple."[64]

A witness's stating "that p" is itself a reason for believing it. How much more so a witness's living "that p," testifying in every possible way, "that you may believe that Jesus is the Christ" (Jn 20:31).

[63]Ibid., p. 367.
[64]Barnabas Lindars, *The Gospel of John* (London: Oliphants, 1972), p. 640.

Ten

Body Piercing, the Natural Sense & the Task of Theological Interpretation

A Hermeneutical Homily on John 19:34

P aul Tillich famously distinguished two types of philosophy of religion by comparing the experience of meeting a stranger with the experience of overcoming estrangement. Reflecting on these two experiences gives rise to two very different types of theology: theism (God as supreme Being) and panentheism (God as Being-itself) respectively. This essay explores a similar parallel with two types of theological interpretation of Scripture: between receiving a person hospitably as a stranger into one's community and socializing a person into a set of authorized communal practices.

How does the distinction between "meeting a stranger" and "overcoming estrangement" bear on our consideration of the task of theological interpretation? In the former case the stranger (read: "text") retains a certain individuality, a degree of over-againstness with regard to the community. A stranger can say things that shock us, things that lead us to view our own community in a different way. In the latter case a person (read: "text") is defined and identified in terms of his designated role and contributes, by performing his designated function, to the good of the whole community. In this respect, socialization resembles "totalization," where the "other" is not allowed to retain its integrity, particularity or difference but is instead forced into the mold of the "same." At issue is whether the text of Scripture has a meaning independent of the community's own culture and language—whether Scripture has a voice of its own and the power to shock and disturb us.[1]

Now this is an oversimplified picture of the contemporary options in theological interpretation. Its purpose is not to give a comprehensive survey, however, so much as to highlight an important area of disagreement concerning the aims and norms of theological interpretation of Scripture. The "socializing" approach lays stress on the priority of the aims and purposes of the reading community. On this view, theological interpretation is a church practice governed by the end of building up the body of Christ in worship and spiritual formation. This contemporary approach is significantly strengthened by an appeal to the ancient Rule of Faith, which acts as a hermeneutical rule—a rule for reading. According to this position, the theological interpretation of Scripture makes edifying use of the Bible—to "form Christians"—in ways that are compatible with the Rule of Faith. The chief purpose of theological interpretation is building up the body of Christ. The other approach focuses on the author as a significant, sometimes strange "other" and continues to speak of the "meaning" of the text, however difficult a notion that is to define.

Must these two aims—to edify the interpretive community and to recover the author's intended meaning—necessarily conflict? Not if, as I shall propose, we view the concept of meaning as an interpretive *norm* rather than as an interpretive aim. Theological interpretation, on this view, is a matter of discovering the divinely authored message in Scripture. This approach draws on church history too, particularly on the wide consensus concerning the authority and priority of the literal sense. As we shall see, the concern for interpretive norms need not lead to a neglect of interpretive aims, though I shall argue that the latter must be tested by the former.

In a somewhat related fashion, Robert Morgan posits a basic dichotomy of interpretive aims between the academic community with its concern with historical reconstruction and literary composition, and the ecclesial community with its interest in reading the Bible as faith-forming Scripture.[2] Is it indeed the case that the aims of scholars and saints must ultimately conflict?

---

[1]The mentions of "culture" and "language" are an oblique reference to George Lindbeck's cultural-linguistic approach to theology, which bears some resemblance to the "socialized meaning" type of my illustration. Interestingly, Lindbeck's more recent work leads me to believe that he may have modified his position somewhat in ways that are congenial to the present essay. See his "Postcritical Canonical Interpretation," especially the favorable remarks about interpreting for authorial discourse, in *Theological Exegesis: Essays in Honor of Brevard S. Childs,* ed. Christopher Seitz and Kathryn Greene-McCreight (Grand Rapids, Mich.: Eerdmans, 1999), pp. 26-51.

[2]Robert Morgan, *Biblical Interpretation* (Oxford: Clarendon, 1988), pp. 1-43. One might think that author-centered approaches find allies among historical critics whereas reader-centered approaches find support among literary critics. In fact, however, this is much too simplistic a picture. Hans Frei has shown how historical critics, in their zeal for reconstructing the history of a text's composition or of the events behind the text, have eclipsed the literary shape of

We are clearly in a dichotomized situation. What is needed, I believe, is an approach to theological interpretation of Scripture that includes both aims and norms, an approach that attends both to edification and to textual meaning. One promising way forward is to focus on what I shall call "the *theological* natural sense" of Scripture. By "natural sense" I refer to what authors are doing with just *these* words in using them in just *this* way in just *this* literary context.[3] By "theological" I refer to what God, as divine author, is doing with just these human words in just this canonical context. The category of the "natural" is, of course, a much-disputed topic in postmodernity. For it is a common postmodern reflex to demythologize talk about the "natural" into talk about the "social." For many postmoderns, all talk about "the way things are" translates into "the way *we think* things are" or "the way *we will* things to be." For better or for worse, then, the term *natural* highlights the specific area of disagreement over the theological interpretation of Scripture in a postmodern, community-oriented context: whose aims will have the upper hand, authors' or readers'?

The goal of this paper is to proffer a strategy for the postcritical retrieval of something like the classic theological interpretation of Scripture. Crucial to this attempt will be the rehabilitation of the natural sense, as well as a correction of certain distortions that have crept into this notion.[4] I begin by examining certain analogies between "bodies" and "texts" and suggest that the "natural" itself is susceptible of theological interpretation. I then return to a consideration of the two types of theological interpretation: the one that relies primarily on the Rule of Faith (and the socialized or ecclesial sense), the other that relies primarily on a reconstituted concept of the natural sense (the author's intended sense). I then examine John 19:31-37 as a practical example of what is involved in theological interpretation. Finally, using John 19:34-36 as a springboard, I make some summary suggestions as to the nature, necessity and norms of theological interpretation of Scripture. The conclusion draws

---

the text. In much biblical criticism, then, the quest for the original sense becomes something other than an attempt to recover the author's intended meaning, if by "author" we mean the person (or persons) responsible for the final form of the text.

[3]Meaning is "determinate" (i.e., it has particularity and specificity) just because of the specificity of the wording and the situation in which the words were used. It does not follow, however, that readers can "determine" with exactitude just what the author said/did. The world's weight is "determinate," but it does not follow that scientists can determine ("find out") exactly what it is. Texts may have "single determinate meanings," but they may have rough edges or, like prisms, many faces.

[4]The reader may be curious as to why I prefer the term *natural* as opposed to "plain" or "literal" sense. On the one hand, treatments of the literal sense (including my own) only partly succeed in distinguishing a literal from a literalistic sense. "Plain" has two disadvantages. First, it suggests that the sense of biblical texts may be obvious and nonfigurative; second, it is now associated with the Yale school's belief that it is determined more by habits of reading in the believing community than by the original authors.

some implications of my thesis for the church as the community of theological interpreters. And the metaphorical red thread running through it all is, improbably
enough, body piercing.

The Postmodern Challenge: "Natural" Bodies?

The basic premise of this essay, as indicated by its title, is that the contemporary fad
for body piercing symbolizes the postmodern concern for identity construction, and
that something similar takes place in biblical interpretation when the aim of the interpretive community is likewise identity construction. To begin with, however, I turn to
the very notion of "natural" bodies and the parallel with the "natural" sense.

"Natural" as an essentially disputed concept. In contemporary ethics and
hermeneutics alike, appeals to categories such as the "natural" or the "proper" often
evoke suspicion and distrust. Such suspicion can be either mild or radical. The milder
suspicion points out that what is often passes as "natural" is actually something culturally and historically relative. It may be "natural" for us to think of marriage in terms
of a legally ratified monogamous relationship between a man and a woman, but a
mild hermeneutics of suspicion will point out the cultural and social contingency of
such an arrangement. The more radical postmodern version of this suspicion insists
that what passes as "natural" is never anything but a social convention.[5]

When it comes to postmodern biblical interpretation, nurture is a clear winner
over nature. According to Stanley Hauerwas, "There simply is no 'real meaning' of
Paul's letters to the Corinthians once we understand that they are no longer Paul's letters but rather the Church's Scripture."[6] Interpretations do not tell us about the plain
or natural sense of the text; they tell us rather about the culture and sociopolitical
location of the reader and the way the reader has been nurtured. Hauerwas's point is
that the church should not be made incidental to the process of biblical interpretation. When he denies that Scripture does not make sense apart from a church that
gives it sense, however, he imperils the very distinction between textual meaning and
community interpretation.

Many postmoderns are happy to deny the text-commentary distinction. There is
no natural sense of words or texts, only senses that have been socially constructed.
Interpretation, like knowledge more generally, has become a thoroughly political
affair, a matter of power, a matter of what individuals or interpretive communities *will*
texts to mean. Postmodernity stands for the crisis of legitimation in interpretation, for
the suspicion of hermeneutics and for the rejection of the very concept of "correct

---

[5]In philosophical jargon, I am describing the demise of metaphysical realism, the notion that
reality, and perhaps textual meaning, is independent of the way we speak and think about it.
[6]Stanley Hauerwas, *Unleashing the Scriptures: Freeing the Bible from Captivity to America*
(Nashville: Abingdon, 1993), p. 20.

interpretation." Richard Rorty, for instance, suggests that we give up trying to "get it right" and concentrate on "making it useful." Is it possible that some of the current proposals that favor reading the Bible in the church for the church may in fact owe more to secular philosophy than to a Christian ecclesiology on which they claim to be based?

Once one abandons the concept of the natural sense, the question of criteria for legitimate interpretation immediately arises. Postmoderns want to know whose reading counts, and why. Why should one prefer the reading of the Christian community to interpretations produced in the secular academy? Why should one prefer a Lutheran interpretation to a Reformed, a Pentecostal to a Puritan? Can we say anything more than "Because I belong to this community"?

Some postmoderns contend that our interpretations, of Scripture or of any other text, are at best relative to the standards of particular interpretive communities and at worse wholly arbitrary. Reading always serves some purpose or other. Interpretation is shot through with ideology and power interests. One's reading is shaped by interpretive interests of gender, race, class and so forth. It has been said that "as there is no such thing as an innocent reading, we must say what reading we are guilty of."[7] Christians can find much to agree with in this statement. Human interpreters are finite and fallen; what we presently know we know as through a glass darkly (1 Cor 13:12).

A. K. M. Adams offers a more neutral definition of ideology: "a description of all the social interactions that ascribe 'significance' to our behavior."[8] On this view, the Christian ideology is learned by participating in ecclesial practices, for it is here that we learn what *divine, holy, evangelical, salvific* and *liberating* mean.

An honest survey of church history—a history that Gerhard Ebeling identifies with that of biblical interpretation—surely leads one to conclude that interpreters in the church are not immune to the temptation of ideological criticism. There are numerous—far too numerous!—examples of communities' forcing their own theological interpretations onto texts that often seem reluctant to accept them. Indeed reading the Bible to "discover" the theology of one's confessional tradition is but another example of what Jacques Derrida calls "ethnocentrism," the attempt to equate "*our* way of reading" or "what *we* see in the text" with "the natural sense." It is an open question, however, whether one should infer from the fact that Christians sometimes pervert the natural sense that the very concept of the "natural sense" has nothing to commend it.

Heavenly bodies. "And let them be for signs . . ." (Gen 1:14). "Nature" includes both the heavens and the earth. Let us begin with the heavens. It would be reason-

---

[7]Louis Althusser, *Reading Capital,* trans. Ben Brewster (New York: Verso, 1970), p. 5.
[8]A. K. M. Adams, *What Is Postmodern Biblical Criticism?* (Minneapolis: Fortress, 1995), p. 48.

able to think that there could be little dispute over the category "natural" when applied to phenomena such as the stars and planets. Not only are they far removed from human life and culture, but their movements, as Galileo discovered, are susceptible to mathematical explanation and objective measurement. Surely if there is a candidate for a nonsocialized natural, it would be these heavenly bodies.

In fact, the conflict of interpretations is all too apparent with regard to heavenly bodies as well. One has only to contrast the approaches of astronomy and astrology. The astronomer (like the historical critic!) wants to distinguish reality from appearance, to state "what actually happens." Astrologers, on the other hand, provide "edifying" interpretations of the celestial bodies. Horoscopes represent ample evidence that it is all too easy to read more into celestial bodies (the positions and alignment of the stars) than is really there. From the perspective of the astronomer, astrology is an example of gross eisegesis.

Christian theologians have had to debunk astrology throughout church history. Augustine's refutation in *The City of God* is both sophisticated and decisive, even appealing to twin studies to refute the premise that heavenly bodies determine human behavior.[9] For our purposes, it is interesting to note that Calvin's objections to astrology are virtually identical to his objections to allegory: both interpret "signs of certain things" to be whatever their fancy dictates. When Moses composed Genesis 1, however, he was writing about the order of nature. Calvin concludes that both astrology and allegory read signs "unnaturally."[10]

While a Christian theological interpretation of celestial bodies will need to include a good dose of demythologizing, it would be a mistake to depict Moses as a naturalist. For it is a mistake to confuse the natural with the naturalistic—with the *only* natural—just as it is to confuse the literal with the literalistic.[11] Christians may reject astrology, but it does not follow that the sun, moon and stars have *no* semiotic value. On the contrary, according to the Bible, "the heavens declare the glory of God" (Ps 19:1 NIV). Nature is God's work, and a complete description of nature requires not

---

[9] Shakespeare too pokes fun at astrology, most notably in Edmond's speech from King Lear: "This is the excellent foppery of the world, that, when we are sick in fortune,—often the surfeit of our own behaviour,—we make guilty of our own disasters the sun, the moon, and the stars; as if we were villains by necessity, fools by heavenly compulsion, knaves, thieves, and treachers by spherical predominance, drunkards, liars, and adulterers by an enforced obedience of planetary influence; and all that we are evil in, by a divine thrusting on: an admirable evasion of whoremaster man, to lay his goatish disposition to the charge of a star!" (act 1, scene 2).

[10] See Kathryn Greene-McCreight, *Ad Litteram: How Augustine, Calvin and Barth Read the "Plain Sense" of Genesis 1-3* (New York: Peter Lang, 1999), p. 129.

[11] I treat this latter confusion in more detail in Kevin Vanhoozer, *Is There a Meaning in This Text? The Bible, the Reader and the Morality of Literary Knowledge* (Grand Rapids, Mich.: Zondervan, 1998), pp. 310-12.

only scientific laws but the doctrine of creation. A "theological natural" interpretation, then, is one that evokes God as a an explanatory hypothesis or factor.

The human body. While disputes over how to interpret heavenly bodies preoccupied a good number of precritical theologians, the more divisive interpretive disagreements have shifted in recent times to something altogether more earthly: the human body. The current craze for body piercing is, I submit, an apt metaphor for how texts, including the Bible, are often treated in the postmodern world. Body piercing is in one sense a flagrant violation of the "natural." The body of the biblical text is similarly "pierced" by those who are concerned less for its natural sense than for its role in constructing personal or communal identity. The question is whether such piercing is ultimately not an act of violence on "the natural": on flesh, in the one case, and on authorial intention, in the other.

The body as cultural construct. At first blush the human body would seem to stand solidly on the side of nature rather than culture. After all, the body is a biological entity whose various systems work involuntarily according to physical and chemical laws. Philosophers and cultural theorists, however, insist that the body is a social, even political construct. They are not oblivious to the body's cellular composition, but their main interest is in conceptualizing the body as the site of multiple, often contesting discourses. For example, social constructionists like Michel Foucault examine the ways society has "shaped" and "disciplined" the body in order to make it meaningful. In itself the body is an underdetermined space, waiting to be written.

Biblical genealogies sketch one type of relation between human bodies: begetting. There is, of course, more to begetting than biology. The purpose of the biblical genealogies is not simply to chart the history of a particular set of human genes. They are also evidence of the faithfulness of God across the generations. In postmodern theory, however, *genealogy* refers to an attempt to "deconstruct" or undo what appears to be something natural by tracing its lineage back to the moment of its social construction.

What does body piercing mean? The body is the physical link between our deepest selves and the outside world, the medium through which we project ourselves into social life. Perhaps nowhere else does the body appear as the site of identity construction more clearly than in the contemporary craze for body piercing. To be sure, body piercing is a global phenomenon that has been practiced for millennia. In many non-Western societies, for instance, tattoos and piercings define one's social status, to "mark" people in long-established social positions. In these tribal contexts, body piercing serves an integrative purpose.

In the social context of the early twenty-first century in the postindustrial West, however, the practice of body piercing may well be of an entirely different order

282

from its function in tribal or primitive societies.[12] In the West, body piercing is a much
more deliberative and reflexive process, often bound up with a person's desire to
stand out from society. During the 1970s body piercing was associated with an aesthetic kerygma that proclaimed one's individuality and *apartness* from society. For
many, tattoos and piercings were marks of dissatisfaction with conventional society.
Body piercings communicate messages both about identity construction and about
the culture in which they circulate. What, then, does body piercing mean?

If there is a language of the body, then body piercing is a peculiarly graphic
speech act. According to one study, body piercings are "acts that ask to be witnessed."[13] Anthony Giddens argues that as the dominant discourses of religion and
family lose their currency, people are attempting to construct a "narrative of self"
upon the only tangible material left: their physical bodies.[14]

Some social theories see the body as an unfinished biological phenomenon that is
transformed as a result of its participation in certain social practices.[15] Body piercing
can be viewed as an attempt to "write the meaning" of the body over and above its
biology. One's body and one's self-identity are viewed as aesthetic projects, underdetermined phenomena that invite further construction, not just passive reception.
There is apparently some satisfaction in the feeling that one has a degree of power
over the project of constructing one's identity.

Postmoderns like Foucault see the human body not only as the site of identity
construction, the canvas with which one expresses one's individuality, but as the site
of a power struggle. Whose interpretive community will be allowed to determine the
body's meaning? Whose reading of sexuality, for instance, will prevail? In our present
situation, marked as it is by the conflict of interpretations, body piercing represents
an assault on the very notion of a "natural" sense. The postmodern assumption,
again, is that human identity is not received but achieved, and body piercing is
viewed as a strategy for "augmenting" body language. Sex-change operations, perhaps the most radical form of body piercing, go far beyond commentary and would
be better construed as radical attempts to "rewrite" the body. Such manipulative
operations, I suggest, are wholesale rejections of a person's particular bodily "text."
As we shall see, such rejections of the natural have their counterparts in hermeneutics and in biblical interpretation.

---

[12]For a general study of body modification practices in the non-Western world, see Arnold
Rubin, ed., *Marks of Civilization: Artistic Transformations of the Human Body* (n.p.: University of California Museum, 1988).

[13]Ken Hewitt, *Mutilating the Body: Identity in Blood and Ink* (Bowling Green, Ohio: Popular
Press/Bowling Green State University, 1997).

[14]Anthony Giddens, *Modernity and Self-Identity* (Palo Alto, Calif.: Stanford University Press,
1991), p. 225.

[15]Chris Shilling, *The Body and Social Theory* (London: Sage, 1993).

A theological interpretation of the body. I have no wish to side with "naturalistic" social theorists who reduce the complexities of social life to some basis in biology. Yet neither do I agree with the social constructionists who contend that the body is a primarily social phenomenon. If the category "natural" has any application to discussions concerning the human body, then, it must be determined by something other than biology on the one hand or sociology on the other. A nonreductionistic understanding of the natural requires nothing less than a theological interpretation. Let us therefore introduce the concept of the "theological natural": nature and the natural as interpreted by the Word of God revealed in the narratives of Israel and the church, and preeminently in the narratives concerning Jesus Christ.

From a theological perspective, the natural is precisely that which accords with the Creator's intention, with what Alvin Plantinga calls the "design plan." Our embodied identity as male or female, for instance, is something we are to receive with gratitude, not something arbitrary that can be made into something else. To reject the natural sense, to rebel against nature construed theologically in terms of the created order, is thus to rebel against God. Further, our bodies are not our own but "were bought with a price" (1 Cor 6:20). The body, says Paul, "is not meant for immorality, but for the Lord" (1 Cor 6:13). A complete theological interpretation of our natural bodies would include the following points: that they are created by God, members of Christ (1 Cor 6:15) and temples of the Holy Spirit (1 Cor 6:19). These theological indicatives lead to a theological imperative: to present our bodies as living sacrifices (Rom 12:1).

What we do with our bodies creates a particular shape of life. Nevertheless, the true or theologically natural meaning of our bodies is more a matter of divine than of human construction. Our true identity—as creatures of God, men and women in Christ, temples of the Holy Spirit—is something we receive and realize, not something we develop or construct. Note too that what the celestial bodies do involuntarily, glorify God, should also be the voluntary aim of human bodily action. While celestial bodies invariably perform their natural function, humans do not. We humans have the terrible capacity to reject the natural, to refuse our divine author's intention.

The body of the text. The body, then, is like a text. Instead of writing one's own meaning onto the body, Christians, I have suggested, should see the body as already inscribed with meaning, with a "natural sense" as it were, by the triune God. Conversely, the biblical text is like a body. We turn now to the parallel assault on the category of the "natural" by some theological interpreters of Scripture. Again, my working hypothesis is that there is an important parallel between the idea of identity construction that underlies the practice of body piercing and the idea of social formation that lies behind a certain practice of theological interpretation of Scripture.

"The body of the text" refers, in common parlance, to the main part of a text. In the hands of some contemporary readers, however, the text appears as an inert, lifeless body on which the interpreter performs various operations. Both bodies and texts can be victims of violence. To anticipate the biblical passage that we will examine below, we may compare what interpreters do to inert texts to what the Roman soldiers did to Jesus on the cross: "The body as object is already being treated as mere flesh, a consumable, a dead, unwanted, discardable thing, before Jesus breathes his last."[16] Similarly, "texts, like dead men and women, have no rights, no aims, no interests. They can be used in whatever way readers or interpreters choose."[17] Dead bodies make no gestures. They do nothing. They are passive, not active. To the extent that the text has no aims or life of its own, it is at the mercy of the reader. It would appear that there is only one active agent in interpretation: the reader. Mark Taylor therefore only slightly exaggerates when he characterizes interpretation as "a *hostile* act in which interpreter victimizes text."[18]

The notion of body piercing, in the context of text interpretation, can actually be applied in two very different ways. On the one hand, one can look at the text, like the body, as the site of identity construction. *This predilection for identity construction is precisely what contemporary body piercers and postmodern interpreters have in common.* There are two problems, however, with viewing interpretation as a means of identity construction. (1) If what gets constructed depends less on the nature of the text or the natural sense than the sense nurtured in the interpreting community, how can what the interpretive community does to the text be defended as more than (an arbitrary?) social convention, especially given the plurality of interpretive communities? (2) To the extent that the community uses the text to construct or reinforce its identity, how can it avoid the charge that its interpretation is nothing more than an imposition, perhaps even a violent one, onto the body of the text?

On the other hand, one can pierce the body (or the text) in the sense of getting beneath the surface and discerning what lies beneath (its "soul" or message). As we shall see, this latter sense of body piercing views the body of the text not merely as a passive object but also as something active—a *communicative* act, to be precise.

What Is Theological Interpretation?

It is both curious and ironic that recent dictionaries of biblical interpretation are virtually silent on the subject of the theological interpretation of Scripture. A two-volume Abingdon dictionary (edited by John Hayes) has entries on "psychoanalytic biblical interpretation," "ideological criticism," "inner-biblical interpretation," even "Ethiopian

---

[16]Graham Ward, "The Displaced Body of Jesus Christ," in *Radical Orthodoxy*, ed. John Milbank, Graham Ward and Catherine Pickstock (London: Routledge, 1999), p. 169.

[17]Morgan, *Biblical Interpretation*, p. 7.

[18]Mark C. Taylor, "Text as Victim," in *Deconstruction and Theology*, ed. Thomas Altizer (New York: Crossroad, 1982), p. 65.

biblical interpretation," but nothing on "theological biblical interpretation."

What, then, is the force of the qualifying adjective *theological* when it comes to biblical interpretation? Obviously such interpretation has something to do with God, but what? There are several possibilities, but I will consider only the two options mentioned in my introductory remarks. The one view sees *theological* as qualifying the *object* of interpretation (Scripture as the Word of God), the other sees it as qualifying the *process* of interpretation (the socialization or identity construction of the people of God). For the first, what makes biblical interpretation theological is the appeal to God as in some sense Scripture's author; according to the latter view, what makes biblical interpretation theological is more a matter of the aim and outcome—living faithfully with others before God.

At present there seem to be two major fault lines that prevent the two approaches from appreciating fully the other's potential contribution. One fault line has to do with the nature of the hermeneutics undergirding the theological interpretation of Scripture (general versus special); the other pertains to contrasting emphases (norms versus aims). I believe that the way forward for theological interpretation of Scripture lies in a fusion of these horizons.

Between general and special hermeneutics. General hermeneutics concerns the principles of text interpretation as such. Many biblical scholars seek to use the best general principles in interpreting Scripture. Benjamin Jowett, for instance, speaks for many historical critics when he exhorts interpreters to read the Bible "like any other book," for "the meaning," which has traditionally been associated with the sense the historical author intended. However, numerous studies have documented how historical critics became sidetracked by attempts to reconstruct either the history of the text's composition (the text's "prehistory" in source, form and tradition criticism) or the real rather than the apparent historical events referred to, thus spending more energy on what lay *behind* the text than in what lay *in* it.

This preoccupation with the history *behind* the text has led other biblical interpreters to relegate the question of authorial intention to secondary status. They argue that textual meaning should not be equated with authorial intention, nor should the quest for "the meaning" define the project of theological interpretation. On the contrary, what makes biblical interpretation *theological* is the specific interpretive interest in using the Bible to build up the community in faith, hope and love. General theories of meaning and interpretation are of little use to these theological interpreters. Of definitions of meaning and approaches to interpretation there is no end. Christians should focus instead on the goal of interpretation: fostering communion with God and others. To put the point slightly differently: the theological interpretation of Scripture, according to this view, is less an epistemological project of coming to know determinate meaning than a political project of trying to shape a particular communal form of life: "The aim of faithful living before the Triune God becomes the standard to which all interpretive interests must measure up."[19]

Is it enough to know the ends of theological interpretation? There is an alternative—often overlooked—to general, often secular theories of meaning on the one hand and the notion that Christian communities read the Bible in their own way on the other. A number of recent writers, myself included, argue for a theological hermeneutic, that is, a theory of interpretation—of the Bible and of texts in general—that is itself formed, informed and reformed by Christian doctrine.[20] This strategy combines the concerns of both general and special hermeneutics by offering a properly *theological* account of "the meaning" of a text.

Interpretive aims: The Rule of Faith as a hermeneutical rule. According to a growing number of community-oriented interpreters, it was only thanks to the ancient church's Rule of Faith that early Christians read the Bible, Old and New Testaments, as a unified canon. While scholars in the academy may read the "Hebrew Bible" in isolation from the New Testament, Christians cannot; for the Rule insists that we make a theological connection between the God of Israel and the Father of Jesus Christ, and hence a hermeneutical connection between the two choirs of witnesses. Proponents of "ruled reading" contend that classic Christian hermeneutics never approached the text with methods only but always with certain rules, rules that ultimately function to aid Christian formation. Such "ruled reading" is the best means for arriving at the end of theological interpretation: a deeper communion with God and others.

The connection between "ruled reading" and "socializing" interpretation (the type that seeks to overcome estrangement) should now be clear. Ruled reading—reading in communion with other saints for the sake of spiritual formation—is a matter of learning authorized community interpretive practices. The *telos* of these practices, we may recall, is to build up the community, not to discover something about the message of the text.

Many who commend ruled reading see theological interpretation of Scripture in terms of politics more than of epistemology. The point, they say, is not to develop general principles of for coming to know texts but rather to foster a certain shape of community life. The Rule of Faith performs three hermeneutical functions in pursuit of this community end: (1) it helps determine the plain sense of the text, (2) it unifies the Scriptures, and (3) it serves as a criterion for interpretation.

---

[19]Stephen Fowl and Gregory Jones, *Reading in Communion: Scripture and Ethics in Christian Life* (Grand Rapids, Mich.: Eerdmans, 1991), p. 20.
[20]See especially Craig Bartholomew, *Reading Ecclesiastes: Old Testament Exegesis and Hermeneutical Theory* (Rome: Pontifical Bible Institute, 1998); Francis Watson, *Text and Truth: Redefining Biblical Theology* (Grand Rapids, Mich.: Eerdmans, 1997); and Anthony Thiselton, *New Horizons in Hermeneutics* (Grand Rapids, Mich.: Zondervan, 1997).

The plain sense. Origen famously rejected the literal meaning of certain Old Testament narratives precisely because he found them unedifying. Is ruled reading simply another name for allegorizing? What happens to the plain sense on this view?

It is common for proponents of ruled reading to assert the priority of the plain sense of Scripture. However, upon closer inspection it becomes evident that they do not consider the plain sense to be a property of the text. The plain sense is rather the sense the text has when read in the context of the believing community.[21] This fits in with the general theme that texts have no intrinsic aims or interests, and with the idea that theological interpretation is primarily a matter of the aims and interests of the interpretive community. According to Kathryn Greene-McCreight, the concept of the plain sense means something slightly different depending on which theologian is speaking about it, but in general she sees two constraints on interpreting for the "plain sense": the verbal sense of the text and the Rule of Faith. The Rule of Faith functions as the sanctioned "preunderstanding" of the subject matter of Scripture and basically sets forth the story of what God was doing in Christ.[22] The Rule's shape is essentially narrative, its substance trinitarian. This ecclesial preunderstanding of what the Bible is fundamentally about, based on the centrality of the narratives of Jesus, enables the church to "rule in" some interpretations and "rule out" others. What is noteworthy is that the plain sense may or may not coincide with the explicit *verbal* sense of the text.

As to the unity of the Bible, here too it is primarily a matter not of some textual property but of the way Scripture is read in community. Unity is less a matter of the coherence of its parts than a byproduct of a habit of reading. Finally, the Rule of Faith functions as a criterion with which to determine which readings are appropriate for the Christian community, as interpretations are finally tested not by the text but by the Rule. This is precisely what one would expect of those who follow Stanley Fish, for whom authority in interpretation is vested in the practices of the interpretive community, not in some alleged inherent textual properties. To the cry "Exegesis! Exegesis! Exegesis!" one wonders whether ruled readers might rejoin "Tradition! Tradition! Tradition!"[23]

---

[21]Hans Frei once commented that if the community had acquired the habit of reading allegorically, then that would have been the "plain sense" (Frei, "The 'Literal Reading' of Biblical Narrative in the Christian Tradition: Does It Stretch or Will It Break?" in *The Bible and the Narrative Tradition,* ed. Frank McConnell (New York: Oxford University Press, 1986), pp. 36-77. See also Kathryn E. Tanner, "Theology and the Plain Sense," in *Scriptural Authority and Narrative Interpretation,* ed. Garrett Green (Philadelphia: Fortress, 1987).

[22]Greene-McCreight, *Ad Litteram,* p. 244.

[23]I acknowledge that all exegesis presupposes some theology or other. The question is whether interpretation provides us with an opportunity to refine, or even correct, our prior theological understanding. I maintain that it does, though it does so only if the interpreter is indeed "virtuous": both scrupulous with regard to the text and suspicious with regard to oneself.

Whose use? Which grammar? A catholic rule. The suggestion that theological interpretation of Scripture take the form of ruled reading is a powerful one. It carries the
venerable weight of ancient tradition and appeals to postmodern sensibilities (the
authority of interpretive communities; interpretation as a mode of identity construction) besides. The main thrust of the proposal is that one view the aims of the interpretive community, that is, the church's interest in spiritual formation, as constitutive
of the practice of theological interpretation of Scripture.

How should we evaluate this proposal? In particular, what should we make of the
eclipse, at least a partial eclipse, of the natural sense of the text itself in favor of the
community's aims and rules for reading Scripture?

To begin with, we may note a certain tension, or irony, built into the claim that
ruled reading caters to the specific aims of the believing community to the detriment
of general theories of meaning. In fact, the notion that one should look "not to the
meaning but to the use" is easily traced back to Ludwig von Wittgenstein, who is neither Fish nor Fowl but the philosophical presence behind both.

Let us assume, for the sake of the argument, that Wittgenstein is correct in his
assumption that we need to attend to the particular uses of words. The question then
becomes: to *whose* use should theological interpreters of Scripture look? Possible
answers to this query fall into three types: (1) the persons (authors, redactors, canon-
izers) responsible for producing the final form of the text, (2) readers seeking to use
Scripture for the sake of edification in accordance with the Rule of Faith, (3) God as
the ultimate author or appropriator of the biblical text. The first option, favored by
historical critics, gets us only as far as the history of religion; we shall therefore consider it no further. The third option will be considered below. Given its prominence,
it is the second option, ruled reading—the method of "socialization" referred to in my
opening paragraphs—that requires further scrutiny.

According to the ruled reading approach, the aims of the biblical text, which is to
say the aims and interests of the individuals and communities responsible for producing it, appear to be subordinate to the aims of the present interpretive community. After all, it is argued, the community, together with its Rule of Faith, preexisted
the New Testament. What books we find in the New Testament are there only
because they cohere with the core beliefs of the church's christological confession:
"Jesus is Lord." The church canonized certain texts "because (when used and used
properly) these writing agree with the Rule of Faith in content and consequence."[24]
Indeed as we have seen, the "plain sense" itself is a result of the verbal (potential)

---

[24]Robert W. Wall, "Reading the Bible from Within Our Traditions: The 'Rule of Faith' in Theological Hermeneutics," in *Between Two Horizons: Spanning New Testament Studies and Systematic Theology*, ed. Joel B. Green and Max Turner (Grand Rapids, Mich.: Eerdmans, 2000),
p. 104.

sense and the community's ruled reading. While it is true that Fowl and Jones refer to the importance of critical biblical scholarship and to "virtuous" interpretation in the context of reading the Bible "over-against ourselves," it is not altogether clear how this can be done in the absence of any stable or determinate textual meaning (the natural sense).[25]

Does the Rule of Faith indeed derive not from Scripture itself but from certain patterns of the believing community's reading of Scripture? Ruled readers apparently agree with Wittgenstein that "interpretation" is a matter of making grammatical remarks about the ways in which texts are used. What sense, then, does it make to speak of the Bible as "canon" (measuring rod, rule)? For ruled readers, the Bible is canonical only when its texts play a certain role for a particular group of people. To be "canonical," then, is less a thing (a list of books) or a property of books than a function or dynamic relation between certain texts and a certain interpretive community. As with "plain sense," so with "canon": neither is a textual property or phenomenon; rather, both are concepts that refer to the *interaction* of text and community.

The Rule of Faith, then, is the "grammar" implicit in the community's interpretive practice. This grammar stipulates the following rules: read the two testaments as a single book; read the story of Jesus as the fulfillment of the story of Israel. The conclusion follows inevitably: "the canon that measures the legitimacy and efficacy of the Bible's interpretation is the church's Rule of Faith."[26] What is Christianly adequate is measured by the Rule of Faith, not by Scripture. The point is that the Rule of Faith becomes a "canonical" rule, the chief criterion for adjudicating between legitimate and illegitimate theological interpretation.

Is it not somewhat disingenuous both to claim that the Christian community reads Scripture in a manner that is *sui generis* and to rely (at least tacitly) on a general theory in support of this claim? Ruled readers say they are not interested in theories of meaning, yet current formulations of ruled reading fit in perfectly with the contemporary turn to reader-oriented approaches in secular criticism, and some of these theorists (e.g., Stanley Fish) are explicitly cited in support. To say that the interpretation of texts is inseparable from the history of their reception *is* to take sides in contemporary debates about textual meaning.

Whose use of Scripture is authoritative, and why? Whence come the grammatical rules of Christian faith? The pressing question is this: *whose* Rule is it? Ruled readers

---

[25]Fowl and Jones commend the "critical virtues" of biblical scholarship for the following reasons: (1) they help us to appreciate the tradition history of the canonical text, and thus of the interests of the Christian communities who first formed the canon; (2) they develop linguistic skills that help in translation; (3) they expose the tradition-bound nature of postcanonical Christian interpretation; (4) they expose the ideological interests (e.g., race, gender, class) brought to bear on the final shaping of the text (*Reading in Communion*, pp. 39-42).
[26]Hall, "Reading the Bible," p. 96.

invariably answer: the catholic church's. "A critical theological hermeneutic requires that every rule of faith must bear close family resemblance to the catholic Rule of Faith."[27] The Rule of Faith is a catholic rule, a summary of how the ecumenical church has, through its history, read the biblical texts. This catholic rule thus affords an anchor in the sea of interpretive possibilities.

At this point we must pose two critical questions. First, just how catholic is the Rule? How do we know the church got the doctrine of God right, or should we simply accept that might, in this case relative catholicity, makes right? Is it simply a contingency of church history that the Rule is trinitarian rather than unitarian?

Second, quite apart from the all too obvious present problem of the plurality of ecclesial communities, the ruled reading approach fails to ascribe supreme authority to the Scriptures because it fails adequately to recognize Scripture as the result of divine authorship. Authority is vested in reading practices and therefore in reading communities. Francis Watson has recently suggested that this approach owes more to postmodernity than to patristic theology. He argues that this hermeneutic actually works against theology by substituting the being of the community for the communicative agency of God. The community must not become the basic principle in hermeneutics.[28] The church itself is derivative; it owes its being to God's prior evocation.

I submit that we must recognize the ecclesial and hermeneutical priority of God, specifically, the priority of his speech agency or "authorship" of Scripture. To interpret the Bible theologically is to interpret it as the verbal communicative action of God that bears witness to God's historical communicative actions in the history of Israel and of Jesus Christ. There are indeed many possible interpretive aims and interests, but the people of God must above all concern themselves with what God is saying, and doing, in and through the Scriptures.

Interpretive norms: The natural sense. In an important article on postcritical canonical interpretation, George Lindbeck comments that Childs's canonical approach, which reads the Bible as an authoritative witness to the Word of God, fails to provide adequate guidance to the Christian community. Lindbeck makes a similar point about

---

[27]Ibid., p. 103. Lindbeck characterizes this as the "Constantinopolian" appeal to unchanging communal tradition ("Postcritical Canonical Interpretation: Three Modes of Retrieval," in *Theological Exegesis: Essays in Honor of Brevard S. Childs,* ed. Christopher Seitz and Kathryn E. Greene-McCreight (Grand Rapids, Mich.: Eerdmans, 1999), p. 39.

[28]Fowl and Jones haltingly accept this point. They do want to acknowledge Scripture as some kind of standard of Christian adequacy. We do not need to believe in divine dictation of Scripture, they argue, but we do need to have a view of providence. This view, sadly, is left unspecified. All Fowl and Jones say is that "the God who has called us to be the Church would not leave us bereft of the resources we need to follow that call faithfully" (*Reading in Communion,* p. 38). It is not finally clear just how God is, on their view, involved with Scripture.

reading Scripture in order to participate in its narrative world. He worries that the canon risks becoming a grab bag for ecclesial interpreters: "The choices tend to range between the three poles of ecclesiastical magisterium, unchanging communal tradition, and private interpretation or, more concretely and inaccurately expressed, Rome, Constantinople, and Wittenberg/Geneva."[29] The first two approaches are unable to lodge an appeal to the text as a basis for preferring one interpretation to another: "For both, choices between alternative patterns of canonical construal are intratextually arbitrary; one must exit the text in order to find grounds for decision; and as to how one does that they seem to have no hermeneutically usable answers."[30]

What Lindbeck's comments bring to light is the need not for another interpretive aim but rather for an interpretive *norm*. Interestingly, Lindbeck himself is intrigued by Nicholas Wolterstorff's authorial discourse model, which represents the required exit from the text that alone and which grounds one's preference for one reading rather than another.[31] While I applaud Lindbeck's openness to the notion of the author's intentional action—a notion I now intend to develop myself—I do not accept that an appeal to the author is an exit from the text. On the contrary, the text *is* an intention (communicative) action. This leads me to privilege not Wittenberg but Gutenberg, for this norm reflects not some community interest but the texts', or rather their *authors'*— human and divine—communicative interest which the written discourse enacts.[32]

Five theses on theological interpretation of Scripture: The role of communicative action. I have argued elsewhere for the cogency of the following theses. Here I will limit myself to a short exposition, in order then to turn to an extended exegetical example. It is worth observing, however, that I have sought to derive these theses from Christian doctrine; the use of speech act philosophy is merely ancillary to my theological purpose.

1. *The ultimate authority for Christian theology is the triune God in communicative action.* Theology is a human response to a divine initiative: communicative action. God makes himself known in word and deed. God is the initiator of this action (agent), the Word or content of this action (act) and the Spirit or power of its

---

[29]Lindbeck, "Postcritical Canonical Interpretation," p. 39.

[30]Ibid., p. 44.

[31]I find it interesting that Lindbeck cites Richard Hays as an exemplar of the "appropriating narrative world" approach in light of the role Lindbeck played in developing it. It appears that Lindbeck may no longer see intratextual theology alone to be sufficient.

[32]David Cunningham mistakenly ascribes to me a belief in the "container" theory of meaning. I do not believe that words, or even texts, "contain" meaning. Rather, I think that they are meaningful because they are used by authors to say and do things. Attention to the way texts are used to perform communicative acts leads to the "action" theory of communication that I here assume. For a more complete account and defense of my theory of meaning as communicative action, see Vanhoozer, *Is There a Meaning in This Text?* chap. 5.

reception (consequence). It is imperative, insofar as we seek to preserve the integrity of the gospel, to respect the difference between the Word of God embodied and enacted in Scripture on the one hand and human commentary on the other. This fundamental intuition—that the gospel of Jesus Christ does not change at the behest of our interpretations—requires nothing less than a distinction between true and false religion, as well as a distinction between right worship and idolatry.

2. *A text's "plain meaning" or "natural sense" is the result of a person's communicative action* (what an author has done in tending to his or her words in this way rather than another). It is the *author's* use of words in communicative action that determines their particular sense. True, words have a range of verbal or conventional senses, but the way authors employ linguistic and literary conventions usually indicates which of the many conventional senses (and there may be more than one) are intended. The natural sense, in short, is the authorially *intended* sense: the sense the words bear when used in *this* context by *this* author. While it is possible to say what readers make of a text, this is not the same as interpreting it. To read Galatians as if I rather than Paul had authored it is to engage in a new act of composition, not commentary.[33]

3. *To call the Bible "Scripture" is to acknowledge a divine intention that does not contravene but supervenes on the communicative intentions of its human authors.* Wolterstorff has recently shown how God could be said to "appropriate" human discourse. That is one way to associate a divine communicative intention with one that is human. There are two other ways: the traditional insistence on the dual authorship of Scripture, an insistence that ultimately presupposes a doctrine of providence; and the more recent insistence that the divine intention comes into its own when the parts of the text are read in light of the canonical context.[34]

4. *The theological interpretation of Scripture requires us to give "thick descriptions" of the canonical acts in the Bible performed by both the human and the divine authors.* The task of literal interpretation is to say what authors have done with their words. If one takes divine authorship of Scripture seriously, then literal interpretation must have recourse to the canonical context, for the meaning of the parts is related to the whole of Scripture. The literal sense of Scripture as intended by God is the sense of the canonical act (the communicative act when seen in the context of the canon). We may recall that the norm of interpretation—the natural sense—is a matter of an

---

[33]We may note in passing that Irenaeus's first problem with heretics had less to do with competing interpretive interests than with their replacing the "natural" sense for some "unnatural" (his term) substitute. Such twisting of words amounts to their being wrenched away from their original authors.

[34]Paul Noble, for instance, comments that Brevard Childs's canonical approach is intelligible only against the background assumption of the divine authorship of Scripture (*The Canonical Approach: A Critical Reconstruction of the Hermeneutics of Brevard S. Childs* [Leiden, Netherlands: E. J. Brill, 1995]).

author's intentional action. What is important to remember is that some features of an action emerge only against a certain context of description. There are many ways to describe what someone has done: we may say that a person moved his index finger, fired a gun, killed someone, assassinated a political figure, precipitated World War I. All of these descriptions are true as far as they go. But the higher level description—"he precipitated World War I"—gives a "fuller" sense of the act than "he moved his index finger." It is only against the larger canonical backdrop that we can discern what God may have intended in particular biblical texts.[35]

5. *The norm of theological interpretation (what an author has intentionally said/done) generates an interpretive aim: to bear competent witness to what an author has said/done.* A certain interpretive imperative follows from the above indicative—the notion that the text *is* an intentional communicative act. "Thou shalt not bear false witness" is only the negative version of this interpretive imperative. The positive version is "Do unto others' texts as you would have them do unto yours."

A canonical rule. "The aim of reading Scripture, to build up Christian faith and practice, should always order decisions about which methods and approaches to adopt."[36] This is a laudable aim. I have argued, however, that this aim needs a norm. There is indeed a rule or norm for theological interpretation, but it is *canonical,* not (at least not primarily) catholic.

What constitutes a theological interpretation of celestial bodies, of the human body and of the body of the text? A theological interpretation, if it is to be authoritative, not to mention true, must involve more than the church's say-so, more than a set of community conventions. It is God's say-so that enables the church's say-so to be properly theological. To give a theological interpretation of celestial, human and textual bodies therefore is a matter of articulating the Creator's intention, an intention realized preeminently in the life and fate of Jesus Christ as attested in the Old and New Testaments.

It is important not to overdraw the distinction between the catholic and canonical rules. Greene-McCreight's suggestion that the community's Rule of Faith is in fact a canonical rule is particularly helpful in this regard. The Rule of Faith—that prior understanding as to what the biblical texts are fundamentally about—is taken from Scripture itself: "Since these rules are drawn from Scripture itself, they are not considered extratextual interpretative devices."[37] This particular account of ruled reading is

---

[35]Note that this account of "thick description" supersedes the notion of *sensus plenior.*

[36]Lewis Ayres and Stephen E. Fowl, "(Mis)reading the Face of God: The Interpretation of the Bible in the Church," *Theological Studies* 60 (1999): 528.

[37]Kathryn Greene-McCreight, "The Logic of the Interpretation of Scripture and the Church's Debate over Sexual Ethics," in *Homosexuality, Science and the "Plain Sense" of Scripture,* ed. David Balch (Grand Rapids, Mich.: Eerdmans, 2000), p. 249.

most congenial to my own approach, insofar as it acknowledges that the community's rule is in fact regulated by the two-testament canon itself, especially inasmuch as it entails the assumption of the divine authorship of Scripture.[38] There are even indications that Greene-McCreight's version of ruled reading is compatible with a *sola Scriptura* approach: "Ruled reading thus allows scripture to interpret itself."[39] All this is to the good, particularly insofar as it makes room both for interpretive aims and for an interpretive norm in the theological interpretation of Scripture.

If the above rereading of what is involved in ruled reading is correct, then we may say that the *catholic* Rule of Faith makes explicit what is already *implicit* in the canonical Scriptures. In this regard, note in passing that each of the rules of "traditional hermeneutics" often cited by proponents of ruled reading is already implied by Paul's use of the Old Testament Scriptures. The rules for theological tradition, I submit, have their origin not in the "Great Tradition" but rather in the apostolic tradition embodied in the Scriptures.

Body Piercing and the Body of Jesus: Interpreting John 19:31-34

Earlier in this chapter I examined the contemporary phenomenon of body piercing as a metaphor of sorts for the eclipse of the natural sense in contemporary biblical interpretation. Body piercing, I claimed, is a means to the end of identity construction. We now turn to an ancient example of body piercing and seek to interpret it in such a way as not to victimize the body of the Fourth Gospel's text. My goal is to pierce the biblical text, not in the sense of inflicting a wound by violently imposing my interpretive will but in the sense of discerning its true intent in order to penetrate its "joints and marrow."

"But one of the soldiers pierced his side with a spear, and at once there came out blood and water" (Jn 19:34). The account of the piercing of Jesus' side is an appropriate case study for several reasons. (1) It occurs at a climactic place in the most theological of Gospels, and it is the only part of the passion narrative that has no parallel in the Synoptics. (2) It involves the relation of both testaments. (3) It raises questions about the extent, and the complexity, of the author's intention, about how determinate it is and about how definite we can be about its determinacy. (4) It touches on a number of theological doctrines, including incarnation, soteriology, ecclesiology, pneumatology and divine providence. (5) Historically, it has generated a rich tradition of theological interpretation. (6) It touches on the postmodern concern for the textuality of the body and the bodiliness of the text.

---

[38]See, in this latter regard, Greene-McCreight's comment on Augustine: "Augustine says that we must acknowledge the prophetic element in the Biblical text because it is 'foremost in God's intention'" (*Ad Litteram*, p. 244).

[39]Ibid., p. 248.

Of the many aspects of the text that could be examined, I wish to focus on just one: how to interpret the natural sense of the result of Jesus' body piercing, the flow of blood and water. Just what is the author of the Fourth Gospel saying/doing at this point? Is the Evangelist describing something that actually happened? If so, does he think it is a natural event or a miracle? If it is a natural event, why is it important to mention? Most important, what does the task of theological interpretation mean when it comes to making (natural!) sense of the blood and water?

History of interpretation: The catholic rule. A number of church fathers understood the blood and water to refer to the "two baptisms": of water (cleansing) and of blood (martyrdom). More commonly, patristic commentators saw the double flow as referring to the two chief sacraments of the church: baptism and Eucharist. It is this latter reading that interests me most, for it raises the issue of whose interest assumes priority in theological interpretation of Scripture—the author's or the interpretive community's. Clearly there is nothing *contrary* to the Rule of Faith in interpreting the blood and water as an anticipation of the sacraments that nourish and give life to the church. On the contrary, such a reading admirably serves the goal of community formation (social identity construction). The issue, however, is whether this "socialized" reading may legitimately claim the authority of Scripture. Is the text speaking of baptism and Eucharist, or is the interpretive aim of the community (the interest in ecclesial edification) here trumping the interpretive norm (the natural sense)? Just what is the Word of God for the church in John 19:31-37?

Augustine. Augustine's interpretation is based on a Latin mistranslation of the Greek. Augustine read 19:34 as "One of the soldiers with a spear *opened* his side." To compound matters, Augustine chose to focus on the significance of this errant term, commenting that the Evangelist used a "wide awake" or suggestive word. Augustine even makes a special point of saying that the Evangelist did *not* say "pierced" or "wounded"! No, the Evangelist said "opened" in order to speak of the door of life that was flung open and from which the sacraments of the church flow. Augustine saw a foretelling of this in the Noah narrative, for Noah was ordered to make a door *in the side* of the ark where those animals that were not going to perish in the flood could enter. (These animals, we may note, prefigured the church).

The idea of an opening in the side suggests another episode from Genesis to Augustine as well: Eve, the mother of the living, came forth from an opening in Adam's side. The crucified Christ is indeed a second Adam who "slept on the cross in order that from there might be found for him a wife—that one who flowed from the side of the One sleeping."[40] Other church fathers work the analogy even more: since

---

[40]Augustine, *Tractates on the Gospel of John 112-24,* trans. John W. Rettig (Washington, D.C.: Catholic University of America Press, 1995), p. 51.

sin came from man's side, it was necessary that from the side should flow the source of salvation. A side for a side . . .

This popular interpretation received official church approval at the Council of Vienne in 1312. More recently, feminist writers have depicted the wound in Christ's side as a lactating breast or as a womb from which the church is birthed. However, apart from the obvious lexical difficulty (the confusion between the terms for "pierced" and "opened"), this reading faces the additional problem of having little or no evidence that a reference to the Genesis account was indeed part of the Evangelist's intentional action in this passage.

An interesting variation on this theme of "opening" comes from J. Ramsey Michaels. He thinks that Mark and the Fourth Gospel give different versions of this same event. Mark's centurion and John's spear-thruster are, he argues, one and the same person. He then reasons that since Jesus' body is the temple (Jn 2:21), the rending of the temple curtain recounted in Mark is the counterpart to the "opening" in Jesus' side.[41] While such a reading does not run counter to the Rule of Faith, there is a real question whether it counts as an *interpretation* of the text. Raymond Brown's verdict is perhaps apt: "Such relationships [between the temple curtain and the wound in Jesus' side] are highly speculative, and more likely the product of the interpreter's ingenuity than of the evangelist's plan."[42]

Luther. Despite its popularity among the "papists," Luther endorses Augustine's interpretation that the sacraments flow from the pierced body of Christ. "For the sacraments have their efficacy from the wounds and the blood of Christ."[43] At the same time Luther says this interpretation is not sufficiently accurate, for it fails to affirm the connection of Jesus' blood to the *gospel.* So, in a kind of hermeneutical variation of the *communicatio idiomatum,* Luther says we "are washed daily through the Word."[44] Moreover, in a 1540 sermon on baptism, Luther claims that it is God—Father, Son and Spirit—who does the bathing. This is what distinguishes baptism from other types of bathing or cleansing. And this, Luther reasons, is why John 19:34 speaks of water being mingled with the blood of Christ. Holy baptism is purchased for us precisely through Jesus' shed blood. Whenever a person receives baptism in faith, then, it is "the same as if he were visibly washed and cleaned of sin with the blood of Christ."[45]

---

[41]J. Ramsey Michaels, "The Centurion's Confession and the Spear Thrust," *Catholic Biblical Quarterly* 29 (1967): 102-9.
[42]Raymond E. Brown, *The Gospel According to John 12-21,* Anchor Bible 29A (Garden City, N.Y.: Doubleday, 1970), p. 945.
[43]Martin Luther, *Luther's Works,* vol. 8, ed. Jaroslav Pelikan (St. Louis: Concordia, 1966), p. 258.
[44]Ibid.
[45]Martin Luther, *Luther's Works,* vol. 51, ed. John W. Doberstein (Philadelphia: Muhlenberg, 1959), p. 325.

Calvin. Calvin considers the idea that the flow of blood and water was miraculous but in the end rejects it. It is natural, he says, for congealed blood to lose its red color and become like water. No, the Evangelist's intention lies elsewhere. In Calvin's view, the Evangelist adapts his narrative to certain scriptural testimonies which he adds in order to make the point that Christ brought with him true atonement and true washing. The Old Testament law prefigured this in its two sets of symbols: sacrifices and ablutions. What the Evangelist is doing in John 19:34 is setting before us a visible symbol of the fact that the law has been fulfilled. Now the sacraments, in their own way, do this too. So though Calvin denies that 19:34 refers to a miracle, he does not object to Augustine's view that the sacraments have flowed from Christ's side.

Brown and Bultmann. Modern scholars disagree over the question of "sacramentalism" in the Fourth Gospel. On the one hand, the Evangelist omits an account of the eucharistic action of Jesus at the Last Supper. On the other hand, some see symbolic references to baptism in passages that mention water and to the Eucharist in passages that mention bread (e.g., Jn 6). Brown nevertheless questions the hermeneutic principle that "since a passage can be understood sacramentally, it was intended sacramentally."[46]

Rudolf Bultmann's commentary on this passage represents an additional twist. While he thinks the phrase "and at once there came out blood and water" is an obvious reference to the sacraments, he attributes the phrase in question to the work of an ecclesiastical redactor, not to the Evangelist. In effect, Bultmann is arguing that the community's interest in spiritual formation was already making itself felt in the very redaction of the Fourth Gospel.

Thin description: The critical rule and the "physical" natural. Reading according to the catholic rule thus appears to stretch the natural sense of John 19:34 to the breaking point. Conversely, reading with modern biblical scholars according to the critical rule ("what actually happened?") tends to evacuate the text of theological significance. Such is the result when one understands the natural sense to refer to the text's ostensive empirical reference only. There is a parallel here with approaches that describe human action in terms of bodily movements only instead of in terms of intentional action. In both cases the result is a reduced, if not reductionistic, or "thin" description.

By "thin description" I mean one that offers a minimal interpretation only, one that confines itself, say, to lexical issues or to issues of historical reference. What gets lost is precisely the dimension of the author's communicative action: what one is doing in using just these words in just this way. The problem with thin interpre-

---

[46]Raymond E. Brown, *The Gospel According to John 1-11,* Anchor Bible 29 (Garden City, N.Y.: Doubleday, 1970), p. cxii.

tation is that it fails to penetrate (to pierce!) the text deeply enough to reach the theological dimension. John 19:34 has prompted more than one medical doctor to try his hand at biblical interpretation, but most of these readings get no farther than blood-thinning.

Brown reminds us that "it is common knowledge that dead bodies do not bleed since the heart is no longer pumping blood through the system."[47] However, most physicians acknowledge that wounds inflicted very shortly after death may yield some bleeding, especially if the corpse is in a vertical position, as was Jesus' case on the cross. What is harder to account for is the flow of water from a corpse, as well as the distinct flow of blood *and* water. Some maintain that the Evangelist is speaking according to the medical conventions of his day. The Mishnah, for instance, asserts, "Man is evenly balanced, half of him is water, and the other half is blood." Similarly, the great Greek physician Galen believed that the right proportion of blood and water in human persons guaranteed good health. On this view, then, the Evangelist would be affirming Jesus' genuine humanity. Jesus had a real physical body and underwent a real physical death—not an incidental point in a context rife with docetic heretics who denied the reality of the incarnation. This thin or physical account, then, does yield some theological fruit. The same cannot be said for most of the others.

The title of W. Stroud's 1871 work promises much: *Treatise on the Physical Cause of the Death of Christ and Its Relation to the Principles and Practice of Christianity.*[48] He argued that Jesus' heart ruptured violently, that Jesus literally died of a "broken heart." Blood from the ruptured heart flowed into the pericardial sac, and after clotting, it separated from the serum. The piercing by the lance opened the pericardial sac, releasing both substances. An interesting explanatory hypothesis, except that medical science today rejects the possibility of spontaneous cardiac ruptures.

Pierre Barbet's *A Doctor at Calvary: The Passion of Our Lord Jesus Christ As Described by a Surgeon* puts forward a slightly different hypothesis.[49] The watery fluid flowed from the pericardial sac, while the blood flowed from the heart itself (rather than from the pericardial sac). This interpretation received the approval of an article that appeared in the *Journal of the American Medical Association* in 1986, authored by consultants from the Mayo Clinic together with a pastor.[50]

It is the argument of A. F. Sava that the brutal scouring of Jesus hours earlier prob-

---

[47]Brown, *Gospel According to John 12-21*, p. 946.
[48]London: Hamilton & Adams, first published in 1847.
[49]Garden City, N.Y.: Doubleday, 1953.
[50]"In the Physical Death of Jesus Christ," cited in George R. Beasley-Murray, *John,* Word Biblical Commentary 36 (Dallas: Word, 1987), p. 356.

ably produced a hemorrhage in the pleural cavity between the ribs and the lungs. This fluid could have separated into a light serous fluid and a dark red fluid. Since the pleural cavity is just inside the rib cage, even a shallow piercing could have released the two parts of blood.[51]

What is fascinating about these varied descriptions is the fact of their disagreements. Even at the most basic level of a purely physical description, we find a conflict of interpretations! The other thing to be said, of course, is that these descriptions are not *interpretations* at all; they do not really help us to understand the Evangelist's communicative intent and action.

Thick description: The canonical rule and the theological natural. The catholic rule orients us as to an important aim of theological interpretation: the building up of the church. Yet it is the natural sense that regulates this aim by providing the norm for acceptable interpretations: a *canonical* rule. Theological interpretations of Scripture that view the Bible as divine discourse will assign priority to the communicative aims of the Scriptures over the interpretive aims of the community of readers.[52] We now turn to a "thick description" of John 19:34 that aims to describe what the author is doing in this text (the intentional action).

The Evangelist is describing something that happened in which he saw considerable theological significance. Whether it was a natural or a miraculous event is a matter of secondary importance. Theological interpreters should ask not "What actually happened?" but rather "What is the author saying/doing with these words?" What the Evangelist is doing, I suggest, is narrating the history of Jesus in a broader canonical and theological framework (that the Evangelist is composing history rather than fiction follows from the appeal to eyewitness testimony in Jn 19:35). The Evangelist's text is a "thick description" of the event of Jesus Christ, and our interpretations must similarly be thick descriptions of the Evangelist's communicative act.

There are three, perhaps four, ways of describing what the author of the Fourth Gospel is doing in this passage; some of these, however, come to light only when the passage is read in the canonical context of the story of Israel and the whole narrative of the Fourth Gospel. As we have seen, it is possible to offer more than one correct description of an action (moving one's index finger, pulling a trigger, etc.). Everything depends on the context in which the action, or in this case the communicative action, is described. I list below what I think the Evangelist is doing in this passage, beginning with the least obvious and proceeding to what, in

---

[51]A. F. Sava, "The Wound in the Side of Christ," *Catholic Biblical Quarterly* 19 (1957): 343-46.

[52]Unless, of course, the aim of receiving and responding to the communicative intent of the text is the interpretive community's chief aim, in which case the interests of the canon and the community coincide.

context, is arguably the best "natural" sense of the text.[53]

1. *The Evangelist is showing indirectly how Jesus' death gives rise to the sacraments that nourish the church.* I have already examined this interpretation. The chief difficulty with it lies in the paucity of internal textual evidence. Not only is the account of the Lord's Supper missing from the Fourth Gospel, but in those places where the Evangelist might well have anticipated the sacraments, the focus is on bread rather than blood (e.g., Jn 6). "Blood" is never by itself used in the New Testament as a designation for the Lord's Supper, except in conjunction with the idea of drinking (see Jn 6:55).[54] There is also a minor problem in associating water from the *side* of Jesus with water baptism.

2. *The Evangelist asserts the reality of Jesus' death and hence his genuine humanity.* According to George Beasley-Murray, the Evangelist "almost certainly" wanted his readers to recognize the reality of Jesus' death and hence the reality of his humanity as a man of flesh and blood.[55] Irenaeus proposed a similar antidocetic interpretation in his *Against Heresies:* "[If he had not been truly man] when his side was pierced, would there have come forth blood and water?"[56] Brown, however, is less certain than Beasley-Murray about the Evangelist's communicative intent because first-century docetism is not well documented; nor does Brown believe that the intent to assert the reality of Jesus' death explains the flow of water.

3. *The Evangelist views the significance of Jesus' death as a "new Passover" and a "new exodus."* With this description of the Evangelist's communicative action we adopt a wide-angle lens—one that encompasses Old Testament testimony. For the stage on which the scene of Jesus' body piercing takes place is set for Passover. It is the Day of Preparation, the day before the sabbath and, according to John 19:14, also the day before the Passover; hence a "great day" (Jn 7:37). Indeed the whole scene is heavily laden with Old Testament imagery. John 19:28 reports Jesus' saying "I thirst"

---

[53]Does a belief in determinate meaning, together with the norm of author's intended meaning, result in a "totalizing" approach to biblical interpretation where one reading is elevated above all others? While it is right to worry about totalizing interpretations, it is wrong to associate it with my position. To say that authors enacted certain communicative intentions rather than others is not to elevate one interpretation above others but to acknowledge that *all* our interpretations—especially mine!—are ultimately accountable and answerable to something other than ourselves and our communities.

[54]So A. E. Brooke, *Commentary on the Johannine Epistles* (Edinburgh: T & T Clark, 1912), p. 132.

[55]George R. Beasley-Murray, *John,* Word Biblical Commentary (Dallas: Word, 1987), p. 356. C. K. Barrett agrees, noting that this is the force of the appeal in John 19:35 to eyewitness testimony. The docetic heresy—which claimed that Jesus only *seemed* to be a man—is addressed even more explicitly in 1 John 5:6-8, where three witnesses to Jesus' incarnation are mentioned: the water, the blood and the Spirit. (As we saw earlier, some ancient thinkers held that the human body consisted largely of blood and water).

[56]Irenaeus *Adversus haereses* 3.22.2.

to fulfill Scripture, and John 19:37 notes that Scripture anticipated the piercing of Jesus' side. The episode therefore takes place in a framework of scriptural fulfillment. The Evangelist describes what happens to the body of Jesus from the perspective of the broader canonical context. To be competent interpreters, we must do no less.

Unless one is canonically tone-deaf, it is virtually impossible not to hear a number of echoes from the Passover ritual in this passage. The Evangelist has already told us that Jesus is the lamb of God (Jn 1:29). He also tells us that Jesus was handed over to Pilate at noon (Jn 19:14), the time at which Passover lambs were slain in the temple. There are further, less explicit clues that provide corroborative evidence of the Evangelist's intent. In the story of Israel's flight from Egypt, for example, hyssop was used to smear blood from the lamb on the doorposts of the Hebrew slaves (Ex 12:22); in the Fourth Gospel, a sponge full of vinegar is placed on hyssop and held to Jesus' mouth (Jn 19:29). Some might dismiss this as an incidental coincidence, but biblically literate readers will find it hard not to hear a faint echo.

The narrator explicitly tells us that these things took place so that Scripture might be fulfilled: "Not a bone of him shall be broken," and "They shall look on him whom they have pierced" (19:36-37). Which Scripture did the Evangelist have in mind in verse 36? Two possibilities strengthen the allusion to the Passover/exodus motif: Exodus 12:46 says that not a bone of the Passover lamb to be eaten must be broken; so does Numbers 9:12. The Evangelist's purpose is to strengthen the reader's faith that Jesus in his death fulfils the significance of the Passover as well as the eschatological hope for a second exodus.

4. *The Evangelist believes that Jesus' death or "exodus" is the condition, now fulfilled, for a new coming of the Spirit, the giver of eternal life.* We have seen that the real interpretive difficulty lies in explaining the conjunction of the blood *and water.* Jesus calls his blood "drink indeed" in John 6:55. Those who believe in him, he says, shall never thirst (Jn 6:35). Jesus says something similar in John 4: those who drink his "living water" shall never thirst, for Jesus' water "will become . . . a spring of water welling up to eternal life" (Jn 4:14).

But we find what is perhaps the most important textual clue to the Evangelist's communicative intent in John 19:34 in John 7:38-39, where Jesus quotes the following passage of Scripture: "Out of his heart shall flow rivers of living water." Some interpreters also hear echoes of Numbers 20:11, where water flows from the rock struck (not pierced, however) by Moses.

The Evangelist interrupts his own narrative flow at this point to make sure the reader is following the speech action: "Now this he said about the Spirit, which those who believed in him were to receive; for as yet the Spirit had not been given, because Jesus was not yet glorified" (Jn 7:39). Jesus is here promising that following his glorification, living water (the Spirit) would be available to those who believe in his glorification (his bloody death on behalf of sinners).

Now the Evangelist has already associated Jesus' body with the temple in Jerusalem (Jn 2:19-21), and he assumes that his readers will be familiar with the passage that speaks of the flow of living water from Jerusalem and the temple at the triumphant day of the Lord (Ezek 47:1-9). We know, moreover, that for the Fourth Evangelist, Jesus is glorified in being "lifted up" on the cross. By calling our attention to the flow of blood and water, then, the Evangelist demonstrates that the promised new life—more specifically, the gift of the Holy Spirit—has now arrived and is available. Passover, we might say, passes over into pneumatology. What the Evangelist is doing in speaking of the flow of blood and water, then, is assuring his readers that the new life of the Holy Spirit flows from the slain body of Jesus.[57]

The Nature of Theological Interpretation
and the Theological Interpretation of the Natural Sense

Let us return to the two types of theological interpretation and to my suggestion that each needs the other. The aim of upbuilding the Christian community, while laudable, risks ascribing priority to the interpretive aims of the community over the communicative aims of Scripture itself. To "socialize" the text so that it fits in with the community's practices may overcome one's sense of estrangement, but it also quenches the text's transformative potential. At worst, it plays into the hands of those postmoderns for whom authority is ultimately rooted in interpretive communities. Body piercing, in the pejorative sense, would thus refer to a community's use of Scripture merely to reinforce a social identity (and agenda?) that it may have obtained elsewhere. As I have argued, the use that must be considered normative is the authors' (and divine author's), not the readers'. The interpretive ends do not justify the means if this means overturning or neglecting the natural sense. In sum: the interpretive aims and interests of the community should not eclipse the communicative aims and interests of God.

---

[57]For an extended treatment of this point, see Larry Paul Jones, *The Symbol of Water in the Gospel of John, Journal for the Study of the New Testament* Supplement Series 145 (Sheffield, U.K.: Sheffield Academic Press, 1999), p. 211. Stephen Moore locates the water flowing from Jesus' side as the site of deconstruction, the place where the text's carefully rendered hierarchy between physical water and living water breaks apart (*Literary Criticism and the Gospels* [New Haven, Conn.: Yale University Press, 1989], p. 162). The flow of water is another symbolic token of the promised living water: "That leaves us with a symbol (the flow of water) of a metaphor (living water) for the Spirit" (p. 162). It is impossible, says Moore, to keep the literal and the figural cleanly separated in this "spiritual material." Two levels of meaning "are collapsed that should have been kept apart" (p. 163). This, I believe, is a somewhat perverse misreading of the natural sense of the text, in which the flow of water from Jesus' side has accrued theological significance but still manages unambiguously to refer to the release of the Spirit of life.

Theological exegesis is best construed as a "thick description" of the natural—that is, the literal, literary, authorially intended—sense. The Rule of Faith works best when viewed as the explicit formulation of a grammar that is implicit in (and intrinsic to) Scripture. The canon is allowed to be itself—respected as a stranger, as an other—only if one follows the hermeneutical rule to read for its natural (authorially intended) sense. As we have seen from our brief hermeneutical exercise on John 19, reading for the author's natural sense need not result in thin, nontheological description. On the contrary, we saw that there were several aspects to the author's intentional action that made for a rich reading, high in theologically saturated fact.

Theological interpretation is neither merely reading with a particular community interest nor *merely* a matter of individuals' describing but not appropriating authorial discourse. Each approach needs the other. To have interpretive aims without norms exposes readers to the danger of inaccurate exegesis; to have interpretive norms without aims exposes them to the danger of incomplete application. To this point, I have argued that it is not enough to have the right aims in interpretation; one must have the right norms as well in order to do justice to the integrity, the otherness, and perhaps the "wholly otherness," of the Christian Scriptures. Yet neither is it enough simply to posit the authority of the natural sense. Merely having the "right" theory of meaning is no guarantee that one will interpret rightly; interpreters must develop the interpretive virtues in order to strive for the aim of edifying reading under the norm of submitting to the intended sense.

What finally keeps the aim and the norm together, I believe, is a vision of the task of theological interpretation of Scripture in terms of giving *true witness*. Let us return to our passage once more, not to solve the problem of the meaning of the blood and water but to reflect on the lessons it holds for the project of theological interpretation as such.[58]

The nature of theological interpretation: Reading for communicative action (John 19:34). Since I have already treated the nature of theological interpretation at some length, I can here be brief. Theological interpretation of Scripture is, in large part but not wholly, a matter of describing what the biblical authors have done in using words this textual way rather than that. To account fully for the author's communicative intent involves describing the action, as it were, against an appropri-

---

[58]My argument is similar to Lindbeck's in calling for cooperation rather than competition between various modes of theological interpretation. How do the three approaches to Scripture that Lindbeck discusses—Childs (canonical witness), Hays (narrative world), Wolterstorff (authorial discourse—relate to my comparison between ruled reading and canonical action? Briefly, I agree with Lindbeck that an authorial discourse approach has the potential to accommodate and clarify the concerns of these other approaches, including ruled reading. Reading for the natural sense of Scripture is a matter of describing the narrative witness of the text in terms of what the author is doing.

ately large background so that it can be seen for what it is. The Evangelist's statement
in John 19:34 is part of a complex testimony whose ultimate aim is to identify Jesus
as the promised Christ and hence to elicit belief.

   ***The necessity of theological interpretation: Reading for true witness (John
19:35).*** Why is it necessary to read the Bible for its communicative action, and for
whom is such reading necessary? The answer to both questions, I believe, is implicit in
verse 35: "He who saw it has borne witness—his testimony is true, and he knows that
he tells the truth—that you also may believe." The Evangelist is a paradigmatic theological interpreter of Scripture, and the passage we have been examining is not simply
an illustration of an interpretive approach but an implicit demand to embody it.

   According to B. F. Westcott, verse 35 is not simply saying that the witness has
given an accurate (factually true) testimony but rather that his witness is *alethine,*
"true to the idea of what a witness should be."[59] The author is not only correct but
competent. He has seen all that there is to be seen—the whole truth. In my terms, he
is a competent and true witness because he gives a sufficiently thick description of
the event. John 19:35 asks readers not only to believe what the witness reports but
also to accept its theological implications (its depth description). The prime interpretive imperative finally amounts to a familiar command: "You shall not bear false witness" (Ex 20:16).[60]

   If interpreters are likewise to be competent witnesses to the subject matter of the
text, our testimony, like that of the narrator, must be sufficiently thick to discern the
theological significance both of the events reported and of the report (the communicative act). After all, testimony is important because of its aim: "that you may
believe." The best theological interpreter of Scripture, then, is the competent witness
to what the author has said/done.

   Could it be that the aim of the interpretive community ultimately coincides with
that of the biblical text? Yes! For it is part and parcel of our Christian identity to be
faithful witnesses. The necessity of theological interpretation is tied up with questions
of Christian identity, after all, and with what it means to be the church. The theological interpreter is the one who testifies truthfully to "that which we have seen and
heard" (1 Jn 1:1-3). Reading before God thus requires interpreters to be faithful—that
is, true—witnesses. Here again we see how the "reading for communion" type of
theological interpretation of Scripture is incomplete without the "reading for communication" type (and vice versa).

   Jesus effaces himself in order to give faithful witness to the Father. Such self-

---

[59]B. F. Westcott, *The Gospel According to St. John* (Grand Rapids, Mich.: Eerdmans, 1971), p. liv.
[60]Who is my neighbor? Can a text be a neighbor? Why not? As I indicated in my opening illustration, the text represents a voice that is not our own—the voice of a stranger, an other.
   The ethical task of the interpreter is to welcome and respect this voice.

effacement is similarly the vocation of the biblical interpreter. "The body of Christ keeps absenting itself from the text. Where does it go to? What the body is replaced by is the witness of the Church."[61] Our faithful witness—a "martyrdom" proper to the biblical interpreter—can itself become a source of life for those who receive it. With this thought we have arrived at the highest task of the theological interpretation of Scripture: to *interpret* "so that they may believe and have life."

The normativity of theological interpretation: Reading for God's canonical action (John 19:36). "For these things took place that the scripture might be fulfilled." The competent witness to what the Evangelist is doing in John 19:31-37 would be remiss not to take account of the significance of the appeal to fulfilled Scripture. For what the Evangelist is doing in this text is ultimately unintelligible apart from a consideration of his entire Gospel, not to mention the Scriptures of the Old Testament. From Jesus' "I thirst" in John 19:28 to "They shall look on him whom they have pierced" (Jn 19:37), the Evangelist has woven a thoroughly biblical framework within which to describe the piercing of Jesus' side. The divine action—in word and deed—fully comes into view only against this broader canonical background. I believe that the concept of *canonical* action—that is, communicative action described in canonical context—ultimately calls for an acknowledgment of divine authorship.

At this point we must pause to consider an objection. Does not the concept of divine communicative action complicate my claim that normativity in interpretation attaches to the natural sense? In particular, what about the natural sense of the Old Testament texts cited in our passage (Ps 69:18; Ex 12:46; Zech 12:10)? Does the Evangelist's use not distort their natural sense? No, but it does recontextualize it. With regard to Old Testament prophecy, we would do well to amend Michael Polanyi's account of tacit knowledge: it is not so much that the prophets "know more than they can tell" but rather that they *tell more than they can know*. The prophets' testimony, when appropriated by the Evangelist, is disambiguated. To place these Old Testament testimonies in the larger canonical context of the story of Jesus Christ is not to falsify their original meaning but to specify their true referents: the body of Jesus (the Messiah), the body of Christ (the church).

Brown's distinction between literal meaning (what it meant to the [human] author), canonical meaning (what it meant to those who accepted the text as Scripture) and what it means today (to those in the church who continue to accept it as Scripture) provides a helpful template from which to distinguish the present proposal.[62] I agree with Brown about literal meaning. However, though it is legitimate to ask what it meant to those who first accepted it as Scripture, I prefer to reserve the

---

[61]Ward, "Displaced Body," p. 174.
[62]Raymond E. Brown, "'And the Lord Said'? Biblical Reflections on Scripture as the Word of God," *Theological Studies* 42 (1981): 3-19.

term *canonical meaning* to refer to the divine intention in the text.[63] The church has historically acknowledged the canon as divine communicative action, the Word of God. As we have seen, *the theological natural* refers to nature—whether celestial, human or textual bodies—as God intends it. With regard to the biblical texts, therefore, *the theological natural* refers to the divine intention enacted in and by the canonical Scriptures. In short: *the theological natural sense* thus refers to the way the words and texts go in their divinely appointed canonical context.[64]

Describing the body of the text requires an expanded canonical context—thick description—as does the narrator's description of the body of Jesus. We pierce beyond the physical to the theological (beyond the human author's intent to that of the divine author) only if we describe what is done and what is said against the broader canonical context. Our role as theological interpreters is to examine the body of the text with piercing discernment. Theological interpretation of Scripture is nothing less than a kind of body piercing, though one that does not absolve but acknowledges the theological natural (divinely intended) sense: what *God* is saying/doing in this text. Theological interpretation of Scripture is finally less a matter of constructing our identity on the basis of the text than of receiving our identity as constituted by the text.

The statement that the events surrounding the piercing of Jesus' side fulfill not one but two Scriptures is itself a claim about the divine authorship of the course of *events*. In quoting Scripture as he has, the narrator puts the passion events in the broader context of divine providence. God has authored both the discourse and the course of events. It should come as no surprise that theological interpretation is tied up with properly theological questions. As Christopher Seitz has observed, "The crisis in hermeneutics is in reality a crisis involving God's providence, a proper ecclesiology and doctrine of the Holy Spirit."[65] Providence is what has perhaps been in view throughout this essay, inasmuch as Scripture, viewed as divine communicative action, is but "providence put into writing."[66]

Piercing the Body of Christ: How to Read Scripture for a Blessing

> For the word of God is living and active, sharper than any two-edged sword, piercing to the division of soul and spirit. (Heb 4:12)

---

[63]James D. G. Dunn rightly points out that it is only as a part of the canon of Scripture that individual documents have functioned as authority for faith and life (*The Living Word* [Philadelphia: Fortress, 1988], pp. 150-51).

[64]To speak of "divinely appointed" rather than "divinely appropriated" discourse might, or might not, distinguish this approach from that of Wolterstorff.

[65]Christopher Seitz, in *Renewing Biblical Interpretation,* ed. Craig Bartholomew (Grand Rapids, Mich.: Zondervan, 2000), p. 63.

[66]This is my counterclaim to radical postmodernity's antihermeneutic, with its "death of God put into writing."

The Bible is a complex, multifaceted but ultimately unified witness to what God was doing in Jesus Christ. Yet it is not enough to equate theological interpretation with "reading for the witness," for this witness is mediated by a variety of literary forms. The contributing act of narrative, for example, is to display a world. However, it is not enough to equate theological interpretation with absorbing the world into the biblical narrative. Fully to describe texts as narrative witnesses or as witnessing narratives finally requires understanding the author as communicative agent and the text as communicative action, with their own intrinsic aims and intentions. One of these aims is to elicit the response of the reader. Theological interpretation of Scripture therefore involves not only describing but responding to and participating in the various forms of communicative intentions enacted in the text. For instance, it is not enough to describe a narrative world from the outside; in order to understand one must indwell the world of the text.

Stephen Fowl and L. Gregory Jones have brought to light the importance of the moral and interpretive virtues for the project of theological interpretation of Scripture. Scholarly exegetical skills alone are insufficient; no amount of grammatical knowledge alone can lead to holiness. It is not enough, for instance, to have the "right" theory about theological interpretation. Knowing the meaning of meaning is no guarantee for correct reading. This is why interpreting Scripture in the believing community matters. Clearly one must approach Scripture as saint *and* scholar or one's scholarship will bear no sanctifying fruit. For it is in the church that we come to Scripture expecting to be taught, encouraged, commanded, blessed. Hence the church is the proper locus for theological interpretation of Scripture. The people of God are called together by God to embody God's Word in worship, witness and wisdom for the sake of the world.

At the same time, however, it is not enough simply to produce edifying readings of the text. For it is one thing to use a text, even for the purposes of edification, and another to interpret it. The task of theological interpretation involves both aims and norms. At present we are probably closer to an agreement concerning the former than the latter. What remains to be done is to secure consensus about the norm of theological interpretation—the communicative intent of the human and divine authors enacted in the text at the literary and the canonical levels. Nevertheless, the prospects for a truly theological interpretation, guided by a theological hermeneutic, have never been better since the inception of *Ex Auditu*.

How, then, can the church read Scripture in order to obtain a blessing? By reading in communion—in agreement about the aims and norms of interpretation—in order (1) to discover the divine communication therein and (2) to be its faithful witnesses. To bear true witness to the text is both an aim and a norm. The best interpreters, to the extent that they become witnesses, participate in the event of meaning and thus become part of the action. The author of the Fourth Gospel thus becomes a paradigm for the contemporary biblical interpreter. We too are to testify to "what we have seen and heard" in Scripture. We too are to be true and competent witnesses, able to hear the music, the echoes, of previous Scripture, able to understand the event of Jesus Christ in the context of the larger story of salvation of which it is the climax and interpretive key.

The specific vocation of the interpreter of Scripture is to be a true witness: one who can not only describe but embody God's communicative intent. The theological interpreter describes what God, the divine author, is doing in and through the works of the human authors. The specific task of theological interpretation, then, is to read the Bible so that one encounters the Word of God. Ultimately, however, theological interpretation of Scripture is a matter not only of reading but of being read by the text; to be a true witness involves not only describing what God is saying/doing in Scripture but embodying this message.

If the church is to be transformed by Scripture—if the body of Christ is to be "pierced" by the Word-wielding Spirit—then we must read so as to open ourselves to its communicative and transformative intent. Theological interpreters of Scripture not only will read in communion with one another but will seek deeper communion with God by laying themselves open to the effects of God's word-acts. Reading in communion with one another is the proper corporate response to God's communication, but it does not constitute that act. On the contrary: the church, as an obedient and competent interpretive community, strives to be a faithful witnesses to what God has done, is doing and will do in, with and through Scripture. Theological interpretation of Scripture is reading for ecclesial communion (the aim) *and* for divine communication (the norm), all for the ultimate purpose of deepening our communion with the triune God.

Eleven

The World Well Staged?

Theology, Culture & Hermeneutics

All the world's a stage
And all the men and women merely players.
They have their exits and their entrances
And one man in his time plays many parts
WILLIAM SHAKESPEARE, *AS YOU LIKE IT*

*S*hakespeare often used the metaphor of the stage to speak of life. Prior to Shakespeare, medieval mystery plays were often three-tiered productions: action on earth was performed on a middle stage (Tolkien's Middle-earth?), stages above and below revealed the attitudes of God and Satan, respectively, toward the unfolding action on the principal stage. "When we are born, we cry that we are come / To this great stage of fools."[1] It is part of theology's task to discover and articulate the way of wisdom through the stage, and the stages, of life with the Word of God—the ultimate set of stage directions. However, no theologian, even one armed with the Word of God, enjoys a God's-eye point of view, for the Word of God must be interpreted. A little lower than the angels, we human players do not have direct access to the things of heaven but must interpret. Those cast as theologians, like those given other parts, play the role of actor and critic simultaneously. Theology is an attempt to evaluate world performance by the criterion of the Word of God. Interpretation is doubly part of theological work: not only the Word but the world itself must be interpreted.

---

[1]William Shakespeare, *King Lear*, act 4, scene 6, line 11.

Culture is a "performance" of one's ultimate beliefs and values, a concrete way of "staging" one's religion. Individuals are the actors, but they are culturally and historically conditioned. They may not be given particular lines, but they are given a particular language. Culture is the scenery, the environment, the world into which one is thrown when one appears onstage. The cultural scenery influences and conditions what the actors see, say, and do. If the world is a stage, culture provides the props that fill it.

Carl Henry has rightly grasped the importance of a theological interpretation and analysis of culture and cultural trends. Indeed Henry opens his magisterial *God, Revelation and Authority* with a perceptive description of "the crisis of truth and word" in our times: "No fact of contemporary Western life is more evident than its growing distrust of final truth and its implacable questioning of any sure word."[2] This crisis—which at its root is a crisis of epistemology and theology—may well be the dusk before the "night of nihilism" and a new Dark Ages.

In an analysis that bears some interesting similarities with that of Jean Baudrillard (see below), Henry suggests that the modern mass media have provided humans, who are by nature idolatrous, with a fantastic mythmaking machinery that is virtually able to shape a new reality (and newly able to create a virtual reality) at will. Nietzsche's belief that humans must be their own gods, creating reality by their will to power, seems to have received a technological verification. For Henry, the situation is dire: "Not alone human culture, but human destiny as well, depend on whether sight and sound are reserved only for human speculation and transitory happenings, or are lent equally to the Word and truth of God" (p. 23). There is at present a growing distrust of the Word, and of words in general. The cult of nonverbal experience threatens the whole cultural inheritance of Western civilization. "To deverbalize an already depersonalized society is all the more to dehumanize it" (p. 26).

According to Henry, every culture has "a certain convictional glue, an undergirding outlook on life and reality that preserves its cohesiveness" (p. 44). Some convictional frameworks, such as that of the ancient Greeks, were able to produce an impressive culture apart from a Judeo-Christian foundation. But the ancient Greeks did believe in an invisible, eternal, spiritual and rational reality that served as a foundation for their attempts to impose this invisible rational order onto the visible worldly order. However, they lacked the spiritual resources to make their vision visible; they lacked the necessary means of grace that would have enabled them to embody the spirituality they discerned. But twenty-first-century cultures are in even worse straits. In the West, industrial and postindustrial societies find it difficult to

[2]Carl F. H. Henry, *God, Revelation and Authority*, vol. 1, *God Who Speaks and Shows, Preliminary Considerations* (Waco, Tex.: Word, 1976), p. 1. Subsequent citations will be made parenthetically in the text.

believe in an ultimate otherworldly order after which earthly life should be patterned.

Where then do the values that shape contemporary cultures come from? People today must either believe their own myths or else view them as convenient and necessary fictions that have pragmatic worth. Either we must think that our values and beliefs about the ultimate are true, or else we must recognize them for the useful fictions they are. Many contemporary Western thinkers are declaring all convictional frameworks to be the fruit of mythmaking and are celebrating them as such. Henry's assessment of the present is a sobering one: "Pragmatism is the last stand for a culture that has lost a true center" (p. 41). In an age without absolutes, humankind's problem is "freely fashioning . . . life, history and nature through self-creativity" (p. 139). Ironically, such sheer creativity will ultimately consume humanity. Like sharks that sense the ebbing of life, modern men and women will feed upon themselves in a kind of "freedom frenzy," desperately trying to stave off nihilism by investing life with values that the underfunded convictional frameworks cannot support. Is there an alternative, a way to life and truth? For Henry, this is perhaps the most pressing question that confronts human being: "The most critical question in the history of thought is whether all the convictional frameworks through which different peoples arrive at the meaning and worth of human life are by nature mythical" (p. 44).

Henry's work provides an excellent introduction to our topic: the relation of theology, culture and hermeneutics. If the theologian is to minister the Word of God to today's world, both the Word and the world must be understood. Theology must engage in both biblical and cultural hermeneutics. Interpretation is one of the fundamental categories of theological thinking.[3] Theology should be in the business (at least part time) of cultural interpretation. Of course we must quickly acknowledge that theology itself is culturally conditioned. The theologian thinks from a particular point in place and time with a language and set of categories that reflect the time and culture in which he or she lives. It is therefore as legitimate to speak of the culture of theology as to speak of the theology of culture. Moreover, because of the present loss of faith in absolutes and in an absolute (God's-eye) point of view, thinkers are happy to speak of interpretation but not of knowledge, particularly the absolute variety. Perhaps more than any previous age, ours is the age of interpretation. That we are not in a position to know things is widely accepted as a given. Absolute knowledge—of good and evil or anything else—unlike the paradisaic tree, is always out of human reach. For this reason we will have to examine the culture of interpretation as well as the interpretation of culture.

In this essay I examine the role of theology in the interpretation of culture and in

---

[3]See Werner H. Jeanrond, *Text and Interpretation as Categories of Theological Thinking* (New York: Crossroad, 1988).

our present culture of interpretation. Next I review some ways culture has been interpreted by historians, sociologists, philosophers and theologians. I suggest that in contemporary culture in the West hermeneutics itself is now considered one of the ultimate values. I speak here of the culture of hermeneutics rather than the hermeneutics of culture, for in the postmodern situation creative interpretation is taken to be one of the prime virtues of human being. In the final section I argue that there is more need than ever for the theologian to be interpreter and critic of contemporary culture, as well as champion of a counterculture that should be embodied in ecclesial existence—that is, in the church. It is only as we interpret Scripture that we will be able to establish an effective counterculture, which itself will be the most effective critique of the dominant culture. Ultimately the interpretation that counts most is one's "performance" of the biblical text. The theologian as interpreter-critic is thus a player on the stage of world history. Theology's "staging" of the world displayed in the Christian Scriptures should constitute a crucial voice, or chorus of voices, in contemporary debates about cultural values and institutions. As players and interpreters of culture, theologians and believers act as social theorists and social activists alike. This, at least, is the demanding role thrust upon Christian disciples, upon the community of those who assemble together to "do" the Word.

Of Nature and Nurture, Cosmos and Culture
The distinction between the natural and the human sciences exposes both the nature of culture as a social phenomenon and the corresponding need for hermeneutical understanding as opposed to causal explanations of culture and society. The natural sciences study, as their name implies, nature. Since Kant, it has been fashionable to distinguish the realm of nature from freedom. Nature is ruled by laws, laws that causally determine what happens in space and time. Nature is marked by a certain necessity: force will always equal mass multiplied by acceleration, no matter what the climate or country. The goal of natural science is thus a catalog of those causal laws that explain what invariably happens in nature. Scientists can "read" the book of nature intelligibly when they have adduced the mathematical causal laws that govern the workings of the "mechanical" universe.

Human beings, on the other hand, are only partially determined by natural laws. Human bodies may be subject to causal laws, but not so the human spirit. Whereas tennis balls have no choice in the way they fulfill their vocation, human beings enjoy a measure of freedom. Human beings have futures—genuine possibilities—in ways that machines, molecules and marbles do not. Human beings also have pasts. Indeed history is the page upon which freedom writes. And one does not understand the book of history, the record of human freedom, by causal explanation. The historian is a human scientist—that is, one who studies humans—and history, along with the other human sciences, searches for understanding rather than explanation.[4]

Now from the point of view of, say, the biologist who studies human beings as a phenomenon of nature, humanity is one. The biologist classifies all human beings as belonging to the same species. But for the historian (as well as for the cultural anthropologist or sociologist), humanity is multiple. No single set of laws, no matter how complex, can explain human beings and what they have done. No unified field theory charts the flow of human freedom. Yet one need not conclude from this that human being and human history are unintelligible. It was Wilhelm Dilthey who argued for a methodology that would study human beings scientifically while at the same time respecting human individuality, freedom and uniqueness.[5] Dilthey aimed at understanding rather than explanation, an understanding that meant reliving the experience and thought processes of individuals who have lived and thought before us. According to Dilthey, the study of history is possible because humans "objectify" or express their thoughts and values (their "spirit") through what they do, through their respective "works." History, which is about the actions of persons in the past, thus becomes the study of signs and the interpretation of traces. Paul Ricoeur's verdict on Dilthey is telling: "History thus becomes the field of hermeneutics."[6] History is the stage for the appearances—the entries and the exits—of the human spirit.

A culture is the objectification, the expression in words and works, of the "spirit" of a particular people who inhabit a particular time and place. The spirit of the age (the *Zeitgeist*) is far from being invisible; on the contrary, it is constantly expressed in concrete forms. Culture is the effort of the human spirit to express itself by building and embodying values and beliefs into concrete forms (e.g., cathedrals, coliseums, cemeteries, cinemas, colleges, cash stations, car washes). Culture is the process (and result) whereby form and meaning are given to material through freedom.[7] A spider's web is not a cultural product because it is not a work of freedom. The spider's web, despite its intricacy, is neither a message nor an expression of a set of values and beliefs. There are no arachnid equivalents of our Gothic, Enlightenment and Romantic—not to mention Cubist— cultural styles. The spider's web has no meaning; rather, it serves an instrumental purpose. The weaving of the web may be admired; it cannot be interpreted.

---

[4]It is a search for understanding because the subject matter of history is the individual particular, not the individual as an instance of a universal and necessary law. In history, one is always conscious that it all might have happened otherwise.

[5]See Raymond Williams, *Culture* (London: Fontana, 1981), pp. 15-16, and Paul Ricoeur, *Hermeneutics and the Human Sciences* (Cambridge: Cambridge University Press, 1981), chaps. 1-2.

[6]Ricoeur, *Hermeneutics and the Human Sciences,* p. 52.

[7]As Herman Dooyeweerd puts it, "Cultural activity always consists in giving form to material in free control over the material" (*Roots of Western Culture: Pagan, Secular and Christian Options* [Toronto: Wedge, 1979], p. 64).

Culture refers to the expressive work of human freedom in and on nature. Unlike any other species, humankind inscribes itself into nature by making meaningful marks—everything from small scratches of black ink on white paper to the scratches of a skyscraper on a sunlit sky. Culture, in its broadest sense, refers to the "world of human meaning."[8] The point about culture is that its "marks," its benchmarks and its landmarks, have meaning. They are to be understood rather than explained. But how? "The Greek culture has left its mark on Western civilization"—well and good, but how are we to understand the "mark" that is Greek culture, or the grandeur that was Rome?

Ricoeur defines hermeneutics as "the theory of the operations of understanding in their relation to the interpretation of texts."[9] Hermeneutics, the art and science of interpretation, pertains primarily to the principles and procedures for making sense of and appropriating the meaning of texts. As we shall see, several thinkers have extended the notion of the "text" to include dreams (Sigmund Freud), film, fashion (Roland Barthes) and culture as a whole (Raymond Williams). And natural sciences have, of course, long referred to the cosmos as "the book of nature."

Ricoeur argues that the human sciences are hermeneutical insofar as their object displays "textual" features, and inasmuch as the method of the human sciences develops the same kind of procedures used to interpret texts. But how are cultures and cultural works like texts? A text is a set of marks (words) that fixes the meaning of the author. The saying of the author may disappear in time, but the marks, and the meaning, remain. Similarly, an action may "leave its mark." Human words and works alike can convey meaning. Max Weber defined the object of the human sciences as "meaningfully oriented behaviour." Studying meaningful human action therefore is like reading a text.[10] Unlike events, which are susceptible to causal explanation, human actions must be understood. Actions are meaningful works inscribed on the fabric of history or nature.

Culture refers to the meaningful actions of an individual, group or whole society. Culture pertains to those human works that express in objective form some value for or shape of human freedom, some meaning or orientation for the wandering human spirit. Culture is not an impersonal cosmos but a meaningful world. As opposed to nature, which is indifferent to human being and human concerns, culture nurtures—cultivates—the human. If meaningful action can be likened to a text, then culture is the library in which these texts are classified by value and shelved in corporate memory.

---

[8]Julian Hartt, *A Christian Critique of American Culture* (New York: Harper & Row, 1967), p. 49.
[9]Ricoeur, *Hermeneutics and the Human Sciences*, p. 43.
[10]See Ricoeur, "The Model of the Text: Meaningful Action Considered as a Text," chap. 8 in *Hermeneutics and the Human Sciences*.

A culture expresses the totality of what a group of humans value. Like a book, culture has a certain unity of plot or thesis. For Williams, culture is a signifying system that communicates and reproduces a social order through its various signifying practices, including the arts, philosophy, journalism, advertising, fashion and so on.[11] We try to express who we are and why we are valuable through our works (our "texts"): paintings, monuments, symphonies. Such cultural anthologies may be the best means of pursuing cultural anthropology. Cultural hermeneutics is the study of how and what these multifarious signifying expressions really mean. By interpreting culture, we try to find the spirit in what has been bodied forth. Cultural hermeneutics is the study of people's beliefs about the meaning of life and about what it means to be human.

Culture is a signifying system that expresses in objective forms what a people take to be the values that guide and sustain human freedom. What aspect of culture is most significant? Kenneth Clark claims that architecture is the best index of the character of a civilization. Hans Rookmaaker says that painting is the most revelatory of a culture's mood. Nathan Scott says that it is literature; T. S. Eliot, that it is poetry. One is hard pressed to decide among these options. For Ricoeur, it suffices to say that culture, unlike economics (having) or politics (power), is established at the level of the imaginary. A culture is a cohesive social group because the individuals in the group share the same imaginative world, the same vision about what is most important and about how the social world should be ordered. At the heart of a society or civilization is a narrative, some story or history or drama, which accounts for its origin and destiny and which enshrines the future in a particular way that gives it a sense of direction and a means of understanding itself. Some call this foundational narrative a "metanarrative"; others call it "myth." Whatever one calls it, I believe that theology should be allowed to tell, and argue for, its metanarrative version of the world too. It is theology's privilege and responsibility to join the conflict of interpretations about the meaning of the human condition and the best means to achieve its fulfillment.[12]

Culture is an ongoing historical drama. The world stage embraces many cultures, many metanarratives, many stories and works that embody various visions and prescriptions for ordering life together. Traditionally, culture has been cherished as an indispensable instrument of nurture for the human spirit. In the preface to the 1873 edition of *Literature and Dogma,* Matthew Arnold defined culture as "the acquainting ourselves with the best that has been known and said in the world, and thus with the history of the human spirit." Arnold was concerned with the perfection of

---

[11]Raymond Williams, *Culture* (London: Fontana, 1981), p. 13.

[12]Abraham Kuyper did this when he suggested that "Calvinism," alongside paganism, Islam, Roman Catholicism and modernism, is one of five main systems of thought in the history of civilization (*Lectures on Calvinism* [Grand Rapids, Mich.: Eerdmans, 1931], p. 32).

the individual. But as T. S. Eliot observed, *culture* may be used with reference to individuals, to a group or class, or to society as a whole. It is on this latter level that studies of culture and social theory intersect and the presence of theology is most needed. For there is a growing chorus of naysayers who deny that there is anything in culture that is worth preserving. Against Arnold's quest for the best, many today argue that what earlier cultures took for the "best" was really a function of male domination, or political imperialism, or even racism. What does it mean to be human? What means should we take to attain genuine freedom? These are currently disputed questions. Theology, with no other credentials than the Word of God and the cultural mandate, must dare to enter the arena of critical discourse and put forth its prescription for culture beside those of the other social theorists.

The Hermeneutics of Culture

Culture is the world of human meaning, the sum total of a people's works that express in objective form their highest beliefs, values and hopes—in short, their vision of what it is to be fully human. Culture is a text that calls for interpretation. But why should we want to interpret culture, and what are the principles that govern its correct interpretation? With regard to the "why" part of the question, I believe we must interpret culture in order first to understand the "other," the culturally distant, and then to understand ourselves, the culturally near.

Can other cultures, distant from us geographically, linguistically or chronologically, speak to us or contribute something to our being? Is it not our belief that we can learn from others that stimulates travel and exploration, not to mention reading? Without this interpretive effort, without this attempt to grasp or comprehend the other, certain values and ways of living would be lost to humanity. *Culture,* for Matthew Arnold, referred to those works of the human spirit that are worth preserving. In some sense humanity would be diminished if the contents of the Louvre were suddenly to vanish. We read, we visit museums, and we listen to music in part to understand how others have experienced and understood life. Culture is a way of sharing what other people consider valuable ways of thinking and living. A given set of ideas and values would disappear unless they were culturally transmitted from one people group, from one generation, to another. A tradition is a kind of ongoing cultural interpretation of certain foundational works. If we would benefit from history, we must interpret in order to overcome cultural distance.

We also interpret culture in order to understand ourselves. The world we live in is so immediate and complex that it is difficult, if not impossible, to gain an objective perspective. We find it difficult to detach ourselves from the immediate so as to inquire after its meaning. And yet we can distance ourselves from our way of life. We may not have objectivity, but we can contemplate the "objectification" of our way of life; for as we have seen, cultures produce works that, like texts, may be interpreted. Similarly, individuals produce works—works of labor, love and art. These various works are expressions of an individual's spirit, a person's desire and effort to exist in one way rather than another. By interpreting what we do (by interpreting our "story"), we have a better understanding of who we are. We may learn that we are far different from what we had imagined. Ancient Israel's inflated opinion of itself, for instance, was shattered by the prophetic interpretation of its history and culture. Things that the Israelites interpreted as signs of God's favor were for Amos signs of Israel's corruption. We therefore see that a certain amount of "distance" is healthy for a hermeneutics that would preserve a critical moment in its interpretation. Though distance can be a barrier to understanding, a certain distance—the distance afforded by the textual productions of a culture—is the condition for honest self-appraisal.

Rudolf Bultmann's question about biblical interpretation—is exegesis without presuppositions possible?—may be applied to the hermeneutics of culture as well. It is evident that there can be false interpretations of culture. French scholars are still debating the causes and meaning of the French Revolution. It is tempting to judge a foreign culture by the standards of one's own. For instance, Enlightenment thinkers cast the medieval era, which relied on divine revelation rather than autonomous human reason, as the Dark Ages. Bultmann himself judged New Testament culture to be primitive compared to the scientific culture of the modern world. Ironically, some philosophers and social theorists are now arguing that "modernity" has run its course. Just what was (is) modernity and what did (does) it mean? This is an important, though disputed, question. Again, we who are in the thick of things see only darkly.

The conflict of interpretations of culture involves a clash of methods as well as disagreements about a culture's fundamental motifs. I have said that culture is the objectified expression, in works of art and styles of life, of a way of being human in the world. These cultural works manifest not only a particular style but also a particular structure and organization. This cultural structure, like the structure of a text, can be observed and explained. One can point to various aspects of the structure as evidence for one's explanation of it. And once one has analyzed the cultural form, one is better able to grasp or understand the cultural content that it carries and expresses. Though different analytic techniques may be used for different types of cultural works, it is quite possible that one will discover the same cultural form shaping, say, an architect's cathedral, a musician's concerto and an artist's canvas. The spirit of an age can be objectified in any number of cultural media. Some cultural interpreters therefore look for the same recurring theses or motifs throughout the various branches of culture. As we shall see, such motif criticism of culture has been especially popular with Christian thinkers.

How does one justify one's interpretation of culture? Take the following perfunctory interpretation of contemporary civilization: the West in the 1990s is a carbohydrate culture. It is fattening, energetic, but ultimately short-lived and unfulfilling. What we need is more protein in our culture, the stuff of life, rather than a carbohydrate diet, which lives on stuff. Is this an insightful interpretation or not? What methods could we use to assess and evaluate such an interpretation? Like human being itself, cultures are susceptible to a number of different disciplinary explanations. For Freud, psychology unlocks the mystery that is humankind. For Marx, there is no mystery, only market economies. Does one academic discipline or scientific method explain culture better than the others? *Positivism* is the term for the belief that all phenomena can be explained with the same scientific method. Culture and the human beings who carry and create it constitute too rich a reality to yield up their meaning to a single explanatory framework, no matter how sophisticated.

Raymond Williams's *Culture* is an example, first, of a hermeneutical approach to culture from a nontheological discipline (sociology); second, it represents a hermeneutics of cultural suspicion, as well as a positivist (in this case "materialist") hermeneutics. Williams shares with Marx a certain skepticism with regard to the stories cultures tell about themselves. Marx argued that these stories are actually cleverly devised strategies for legitimating a certain political order and power structure. Even religion, Marx argued, serves a political purpose, distracting the masses from social injustices by encouraging them to project their hopes onto an otherworldly future. Religion, along with other cultural institutions, thus served, wittingly or unwittingly, an ideological function.

For Marx and Williams, an ideology is the principal set of beliefs and ideas that justify a certain social order. Ideology includes a group's conscious beliefs, as expounded in its philosophy, economics, law and so forth, as well as its less formulated attitudes and feelings, displayed in its drama, poetry, painting and other arts. Williams believes, as did Marx, that ideologies, while making a pretense to the status of objective knowledge, mask the real interests of those who wield cultural and political power. For Marx and Williams, one must approach culture with a hermeneutics of suspicion. The supposed values embodied in culture may only be a disguise for economic and political interests.

Williams is a cultural materialist. While acknowledging that culture pertains to the cultivation of a particular way of life, his real interest is in the (material) means and processes by which culture and even ideology develop. Whereas the cultural idealist lays emphasis on the "spirit" that informs cultural practices, Williams reverses the order and focuses on the cultural practices that constitute a culture's "spirit." For Marx, as for Williams, a society or culture can be explained only in historical and empirical terms. In other words, culture should be studied as a concrete form of life, in relation to rather than abstracted from the economic, technological and political forces of the day.

Williams's focus on cultural practices leads naturally to his adopting sociology as his method of choice. Sociology yields a method of observational analysis: "A *sociology* of culture must concern itself with the institutions and formations of cultural production."[13] As a sociologist of culture, Williams is more interested in explaining how cultural institutions such as universities and churches work to produce ideas and practices than in the truth or the rightness of these ideas and practices themselves. By explaining how cultural conditions change, Williams believes he can better account for a culture's *Zeitgeist*. This is a hermeneutics of suspicion. Williams believes he can unmask the lies cultures tell about themselves by discovering the material laws that govern their social conditions and relations. For instance, he believes that both the form and the content of the eighteenth-century realist novel can be "explained" in terms of certain social facts, such as the increasing importance of the bourgeoisie.

If Williams's sociological interpretation tends toward a materialist explanation of culture, speculative philosophers of history and philosophically oriented historians have traditionally fallen into the camp of the cultural idealists. Philosophical historians have tended to see ideas as the generative forces behind cultural practices, rather than the converse. Cultures are deemed to be understood if one can uncover the ideological basis or the root ideas that undergird and fund cultural production and social practice. The structure of cultural works reveals a more basic intellectual ground. A Mozart symphony, for instance, displays the "classical" mind, marked by a love of order, symmetry and balance—values that informed the politics and religion of the eighteenth century as well as its art. Speculative philosophers of history claim to have discovered overall patterns in the history of culture and civilization. Some believe the history of civilization to be progressive and linear; others believe it to be cyclical. In any case, these are further attempts to offer full-blown interpretations of world history. Interestingly enough, most speculative philosophers of history have tried to discover the purpose or meaning behind the pattern. Does the ebb and flow of culture and civilization have some ultimate purpose? With this question, the philosophy of history becomes positively religious in its hermeneutics of culture.

Enlightenment philosophers of history were generally not only cultural idealists but optimists as well. As cultural idealists, they believed that ideas tell the main story about culture. As cultural optimists, they believed that the march of ideas that informed culture was onward and upward. G. W. F. Hegel represents perhaps the clearest illustration of an idealist philosophical reading of the history of human culture. For Hegel, the history of culture is simply the story of the outworking of philosophical ideas. Hegel viewed human history as the progressive development of Mind or Spirit *(Geist)*. The "spirit" of an age is only one stage in the unfolding of Spirit,

---

[13]Williams, *Culture*, p. 30.

which is for Hegel the rational idea of freedom. For Hegel, the Spirit that animates human beings, the Spirit of reason, is moving inevitably toward absolute truth and freedom. Hegel believed that world history manifests this development of human freedom through successive types of social organizations, from the earlier master-slave organization through Stoicism and Christianity to, at last, Enlightenment rationality. Hegel immodestly viewed his own philosophy as the culmination of the whole process. He believed that his philosophy had absorbed whatever was of value in previous manifestations of Spirit, and that the history of ideas and culture alike had reached its peak around the year 1821, when he published his *Philosophy of Right*.

Hegel's philosophy is generally considered the last, and the greatest, attempt to gain a God's-eye point of view on human history. For Hegel, there is only one way to view the world—with the mind's eye. Hegel believed that he had not merely offered an interpretation of human history but actually attained absolute knowledge about it.

Hegel's example is instructive: human beings cannot adopt a perspective outside history from which to observe and interpret it. It was Hegel's obliviousness to the interpretive problem that led him to make pretentious claims to have discerned the one true "Spirit" that progressively informs every human culture.

After World War I, philosophers of history were less willing to speak of the "development" of ideas or culture. There was also an attempt to make the study of history more scientific and less speculative. Oswald Spengler represents both trends. Spengler believed that an inductive study of history would lead to the discovery of the laws that govern cultural development. These laws could then be used to predict what will happen in one's own culture. Spengler considered explanation by laws to be constitutive of science in general, including the human sciences. His was an attempt to overcome the dichotomy between the natural and human sciences in order to give his historical interpretation the prestige of the "hard" sciences such as physics. Accordingly, in his *Decline of the West* (1918-1922), Spengler argued that culture invariably passes through four stages (birth, maturity, old age and death) and that his own culture was no exception.

Several recent examples of historical and philosophical interpretations of society well demonstrate that the debate between cultural idealists and materialists is far from over. Again, the question concerns the relative priority of idea over the material conditions of social existence. As we try to make sense of a culture and its development, which do we say comes first, the principle or the practice?

For Arnold Toynbee, the proper object of historical study is not great individuals nor cultures but civilizations. Unlike Hegel, Toynbee viewed history as a series of back-and-forth movements in which civilizations rise and fall. Their fall is as much from internal failures as from external attacks. Toynbee's major project, his twelve-volume work entitled *A Study of History* (1934-1961), began when, at the beginning of World War I, he noted some striking similarities between ancient Greco-Roman and modern European civilizations. Toynbee found that civilizations, like texts, have certain structural similarities, certain recurring themes. He tended to portray his study of history as scientific and inductive. He looked at twenty-one civilizations, from Sumerian and Egyptian to the present, and discovered the same ebb-and-flow pattern. His critics have accused him of cultural eisegesis, of reading a pattern derived from ancient Hellenic culture into other, very different, civilizations. Again, the conflict of interpretations over civilizations is very much like debates between literary critics over texts. Disputes over how to identify a civilization are similar to debates over identifying a literary genre. Such identification is crucial to Toynbee's task, since the twenty-one civilizations he examined are species of the same genus.

Arthur Lovejoy, the first editor of the *Journal of the History of Ideas,* believed, as Francis Schaeffer did after him, in the efficacy of ideas. For Lovejoy, we understand a culture when we grasp its leading ideas. He was particularly intrigued when certain ideas, such as romanticism or evolution, migrated into fields with which they had no logical connection. An idea that began its life in biology (e.g., evolution) might turn up in art, logic or even religion. In the nineteenth century, for example, not only nature but also religion was thought to be subject to evolutionary development.

Ideas inform many aspects of a culture. In a similar vein, Franklin Baumer has written a history of ideas from the seventeenth to the twentieth centuries that tells the story of the gradual victory of the category of "becoming" over the category of "being." Baumer explains a wide number of cultural phenomena—including art, literature and theology—in terms of this ideological drama. What's in an idea? For Baumer, if "becoming" or flux is king, then all fixities and absolutes are banished: "It is hard to see how a civilization can long endure on becoming alone."[14]

By contrast with philosophers who believe that ideas are the hermeneutic key for unlocking the meaning of culture and its development, Fernand Braudel, the founder of the Annales school of French historiography, maintained that we understand history best by attending to the works of "Everyman" rather than "the Great Man." Instead of focusing on the acts and documents of kings and philosophers, Braudel investigates the documents of ordinary life: laundry lists, church registers and so on. Members of the Annales school believe that the history of culture must be written "horizontally"—that is, with reference to the broad social setting—not "vertically," with reference only to the ideas of great thinkers (mostly philosophers) who somehow transcend their times. The cultural historian should be just as interested in the opinions of the peasant as in the arguments of the philosopher. The

---

[14]Franklin Baumer, *Modern European Thought: Continuity and Change in Ideas, 1600-1950* (New York: Macmillan, 1977), p. 23.

"texts" that convey the meaning of culture are not only the great books but also the artifacts of day-to-day existence.

Theological Interpretation of Culture

Cornelius Van Til never tired of telling his theology students that created reality does not exist as brute, uninterpreted fact. It is always already meaningful because it is interpreted by God. The theologian's task is thus to "think God's thoughts after him." The contrast between a secular and a theological hermeneutics of cultural history may be illustrated by comparing Edward Gibbon's and Augustine's interpretations of the fall of ancient Rome. Gibbon's *History of the Decline and Fall of the Roman Empire* (1776) is one of the greatest histories ever written in English. Gibbon's thesis is that Christianity was the central destructive force in the Empire's collapse, a collapse that meant the triumph of barbarism and religion. Christianity, in Gibbon's view, far from leading to a Protestant work ethic (Max Weber's idea to explain the culture of European capitalism), led to the undermining of the Roman ethical system—that is, their rational pursuit of virtue and rewards. Gibbon thus offers a naturalistic explanation of the fall of Rome that casts the Christian faith as the villain.

Augustine's interpretation, on the other hand, is supernaturalistic. His *City of God* (412-426) is not simply a history of Rome; it is a Christian philosophy of world history in general as well as a penetrating theological analysis of human culture and its religious roots. Augustine envisaged the course of human history as a struggle between two communities: the earthly city of Man and the heavenly city of God. Through divine revelation we know that the city of God (i.e., the church, which has better claim to the epithet "the eternal city" than Rome) will ultimately triumph. Augustine's interpretive framework, with divine providence as its essential feature, is theological and supernaturalistic. History includes the marks of *God* in the past, and all human culture is to be interpreted as either aiding or hindering the progress of the city of God.

Augustine's *City of God* is often treated as a speculative philosophy of history because it applies a conceptual framework to experience. For Augustine, it is the mind's eye, illumined by faith, that perceives the meaning and significance of the historical process. Where empirical observation may perceive historical cycles, it cannot explain the reasons behind these cycles. The goal that gives meaning to history is itself outside history. It is an eschatological work of God in the future. Here we may indeed speak of the world as "well staged," for Augustine presents world history as a drama that has a divinely appointed beginning, climax and conclusion. History is not cyclical; rather, it is a progressive linear sequence, with humankind as a "subplot" in the divine comedy.

A large part of the *City of God* consists in debunking pagan myths and earthly values, which for Augustine are temporary and therefore of only relative worth. The fall of Rome is the indictment not of Christianity but of sin, for the city of Man is characterized by self-love rather than by love of God. True freedom and goodness can never be attained on the basis of self-love, for human fulfillment ultimately depends on something greater than humanity. Human being is fulfilled only by the love of God. This is the meaning of pagan culture for Augustine: self-centered humanism is ultimately self-defeating.

In the twenty-first century, Augustinian interpretation of culture is perhaps best represented by Dutch-American Reformed theology. To be Reformed in the Dutch-American tradition means taking Calvin's principle of the sovereignty of God and applying it to all areas and aspects of life. Christ is Lord of culture. Evangelicals such as Carl Henry have agreed with Abraham Kuyper and Herman Dooyeweerd that the Christian world and life view must be related to all areas of culture.[15] For Kuyper, Calvinism means recognizing the lordship of Christ over all areas of life. This recognition led him in 1880 to found the Free University of Amsterdam as a place where the Bible may be applied to all aspects of life and thought. Culture is not some neutral, nontheological activity but an activity that is inherently religious. Every sculpture, every film, every novel, every building, every expression of human freedom in some concrete form presupposes some worldview, a set of beliefs and ideas about the nature of ultimate reality and the good.

For Kuyper, the dichotomy between sacred and secular is misbegotten if the earth, and all that is in it, is indeed the Lord's. No human activity is religiously neutral: "I maintain that it is the interpretation of our relation to God which dominates every general life system."[16] Kuyper pictures not two cities but two world and life views engaged in mortal combat: modernism, which builds its worldview on naturalistic principles, and Calvinism, which constructs its worldview from Christian principles.[17] Kuyper argues, for example, that though Calvin himself was not artistically inclined, his theological principle of the lordship of Christ allowed him to view art as a divine gift. Art for Calvin is not simply an imitation of nature but a means of disclosing a higher reality than our present fallen world. Art gives us a taste of creation and restoration, of the beauty that was God's original intent for the world. Art that points back to creation and forward to redemption is thus truer than art that merely imitates our fallen present. The values embodied by art are inescapably religious; art makes theological statements.

---

[15] See George M. Marsden, "Reformed and American," in *Reformed Theology in America*, ed. David F. Wells (Grand Rapids, Mich.: Eerdmans, 1985), pp. 1-12, for the "culturalist" tradition in Reformed theology.

[16] Kuyper, *Lectures on Calvinism*, p. 24.

[17] Kuyper believed that Calvinism embodies the Christian principle—the lordship of Christ—more purely and consistently than other Christian movements (ibid., p. 17).

Dooyeweerd, another Dutch Calvinist, similarly argues that the roots of culture are always religious. Dooyeweerd claims that every culture is animated by a religious "ground motive."[18] This ground motive is the basic direction of an individual's or society's life, the source of its energy and direction—its "heart." On the deepest level, every culture is driven by either a God-affirming or a God-denying ground motive. These ground motives are not only the forces that shape cultures and communities; they are also the "hermeneutic keys for understanding and interpreting periods and patterns of history and culture."[19] Dooyeweerd thus interprets the history of Western civilization in terms of the religious ground motive that shapes a given culture. If cultures are texts, then Dooyeweerd's ambition is to uncover their "deep grammar."

What other thinkers have called the "spirit" of the age is for Dooyeweerd a religious spirit, one that either accepts or denies God's lordship over culture and creation. For Dooyeweerd, the Christian's ground motive is creation-fall-redemption. Fallenness means that human culture will always be, at best, "on the way." Redemption means that human culture should actively affirm, in the power of the Spirit, God's rule over all creation. In Dooyeweerd's scheme, modern culture stems from Kant's "nature and freedom" ground motive, a motive that denies the religious character of life and thought. Instead of recognizing the authority of God over all areas of life and thought, modern culture, animated by the religious ground motive of freedom and nature, has declared its autonomy. The world stage includes only nature and natural facts on the one hand and free human beings with their self-made values on the other. Modern human beings are therefore a law unto themselves. Modern culture is simply an expression of this ground motive.

Two other thinkers, from different theological traditions, largely agree with Augustine and Kuyper with regard to the essentially religious nature of culture. T. S. Eliot, in his *Notes Towards the Definition of Culture,* suggests that culture and religion are roughly synonymous: "We may ask . . . whether what we call the culture, and what we call the religion, of a people are not different aspects of the same thing: the culture being, essentially, the incarnation (so to speak) of the religion of a people."[20] For Eliot this implies two things: (1) that culture cannot be preserved in the absence of religion and (2) that religion cannot be preserved in the absence of culture. What then is culture? Eliot suggests that it refers to that which makes life worth living, that which creates a meaningful home out of an otherwise impersonal cosmos. *Culture* refers to the characteristic interests and activities of a people; for Eliot, an English-

---

[18]See C. T. McIntyre's chapter on Dooyeweerd in *Reformed Theology in America,* ed. David F. Wells (Grand Rapids, Mich.: Eerdmans, 1985), pp. 172-85.

[19]Dooyeweerd, *Roots of Western Culture,* p. x.

[20]T. S. Eliot, *Notes Towards the Definition of Culture* (London: Faber & Faber, 1948), p. 28. Subsequent citations will be made parenthetically in the text.

man, these included the annual Henley Regatta (a boat race), the dart board, Wensleydale cheese, nineteenth-century Gothic churches and the music of Edward Elgar.

According to Eliot, culture is lived religion: "behaviour is also belief" (p. 32). Where does one learn patterns of behavior? For Eliot, the primary channel of transmission of culture is the family. It is in the life of the family that religion is "interpreted" in terms of daily life. Can there be a family of nations united by Christian faith? Some forty-five years before the founding of the European Economic Community, Eliot raised the question of the unity of European culture. The problem he correctly foresaw was this: true religious reunion involves a community of culture, not simply a common profession of faith. Without a common faith, "all efforts towards drawing nations closer together in culture can produce only an illusion of unity" (p. 82). Cultures themselves are mired in a conflict of interpretations about the way to the good life. The only common point is the common spiritual heritage of Europe—the Christian Scriptures and the Christian faith: "I do not believe that the culture of Europe could survive the complete disappearance of the Christian faith" (p. 122). The greatest task at hand, according to Eliot, is preserving our common culture and our spiritual heritage. Europe's very survival depends on its continual mining of culture for the religious roots that sustain it.

Yet another Protestant theologian, Paul Tillich, also believes that culture is essentially religious. Tillich produced what was perhaps the most comprehensive theology of culture in the twentieth century. In his view, simply being human is a fundamentally religious enterprise. To be or not to be, to exist as finite, raises ultimate questions for any human being who pauses to consider his or her situation. What is our situation? Danger lurks just offstage; our being is threatened in many ways. First of all, there is the threat of nonbeing—that is, death. Second, we find ourselves morally responsible for our being, and this leads us to the threat of guilt and condemnation. And finally, there is the threat that we will find no meaning to our lives. Tillich calls these the anxieties of death, guilt and meaninglessness, respectively.[21] Furthermore, Tillich interprets the history of Western civilization in terms of a progression through these three anxieties. Ancient civilizations were preoccupied with death and immortality; medieval cultures centered their reflection and activity on the problem of sin and salvation; and the modern age desperately seeks alternatives to the despair of spiritual emptiness.

Tillich believes that the human condition as such, whatever the age or culture, provokes religious questions. Ordinary human experience is anxious; human being is always a question, and a religious question at that. This is so because for Tillich

---

[21]See Paul Tillich, *The Courage to Be* (New Haven, Conn.: Yale University Press, 1952), pp. 40-63.

religion has to do with an individual's or a people's ultimate concern. Religion has to do with the "depth dimension" of all human experience. What does Tillich mean by "depth"? "It means that the religious aspect points to that which is ultimate, infinite, unconditional in man's spiritual life."[22] *Religion* is the name for that which concerns us ultimately.

Tillich's interpretation of the human condition and human culture is ontological or existential. An analysis of the human situation inevitably leads to the question of how we can overcome the anxieties that are part and parcel of our being human. This is a religious question, a question about something that concerns us ultimately. Religion is the state of being grasped by an ultimate concern. In Tillich's concise but important formula, "religion is the substance of culture, culture is the form of religion. . . . He who can read the style of a culture can discover its ultimate concern, its religious substance."[23]

Each of the theologians surveyed here shares the conviction that culture is a form of lived religion. We learn what a people really believes and values by interpreting that people's works, art and forms of life. However, the principles of cultural hermeneutics differ from theologian to theologian. Augustine, Kuyper and Dooyeweerd are tied to biblical motifs in a way that Tillich is not. But common to all of them is the belief that there is no such thing as a purely secular culture; the way people live and express themselves in their works has religious meaning. "By their fruits ye shall know them" (Mt 7:20 KJV). Culture is thus the fruit of a theology or a worldview.

After noting the Thomism of Dante, the Calvinism of Rembrandt, the Lutheranism of Bach and the Puritanism of Milton, Denis de Rougement remarked that neither nineteenth- nor twentieth-century liberalism had similarly inspired any great artist or poet.[24] If culture is the fruit of theology, what happens to culture when God is not merely debilitated but dead? Nietzsche announced God's demise in the late nineteenth century, and the message was repeated in the 1960s. If culture is a form of lived religion, what might a posttheistic culture look like? I believe it looks something like our present culture of radical hermeneutics. After all, if there is no God, as Dostoyevsky said, everything is permitted . . .

The Culture of Hermeneutics
To this point we have been considering culture as a hermeneutical phenomenon. Culture, that shared set of meaningful human activities and works that express ultimate beliefs and values, is a "religious" text that calls for theological interpretation.

---

[22]Paul Tillich, *Theology of Culture* (London: Oxford University Press, 1959), p. 7.
[23]Ibid., pp. 42-43.
[24]Recounted in Bernard Ramm, *After Fundamentalism* (San Francisco: Harper & Row, 1983), p. 175.

We have seen how theology functions in the hermeneutics of culture, but what of theology's role in the present culture of hermeneutics? By speaking of the "culture of hermeneutics" I mean to call attention to the fact that more and more academic disciplines (including theology) have become increasingly aware of their own hermeneutic status. Epistemology, the study of the nature and means of knowledge, has taken on a hermeneutical hue. *Homo sapiens* has given way to *Homo interpretans*. We humans see very little of reality directly; we see neither its ultimate subatomic components nor its meaning. What knowledge we have is not direct but indirect—that is, the world comes to us mediated through language. Hermeneutics is an interdisciplinary phenomenon because all disciplines meet on the common ground of language.

The extension of hermeneutics beyond its original home in literary criticism reaches even into the natural sciences.[25] Thomas Kuhn has argued that even the scientist's eye is not innocent: all observations are theory-laden. The scientist comes to "objective data" with some kind of interpretive framework already in place (Kuhn calls it a "paradigm"). "An apparently arbitrary element, compounded of personal and historical accident, is always a formative ingredient of the beliefs espoused by a given scientific community at a given time."[26] In other words, scientists are caught up in the hermeneutical circle with the rest of us.

Recent philosophers of science acknowledge the hermeneutical dimension of the natural sciences by speaking of theories as "models." Ian Barbour defines a model as "an imaginative tool for ordering experience, rather than a description of the world."[27] Barbour says that scientists take their models seriously but not literally. They are heuristic devices—"useful fictions." Max Black has compared scientific models to poetic metaphors: both the scientist and the poet explore various aspects of reality by using language in a creative way.[28] Science involves inventing and interpreting metaphorical models of the real. Mary Hesse is quite explicit about the hermeneutical dimension of the natural sciences: "My thesis is that there is . . . a linear continuum between the empirical and the hermeneutic. . . . At each stage of the continuum, appropriate interpretive conditions enter the process of theorizing."[29] Truly, the book of nature has become a text.

"Textuality" is indeed one of the leading notions that distinguish the contemporary "postmodern" situation from the "modern" era. Everything from dreams to denim is

---

[25]See Vern S. Poythress, *Science and Hermeneutics* (Grand Rapids, Mich.: Zondervan, 1988).
[26]Thomas Kuhn, *The Structure of Scientific Revolutions* (Chicago: University of Chicago Press, 1970), p. 4.
[27]Ian Barbour, *Myths, Models and Paradigms: A Comparative Study in Science and Religion* (San Francisco: Harper & Row, 1974), p. 6.
[28]See Max Black, *Models and Metaphors* (Ithaca, N.Y.: Cornell University Press, 1962).
[29]Mary Hesse, *Revolutions and Reconstructions in the Philosophy of Science* (Bloomington: Indiana University Press, 1980), p. 225.

today regarded as text. Not only words but the clothes we wear and the cars we drive are "signs" in a system of signs. The study of sign systems, or "semiotics," derives from a series of lectures on linguistics delivered by Ferdinand de Saussure at the University of Geneva between 1906 and 1911. Saussure argued that the relation of signs (signifiers) to things or concepts (signified) is a matter of arbitrary social convention. It just so happens that the sign GOD signifies a supreme being and DOG a canine being. More recently Roland Barthes and Umberto Eco, among others, have argued that the theory of semiotics may be applied beyond words to a whole range of cultural phenomena. Everything in culture is a signifier in some system of signs. A Ford Escort sends one signal about one's social status, a Porsche quite another. Perfumes, hairstyles, movies, toys, margarine, shoes—all signify.

Augustine and other Christian theologians would be happy to accept, I think, this "textuality" of culture. A dividing of the ways appears only when one asks whether such and such a text has a determinate meaning.[30] A number of French thinkers in the 1960s applied Saussure's insights into the arbitrariness of language to texts in general. Every text is an indeterminate signifying system, a network of signs that refer to one another. Furthermore, it is impossible to stop the "play" of signs and say decisively what a text means. Why? Because the signs do not refer to reality but to one another; they gain their meaning precisely through their opposition to other signs (*hot-cold, green-red,* etc.). A text has a "texture" but no substance. Its meaning is indeterminate. To define "the" meaning of a text would be considered the height of hermeneutic pontification; there is simply no one correct order of an arbitrary sign system.

For Barthes, this is a liberating discovery because the reader is freed to be creative. Like Nietzsche, Barthes believes we are never more human than when we are creating our own meaning and values. The alternative is the hermeneutic bondage of having to discover the "correct" interpretation of a text. Barthes maintains that sign systems are open, susceptible to many combinations. The point, after all, is to play with the text as one would with a Rubik's cube that had no one solution. In order to achieve total interpretive freedom, however, Barthes has to get rid of the idea of an "author." Barthes says the author must die so that the reader may live. But this is simply a repetition on the textual level of the death of God (the Author of all) on the metaphysical level. What is the meaning of life? If there is no Author, no authority, who can say? Once one abandons the idea of determinate textual meaning and correct textual interpretation, everything in interpretation is permitted. The death of God thus leads to the cult of Hermes.

---

[30]See Kevin Vanhoozer, *Is There a Meaning in This Text? The Bible, the Reader and the Morality of Literary Knowledge* (Grand Rapids, Mich.: Zondervan, 1998).

Postmodern is the name many give to the present culture of hermeneutics.[31] John Caputo believes that the postmodern world has abandoned modernism's metaphysical quest and embraced a radical hermeneutics. Metaphysics is the attempt to answer rationally the ultimate questions concerning life and reality. The modern world believed that reason in its metaphysical mood could reach and formulate these universal truths. Hermeneutics, on the other hand, restores life to its "original difficulty," to use Caputo's phrase. Radical hermeneutics "exposes us to the ruptures and gaps, let us say, the textuality and difference, which inhabit everything we think, and do, and hope for."[32] To have answers for the ultimate questions of life is to have the "one true perspective," the one true interpretation of the book of life. And this is precisely what postmodernist thinkers deny to human beings. Human being is irremediably perspectival. The way we think, talk, perceive, communicate, act, marry, play—all these activities, including knowing, are conditioned by our "place." One's outlook on God, self and world is affected by the time and place in which one lives, one's upbringing, one's social class, one's sex, one's biochemistry and so on. Metaphysics is a hopeless quest for an epistemological grail. The most a thinker can hope for is not knowledge but an interesting interpretation.

The postmodern mindset and culture alike are characterized by self-consciousness. Postmodern authors and artists are all too aware of the fact that they are writing, that they are painting—so much so that their writing and painting represent not reality but rather writing and painting! Postmodern writing, art and television call attention to their artificial, human-made nature. For Jean-François Lyotard, the postmodern condition is suspicious of all "metanarratives," those stories that pretend to explain everyone else's story and tell it the way it is.[33] Postmodern culture no longer believes in such metanarratives, be they Marxist, rationalist or Christian. What this means is that there is no overarching story that will inform culture. Instead Lyotard looks forward to a way of life that would celebrate "tribal" diversity. For Lyotard, freedom means that everyone can tell, and enact, his or her own story or narrative. In the postmodern world reality disintegrates into myriad stories and systems of signs.

Jean Baudrillard believes that the television screen is the most appropriate meta-

---

[31]Scott Lash believes postmodernism is a kind of culture and thus is open to sociological description. He believes that whereas modern culture differentiated between the theoretical, ethical and aesthetic realms, postmodern culture is characterized by "de-differentiation." In postmodernism the lines between the theoretical, moral and aesthetic begin to blur, as does the line between reality and its representation. See his *Sociology of Postmodernism* (London: Routledge, 1990), pp. 9-13.

[32]John Caputo, *Radical Hermeneutics: Repetition, Deconstruction and the Hermeneutic Project* (Bloomington: Indiana University Press, 1987), p. 6.

[33]See Jean-François Lyotard, *The Postmodern Condition: A Report on Knowledge* (Manchester, U.K.: Manchester University Press, 1984).

phor for postmodern culture. Instead of the permanence of a painting, television is an electronic field of flickering images. Television is "a world of simulations detached from reference to the real, which circulate and exchange in ceaseless, centreless flow."[34] One clear instance of this is the rock video, where images of past and present, dreams and waking ceaselessly intermingle, thus short-circuiting any attempt to privilege one image and use it as an interpretive key of the whole.

Theology is not immune from the influence of its surrounding culture. A number of theologians have been hard at work on a hermeneutical or postmodern theology. David Tracy understands *modern* as referring to the conviction that the human subject is rational and can attain knowledge and truth. But this Enlightenment "faith" is now at an end. Tracy acknowledges, with other postmodern thinkers, the finite and perspectival nature of all human knowing. We must interpret because of the plurality and ambiguity of language and history. Though all cognition is interpretation, Tracy believes that a more modest form of rationality survives the passing of modernity: conversation. In conversation one respects the other's interpretation as much as one's own. Rationality is the art of conversing about texts; rationality is hermeneutical. Religion here performs an invaluable service according to Tracy: its object—the Transcendent—serves as a permanent reminder that our attempts at knowing will always be incomplete. Religion reminds us that no one is in a position to dominate or end the conversation. For Tracy this means that the Christian theologian cannot assume that the Christian metanarrative—the gospel—is superior to the stories of other religions. There is no room for absolutes in the hermeneutic inn.[35]

Don Cupitt welcomes the end of modernity and its myth of a transcendent rational order. For Cupitt, postmodernism means ceasing to believe in any absolute Beginning or End, Ground or Presence. Augustine's world, where everything is a sign for something eternal, has been stood on its head. Or better, his world has been declared flat. Cupitt writes: "The interpretive movement is not from sign directly on to thing signified, but sideways from sign to sign."[36] The end of fixed views and the reign of flux means that humans are free to be creative: "It is up to *us* to reimagine Christianity, to re-invent faith for our time" (p. 2). Theology, like poetry, must conjure up a meaningful world out of nothing. Creation ex nihilo characterizes the theologian's work, not God's. Worldviews are imaginative creations. Modern metaphysics was just pretentious poetry.

---

[34]Jean Baudrillard, quoted in Steven Connor, *Postmodernist Culture: An Introduction to Theories of the Contemporary* (Oxford: Blackwell, 1989), p. 168.

[35]See David Tracy, *Plurality and Ambiguity: Hermeneutics, Religion, Hope* (San Francisco: Harper & Row, 1987).

[36]Don Cupitt, *The Long-Legged Fly: A Theology of Language and Desire* (London: SCM Press, 1987), p. 21. Subsequent citations will be made parenthetically in the text.

But if we are honest about the fictions we fabricate, can we really believe and respect them? Imaginative visions can after all be generated from reason as well as madness, and indeed, who is to say which is which?

One of the aims of culture is the preservation of knowledge, creative achievements and values. Those who contribute to culture believe that there is a meaning that is worth transmitting to others. But Cupitt questions whether culture really expresses timeless truths. Both philosophy and theology have claimed to teach truth, and in the case of Christianity the church has often exercised a cultural hegemony: "God was the absolute Memory, the guarantor of lasting knowledge and value and the refuge from the mere contingency that people need if life is to have worth" (p. 84). But for Cupitt, an apostle of postmodernism, the use of God to validate cultural norms is illegitimate. "Language and interpretation are beginningless and endless in a way that rules out ideas of indisputable first principles and final truths" (p. 88).

Cupitt's cult and culture of Hermes lead, ironically, to the annihilation of the very idea of culture. In the end, he must conclude that nothing is worth preserving. Anything permanent would be a burdensome restriction on his freedom to create endlessly his sideways world. The culture of hermeneutics is one of free play, where everything is turned sideways, upside down and inside out. Devotees of the cult of Hermes thus lead lives of riotous interpretive play; their worship is neither in spirit nor in truth, but in the carelessness of carnival.[37]

Theology and the Critical Reconstruction of Culture

A critical hermeneutics of culture is committed, first, to discovering what a civilization is up to. Theological criticism of contemporary culture discovers that the "lived religion" behind postmodern culture is the religion of Hermes, the winged messenger, god of mystical doctrines and patron of thieves. It celebrates rather than confesses its article of faith—that there is no authorized version of reality, only interpretation. Postmodernism means the priesthood of all believers minus a text in which to believe.

If the Author is dead, does all authority disappear too? Not necessarily. In the postmodern world, the priesthood of all believers leads to mass culture. In mass culture authority becomes a function of popular opinion. Indeed Julian Hartt defines mass culture as "the elevation of popular taste and conviction to an effectively unchallenged supremacy over all the principal modes of action and thought in our civilization."[38] How can such a culture be criticized or reformed? Hartt laments the church's loss of

---

[37]For an explication of the suitability of this metaphor, see Nathan Scott, "The House of Intellect in an Age of Carnival: Some Hermeneutical Reflections," in *The Whirlwind in Culture: Frontiers in Theology*, ed. Donald W. Musser and Joseph L. Price (New York: Meyer-Stone, 1988), pp. 39-54, esp. p. 42.

[38]Hartt, *Christian Critique*, p. 391.

prophetic voice: "Popular Christianity is rapidly approaching the state of perfect homogenization. It is religiousness rather than faith; it is geniality rather than love; it is wish rather than hope; it is opinion rather than truth."[39] The Christian criticism of mass culture must begin with the church, with those in the household of faith.

In a culture of hermeneutics, there is more need than ever for theology—even in the church. But what can theology offer? What should be its reaction to the deconstruction of stories, texts and whole cultures? Theology must become involved in the reconstruction of culture. Theology must lay the intellectual foundations for lived biblical religion. It must serve the community of interpreters who believe that the Bible witnesses to God's acts in the world and in his Word, Jesus Christ. Amid the ruins of our age, biblical interpretation is the best means of rebuilding the walls of a culture originally built upon the Book.

The community of biblical interpreters is, of course, the church. The church is a hermeneutical community, a community of interpreters constituted by the Word and enlivened by the Spirit. Indeed the Spirit is the enabling power that ministers the Word and renders it effective. Hermeneutics, we may recall, involves not only the explanation of textual meaning but also its appropriation. It is not enough to explain what a text once meant; one must decode what it means today. Meaning must be *applied*—to the church, to the world, to oneself. Hermeneutics, in the broadest sense of the term, pertains not only to "hearing" but also to "doing" the word. The most important interpretation of the Bible is the way we live our lives. We appropriate the meaning of a text when we let its world into ours, when we put its pages into our practice. We apply a text's meaning to our lives when we perform the text. Our response to a text constitutes its "lived meaning."

We have examined the hermeneutics of culture and the culture of hermeneutics. What I am now proposing to consider is hermeneutics itself as a means of constructing culture. A community's performance of a text gives rise to a particular way of life and thus to a particular culture. Augustine's rules for biblical interpretation, for example, yielded a Christian culture that lasted almost a thousand years.[40] Hermeneutics—the art and science of applying as well as interpreting texts—is thus an important aspect of creating cultures. Ricoeur speaks of living in the "world" of the text. If we dwell in a text's world long enough, it will begin to shape our vision and our values. This is the function of culture—the world of meaning—too. It is by faith that the community of biblical interpreters believingly enters the text; it is the Spirit who enables the Word's world to cultivate the image of God that we bear and that we are. The church's aim should be to render a faithful interpretation of Scripture.

---

[39]Ibid., p. 394.
[40]See Augustine's *On Christian Doctrine*, trans. D. W. Robertson Jr. (Indianapolis: Bobbs-Merrill, 1958).

Augustine's rule for biblical interpretation can be neatly extended to the church's interpretive performance: when faced with a plethora of possible meanings, choose the interpretation that fosters love of God and love of neighbor. "Correct" interpretation of Scripture means living a life of love and service to God, to the church as the people of God, and to the world. We really understand the story of Jesus only when we perform it.

Performing the story of Jesus leads to an interpretive practice that challenges the predominant cultural trend. The story of Jesus is one of humiliation and exaltation, in that order. Hearing and doing the story of Jesus produces a style of life characterized by humility, service and love. But these theological virtues must characterize our hermeneutic practice too. The church should strive to exemplify what for lack of a better term we might call the "hermeneutics of faith," a hermeneutic not of irresponsible iconoclasm nor of prideful play but of charity and humility. A theological hermeneutics of faith will resist both dogmatism (interpretive pride) and skepticism (interpretive sloth). On the one hand, it will not claim too much for itself; its commentary must never presume to usurp the primary text. On the other hand, a hermeneutics of faith respects the text as a given. A hermeneutics of faith will work to seek textual understanding. This means attending to and respecting the text's voice rather than one's own.

This last point is important. The church is not immune to the conflict of interpretations. Are there any norms that may help us decide which community's reading or performance of Scripture is the most adequate? There are, I believe, two such criteria. The first is the text itself, the fixed point from which various interpretations may be challenged. As Martin Luther successfully demonstrated during the Reformation, the text can be used *against* the community of its interpreters. Second, some interpretations or performances of a text may be more "fruitful" than others. But what does "fruitful" mean in the context of biblical hermeneutics? It means, first, a reading that explains more of the text and displays more of its rich internal coherence. But second, an interpretation may be judged to be fruitful if it disperses the riches of the text among its readers. Augustine pointed to charity as a kind of criterion for a good reading of the Bible. Jesus said we would recognize his disciples by their love. Should we not therefore prefer the reading that gives rise to a way of living that most approximates the life of Jesus himself, the harbinger of the kingdom of God? Orthopraxis—right living—is a sign of the Spirit's enlivening presence with the Word. Christian culture is not just a means to preach the gospel; it is rather the means for us to come to know the gospel and to know what it means. Christ must be not only the eternal Word but also the church's "living idiom."[41]

---

[41]Hartt, *Christian Critique*, p. 353.

Culture and readers alike are restored only by God's grace. The story of Jesus Christ, his "lived meaning," has been staged in our world through the centuries by his body, the church. Again, it is the Spirit who animates this life. We can perform the gospel only because the gospel has been lived by Christ and then enabled by his Spirit. It is for these reasons that Donald Bloesch can speak of "God the Civilizer."[42] Culture, according to Bloesch, "is the divinely appointed means for men and women to realize their humanity."[43] As such, culture is both human achievement and divine gift.

It is the church's role to be a light to the nations. The church should be the model for the right use of human freedom; the church should be the civilized society par excellence. The community of believers represents a prophetic counterculture that challenges the gods and myths of the day with regard to which world and life view best fulfills humanity. The church's challenge will only be as strong as its expression of the biblical world and life view. Again, this is not only a matter of correct doctrine but also a matter of faithful biblical performance. The church must be the cultural incarnation of the story of God in Christ. Bloesch is careful to note that the church is in no position to lord it over secular culture; its performance of Scripture will also be reviewed. Karl Barth viewed the world as the field, but not the source, of the redemptive activity of God. Though human culture can be influenced by the divine command and the divine promise, the kingdom of God will always "outrun" human achievements.[44] The church is to be a humble witness to the kingdom of God, not its political administrator.

The believing community "reads" the world in light of the Word of God. In other words, the church interprets the world and the surrounding culture through the lens of the biblical text. But just as important, its hermeneutics of faith issues in a community performance of the biblical texts. To repeat: it is not enough to hear and understand; one must also appropriate the meaning of a text and "do" the words. To understand the Bible properly is to "follow" it, and this in two senses. First, we follow a text when we understand it, when we grasp its meaning. But "follow" also means going along a particular path or way. To follow the Word in this sense is to put it into practice, to perform it. The hermeneutics of faith demands nothing less than discipleship. Faith comes from hearing and reading the Word of God. To have Christian faith means having your thinking, imagining, language and life shaped by the biblical texts—by biblical law, wisdom, songs, apocalyptic, prophecy, gospel and doctrine.

---

[42]Donald Bloesch, "God the Civilizer," in *Christian Faith and Practice in the Modern World: Theology from an Evangelical Point of View*, ed. Mark A. Noll and David F. Wells (Grand Rapids, Mich.: Eerdmans, 1988), pp. 176-98.

[43]Ibid., p. 177.

[44]See Karl Barth, "Church and Culture," in *Theology and Church: Shorter Writings, 1920-1928*, trans. L. Pettibone Smith (New York: Harper & Row, 1962).

These literary forms of Scripture are constitutive of Christian identity and practice alike. Literary critic William Beardslee wrote: "A particular literary style is not only appropriate to, but generative of, a life style."[45] An "evangelical" is one whose life and thought conform to the gospel of Jesus Christ. The believer performs the gospel (*euangelion*) when he or she puts it into practice, following the Word to grace and freedom in Christ, and then showing and telling others the way to follow.

The way of life generated by the biblical texts is not, ultimately, the way of this world. Insofar as the church successfully performs Scripture, it will produce a culture that far from being in easy complicity with the world, will be a permanent revolution. The world is the theater of action for the people of God, not their final home. It is at best a staging area for a group of wandering pilgrims and minstrels who perform parables of the kingdom of God. Culture that is genuinely evangelical accepts the gospel as the given from which it first derived its life and upon which it continues to draw for its intellectual, imaginative and practical resources. Culture is evangelical if it accepts the revelation of God in Christ and the salvation of God in Christ. Its response to God's grace (*charis*) should be *eucharist*—thanksgiving and gratitude. *Evangelical culture is the eucharistic response to the gift of Christian freedom.*

Culture is, as we have seen, the sphere in which freedom manifests itself. Cultivating Spirit-given freedom is perhaps our greatest privilege; it is certainly our greatest responsibility. The most important interpretive task of the church is to create an evangelical, eucharistic culture in which Christian freedom would be expressed in obedience to God and oriented to God's glory. It is neither trivial nor irrelevant that Johann Sebastian Bach concluded each of his musical compositions with the dedication "Sola Dei Gloria."

A hermeneutics of faith concerns itself with the interpretation of texts that purport to engender and give shape to human freedom. After all, culture is about shaping human freedom into social practices that express ultimate values and fulfill human beings. A hermeneutics of Christian faith interprets the world in terms of the literary framework of the Word. In light of this Word, we must conclude that the so-called freedom of our contemporary culture of hermeneutics is illusory. Freedom that leads to the frustration rather than fulfillment of human being is not true freedom at all.

But this is only the negative, critical side of a hermeneutics of faith. Its positive agenda is expressed by two phrases: "faith seeking understanding" and "understanding seeking faithful performance." To be an interpreter means to be an incessant seeker. If we no longer needed to search for meanings, we would have absolute knowledge, and interpretation would no longer be needed. If we no longer needed

---

[45]William Beardslee, *Literary Criticism of the New Testament* (Philadelphia: Fortress, 1970), p. 76.

to criticize our performances, we would have absolute goodness. We who live on Middle-earth, however, have neither absolute knowledge nor absolute goodness; hermeneutics is thus our common human lot—our privilege and our responsibility.

The interpretations and performances of saints and sinners will always fall short. But through Christ, a new "culture" has entered the world and is growing at a fabulous rate, a benign bacterium with the power to heal humanity. I refer of course to the culture engendered by the Word of God and sustained by the Spirit. At first no louder than a whisper, the Christian story quickly toppled empires and gave birth to civilizations. Our Christian performances are not in vain because of the living Word's performance in the first act. The community of faith continues the story, sustained by memory and hope. It lives in the second act—commemorating the first, holding its breath for the last. Christian interpreters perform not gospel but apocalyptic when they contemplate that glorious Finale, when the world will indeed be well staged and all manner of things shall be well.

Twelve

The Trials of Truth

*Mission, Martyrdom &
the Epistemology of the Cross*

*W*hat might Christian theology have to contribute by way of response to the epistemological predicament of postmodernity? This essay explores a number of parallels and contrasts between the narrative of the trial of Jesus and the contemporary trials of truth by the postmodern masters of suspicion. "The trials of truth" signals, in the first place, the severe troubles faced by the concept of truth in contemporary culture and contemporary thought. Second, the notion of the "trials of truth" leads to a renewed appreciation of the role of the person in staking a claim and to a focus on "testifying" as a speech act, rather than restricting the discussion either to basic propositions or to justificatory procedures.

My goal is to offer an expansionist account of epistemology by thinking through its relation with ethics. This leads to a reflection on recent "virtue epistemologies" that highlight the role of intellectual virtues in achieving justified belief and that make wisdom rather than mere knowledge the ultimate goal of cognitive endeavor. Rationality, I argue, is a matter of developing epistemic virtue and wisdom rather than merely acquiring knowledge. Finally, a contrast of the trials of Socrates and Jesus brings my discussion of the intellectual virtues into relation with the so-called theological virtues, highlights the importance of the concept of testimony, and clarifies the peculiar intellectual virtues associated with the "epistemology of the Cross."[1]

---

[1] I offer these reflections in part to commemorate the one hundred fiftieth anniversary of the publication of Søren Kierkegaard's "On the Difference Between a Genius and an Apostle" (1847), an essay that has proven to be of seminal value in regard to the conception of the present work.

Crusade, Pilgrimage or Missionary Journey?

Knowledge claims are today poised unsteadily between epistemology, missiology and ideology. A truth claim is a statement on a mission—to be precise, a statement on a mission of truth, whose goal is to procure universal acknowledgment.[2] The problem is how to construe the nature of this mission: Is it heroic or hopeless, imperialistic or impotent? Will the claimant return covered in glory or empty-handed?

The project: The evangelical truth claim. The theologian's primary task is faithfully and intelligibly to render the claim that "God was in Christ reconciling the world to himself." But there is an important preliminary task as well.

Today it is not discrete packages of truth content that need to be defended so much as the concept of truth itself. How can truth claims fulfill their mission in a postmodern world? Three intimidating obstacles bar the way to success.

1. *The problem of perspective and partiality.* What people see is affected by where they are standing, when they are living, why they are looking and who they are.

2. *The problem of power.* Both propositions and the processes of legitimating them as knowledge are commonly seen as implicated in the material conditions of social life. Language and ideas, that is, intersect with and are complicated by relations of domination.[3]

3. *The problem of pluralism.* For many today, the one clear, distinct and incontrovertibly true idea is that the contemporary situation is marked by rival truth claims that compete and conflict with one another. To some it follows that truth is exclusivistic and thus that claims to truth are necessarily oppressive. To others it follows that truth must be inclusivistic, embracing all claims in its fullness.

In response to these and other problems, it has become fashionable to abandon talk about truth and to limit one's claims to justification instead.[4] This approach con-

---

[2]Cf. Alistair McFayden, who argues that if something is true, it is true for everybody and will be seen to be true once all the distortions and limitations of partiality are stripped away ("Truth as Mission: The Christian Claim to Universal Truth in a Pluralist Public World," *Scottish Journal of Theology* 46 [1993]: 437-56).

[3]See John B. Thompson, *Studies in the Theory of Ideology* (Cambridge: Polity, 1984). Later in this essay I shall contrast the postmodern tendency to link ideology to power relations to the biblical ideology of vulnerability and suffering.

[4]Hilary Putnam is a good example of this trend: "*Truth is not the bottom line:* truth itself gets its life from our criteria of rational acceptability" (*Reason, Truth and History* [Cambridge: Cambridge University Press, 1981], p. 130). Kierkegaard would doubtless reply that if truth is neither more nor less than rational acceptability, then it's "good night, Christianity" (see his "On the Difference Between a Genius and an Apostle," in *The Present Age and Two Minor Ethico-religious Treatises,* ed. Alter Lowrie and Alexander Druanda [Oxford: Oxford University Press, 1940], esp. p. 139).

signs authority to a material norm (foundational beliefs), a rational procedure (tradi-
tion-based fallibilism) or a reliable belief-forming mechanism (reliabilism). However,
there is considerable dispute over what it is that makes one's believing *right*. Moreover, to restrict one's epistemological mission to showing that one is entitled to hold
certain beliefs removes one of the most important reasons for believing something:
because it is true. The Christian theologian must today show how truth is accessible
and why truth matters.[5]

What is truth? According to William Alston, a proposition (what a statement
asserts) is true if the world is the way the proposition says it is, if, that is, the state of
affairs asserted *obtains*.[6] Jesus, one might say, is God's truth claim: the divine self-
revelation in history, the Word above all words that can be relied on—the Word (a
person rather than a proposition) whose life, death and resurrection, taken together,
displays how things (ultimately) are (or will be).[7] The truth of Jesus Christ has a
propositional component, summed up by his names—Savior, Messiah, God with
us—and by the New Testament confession that "there is no other name under
heaven given among mortals by which we must be saved" (Acts 4:12 NRSV). Specifically, Christian theology makes a truth claim about Jesus' passion: God was in Christ,
reconciling all things to himself (see Col 1:19-20). I call this the "evangelical" truth
claim, and I contrast it with merely empirical or existential claims, for it is primarily a
claim about the reality of God.[8] This theological claim arises from a tradition that
ultimately goes back to the authors of the New Testament (the apostolic preaching),
yet it is also a universal truth claim, because it is a claim about the one Creator God
and hence about the nature of ultimate reality.[9] The evangelical truth claim is thus a

---

[5]William Alston offers an apology for the concept of truth, even for the epistemological purposes of justification, in his *A Realist Conception of Truth* (Ithaca, N.Y.: Cornell University
Press, 1996), chap. 8. Truth matters, he says, "because it is important for us to determine
what states of affairs obtain where that has a bearing on our practical or theoretical concerns" (p. 235). It should be obvious that theological statements meet this latter requirement.
Alston also argues in the same chapter that "doing without truth leaves us without any way
of framing an adequate concept of epistemic justification" (p. 255). It is an important part of
virtue epistemology that epistemic virtues are motivated by a desire for truth.
[6]Alston names his theory a "minimalist realist theory of truth" because while he maintains that
truth is a matter of the relation between propositions and facts, he does not undertake to
specify the nature of the correspondence relation between the two. See ibid., chap. 1.
[7]Bultmann famously commented that the riddle of the New Testament is how the proclaimer
became the proclaimed. My view is similar, but slanted toward epistemology rather than
homiletics: how did the truth-teller come to be identified with the truth itself?
[8]As we shall see, this reference to God—the transcendent—is for Kierkegaard what sets the
apostle and the witness apart from the philosopher-genius.
[9]McFayden and Wolfhart Pannenberg both defend the universality of Christian truth claims by
appealing to monotheism: the unity of the world, even if it is an eschatological unity, ultimately finds its unity in God. Universality is implicit in what I have called the evangelical
truth claim: God through Christ reconciles *all things* to himself.

claim about *the meaning of the whole.* To do justice to the nature of theological truth claims, therefore, it will be necessary to recover two notions that have been rather neglected in contemporary epistemology: understanding (a grasp of meaning) and wisdom (an understanding of the whole).

How can we rationally commend Christian truth? Are theological truth claims inherently oppressive, in which case staking a truth claim would be like waging holy war? Is the apologist a crusader, with the cross emblazoned in crimson upon her breast? There is a real danger of making truth an instrument of power and ideology, turning the cross into "the swastika on our breasts." Perhaps we should rather think of theology as a pilgrimage, in which case staking a truth claim would be what happens at the end of a quest for the epistemological Holy Grail. On this model, we will exchange tales with our fellow pilgrims, and it is possible that our journey will lead to Birmingham rather than Canterbury, or to Delhi rather than Jerusalem. Philosophy has traditionally been conceived as a quest in which the philosopher-pilgrim seeks wisdom. Theology, in my opinion, is different. An incarnational theology that confesses the Word made flesh contends that wisdom has found a way to us.[10] An apprentice of wisdom, theology now carries a double burden: to seek understanding (rendering faith for ourselves) and to share the good news (commending faith to others). I shall therefore picture the theologian neither as pilgrim nor crusader, but as an itinerant evangelist on a never-ending missionary journey. The task of the theologian is to make evangelical truth publicly accessible. I shall argue, however, that more will be involved in staking a truth claim than proclaiming it.

At stake: A way of wisdom. How can we make the idea of truth intelligible in an age rife with suspicion and cynicism? Today it is no longer enough merely to justify propositional truth claims. For what is at stake is the very concept of truth, that is, the notion that truth is meaningful and that truth matters. What Kierkegaard said of individuals can be stretched to apply to whole communities: what is needed in an apathetic age is a truth for which we can live and die. But before we can articulate this "saving" truth we need first to secure the very idea of truth. Truth matters because "truth is that on which we necessarily or ultimately rely."[11]

The truth claims that will here be of interest are those that are implicit in our way of life. This is another reason for redirecting epistemology toward wisdom rather than

---

[10]This is yet another way of articulating what Kierkegaard saw as the crucial difference between the apostle and the genius: the apostle proclaims a message that is not a product of his own devising.

[11]I am here adapting Rowan Williams's definition of metaphysics as discourse about the underlying intelligible structure of our commitments, "what constitutes them as more than arbitrarily willed options" ("Between Politics and Metaphysics: Reflections in the Wake of Gillian Rose," *Modern Theology* 11 [1995]: 6).

knowledge only.[12] This expansionist approach to epistemology is in accord with Kierkegaard's view that philosophy, especially in its Greek origins, is not so much a subject as a way.[13] What is at stake in a theological truth claim, I contend, is whether we can gave an explicit account of those Christian convictions about the meaning of the whole that our most important practices implicitly presuppose. Articulating the meaningfulness of the idea of truth involves showing how truth claims are implicit in the way we live, in our commonsense practices—what might be called our "metaphysical competence" (wisdom).

A theological truth claim will be a statement about the meaning of the whole and as such *will matter to everyone*. Such a claim must involve propositions (objectivity) and passion (subjectivity). A theological truth claim will ultimately be about the Word of God and the difference it makes to human being. What is finally at stake in the epistemological crisis of Christian mission is the wisdom and way of Christ. As we shall see, to stake a theological truth claim is to undertake a missionary journey that ultimately involves both propositions and passion and participates in the trinitarian "missions" of Son and Spirit.

Theology as passion for the truth. Theology is the discipline that cultivates Christian wisdom and makes disciples. But surely, one might object, Christian theology has no monopoly on passion, or truth, or wisdom for that matter. Jesus and Socrates alike aim at inculcating wisdom in their followers. In what follows therefore we shall have to be sensitive to what, if any, difference there may be between philosophical and theological truth claims. An examination of the respective trials of Socrates and Jesus may prove to be of help in this regard. For the moment, let us define theology as the discipline that trains disciples (1) how to render for ourselves and commend to others the utter reliability of the Word of God, (2) how to render for ourselves and commend to others the meaning and truth of the claim that God was in Christ reconciling all things to himself, and (3) how to render for ourselves and commend to others the wisdom of the cross.

The challenge: Trial by Nietzsche. Staking a theological truth claim requires a three-dimensional strategy. There is first a negative moment of exposing the beliefs of my conversation partners (call it "the moment of truth"), a moment that may involve naming the idols (e.g., ideology critique). This corresponds to Socratic "examining." There follows a positive moment when one seeks understanding by establishing one's own reading of reality. With this second stage, one effectively stakes a claim about

---

[12]The Christian way may involve countercultural wisdom (e.g., the first being last and the last being first) but this is not the same as irrationality. It may well be, however, that the apostle will appear less like a genius and more like a fool (though of the Shakespearean variety).

[13]So David J. Gouwens, *Kierkegaard as Religious Thinker* (Cambridge: Cambridge University Press, 1996), p. 28.

how things are. Third, one gives an account of how the evangelical truth claim can be rationally established and if need be defended. It follows from the nature of the claim, however, that the person making it, as well as the proposition, must be tried and tested. The present essay focuses on the third of these stages.[14]

I have elsewhere in this volume set out the contemporary epistemological predicament. To that general sketch I now wish to add a few concrete conversation partners. This is better than debating with straw men; there is little virtue in staking truth claims in undisputed territory. I will therefore stake my claim on ground contested by Van Harvey, a historian who is representative of modernity's passion for the truth (autonomy, criticism), and Friedrich Nietzsche, representing postmodernity's hyperbolic hermeneutics, for whom there are no facts, only interpretations. Both Harvey and Nietzsche have tried traditional ways of staking the evangelical truth claim and found them wanting.

Harvey's *The Historian and the Believer* represents one of the most powerful modern challenges to the evangelical truth claim.[15] Harvey believes that rational thinkers should be committed to an ideal of judgment which is also a morality of knowledge. Rationality for Harvey is a matter of one's doing one's intellectual duty. He appeals to the metaphor of the law court and casts the historian in the role of a prosecuting attorney who cross-examines witnesses and tears their stories apart.

For his part, Nietzsche represents a hermeneutics of extreme suspicion, for whom all truth claims are really reflexes of the will to power. He contends that Christians inhabit a fictional world rooted in the hatred of everything natural and life-enhancing. The idea that one has to die in order to live is for him the denial of reality. Nietzsche represents an explicitly anti-Christian interpretation of reality, and in particular a misreading of the cross of Christ. In attacking truth in general and Christian truth in particular, therefore, Nietzsche stakes an important counter-theological claim.

My last dialogue partner is, appropriately enough, Socrates. We have already seen that Socrates stands for philosophy's independent attempt to cultivate the way of wisdom, to reach the truth about the whole by means of unaided reason. He too is

---

[14]I have rather freely adapted a model drawn from ancient biblical hermeneutics: *explicatio* (unfold the hidden theological presuppositions that undergird one's interpretation of the world), *meditatio* (establish one's interpretation of reality by reflecting on parts in the light of the whole) and *applicatio* (apply the interpretation by demonstrating its practical implications). My method thus includes the three moments that John Frame calls offense (exposing belief/unbelief), proof (presenting a basis for belief) and defense (answering objections to belief) in his *Apologetics to the Glory of God: An Introduction* (Phillipsburg, N.J.: Presbyterian & Reformed, 1994). It is also similar to the development of a chess game, with opening moves, consolidating the position and an end game.

[15]Van Harvey, *The Historian and the Believer: The Morality of Historical Knowledge and Christian Belief* (Philadelphia: Westminster Press, 1966).

engaged in mission (so, for that matter, are Harvey and Nietzsche). Socrates represents both philosophy's passion for truth and philosophy's sustained examination of every claim to truth. Accordingly Socrates symbolizes both rationality's constitutive principle and its intrinsic limitations.

Expository Epistemology

As its name indicates, this is an epistemological first step that *exposes* (Latin *exponere,* "to put off"). It is a preeminently postmodern move, but postmoderns were hardly the first to make it.[16] Indeed, Socrates exemplifies this negative hermeneutic of suspicion for like Nietzsche and the postmoderns, he is concerned to expose what is falsely called knowledge.

Expository epistemology aims to uncover one's ultimate beliefs or presuppositions. The theologian takes Bultmann's hermeneutical maxim—exegesis without presuppositions is impossible—and translates it into epistemology: behavior without belief is impossible. Rowan Williams has defined metaphysics as the attempt to clarify those basic insights into the nature of the real to which our practice commits us.[17] What is to be examined and exposed are those commitments about the way things are which are implied in our most familiar and most important practices. If we ask why these practices are other than arbitrary, the discussion quickly becomes metaphysical. Expository epistemology must include a "hermeneutics of practices." In short, the transcendental question exposes that on which one's belief, or suspicion, is ultimately grounded.

Socrates' expository method is grounded in his sense of mission: to show people who think they are wise that they are not. The goal of the typical Socratic dialogue is to demonstrate that Socrates' interlocutors do not actually know "the most important things" they think they know (what is holiness, goodness, knowledge, justice, etc.). Socrates puts his dialogue partners to the critical test and finds them wanting. This epistemological method is the subject of Kierkegaard's study *The Concept of Irony, with Constant Reference to Socrates.*[18] Socrates feigns ignorance in order to show the wise that they are not really wise about "the things that really matter." For Kierkegaard, the irony of this epistemology is more a quality of Socrates' person than of any single argument. It is Socrates' ignorance that challenges knowledge, offers no answers and then claims to make wise. For Kierkegaard, Socrates' epistemological midwifery is "infinite negativity": Socrates prepares the way for the truth by decon-

---

[16]John W. Cooper rightly reminds us that twentieth-century Dutch Calvinists (e.g., Cornelius Van Til, Hermann Dooyeweerd) had earlier challenged the alleged neutrality and autonomy of human reason ("Reformed Apologetics and the Challenge of Post-modern Relativism," *Calvin Theological Journal* 28 [1993]: 108-20.

[17]Rowan Williams, "Beyond Politics and Metaphysics," *Modern Theology* 11 (1995): 3-22.

[18]Søren Kierkegaard, *The Concept of Irony,* trans. Howard V. Hong and Edna H. Hong (Princeton, N.J.: Princeton University Press, 1989).

structing the false opinions of those who think themselves wise.

Nietzsche also uses irony to question assured beliefs.[19] Like Socrates, he wants to show his readers that they do not really know "the most important things." Whereas in verbal irony one does not say what one really means, in what I call *metaphysical irony* one does not believe that one's concepts and theories actually correspond to the world. Humans are "all too human" either to know God or to know as gods. Unlike Socrates, however, Nietzsche was persuaded of the fundamentally nonrational character of the world and of human life. In this he anticipated the postmodern preoccupation with the "all too human." What is left of epistemology in postmodernity is rationality among the ruins.

Socrates and Nietzsche yield only an ironic wisdom concerning the limits of reason, a "wisdom" that ultimately undoes the picture of knowledge as justified true belief. Philosophical examination in the mode of irony instead becomes never-ending critique.[20]

Nietzsche and his contemporary followers believe that religion is an imaginative projection that sacrifices the truth—namely, that all is metaphorical projection and interpretation—for a lie. He assumes the prophetic mantle against Christianity and presents himself as the defender of the truth: the world is not a good creation but a field of conflicting forces without any inherent structure or final purpose. Ironically enough, Nietzsche speaks as if he knows what the truth is (*not* Christianity). Absolute suspicion, like absolute skepticism, is impossible in practice. What we have in Nietzsche and his ilk is finally an apologist for *another* faith.

Unlike much modern Christian apologetics, I am concerned in the first instance not to expose *unbelief* but rather alternative control beliefs. The risk of offending is just as great, perhaps; no one likes to be shown to be inconsistent or idolatrous (or metaphysical!). Yet this is the aim of this initial expository work: to make explicit the fundamental commitments to which our most important practices implicitly commit us.

Hermeneutical Epistemology: Reading Reality

Expository epistemology must be balanced by a positive moment (*ponere,* "putting

---

[19]Friedrich Schlegel's definition summed up the Romantic variation of irony popular in the late eighteenth and nineteenth centuries: "the recognition of the fact that the world in its essence is paradoxical and that an ambivalent attitude alone can grasp its contradictory totality" (quoted in René Wellek, *A History of Modern Criticism (1750-1950): The Romantic Age* [New Haven, Conn.: Yale University Press, 1955], p. 14).

[20]In the light of Kierkegaard's analysis, we might venture to suggest that the deepest irony in Socrates, and perhaps in all philosophy, is that it seeks infinity within human being itself. As we shall see, Kierkegaard associates Socrates with the religion of immanence. Perhaps irony is the inevitable result of an approach that seeks transcendence through introspection. The question that Kierkegaard poses is whether the philosopher can ever get beyond immanence, that is, whether the philosopher can ever know more than his own mind.

[forward]") that establishes one's own position.

Positive has another meaning as well. The core beliefs of Christianity are "positive" in the sense that they are grounded not on universal reason but on testimony to specific historical figures and events (revelation). The scandal of the cross is epistemological, at least in part, and from this follows positivity and particularity of the gospel. Yet it is precisely this positivity that, according to Kierkegaard, gives rise to the difference between the apostle and the genius. The nature of the theological truth claim is such that neither its source nor its norm can be located in the sphere of immanence "within the limits of reason alone."

There are a number of reasons for discussing theological truth claims under the rubric of hermeneutics. First, hermeneutics is a viable alternative to the either-or of objectivism and relativism. Objectivism is the belief that there is some permanent framework to which we can appeal in determining the nature of rationality, knowledge, truth and rightness. An objectivist might say that philosophy's job is to identify and defend the objective structures of reality and rationality alike. My counter-thesis is that while we may not have such a universal framework, we do have a number of relatively adequate frameworks for this enterprise.[21] As Paul Ricoeur puts it, we must choose between absolute knowledge and hermeneutics. Our age acknowledges the theory-ladenness of data, the "impurity" of reason. It is increasingly difficult to take seriously those who maintain that their thought is free of cultural, historical and linguistic conditioning. Yet we can continue to stake theological truth claims in the hermeneutical age of reason.

Second, hermeneutics is perhaps the discipline that best corresponds to the nature of a theological truth claim, not only because the latter concerns biblical testimony but because it deals with the *meaning of the whole*. Hermeneutics thus allows us to recover a neglected theme in epistemology, namely, understanding.[22] This involves leaving behind "the Cartesian perspective," in which the focus is on the individual

---

[21]I am thinking here not only of diverse disciplinary perspectives but also of the diverse literary forms of biblical discourse, each of which constitutes a way of experiencing and seeing the world. See Kevin Vanhoozer, "Language, Literary, Hermeneutics and Biblical Theology: What's Theological About a Theological Dictionary?" in *The New international Dictionary of Old Testament Theology and Exegesis,* ed. Willem A. VanGemeren (Grand Rapids, Mich.: Zondervan, 1997), vol. 1, chap. 1.

[22]Linda Trinkaus Zagzebski observes that contemporary epistemology neglects both understanding and wisdom. When understanding is mentioned, she says, it is usually identified with a minimal grasp of the sense of an isolated proposition. My definition of theological truth claims as claims about the meaning of the whole enable me to amend both of these oversights. In this section the focus is on understanding, but in the penultimate section, on the "epistemology of the cross," I shall return to the theme of wisdom. See Zagzebski, *Virtues of the Mind: An Inquiry into the Nature of Virtue and the Ethical Foundations of Knowledge* (Cambridge: Cambridge University Press, 1996), pp. 43-51.

beliefs of a single person and the goal is to attain propositional knowledge.[23] On the other hand, understanding, according to Linda Zagzebski, "is not a state directed toward a single propositional object at all. . . . One understands *p* as part of . . . one's understanding of the whole pattern of a whole chunk of reality."[24]

To see knowledge as a form of interpretation, then, is to *expand* and *enrich* the traditional notion of epistemology. It allows us, moreover, to reclaim the imagination—the capacity to see things together, in terms of whole patterns. This self-conscious appropriation of the imagination is crucial, for the most intimidating obstacle to the Christian apologist is not this or that argument but rather the monolithic secular culture or framework that has taken thought captive to a flattened-out naturalism that pretends to be comprehensive. In sum, a hermeneutical model of reasoning allows for both a negative and a positive moment in one's theology (exposing and proposing), as well as for critical testing, as we shall see in due course.[25]

Text and interpretation as epistemological concepts. The world has rightly been called the Book of Nature. For those who subscribe to naturalism, the world does not mean, it just is; but for others, including Christians, the world cries out for interpretation. Nietzsche insightfully portrays human beings as "*homo hermeneutics,* an organism that invariably and necessarily interprets," though he mistakenly denies that interpretation can be a form of knowledge.[26] Knowledge in the hermeneutical age of reason may be a context-dependent affair, relative to paradigms and frameworks, though in a critically realist account it is nonetheless knowledge for that.

According to Martin Buber, however, it is Christianity that gives the world hermeneutics, that is, the confidence that there is a correct interpretation of the Word and of the world: *God's* interpretation. The Word of God is, for Christians, the basic text that provides the lenses through which one seeks to understand God, the world and oneself. The revelation of God in Christ, together with the witness of Scripture, generates a distinctively Christian worldview. This basic text provides concepts for the descriptive task of understanding the "most important things" and imperatives for the prescriptive task of living them out.

---

[23]For an account and critique of "the Cartesian perspective," see Jonathan Kvanvig, *The Intellectual Virtues and the Life of the Mind* (Lanham, Md.: Rowman & Littlefield, 1992), pp. 181-82.

[24]Zagzebski, *Virtues of the Mind*, p. 49. It is important to add that the "whole" that understanding grasps is not simply a matter of theory or of propositions but includes different kinds of facts and contexts. Hermeneutics is also holistic in the sense that it looks at the speech act as a whole and not only at its propositional content.

[25]I am here correlating expository theology with the hermeneutics of suspicion and positive theology with the hermeneutics of belief.

[26]Karen L. Carr, *The Banalization of Nihilism: Twentieth-Century Responses to Meaninglessness* (Albany, N.Y.: SUNY Press, 1992), p. 28.

A worldview is a comprehensive interpretation of individual, social and cosmic reality. It is a comprehensive interpretation of the "meaning" of life: its origin, its nature and its destiny. Let me propose yet another definition of theology as *the reflective and active rendering of the Christian interpretation of reality.*[27] The Christian interpretation of reality is a function of its interpretation of Scripture, those books set aside as authoritative testimony to the gospel—call it a philosophy of "canonical sense." It is the sum total of the biblical books, the various parts in their interrelatedness, that communicates the wisdom of the Christian way, which is to say, the wisdom of Christ and the wisdom of the cross. Faith in the God of Israel and of Jesus Christ commits Christians to a supreme interpretive norm: the Scriptures. Yet all attempts to secure this canonical norm philosophically are bound to fail. So while one may have an absolute commitment to Christ, one need not be committed to a single conceptual scheme: objective truth need not entail objectivism. A hermeneutical theology neither aspires after certainty nor rests content with faith, but makes a case for or against various proposed interpretations of that to which our most important Christian practices, generated by Scripture, ultimately commit us.

The only kind of fideism to which I might subscribe therefore would be a *hermeneutical fideism:* not "I believe in order to avoid thinking"; not "I believe in order to lord it over others"; not "I believe in order to immunize myself from criticism"; but rather "I believe *in order to understand.*"[28] What we are exposing, and proposing, as theologians who stake truth claims, is ultimately the rationale for one's beliefs and actions; hermeneutical theology is about the justification of the ways of wisdom that are generated by and embodied in our canonical texts and community practices.

Training in imagination: Cultivating Christian phronesis. "Christianity is *praxis,* a character task" (Kierkegaard).[29] To sum up the argument to this point: I have argued that formulating and defending the Christian worldview is like interpreting a text. We expose our presuppositions and we propose an interpretation, a way of describing, knowing full well that there are other interpretations that arise from other perspectives. How then do we cope with the conflict of interpretations?

Nietzsche thought that because religion is an imaginative projection it is necessarily false. Ironically, the self-proclaimed champion of creativity turns out to have a low

---

[27]Note that this entails a new definition of truth as well: truth is God's interpretation of reality. Cf. Kant's tacit understanding of the noumenal as the object of God's knowledge (Immanuel Kant, *Critique of Pure Reason,* trans. Norman Kent Smith [London: Macmillan, 1933], p. 90).

[28]I shall return to fideism toward the end of the essay and ask whether the *Shorter Oxford* definition is correct: "a mode of thought in which knowledge is based on a fundamental act of faith." Kierkegaard's distinction of the apostle from the genius obliges us to ask whether it is rational to believe what the apostle tells us. Can fideism—the position that religious truth is based on faith rather than evidence or a process of reasoning—nevertheless be rational?

[29]Quoted in Gouwens, *Kierkegaard as Religious Thinker,* p. 209.

view of the imagination: imaginative projections are fictive constructions and do not correspond to the way things are. His criterion for preferring one interpretation rather than another had to do with its "life-value" (does it enhance life?), not its truth value. In contrast, I argue for a perspectival realism: the imagination, formed and guided by the canon, may be an organ of truth. *It may be that some of our perspectives—the biblical "word views," to be exact—allow us to imagine reality rightly.* The worldview one holds, however, is a matter of one's moral and spiritual positions as well as one's cultural and linguistic position. A worldview, that is, is not merely an intellectual tool but the product of an intellectual outlook which, I shall argue, is ultimately a matter of ethics, even spirituality.

Right interpretation depends not only on having the right procedures but on having the right habits of perception as well as a desire to understand the whole.[30] We often need to be trained in order to perceive things correctly. Theology both announces past fact (indicative) and draws our attention to what should follow from it (imperative). The intelligibility of the claim, however, is a matter of both theory and practice. To stake a theological truth claim ultimately demands practical reasoning, something akin to Aristotle's *phronesis*. It is a matter of grasping the significance of the biblical story and of the contemporary situation, so that we know what a particular situation requires of us as persons staking the evangelical truth claim. Staking theological truth claims is a product neither of instrumental nor of speculative reason but of practical reason: a type of reasoning about moral action and a type of reasoning for which one may be held morally responsible.[31] Indeed, according to some recent virtue epistemologists, rationality just is a form of being moral—of ethics applied to the intellect—a point to which I shall return below.[32]

The above leads me to my major thesis in this section: *theology in postmodernity must reorient itself to wisdom rather than knowledge.* Wisdom, I believe, is the means of integrating what modernity and postmodernity alike have torn asunder: metaphys-

---

[30]A hermeneutical model oriented to understanding and right interpretation can easily assimilate commonly cited epistemological criteria—personal disclosure value, empirical fit, logical coherence, to name but a few. Rationality in hermeneutics, as in science, is a matter of submitting one's interpretation to critical tests in a free and open conversation. It is this willingness to submit one's interpretation to critical tests that prevents hermeneutical theology from becoming an irrational fideism.

[31]Paul Helm suggests that *believing* too can be a species of practical reason: "The practice of believing may be considered a means of gaining a chosen end, the possession of the truth" (*Belief Policies* [Cambridge: Cambridge University Press, 1994], p. 143). I further explore the ethical dimensions of epistemology below.

[32]See, for instance, Linda Trinkaus Zagzebski, "The Place of Phronesis in the Methodology of Theology," in *Philosophy and Theological Discourse,* ed. Stephen T. Davis (New York: St. Martin's, 1997), pp. 204-23; James A. Montmarquet, *Epistemic Virtue and Doxastic Responsibility* (Lanham, Md.: Rowman & Littlefield, 1993).

ics and morals, theory and practice, fact and value. Wisdom is a matter of knowing certain things but also of making one's knowledge fruitful. It is a matter of being able to apply truth appropriately to the matter at hand. Wisdom provides an effective means for integrating seeing and doing, judging and acting. The wise person knows what to do in a given situation; the wise person understands. Wisdom thus provides a way of integrating universals and particulars. Truth and metaphysics return to post-modernity on this view not as correlates of *episteme* or theoretical reasoning but rather as correlates of *phronesis*.

Scripture, inasmuch as it trains the imagination and generates interpretive frame-works for describing experience, is the central means for cultivating Christian *phro-nesis*. The task of the Christian theologian is to demonstrate the rational superiority of the Christian way and Christian wisdom in whatever situation one finds oneself. One who would stake a theological truth claim, then, must show that its descriptions and prescriptions make wise unto creation. What the theologian ultimately defends, I sub-mit, is not so much the existence but the *wisdom* of God.[33]

Can Christian truth claims be verified? Not, perhaps, according to *episteme* or *techne*. There is no proof or process that can conclusively verify a theological truth claim. If reason were ultimately the judge of revelation, says Kierkegaard, then "God and the Apostle have to wait at the gate, or in the porter's lodge, till the learned upstairs have settled the matter."[34] There may nevertheless be a kind of verification in the domain of practical reason or *phronesis*. We verify or corroborate biblical wisdom in situations where, in the light of a Christian vision of the whole, we are able to act well. Disputes with non-Christians about how to live well usually turn on competing descriptions of the situation in which we find ourselves. The theologian offers bibli-cal perspectives on the world. Those who wish to stake theological truth claims must show that folly follows the bad descriptions of an atrophied imagination: descriptions of sexual intercourse as mere physical encounter and bodily movements, of justice as the will of the majority, and so on. If theology is the discourse that articulates the underlying intelligible structure of our commitment to the Christian way, truth and life, the "proof" of its nonarbitrariness is in the following ("follow the argument where it leads"). We begin to understand and to commend theological claims only as we begin to take up our Procrustean beds and walk. In short: the getting of wisdom is the payoff of Christian interpretations.

One cannot force the truth on others. This is the crusader model of staking a

---

[33]Belief in the existence of God may be a necessary component of the evangelical truth claim, but it is hardly sufficient: "even the demons believe—and shudder" (Jas 2:19). Assent to propositions, in other words, is not yet wisdom. I discuss below the question whether one can be held culpable for unbelief in God.

[34]Kierkegaard, "On the Difference," p. 148.

claim, and it does not work. Theological knowledge is ultimately gained through obedient action (Jn 7:17). Again, right imagination is needed for right action; *phronesis* is a matter of seeing well and doing well. We can fit into a situation appropriately only if we are able to envision it aright. The imagination, the faculty of perceiving the whole, is an integral ingredient in wisdom. The wise person relates herself to God, the world and others in a way that is fitting, and hence in a manner that leads to human flourishing (and to the glory of God): "In all that he does, he prospers" (Ps 1:3). Theories, worldviews and ways alike can be tested and tried to see if they are progressing or degenerating: "You shall know them by their fruits."

Wolfhart Pannenberg comments: "All interpretation, whether private or official, is measured against the truth of the subject matter, which is not decided by any one expositor but in the process of the expository debate."[35] True enough. And yet when it comes to trying a theological truth claim the Christian way, the ultimate test is not debate but a trial of life and death. Christian wisdom is fruit-conducive.[36]

An Epistemology of the Cross: The Witness to Wisdom

To this point I have argued that theology's task is to read reality rightly, with the goal of showing how human beings may fit in or relate to it for their own good and for the glory of God. But can we really dignify this hermeneutical approach with the epithet *epistemology?* Is it possible rationally to justify the evangelical truth claim? The obstacles to doing so appear formidable. Who, after all, is in a position to know whether God was in Christ reconciling all things to himself? And in a pluralistic world, why should we attend to the Christian testimony about the meaning of the whole (assuming there is one) any more than another?

I began this essay by asking what Christian theology could contribute to the project of staking truth claims given the contemporary epistemological predicament. Surely I am not suggesting that theology, a specific academic discipline with a peculiar remit and a very distinct subject matter, has something to say to epistemology in general about how to sort out knowledge from opinion or to justify belief? Athens and Jerusalem we know, but the epistemologist is apt to be as incredulous as Nathanael and ask: "Can anything good come out of Nazareth?" (Jn 1:46). The simple answer is "Yes, Jesus Christ."

Jesus associates his own person and work with the concept of truth in the clearest possible way: "For this I was born, and for this I have come into the world, to bear witness to the truth" (Jn 18:37). A consideration of the narrative of Jesus, and espe-

---

[35]Wolfhart Pannenberg, *Systematic Theology* (Grand Rapids, Mich.: Eerdmans, 1991), 1:15.
[36]Note the integral connection between ethics and epistemology. As we shall see below, an intellectual virtue is epistemically privileged because it is truth-conducive. Conversely, wisdom is ethically privileged because it is fruit-conducive.

cially of his trials, yields an enriched account of what is involved in making, and staking, truth claims.[37] In the Christian tradition, testimony is a way of knowing, and the Greek term for one who testifies—*martyr*—captures both the aspect of "giving witness" and that of "giving one's life" for the truth. Martyrdom, I shall contend, is ultimately what is required in staking a theological truth claim, for it is the whole speech act of testifying, not only the proposition, that ultimately communicates truth claims about the way of wisdom. The martyr's witness responds both to the postmodern critique of traditional modes of justification and to the postmodern indifference toward the concept of truth. I shall be particularly interested in noting the ways martyrdom contributes to a virtue-based epistemology. Finally, I shall contrast the trials of Socrates and Jesus in order to consider the objection that a martyrological approach is neither unique to theology nor truth-conducive, since passionate commitment alone is an insufficient criterion of rationality ("the fanatic you shall always have with you"). Before I can show how theology qualifies epistemology, however, it is necessary to introduce the notion of an intellectual virtue.

Virtue epistemology and the desire for truth. Virtue epistemology may be said to begin with the insight that we are responsible for what we believe. Since believing is something we do, it is subject to evaluation; it can be right or wrong, done poorly or done well. A virtue is an acquired excellence and involves "a characteristic motivation to produce a desired end and reliable success in bringing about that end."[38] It was Aristotle who first distinguished the intellectual from the moral virtues.[39] The intellectual virtues differ from their moral counterparts in two important respects: (1) the intellectual virtues arise from the general motivation for truth, and (2) the intellectual virtues cultivate habits that reliably attain the aims of this motive.

Virtue epistemology aims to elucidate the normative element in believing: what makes believing *right*. The basic idea, roughly, is that truth is acquired through acts

---

[37]My wager in what follows is that just as a study of biblical interpretation yields insights for general hermeneutics, so an examination of what is involved in making a theological truth claim yields dividends for epistemology in general. Theology's contribution to the discussion is best seen, I contend, if one espouses virtue epistemology, though this is hardly the only reason to subscribe to such an approach. Virtue epistemology appears to be especially well suited to staking the evangelical truth claim, provided that epistemology is informed by the properly theological virtues as well (see below). To anticipate: if, as Montmarquet says, "the epistemic virtues turn out to be qualities that a truth-desiring person would *want* to have" (*Epistemic Virtue,* p. viii), might not the epistemic virtues be more completely displayed by qualities of a person with a *passion* for the truth?

[38]Zagzebski, *Virtues of the Mind,* p. 137.

[39]Cf. his *Nicomachean Ethics* 6. It is important to note, however, that virtue epistemologists dispute Aristotle's claim that intellectual virtues differ from their moral counterparts in kind. Both Zagzebski and Montmarquet, for instance, argue that rationality is a way of being moral and that morality and rationality alike should be governed by *phronesis.* See Zagzebski, *Virtues of the Mind,* pp. 137-58, and Montmarquet, *Epistemic Virtue,* chap. 2.

of intellectual virtue.[40] An intellectual virtue—open-mindedness, conscientiousness, impartiality—is one that is conducive to knowledge and truth, that is, to "cognitive contact with reality."[41] It begins with the desire to attain truth. According to Zagzebski, "the motive for truth is a component of epistemic goodness."[42] It is important not to confuse an intellectual virtue with an intellectual skill: the latter is a capacity, the former an excellence. Moreover, a virtue is a character trait: a deep and enduring acquired excellence that is learned primarily by imitating virtuous persons.[43] Epistemic virtues, then, are traits of character "generally conducive to the discovery of truth, irrespective of subject matter."[44]

The concept of an intellectual virtue thus focuses on persons rather than processes and means that virtue is the most useful criterion for determining the rightness of an act (ethics) or a belief (epistemology).[45] A belief is justified, in other words, when it is held by a person with epistemic virtue: "An 'epistemically responsible' person, then, will be *trying* (her best or reasonably hard) to arrive at the truth and to avoid error."[46] It follows, then, that justification—that extra something that makes a belief *right*—is a secondary trait that emerges from the primary, inner traits of persons of intellectual virtue.[47]

For my purposes, virtue epistemology highlights one especially noteworthy idea,

---

[40]Montmarquet offers the following definition: "*S* is justified in believing *p* insofar as *S* is epistemically virtuous in believing *p*" (*Epistemic Virtue*, p. 99).

[41]Zagzebski, *Virtues of the Mind*, p. 168. Note her definition of *knowledge:* "a state of cognitive contact with reality arising out of acts of intellectual virtues" (p. 270). Note also that virtue is a "success" term that refers to a competence to achieve a result (e.g., the competence to arrive at true beliefs).

[42]Zagzebski, "Place of Phronesis," p. 209.

[43]Zagzebski doubts that the virtues can be learned through following rules or procedures. It is better to be apprenticed to those who have the virtue or, what is second best, to read narratives about such persons (ibid., p. 181).

[44]Montmarquet, *Epistemic Virtue*, p. 19.

[45]Cf. Ernest Sosa, "The Raft and the Pyramid: Coherence Versus Foundations in the Theory of Knowledge," in *Studies in Epistemology*, Midwest Studies in Philosophy 5 (Notre Dame, Ind.: University of Notre Dame Press, 1980), and "Knowledge and Intellectual Virtue," *Monist* 68 (1985): 226-45, for earlier statements of the proposal that epistemologists focus on intellectual virtue, the property of a person, rather than on properties of belief (e.g., foundationalism) or of rational procedures (e.g., coherentism).

[46]Montmarquet, *Epistemic Virtue*, p. 21.

[47]How do we know which personal traits are truth-conducive? Why, for instance, are lucky guesses not epistemic virtues? Zagzebski believes it is because guessing is not a reliable procedure for producing true beliefs. Moreover, "an awareness of the unreliability of guessing is something within my sphere of responsibility" ("Place of Phronesis," p. 209). Which processes are reliable? This is determined by "the nature of the believer and the 'fit' between the believer and the knowable world" (p. 210). Montmarquet concurs: the epistemic virtues are qualities that a truth-desiring person, given the conditions that obtain in the world, would want to emulate (*Epistemic Virtue*, p. 30).

that epistemology is an affair of the heart. Everything begins with a desire for truth. Though as we shall see, this desire by itself does not suffice for rationality, it has been said that genius is nine-tenths passion. Certainly a passion for the truth is requisite when it comes to the knowledge of God, which is also a whole-person affair: "You shall love the Lord your God with all your heart, and with all your soul, and with all your mind" (Mt 22:37). Insofar as there is an incipient epistemology implicit in Scripture, it deals not only with the head but with the core of one's personal being: "For man believes with his heart and so is justified" (Rom 10:10). Virtue epistemology thus has the merit of admitting long-neglected factors back into the conversation about knowledge, truth and rationality.

The epistemology of the cross and the epistemology of glory. It is but a short step from the notion of epistemic virtue to that of epistemic vice or noetic sin. One besetting epistemic vice is intellectual pride, the tendency to think too highly of one's arguments or conclusions. Theologians in particular should beware what we might call, after Luther, an "epistemology of glory": the belief that human beings through their native powers of ratiocination and intellectual works can achieve knowledge of God (and thus of the evangelical truth claim).[48] Kierkegaard's careful distinction between a genius and an apostle could likewise be taken as an attack on an epistemology of glory and on the idea that one can "by reason find out God."[49] The glory of the genius shines only in the realm of immanence, and that only for a time; the genius is simply the first to discover what humanity will eventually learn anyway as it develops.

An epistemology of glory is a strategy for self-transcendence whereby a knower surmounts his or her own subjectivity by means of some process (justification) that purges beliefs of the wrong kind of supports. For instance, modern philosophy tended in its heyday to equate Reason with a God's-eye point of view. The more muted postmodern epistemology of glory is content with the severely limited transcendence of intersubjectivity: communities can achieve what the individual cannot (it takes a village . . .). But is community consensus sufficient insurance against the

---

[48]An "epistemology of the cross" is implicit in Luther's "theology of the cross." In his *Heidelberg Disputation* (1518) he contrasts scholasticism's natural theology with his own attempt to know God through God's self-revelation in the life, work and especially death of Christ. Luther's contrast of the two epistemologies is his way of pointing up the differences between philosophy and theology as ways of knowing God. My own adaptation of Luther's phrase, developed below, puts the accent in a slightly different place: the importance for epistemology of the theological virtues (including humility) and of discipleship.

[49]The notion of epistemic virtue provides another way of drawing this distinction. The genius is one gifted with intellectual skill; being an apostle—one who believes reliable authority and responsibly gives testimony—is not so much a matter of intellectual skill as of intellectual (and moral) virtue.

possibility that our beliefs are more than mass opinion? It is widely believed that either the quality of the evidence or the process of testing it justifies belief. But who, and what, guarantees the evidence and the justificatory procedures?

Paul Helm suggests that belief policies are not themselves determined by evidence (or by procedures of justification) but are rather a matter of choice and thus subject to the possibility of weakness of will and self-deception.[50] An example of weakness of will, says Helm, is "when a person does not believe when there is good reason to believe."[51] It is not enough, then, to want to avoid error; one has to love the truth more than one's own ideas. Blaise Pascal notes that everyone has an aversion for the truth in different degrees "because it is inseparable from self-love."[52] One displays a distinct lack of virtue, for example, by ignoring the evidence. Moreover, according to Montmarquet, such ignorance results not in bliss but in blameworthiness.

Virtue epistemology provides a fascinating lens through which to read familiar passages such as Romans 1:18-23. The apostle Paul speaks of those who "by their wickedness suppress the truth" (Rom 1:18). Though what can be known of God is plain, leaving unbelievers without excuse, the crucial evidence is neglected, apparently for moral as much as intellectual reasons. False beliefs arise not only from error but from "leaving undone the things we ought to have done." It would appear that Luther's *simul iustus et peccator* has important epistemological implications; moreover, it applies to philosophers and theologians alike.

Justifying belief is not an impersonal intellectual procedure but is rather a person-relative process. Different people work with contrasting styles of assessment; for instance, willing believers have a lower threshold of justification. Helm views the adoption of a belief policy as an action for which individuals are responsible.[53] After considering the skepticism of Sextus Empiricus, Helm formulates the following belief policy: "Believe only what keeps you from disquiet or anxiety."[54] Now it is an open question whether belief in God fosters peace or disquiet. To many, like Nietzsche, the notion of a creator-redeemer God is distinctly unsettling (cf. Jean-Paul Sartre's "either God or human freedom"). The volitional component in belief policies may explain why the most intransigent resistance to Christian truth claims is located not

---

[50]Helm, *Belief Policies*.

[51]Ibid., p. 148. Helm does not explicitly relate his account to virtue-based epistemology (though see p. 4), but the connection is easily made. Self-deception, for instance, is ethically qualified ignorance; it is an intellectual vice. It would be interesting to rethink Helm's account of belief policies in terms of Zagzebski's account of the intellectual virtues. Unfortunately, neither author seems aware of the other.

[52]Quoted in Zagzebski, *Virtues of the Mind*, p. 147.

[53]Helm, *Belief Policies*, p. 164.

[54]Ibid., pp. 159-60.

on the plane of intellectual argument but on the ethical level. Unbelievers resist, sometimes culpably, theological truth claims. However, to be fair, we should acknowledge that perhaps the biggest single reason for resisting the evangelical truth claim is Christians themselves, because of the way they stake the claim. The most frequent objection to the Christian faith, at least in the popular if not the philosophical arena, is an account of what some Christians or the church have done. Actions refute louder than words.

If justification is to some extent a matter of adopting a certain belief policy, and if individuals and groups allow interests other than an interest in truth to determine their choices, then the theologian should be wary of adopting an epistemology of vainglory that pretends to represent reason alone. The epistemology of the cross is far more deconstructive of human ideologies and belief policies than anything postmodernity has yet produced. That God reveals himself on Christ's cross as One who suffers and dies is an implicit correction, if not outright rejection, of the attempt to think of God on the basis of reason alone: "Has not God made foolish the wisdom of the world?" (1 Cor 1:20).[55] This is why the confessions of Reformed churches recognize the inherent corrigibility of theological formulations. The confessions themselves have only relative and provisional authority; they are under the Word of God and thus subject to correction from it. There is a built-in iconoclasm, an intrinsic guard against the tendency to let a community's language and concepts dictate what can be known of God. An epistemology of the cross incorporates ideology critique into its very fabric.

Epistemology and martyrology: The rationality of testimony. Staking the evangelical truth claim, I submit, is a matter of demonstrating wisdom rather than knowledge, and so demands that one justify not only particular propositions but a certain kind of practice, both in order to be make wisdom intelligible and in order to "try" it. In short, staking a theological truth claim requires the (virtuous) practice of "taking up one's cross." This is the probationary moment of practical reason, the moment where the theological truth claim is tried and tested. What happens to virtue epistemology when it encounters the peculiarly theological virtues—faith, hope and love—associated with Christian discipleship and martyrdom?

In this section I reclaim the category "martyr," in its dual sense of witnessing and suffering, for the sake of an enriched concept of knowledge that privileges neither epistemology nor ethics but rather seeks to preserve both propositions *and* persons, procedures *and* practices. *Witnessing is the way to put others in the position of coming to know (believe and understand) evangelical truth.*

---

[55]At the very least the cross represents a significant correction to the concept of perfection with regard to God as the "most perfect being."

In a postmodern setting it is no longer enough to justify truth claims proposition-ally. An epistemology of the cross will not be merely evidentialist. It is not enough to state a proposition; one must stake a claim, and ultimately oneself, and this for two reasons. First, the truth of this claim is not a matter of propositional content only. What is at stake is the very notion of truth, as a way of life, and thus the notion that truth matters (individually and socially). What is needed in an apathetic age, in a sit-uation of ironic indifference, is a truth for which one can live and die (Kierkegaard). In the second place, the martyr displays several character traits related to the epistemic virtues. If justification arises from acts of intellectual virtue, it may be that martyrdom could serve as a normative component of justified true belief. Indeed martyrdom may well be an instance of epistemic responsibility taken to the limit. A belief is justified, in other words, when it is held by a person with epistemic virtue: one who knows of what she speaks and is willing to suffer on its behalf.

The trial of Jesus and the trials of life. Jesus' theological truth claim—"I am the way, and the truth, and the life; no one comes to the Father, but by me" (Jn 14:6)—seems to have led directly to his trial.[56] Jesus' passion for the truth ultimately resulted in his passion and death. As Jürgen Moltmann observes, "At the center of Christian faith is *the passion of the passionate Christ*."[57] Jesus staked his claim, then went to the stake for it. Both stakings were integral to his mission, which was in part epistemo-logical: to make known the truth about God and about salvation.

How does one "try" Jesus' claim to be "the way, the truth, and the life"? "To try" admits of an interesting double meaning, which I shall explore below. Here I want only to point out that what is on trial is Jesus' whole life. The trial narratives make this explicit. The various trials of Jesus recounted in the Gospels oblige us to take the role of judge or jury and to make judgments about the whole of his life. In so doing, the story tests the reader for practical wisdom.

The judiciary: The economy of works (law) and the sphere of immanence (Religion A). The trial of truth involves certain judicial procedures, procedures for making right legal judgments. To make such judgments is to speak in the name of the law. But

---

[56] I cannot here deal adequately with the historical reconstructions of the accusation against Jesus: was it blasphemy (a religious charge), sedition (a political charge) or perhaps the claim to be and do all the temple was and did, in which case it would be both religious and political (see Bruce Chilton, *The Temple of Jesus* [University Park: Pennsylvania University Press, 1992])? There is a similar ambivalence over the charge against Socrates as to its reli-gious or political motivation (see Thomas C. Brickhouse and Nicholas D. Smith, *Plato's Socrates* [Oxford: Oxford University Press, 1994], chaps. 5-6). What we can say with some certainty is that the charges against Jesus and Socrates were attempts to defeat their respec-tive missions.

[57] Jürgen Moltmann, *The Way of Jesus Christ: Christology in Messianic Dimensions* (Minneapo-lis: Fortress, 1993), p. 151.

which law? What kind of authority gives these judiciary procedures legitimacy? In modernity, philosophers like Kant happily spoke of reason in juridical terms. Not so in postmodernity. According to the postmodern critique, reason is not blind but biased. Hence the difficulty: we have to make judgments in the absence of an impartial judge. Some philosophers, like Gary Habermas, appeal to the regulative notion of an impartial communicative process. The account of Jesus' trial, however, is far from picturing the ideal speech situation. On the contrary, it illustrates how religious and political interests and perspectives affect the participants' judgments despite the presence of evidence and the existence of judicial procedures. The trial of truth by the judiciary is something of a travesty. Doing one's intellectual duty, I shall argue, involves more than following procedures.[58]

Jesus was in fact tried more than once, before different "publics," and was thus subjected to more than one judicial procedure.[59] Before Caiaphas and the Sanhedrin Jesus was judged according to the law and the prophets (though in fact it was tradition rather than Scripture that ultimately carried most weight). Before Pilate Jesus was judged according to a different, explicitly political standard, though the procedure still aimed at rendering justice. Jesus' third trial, before Herod, seems to have been conducted according to more eccentric standards. Herod, aware of the plurality of pretenders claiming to be Christ, "was hoping to see some sign done by him" (Lk 23:8). The fourth "trial," before the crowd, was conducted according to the slimmest of judicial procedures only. It was trial by mass opinion, and the mob duly displayed its lack of practical wisdom by choosing Barabbas over Jesus. Interestingly, the Evangelists highlight the mockery displayed during *all* of Jesus' trials. Jesus was correctly hailed "King of the Jews" but for entirely the wrong reasons; the soldiers' ironic identity description of Jesus does not therefore count as justified true belief. In the final analysis, it is difficult to say whether any of these judicial procedures satisfied their epistemic duties by rendering a true judgment.

In the context of epistemology, "the judiciary" refers primarily to the procedures by which beliefs are deemed right. Rationality here appears to be a matter of due process or of doing one's epistemic duty. Zagzebski points out that almost all contemporary epistemic theories take an "act-based" moral theory as their model.[60] However, this focus on justifying individual beliefs has led to the neglect of understanding

---

[58]Zagzebski notes that the traditional view of epistemology "identifies justification with both the component of knowledge in addition to true belief and the idea of doing one's epistemic duty" (*Virtues of the Mind*, p. 31). She is quick to point out that deontological theories do not exhaust the nature of morality. Virtue theory and consequentialism represent other approaches to morality that have their epistemological analogues as well.

[59]Again, I do not have time to go into the historical dimension of Jesus' trial (e.g., the question whether the Sanhedrin had the authority to try Jesus as it did, at night).

[60]Zagzebski, *Virtues of the Mind*, pp. 1-15.

and wisdom in much contemporary epistemology. I share this concern but see an additional one as well: To what extent are the judicial procedures of reason confined to the sphere of immanence, to what Kierkegaard calls Religion A? How successfully can traditional epistemology cope with Jesus' fifth trial, the one he endured before the world, on the cross? Significantly, Karl Barth discusses the resurrection of Jesus under the heading "the verdict of the Father."[61] Given the intrinsic limits of human reason (Kant), can reason alone do justice to the evangelical truth claim?[62]

The fiduciary: The economy of witness (testimony) and the sphere of faith (Christianity). Is the epistemology of the cross then fideistic? Yes, in the sense that faith yields knowledge of God; no, in the sense that I am not saying that one may justifiably believe irrationally or against the evidence. On my view, fideism is a matter of belief policy where one decides that accepting certain forms of evidence—apostolic testimony, to be exact—is a rational, intellectually virtuous knowledge-producing act. The epistemology of the cross I am here trying to sketch is fideistic in the sense that with regard to the evangelical truth claim it displays a certain epistemic humility as to the unaided powers of human reason and makes a *reasoned* case for the necessity of trust.[63] From another angle, an epistemology of the cross does not renounce the role of evidence but *expands* it to include testimony. Trusting testimony, however, is more than a matter of epistemic duty; it is, as we shall see, a matter of epistemic virtue. To anticipate: in an epistemology of the cross, faith is not only the first theological virtue but a prime epistemic virtue as well.

Testimony (the first sense of *martyrdom*) occupies a central place in the narratives of Jesus' trial. Indeed, the Fourth Gospel as a whole is an extended testimony to God's truth claim that aims to persuade its readers to make the judgment for themselves "that Jesus is the Christ, the Son of God" (Jn 20:31). The Fourth Gospel parades a host of witnesses on Jesus' behalf. John the Baptist "bears testimony" to Jesus as the Savior of the world (Jn 1:7-8; 3:26). The so-called testimonies of the Old Testament are adduced as additional evidence as to Jesus' true identity. Moreover, the works that Jesus does constitute testimony of his origin (Jn 5:36); in the

---

[61]A number of commentators have observed that in the Fourth Gospel it is the world that is ultimately on trial. As in the Old Testament, God in Christ is prosecuting a kind of cosmic lawsuit, and the way people respond to his Word provokes a judgment on themselves ("he who does not believe is condemned already, because he has not believed in the name" Jn 3:18).

[62]The reader must keep in mind that I am considering the evangelical truth claim. I agree with Helm that "it is extremely difficult to maintain most forms of fideism consistently as belief-policies across the whole body of a person's beliefs" (Helm, *Belief Policies*, p. 192). I am not therefore suggesting that rational procedures are unhelpful in most domains but only inquiring into their role in judging "the most important things."

[63]Helm speaks of a "second-order" or rational fideist "who provides reasons and arguments for fideism" (ibid., p. 210).

same way, Jesus' miracles are "signs" (*semeia*) that confirm his identity and mission. The Spirit of truth is an "Advocate" who bears witness to Christ (Jn 15:26), and even God the Father is said to bear witness to Jesus (Jn 5:37). Of course there were many at Jesus' trials who bore false witness as well. Nevertheless, the centrality of testimony, together with the possibility of false witness, requires a more careful analysis of what I am calling "the fiduciary."

Contrary to Plato and Locke, testimony yields not mere opinion but evidence, even a way of knowing. C. A. J. Coady's *Testimony: A Philosophical Study* argues that testimony as a mode of knowledge fell out of favor in modernity, due in large part to the dominant individualist ideology: "It may be no accident that the rise of an individualist ideology coincided with the emergence of the theory of knowledge as a central philosophical concern but, accident or not, the coincidence was likely to cast into shadow the importance of our intellectual reliance upon one another."[64] Coady's thesis is as simple as it is bold: "Our trust in the word of others is fundamental to the very idea of serious cognitive activity."[65] It may also be fundamental to our ability to make cognitive contact with reality.[66]

David Hume maintains that one can always reduce testimony to some other, more basic form of evidence (e.g., observation). His critical attitude toward testimony is shared by a good number of modern philosophers who agree that we need sufficient reason before believing in testimony.[67] Neither Hume nor Harvey allows testimony itself to count as a sufficient ground for believing what we have been told. Indeed they reckon one who believes something on the basis of testimony alone to be epistemically irresponsible. The main difficulty seems to be their assumption that testimony does not constitute "sufficient evidence" for belief. This is problematic on two counts. First, what is the warrant for that assumption? Second, is there an obvious answer to the question of what sufficient evidence amounts to?

Testifying—giving testimony—is a speech act. We are invited to accept *p* because *A* says that *p*, and because *A* is in a position to say so; in other words, *A*'s stating *p* is offered as grounds for accepting *p*. The legal act of testifying only "adapts and solemnizes an everyday phenomenon."[68] Thomas Reid classifies testimony, along with other speech acts such as promising, as "social operations of the mind" and complains that philosophy has overlooked their significance.[69] Testimony, like language

---

[64]C. A. J. Coady, *Testimony: A Philosophical Study* (Oxford: Clarendon, 1992), p. 13.
[65]Ibid., p. vii.
[66]I am here anticipating Zagzebski's definition of knowledge as "a state of cognitive contact with reality arising out of acts of intellectual virtue" (*Virtues of the Mind*, p. 270).
[67]See W. K. Clifford, "The Ethics of Belief," in *Lectures and Essays* (London: Macmillan, 1886), and Nicholas Wolterstorff, *John Locke and the Ethics of Belief* (Cambridge: Cambridge University Press, 1996).
[68]Coady, *Testimony*, p. 26.

itself, is essentially social. Coady similarly argues that trusting the word of others is implicit in our actual cognitive procedures.[70] In believing testimony, then, we are *believing in* the speaker. This need not lead to blind faith: "We may have 'no reason to doubt' another's communication even where there is no question of our being gullible; we may simply recognize that the standard warning signs of deceit, confusion, or mistake are not present."[71] Significantly, no such warning signs seem to be present in the apostolic testimony to the event of Jesus Christ.

H. H. Price's "principle A"—"Believe what you are told by others unless or until you have reason for doubting it"—is a restatement of sorts of Reid's "principle of credulity."[72] Trusting the word of others is socially expedient and socially indispensable. Trust is an intellectual virtue because relying on what other people say is often truth-conducive. The knowledge we gain from others is not inferential but properly basic; in many cases there are no other grounds for a belief.

There are additional reasons, however, that trust is important in discussions concerning the evangelical truth claim. As I have already suggested, there are good reasons to acknowledge that knowledge about God may be beyond the reach of unaided human reason. Significantly, Zagzebski lists "reliance on truth-worthy authority" on her list of intellectual virtues.[73] A person with a passion for truth should count divine revelation a reliable authority, though of course identifying divine revelation with Scripture requires *phronesis*. Trust is the virtue of "knowing when to rely on others" and is the "reverse side of autonomy."[74] Montmarquet unifies the virtues under two headings: honesty (a regard for the truth as such) and charity (a regard for others, not least as potential sources of truth). It remains to be seen whether faith is not the intellectual virtue that involves a proper regard for God. In any case, I have established that belief in apostolic testimony may well be the rational response of a person of epistemic virtue.

Hume reduces testimony to first-person observation. In other contexts, however,

---

[69]Thomas Reid, *Essays on the Intellectual Powers of Man,* ed. Baruch Brody (Cambridge, Mass.: M.I.T. Press, 1969), essay 1, chap. 8.

[70]We may relate this to George Steiner's suggestion that belief in God underwrites language (*Real Presences* [Chicago: University of Chicago Press, 1989]).

[71]Coady, *Testimony,* p. 47.

[72]H. H. Price, *Belief* (London: Allen & Unwin, 1969), chap. 5. Reid acknowledges that our propensity to believe others will be qualified by experience. On the basis of my experience, for instance, I am more likely to believe what I am told in *Time* than in the *National Enquirer.*

[73]Zagzebski, *Virtues of the Mind,* p. 98.

[74]Ibid., p. 160. Credulity should not be confused with gullibility. In the first place, we are only rational in trusting others who are reliable in showing us the way or in giving us the truth. Most to be trusted therefore are those who are demonstrably knowledgeable or wise. Second, credulity, as an intellectual virtue, should not stand alone but must always be tempered by the other intellectual virtues.

he appeals to natural laws, which are but inferences from the observations of a large number of people. He has here to rely on a notion of the common experience of humanity rather than his own individual experience. This is highly problematic, for the notion of "common human experience"—the criterion with which Hume evaluates reports of miracles—ultimately relies on testimony, what others have reported to be common in their experience. Hume's distrust of reports of the miraculous is therefore a performative contradiction. The only escape would be to check the experience of others against our own individual experience. But this is to be mired in the worst kind of solipsistic relativism. Our reliance on testimony "goes beyond anything that could be justified by personal observation."[75] Coady thus concludes that testimony is an irreducible form of knowledge.

Justification in a fiduciary scheme has to do not with "founding" the evidence given by a witness but with trusting it. Testimony makes past and present perception of others available to those who did not, or could not, perceive for themselves. Propositional truth—a report about what happened in history—is thus one element in testimony. As Coady observes, reporting "is probably the dominant form of assertion."[76] Yet my argument is that the witness's whole speech act, taken as part of a broader way of life, is part of the package that certifies the validity of the claim being made. At least with regard to claims about ways of wisdom such as the evangelical truth claim, the life of the witness and the testimony itself are inseparably intertwined. To stake a theological truth claim is to make a self-involving speech act that requires the speaker to take a stance toward her own words, toward others, toward the world and perhaps toward God. One who testifies must redeem Habermas's validity conditions for communicative acts in general as well as an additional validity claim, that this is a truth for which one is prepared to live and die.

To repeat: in the current epistemological climate of postmodernity, justifying propositions is not enough. What needs to be validated is not only the proposition but the entire speech act of testifying. The present expansionist account of epistemology requires us to consider not only procedures but practices, the performance not only of epistemic duties but, more important, of epistemic virtues.

Testimony and "incredible" reports. Hume and others of his ilk would like a criterion with which to rule certain types of testifying out of court without having to consider the particular circumstances of the speech act. Harvey agrees with R. G. Collingwood: "In so far as an historian accepts the testimony of an authority and treats it as historical truth, he obviously forfeits the name of historian."[77] Testimony must be tested because there is false testimony, as the penultimate prohibition of the

---

[75]Coady, *Testimony*, p. 93.
[76]Ibid., p. 154.
[77]R. G. Collingwood, *The Idea of History* (Oxford: Oxford University Press, 1946), p. 256.

Ten Commandments reminds us: "You shall not bear false witness" (Ex 20:16).

No witness, of course, hands down a complete, photographlike description of an event. Rather, one selects and interprets what one reports. Here most moderns and postmoderns are in agreement. An element of judgment is necessarily present. These judgments, as F. H. Bradley pointed out, presuppose other judgments and beliefs influenced by one's culture and worldview. The task of the critical historian is to cross-examine the witness with the goal of removing obsolete worldview accretions and recovering the literal core: what a person today would have observed had she been there. In this fashion, says Harvey, "the historian *confers* authority upon a witness."[78]

Bradley argues that all testimonies to the "non-analogous" should be rejected.[79] Unless the witness's experience is like our experience, it does not count as evidence. Critical history involves rethinking the judgments of others according to the criterion of present knowledge and experience.[80] This is a rather legalistic "morality of historical knowledge," to say the least, one that partakes of the judiciary and privileges the desire to avoid error to the exclusion of the fiduciary and the desire to gain truth. Is it necessarily a defect of testimony that a past witness "saw" things differently from the way we might have seen them? Is this not simply to acknowledge that *testimony itself is an interpretation?* And might it not be that the witness's judgments and interpretive framework are as indispensable for our appreciation of a claim as a mere report of a raw perception? It seems unlikely, for instance, that we could ever assess the claim "Jesus is the Christ" without some appreciation of the Hebrew Scriptures. One could never directly observe Jesus as the Christ; that claim—and perhaps the evangelical truth claim as well—is more of a judgment than an empirical observation. By treating common human experience or universal natural laws as our critical criteria, then, we are choosing to attend to testimony with a blind eye and a deaf ear.

In testimony there is both "mere observation" and "worldview." *Both* have to be tested, and we have to be clear about which we find objectionable and why. Coady states, "Unless we register quite a lot we cannot act, select, and interpret at all. The real story is quite complex and multi-layered: neither the picture of wholly passive registration nor that of furiously active invention is adequate."[81] Witnessing involves fact (reporting events) and interpretation (describing their meaning). What, after all is more marvelous: that a dead man came back to life or that God is described as one who forgives sinners?

---

[78]Harvey, *Historian and the Believer*, p. 42.

[79]F. H. Bradley, "The Presuppositions of Critical History," in *Collected Essays* (Oxford University Press, 1935). Harvey cites Bradley's essay with obvious approval.

[80]Bradley states: "The view I have put forward is this, that every man's present standpoint ought to determine his belief in respect to *all* past events" (ibid., p. 2).

[81]Coady, *Testimony*, p. 268.

Testimony need not be exhaustive in order to yield knowledge. A critical realism of testimony recognizes the value of multiple perspectives or voices and insists that through serious interpretation the reader can make cognitive contact with that to which the witnesses testify.

The theologian as witness. "Is the cross an argument?" (Nietzsche, *The Antichrist* §53). The witness is one who first acquires a belief and then attempts to pass it on. While testimony may or may not be the source of the witness's belief (the mechanism by which the belief is acquired), it is certainly the result. The reliable or authoritative witness becomes a conduit of rationality. One important aspect of the vocation of the theologian is to witness to the truth: not just to the evangelical truth claim but to the notion of truth itself.[82] Moreover, bearing witness to truth involves a way of life. The witness, especially the martyr, displays the meaning of the evangelical truth claim by readiness to stake not only the claim but herself. This involves courage, moral and intellectual. *Bearing witness is ultimately a matter not of epistemic duty but of epistemic virtue.*[83]

In Kierkegaard's view, the problem with Christianity is that it has too many teachers and not enough witnesses. For the teacher, Christianity is essentially doctrine. This takes us only as far as *episteme* and *theoria* (theoretical knowledge), not as far as *phronesis*—the way, the truth and the life. It is important to note that for Kierkegaard the witness speaks not a private but a public language. Though Kierkegaard never abandons his emphasis on inwardness (one's subjective passion for the truth), he does develop the implications of inwardness *outward*. One's life must conform to one's message. A politics must follow from a passion. The witness unites in his or her person the private/passionate and the public/political realms, for the sake of the wider community. In this way private responsibility and public accountability alike are satisfied. A witness with personal integrity stakes himself in a public manner. Accordingly, the "witness" is the fullest expression of "the individual," yet not in a way that leads to privatization.

Witnessing is a practice that displays not only the witness's sincerity with regard to the truth claim but often its very *matter:* "the self, language, and world coexist in relations of mutual implication."[84] Questions about meaning and truth—about God as well as about everything else—will be related to the way we actually live. One's active wit-

---

[82]This is particularly so given Jesus' claim to be the truth (Jn 14:6). Can persons as well as propositions be truth-bearers? Perhaps so, if the truth concerned is a matter of that on which a "way and life" ultimately relies.

[83]I am not sure what Zagzebski, to whom my account of epistemic virtue is largely indebted, would make of this claim. She does recognize that courage is an intellectual virtue, but there is no discussion of testimony and no index entry for "credulity" in her work.

[84]James Fodor, *Christian Hermeneutics: Paul Ricoeur and the Refiguring of Theology* (Oxford: Clarendon, 1995), p. 11.

ness therefore can disclose to others not only the meaning of the evangelical truth claim but the intelligible structure of the world as interpreted by Christians as well. Doing the truth is one way of showing what the truth is, what the world is really like.

Living the Christian way helps form sensibilities that allow others better to perceive the summons that a situation represents. Aristotle says that moral education begins with a child's learning to be appropriately ashamed at what is shameful. We might similarly say that Christian education begins when a disciple learns why one need *not* be ashamed of the gospel. My thesis is that Christian discipleship is conducive to forming certain epistemic virtues, especially the theological virtues of credulity and humility, and that these virtues in turn are conducive to appreciating the truth that God was in Christ reconciling the world to himself.

Martyrdom as communicative action. "The martyrs have *harmed* the truth" (Nietzsche, *The Antichrist*). Christian witnesses are not only speakers but sufferers too. This was a constant theme in Kierkegaard's works. Neither orthodoxy nor "Christendom" is enough; Christian truth demands passion or inwardness. Yet subjectivity is not the whole story for Kierkegaard either. In his later writings, discipleship becomes more and more important. "Dying from the world" means not withdrawing from the world but following Christ without being dominated by worldly matters. Being a Christian is recognizable "by the opposition one suffered."[85] Discipleship inevitably leads to suffering.

Kierkegaard speaks of "suffering for the truth" or "suffering for the doctrine." The truth *has* to suffer; Christ's persecution was not accidental. The cross of Christ symbolizes what is involved in having a passion for the truth. It is not that the disciple seeks suffering but rather than the world inevitably persecutes the truth. Why should this be so? Because the truth is not ultimately of this world. It is eschatological, not immanent, and cannot be contained within a worldly framework.

Both the form and the content of the evangelical truth claim work against the notion of "Christendom" and its imperialistic overtone of imposing truth on others. Those who stake theological truth claims, then, should expect not to oppress but rather to suffer oppression. To associate the theological truth claims with expressions of the will to power is effectively to contradict Christian witness. The power associated with Christian truth has little to do with force (except the force of testimony and perhaps the force of the better argument) and nothing to do with violence. The power of the cross is the weakness and wisdom of God (1 Cor 1:23-25). From the perspective of an epistemology of the cross, truth—even rationality—is vulnerable.

Christ's passion becomes for Kierkegaard the pattern for Christian witness. When Kierkegaard declares "truth is subjectivity," he is speaking the language not of post-

[85]Quoted in Gouwens, *Kierkegaard as Religious Thinker*, p. 214.

modernity but of the gospel. Subjectivity for Kierkegaard is an intellectual virtue that calls people to relate to the truth as if their lives depended on it (which they do). To say truth is subjectivity is just another way of talking about "passion": about passion as an epistemic virtue (a burning desire for the truth) and about the passion of Christ (a definitive suffering for the truth). Christ's passion is a model for how we should stake truth claims today—as a suffering witness: "Christ is the truth [but] to *be* the truth is the only true explanation of what truth is."[86] The witness to the truth is one whose life displays the rightness of the believing, and thus the rightness of the belief. Only personal witness—an integration of speech, belief and life—can ultimately legitimate the wisdom of the Christian way. George Malantschuk's comment is apt: "Kierkegaard's subjectivity is a blend of truth and what is individual, whereas Nietzsche's subjectivity is a blend of what is arbitrary and what is individual. For Kierkegaard, it is truth which determines and transforms the individual; for Nietzsche, it is the individual who determines what truth shall be."[87]

Martyrdom can be a powerful form of truth-disclosive action. Christian martyrs bear witness to the love of God and the lordship of Jesus Christ: twin convictions that undergird the Christian way of life. As a practice that is peculiarly transparent to the ultimate commitments that fund it, martyrdom displays the shape of Christian metaphysics as well as that of Christian morals. Coady aptly observes that we are oriented to reality by others as much as by our own intellectual powers. The Christian martyr not only declares but displays what it means to say "Jesus is Lord" or "God is love." Indeed one might go further and say that without martyrs we simply would no longer have the meaning of these propositions. Martyrdom appears to be a form of what Kierkegaard calls "indirect communication" and is thus an appropriate response to the epistemological predicament of postmodernity. The evangelical truth claim, precisely because it is as concerned with the way to live as with correct ideas, is staked best not through direct communication (theoretical knowledge) but indirectly, through the expansive category of the speech act "testifying."

Of course if we ask whether the commitments implied by one's testimony are arbitrary, we begin to do metaphysics. But this is precisely my point: martyrdom is a form of "indirect metaphysics."[88] Faithful Christian witness thus involves naming God *and* a particular way of being-toward-death. Speaking the truth in love is tied up with bearing witness, that is, with learning how to be a Christian martyr.

---

[86]Ibid., p. 218.

[87]George Malantschuk, "Kierkegaard and Nietzsche," in *A Kierkegaard Critique,* ed. H. A. Johnson and Niels Thulstrup (New York: Harper, 1962), p. 124.

[88]It would be a misunderstanding of my proposal to see it as reducing truth to truthfulness or correspondence to sincerity. Speech acts have various kinds of validity conditions, and sincerity is only one of them. I shall consider below the objection that my proposal is unable to distinguish the martyr to truth from the foolish fanatic.

Cross-examination: Passion and truth. "A man's virtues are called *good*
depending on their probable consequences not for him but for us and society. . . .
When you have a virtue . . . you are its victim" (Nietzsche, *The Gay Science*). The wit-
ness/martyr, I have argued, has a passion for truth. Is this fact of any epistemological
significance? We have seen that virtue epistemology conceives justification as something that emerges from the inner traits of persons rather than something that
attaches to impersonal processes. Did not the Greeks develop an interest in philosophy and epistemology, precisely in order to get beyond subjectivity and to counter
the irrational force of the passions? In giving pride of place to passion, am I not playing into the hands of the postmodern relativists? On the contrary, I view passion as
the epistemic virtue that is perfectly suited to staking the evangelical truth claim in an
age marked by irony and indifference toward the truth. Passion, I shall argue, is an
epistemic (and ethical) virtue that, just because it is truth-conducive, leads also to
martyrdom.

"Here I stand." "Stand firm in your faith" (1 Cor 16:13). Luther's terse formula
"Here I stand," allegedly spoken in the context of his own trial, displays two important intellectual virtues: humility and conviction. *Here* I stand. This is a confession of
humility, an admission of the contextual conditioning of one's thought.[89] Humility, as
an intellectual virtue, recognizes that in some areas I must think others more epistemically privileged than myself. It predisposes me to trust the testimony of those who
are reliable authorities. It also means that I must stand prepared to be corrected by
better arguments (or, in Luther's case, by the Word of God). Humility is perhaps the
prime feature of an epistemology of the cross.[90] Epistemic humility leads to an aban-
donment of the epistemology of glory, the project of finding out God through theoretical argumentation or of thinking that one can, through reason, attain a context-
free God's-eye perspective. Intellectual humility means that I, and my whole community, must acknowledge the provisionality of our claims ("Here *we* stand, in the West,
at the beginning of the twenty-first century"). To stress humility is thus to emphasize
the corrigibility of interpretive traditions. Yet humility remains an intellectual virtue;
those who have it stand a better chance of apprehending the truth—of knowing
God—rather than their own ideological projections.

"Here *I* stand." Luther can also be read as displaying a second epistemic virtue:

---

[89]The incarnation, especially the *kenosis* of Christ, shows that even God's truth claim was con-
textualized in "the form of a servant . . . in the likeness of men" (Phil 2:7).
[90]Interestingly, Aristotle (whom Luther calls the philosopher behind the theology of glory)
appears to have thought humility a vice (see Zagzebski, *Virtues of the Mind*, p. 88). Zagzebski, however, is not so negative: "But if humility is the virtue whereby a person is disposed
to make an accurate appraisal of her own competence, intellectual humility could reasonably be interpreted as a mean between the tendency to grandiosity and the tendency to a
diminished sense of her own ability" (p. 220).

intellectual courage, the courage of one's convictions. Sometimes one has literally to stand in order to stake a claim—to stand and be counted. Luther's standing was a sign of his conviction and commitment to the truth.

One stands for truth because truth is for everyone. Luther the private individual had a passion for public truth. The evangelical truth claim, of all possible truth claims, is eminently public: it is good news for the whole world. In standing for Christian wisdom, then, one proclaims its ability to transform any situation or society where people are willing to take it seriously and follow its way.

Endurance as a criterion of truth (Jas 1:12). "What does not destroy me makes me stronger" (Nietzsche). These two virtues, each an aspect of passion, are, I submit, the virtues of the martyr who bears witness to and suffers for something that she has received from another. But why should passion, which in this context refers to suffering, be truth-conducive? And what distinguishes Jesus' passion from that of Socrates, the Christian martyr from others who are willing to die for the truth, not to mention the fanatic? This is an important query. My thesis is that *humility and conviction are epistemic virtues, and so truth-conducive, because together they lead one to believe that which can be relied on ultimately*. The belief policy of the Christian martyr is not "believe whatever you're told no matter how seemingly ridiculous" but rather "believe what you are told about God by those who have it on good authority and whose testimony—which includes their lives (and deaths)—are reliable indicators of practical wisdom." If I may again appeal to Luther: properly to state Christian truth involves *oratio* (prayer), *meditatio* (interpretation) and *tentatio* (the experience of testing through affliction). In brief: the connection between humility, conviction and rationality is to be found in the critical test of *endurance*.

To stake the evangelical truth claim means to be able and willing to render Christ in one's daily living—or better, to *surrender* everything for the sake of this claim. In particular, theologians, in imitation of Christ, must humble themselves and not retreat to commitment or hide behind ecclesial authority.[91] No special privileges or prerogatives should be allowed to insulate theological truth claims from the crucible of testing. To pour oneself out for the sake of the evangelical truth claim means making the way of Christ intelligible, both theoretically and practically. It means living a life that embodies the Word in the power of the Spirit in a way that is able to meet, and pass, the critical tests of human reflection and human existence.

Displaying humility and conviction is analogous to fallibilist theories of rationality according to which justification involves a process of critical testing. Epistemic humility means being tolerant, not in the sense of embracing plurality and difference, as

---

[91]This seems to be the application to epistemology of Jesus' renunciation of divine glory or "equality with God" (Phil 2:6).

would a postmodern relativist, but rather in the sense of enduring it. This is, in part, what it means to suffer for the truth. The epistemically virtuous person endures critical testing of beliefs. The virtuous believer/witness tries to pass the greatest test of all: the test of time.[92] Ultimately to stake a Christian theological truth claim is to embark on an endurance test for which we have only the firstfruits of verification.

The witness implicit in this standing is that the truth is strong enough to absorb everything the world has to throw at it. Endurance does not mean duration, for truth is not merely a matter of *surviving* critical testing. On the contrary: to "endure" means "to harden"; it is not merely a matter of staying the same over time but of becoming stronger. The truth is that which endures and that which edifies. The steadfast faith is the faith that stands fast (Col 2:5; Jas 1:3). Knowledge, then, is neither a pyramid nor a raft, but a tree whose roots extend ever deeper and whose branches bear ever more fruit.

As did Jesus in his trials, his disciples often have to stand and take it. As we have seen, this is precisely the way the virtues are learned: through doing what a person with *phronesis* would do in similar circumstances, through imitating a master. Christian discipleship is, at least in part, an apprenticeship in the intellectual as well as the properly moral virtues.

Jesus and Socrates. "If this . . . undertaking is of men, it will fail; but if it is of God, you will not be able to overthrow them" (Acts 5:38-39).

Surely I have proved too much. Every faith has its martyrs, yet unless we side with postmodern relativists, not all faiths can be true. To what extent then does an epistemology of the cross really help in discerning true knowledge from knowledge falsely so called? In particular, why should one not follow a genius like Socrates rather than an apostle like Paul?[93]

Socrates, we may recall, was on an epistemological mission too, one that was commissioned by a god (though philosophers do not like to be reminded of it). Indeed at his trial Socrates claimed to be "god's gift to Athens."[94] His task was to make people wise. Like Jesus, Socrates was brought to trial because of his single-minded passion for his mission, though he claimed, again like Jesus, that he had never done anything wrong and had never acted against the gods.[95] Furthermore, Socrates, again like Jesus, chose to die for his mission; even Kierkegaard admired Socrates' passion.

---

[92]There is a sense in which endurance is formally analogous to Alistair MacIntyre's suggestion that traditions are best tested over time. To highlight humility is to make "willingness to submit one's beliefs (or oneself) to critical testing" an epistemic virtue that is conducive to truth.
[93]"Apostle" here means "one sent on a mission." Though Jesus sent others, he too was sent, by the Father (cf Jn 15—17).
[94]Plato *Apology* 30d7-e1.
[95]Ibid., 37b2-5.

How then does Jesus' martyrdom differ from that of Socrates, or from that of a fanatic? Let us begin with Socrates. For what did Socrates die? In the first place, he died to maintain his personal integrity. He had the courage of his convictions. Kierkegaard, however, rightly observes that Socrates did not die for the truth—that is, for some positive message—but rather for a principle, for the sake of making a formal protest. In other words, he died for negativity, and the wisdom he left his students was largely negative too (dialectic, critical thinking). On the one hand, he lived a life free of the evil of thinking that he was wise when he was not; on the other hand, he had not achieved a positive truth. He died for a question, not for an answer. Socrates, in the end, is only half a martyr; he died, but his was the death of a genius, not of a witness, and certainly not of an apostle.[96]

Socrates died, moreover, in the vague belief that he would not be worse off in death than he is in life. Thomas Brickhouse and Nicholas Smith observe, "Although he never claims to be wise in this all-important matter, Socrates believed there is good reason for thinking everyone will be better off dead."[97] While he may well have been right about eternal life, he could surely not be said to have had knowledge of it. As Kierkegaard observes, the difference between transcendence and immanence is that when Jesus and Socrates both say, "There is eternal life," only Jesus has the authority to do so; only Jesus *knows,* for only he has it on reliable authority.[98] Last, Socrates dies in his old age with a joke on his lips.

In the final analysis, Socrates' parting wisdom about life and death lacks authority. In short: his testimony is nonapostolic, a proud protest limited to the sphere of immanence, to what unaided human reason can know. On closer inspection, then, there is reason to question whether Socrates' death displays the epistemic virtues associated with passion (credulity, humility, conviction). Socrates does not give his followers a sufficient reason to follow his example. It is thus questionable whether he is an example of one who lives, and dies, well.

In contrast to Socrates, Jesus died in anguish, in his prime, at the hands of others. In submitting to an unjust penalty, in being willing to die for a message (concerning the kingdom of God) he had received on authority, Jesus put those who observed his life and death in a position to see, and to *feel,* the force of his claim. Jesus' martyrdom was therefore not only truth-conducive but transcendence-conducive: the cross—the way Jesus lived and the way he died—communicated to and

---

[96]Significantly, though his *daimonion* tells him what *not* to do, Socrates does not really receive any other positive revelation than the original Delphic oracle that pronounced him the wisest of men!

[97]Brickhouse and Smith, *Plato's Socrates,* p. 202.

[98]Christ was not a genius who communicated his own ideas. As Kierkegaard points out, the statement "There is eternal life" is not profound; that's not the point. What counts is that it is the One sent from God who said it ("On the Difference," pp. 156-57).

convinced others of the truth of his claims. The centurion at the foot of the cross, when he saw how Jesus died, confessed, "Truly this man was the Son of God" (Mk 15:39).[99]

An objection: The epistemic fanatic. To stake a claim is to act as a witness to some state of affairs. My thesis is that the way one witnesses is an important part of assessing the content of what is said. But could it not be argued that fanatics have the same kind of passion as that evidenced by Jesus? If the intellectual virtues arise out of a love of the truth, must we not say that the fanatic is a person of epistemic virtue?

The first thing to determine is whether the fanatic really desires the truth rather than the truth of his own ideas. To be passionate only about one's own ideas is to lack the epistemic virtues of humility and open-mindedness. This kind of love for the truth partakes more of *eros* than of *agape.* Let us assume for the sake of discussion, however, that the epistemic fanatic really desires truth. The first thing to be said is that the mere desire for truth is not enough to qualify one as epistemically virtuous. Sincerity alone is insufficient, for sincerity alone is not necessarily truth-conducive. One can be sincerely wrong. Second, the epistemic fanatic is often not a martyr. Take the members of the Heaven's Gate sect. No one persecuted them; they were not martyrs. Their suffering was self-inflicted. In choosing death, they witnessed only to their own confusion.

Third and most important, the fanatic's passion for the truth is untempered by the other intellectual virtues. This is a most important point. Though passion for the truth can be a virtue, when unchecked by the other epistemic virtues it ceases to be truth-conducive. The fanatic is, epistemologically speaking, a tragic hero whose downfall is due to an excess of one intellectual virtue.[100] As Montmarquet points out, the desire to attain truth must be regulated by the other epistemic virtues.[101]

Fanaticism therefore is best described as a *deregulated* passion for the truth. The epistemic fanatic, to put it another way, is one who fails to integrate and unify the intellectual virtues in his or her person. In short, the fanatic lacks *phronesis,* practical wisdom, the supreme regulative virtue. It is the task of *phronesis* to balance the virtues and to judge, say, when to persevere with a belief and when to give it up. A person of epistemic virtue must believe what a person with *phronesis* would in similar

---

[99] Jesus' sufferings were for others—for the whole world: "Jesus suffers them in solidarity with others, and vicariously for many, and proleptically for the whole suffering creation" (Moltmann, *Way of Jesus Christ,* p. 152). Of course not everyone could see the truth in Jesus' death, for many lacked the right imagination, not to mention the requisite epistemic (and spiritual) virtues. Knowers require not only training but sanctification in order to acquire the virtues that put them into cognitive contact with divine reality.

[100] The analogy with moral tragedy may be helpful. Othello's love for his wife, taken to the extreme, becomes jealousy (a vice).

[101] Montmarquet, *Epistemic Virtue,* p. 25.

circumstances.[102] Fanaticism, to the extent that it is a matter of unregulated passion and therefore of what can ultimately only be foolishness, is a downright epistemic vice.

Epistemic and theological virtue. In Jesus' passion we see the wisdom of God personified, the divine *phronesis* made flesh. Jesus displays epistemic virtues in his martyrdom, then, that Socrates and fanatics do not. In particular, Jesus personifies the antidote to fanaticism, namely, humility: his teaching witnesses to what he has received, and his life is a pouring out on behalf of this same message.

Epistemic humility, I suggest, is the intellectual virtue needed if we are to make cognitive contact with transcendent reality by trusting apostolic testimony. As I have argued, such trust is eminently rational, since credulity is an intellectual virtue. The witness acquires beliefs through credulity but commends them to others through humility, that is, by submitting them to critical tests. Christians testify not only to a set of propositions but to a way, and this way must be subjected to Socratic examination, perhaps even to persecution.[103] Only by such trials can this way be deemed wise and reliable rather than foolish and misleading.

Jesus' ability to endure critical testing stems not only from the character traits typically mentioned by virtue epistemologists but from the properly theological virtues as well: faith, hope and love. Faith: Jesus accepted and held on to beliefs acquired through trusting the Word of God. Hope: Jesus' implicit trust in his Father and in the divine promise of new life allowed him to complete his mission. In turn, Jesus' resurrection inspires contemporary witnesses to hope that the evangelical truth claim will ultimately be vindicated by God himself. Love: it was Jesus' love for others, even for those who opposed him, that not only inspired his passion but enabled him to endure it. As Paul has written, "Love bears all things, . . . endures all things" (1 Cor 13:7).

An epistemology of the cross is humble yet at the same time hopeful. Testifying, like promising, is a speech act in which speakers commit themselves to an eventual fit of words and world. Now even an enriched epistemology will not be able to prove the evangelical truth claim. Yet we need not go so far as to suggest that the

---

[102]There are prima facie problems with the criteria for recognizing *phronesis*. Zagzebski appears to think that good intellectual practice is, if not self-evident, at least widely acknowledged. More work probably needs to be done in this area. Zagzebski's comment is relevant, however: "It is often a difficult matter to decide what theological propositions to believe, but this is no objection to the appeal to practical wisdom unless it is a condition of adequacy of a methodology of theology that it make the difficult business of deciding what to believe easy" ("Place of Phronesis," p. 221).

[103]Moltmann comments, "The ancient church knew her martyrs, and knew also how to interpret the martyrdom of the witnesses theologically" (*Way of Jesus Christ,* p. 197). See also 2 Corinthians 4:10, Philippians 3:10 and Colossians 1:24.

cross fails to get us beyond the level of immanence.[104] On the contrary, the Fourth Gospel suggests that the cross itself is the moment of Christ's glorification (his being "lifted up"). In the final analysis, we must say that the cross is an *indirect* communication of divine transcendence. Jesus' resurrection is both testimony and promise: testimony to the fact that God was in Christ reconciling all things to himself and a promise that all things shall indeed be reconciled. The cross is ultimately an apocalyptic witness to the meaning of the whole of world history.

Martyrs, says Moltmann, "anticipate in their own bodies the sufferings of the end time. . . . They witness to the creation which is new."[105] To testify to the resurrection is thus to participate, in anticipatory fashion, in the promise of the kingdom of God. The Christian martyr, unlike Socrates, thus testifies in concrete terms to hope. This too is a matter of *phronesis:* knowing how, in every situation, to live in a way that testifies not only to the wisdom of Christ but to hope in his resurrection.

Barth spoke of resurrection as the "verdict" of the Father. Perhaps there a lesson here for the contemporary minister of the Word as well. We can stake claims with humility and conviction and show their reasonableness and wisdom by enduring trials and critical testing, but it is ultimately up to God to validate them. God raised Jesus from the dead; the apostles were only witnesses of this fact (Acts 2:32). The trial of truth may admit of no worldly resolution. The church today continues to witness to resurrection, not by eyewitness but by existential testimony that attests the promise and its power.

Those who stake theological truth claims, then, need not wield the sword; truth will be victorious, but its victory is not gained through an overpowering of its opponents. As Oliver O'Donovan says, "The church does not philosophize about a future world; it demonstrates the working of the coming Kingdom within this one. . . . This may lead to mutual service, or to martyrdom."[106]

Witnessing, I submit, is the epistemologically correct way of staking a theological truth claim. For postmodernity in some respects has not advanced beyond Socrates. Both are philosophies of immanence that fail to do justice to the absolute significance of the historical particular. Martyrdom, I suggest, is the most appropriate form of a claim that concerns the extraordinary in the ordinary: the eternal quickening of human history.

Conclusion: The Theologian as Interpreter-Martyr

The vocation of the Christian theologian is to be an interpreter-martyr: a truth-teller, a

---

[104] As Anthony Thiselton apparently suggests in *Interpreting God and the Postmodern Self* (Edinburgh: T & T Clark, 1995), p. 147.
[105] Moltmann, *Way of Jesus Christ,* p. 204.
[106] Oliver O'Donovan, *The Desire of the Nations: Rediscovering the Roots of Political Theology* (Cambridge: Cambridge University Press, 1999), p. 217, order slightly changed.

truth-doer, a truth-sufferer. Truth requires evangelical passion, not postmodern passivity; personal appropriation, not calculation. The theologian is to embody in his or her own person the core of Christian culture, in order to provide a focus for Christian wisdom. Making Christian truth claims is ultimately not a crusade nor a pilgrimage nor even a missionary journey, but rather a *martyrological* act. Genuine theology is not only about the art of reasoning well (rationality) but about living well (wisdom) and dying well (martyrdom). Martyrdom is a form of indirect epistemology that arises from acts of intellectual virtue (e.g., humility, conviction) motivated by the passion for truth.

Questions about the truth of our theology are thus tied up with questions about the effectiveness of our discipleship and martyrdom. There is a tie between defending the truth and living faithfully. The challenge of Christian mission today, the challenge of staking a theological truth claim, is nothing less than displaying in one's life the way of Jesus Christ: not Heidegger's (or Socrates') being-toward-death but a distinctively Christian *being-toward-resurrection*. This is not a matter of epistemological foundationalism so much as a demonstration of the integrity and uniqueness of Christian wisdom. Such a demonstration can be made, of course, only by those who are willing to be martyrs. Staking a theological truth claim is a costly affair. To refer truly to God *is* to bear faithful witness to the way of Christian wisdom, a witness that embodies the Christian metaphysic.

Epistemology in the service of Christian mission means not only doing one's epistemic duty but displaying intellectual virtue and pursuing epistemic excellence. Making a truth claim is both a relational and propositional affair, involving persons and procedures. What theology gives back to epistemology is an expanded set of intellectual virtues (faith, hope, love and humility) and the model of the martyr/witness who is prepared to endure anything for the sake of the truth. To stake a theological truth claim humbly yet hopefully is, finally, to *be* a truth to one's neighbor.[107]

[107] I am grateful to my Edinburgh University doctoral students and to Fergus Kerr, who made up the Whither Theology? discussion group, for their comments and suggestions on an earlier draft of this paper.

Index of Subjects